CE

D0592910

THE LIBERAL TRADITION
IN AMERICAN THOUGHT

The
Liberal Tradition
in American Thought

AN ANTHOLOGY

SELECTED AND EDITED BY

Walter E. Volkomer

G. P. PUTNAM'S SONS

NEW YORK

To

Edward McNall Burns—gentleman and scholar—who first introduced
me to the study of American political theory

PREFACE

Turmoil and doubts have marked America's presence in the second half of the twentieth century. Internal violence and ideological conflict have increased among a minority in the society while the majority has been beset by confusion and uncertainty about America—about its meaning and purpose. As in the case of the youth who discovers that all too quickly he has grown to adulthood and must reevaluate his relationship to the past, present, and future, the United States since World War II has had to search for its identity during a time of rapid political, social, and economic change. In such an age it is especially important for a society to study its history and development, and this book on America's liberal experience (along with its companion volume on the conservative experience) is designed to be of assistance in the search for understanding and comprehension.

This volume is not designed to present an argument in behalf of a single interpretation of American liberalism. In the selection of material there is a frank acceptance of the fact that liberalism has been identified with different ideas during different periods of American history. This is not to suggest that the student of American political theory should abandon the search for political ideas that have been held in common by liberals throughout American history. The author's personal struggle with this problem is revealed in an introductory essay which is probably more successful in showing the contradictory aspects of liberalism than in stating the intellectual elements common to this tradition.

No attempt has been made to make any novel or original interpretations, nor have choices of selections been made on the basis of a specific ideological view of American liberalism. The selections are designed to present political thinkers in relation to the prevailing intellectual climate of their times. It is possible to interpret Jefferson's political theory, from the perspective of the mid-twentieth century, as a conservative philosophy. Jefferson, for example, opposed centralized and active government, and these beliefs are accepted by many present-day conservatives. But, considering his many disagreements with Federalist thinkers such as Alexander Hamilton and John Marshall, it is impossible to understand Jefferson in the perspective of his own time as other than a liberal political thinker. The reader is, of course, encouraged to challenge the legitimacy of individual selections which have been presented as part of American liberalism and to formulate his own views on the nature of liberalism.

This work would not have been possible without the help of Charles Sherover of the Department of Philosophy of Hunter College, whose editorial assistance has been invaluable, and Dr. Jerome M. Levine of New York City, whose analytic insight has enabled the author to complete this study. The author would also like to thank Paula Kiff Spector of Hunter College for her help in the preparation of the manuscript. Finally, he would like to thank his students of American political theory at Hunter College for their thoughts and questions that have helped to formulate and clarify his ideas and understanding of the subject. The author is, to be sure, solely responsible for the organization and content of the material presented in the book.

CONTENTS

INTRODUCTION

American Liberalism — An Interpretation

A less than optimistic view of human nature and the possibility of progress—a secular pragmatic philosophy—the pursuit of positive liberty and equality as the primary goals of public policy—support for a strong, positive central government—a defense of energy in the executive branch of government—praise for the United States Supreme Court and for its role in promoting and protecting individual rights and liberties—internationalism in foreign affairs. These doctrines constitute the main tenets of contemporary liberal political thought in the United States. They are the beliefs which have been stated by the theoreticians of liberalism in recent decades, acted upon by its practitioners in public life, and associated with the term liberalism in the minds of most Americans.

Liberalism's supporters frequently seek to sanction its principles by appealing to tradition and to the wisdom of liberalism's early spokesmen—Jefferson, Jackson, and Lincoln. But, viewed from the perspective of America's more than three hundred years of political history, what is most striking about present-day liberalism is the relatively recent origin of its main beliefs. Rather than being a current manifestation of a long intellectual tradition, liberalism, as it is understood today, is largely a product of the twentieth century. Its roots were formed late in the nineteenth century, and it has been nurtured and shaped by the domestic and international events and developments of this century.

A comparison of the principal doctrines of contemporary liberalism with the beliefs held by liberals in the seventeenth, eighteenth, and nineteenth centuries reveals the fundamentally different character of liberalism in the present century. In the past, for example, liberal

1

political theorists advanced a generally optimistic view of human nature. While avoiding a Utopian vision of man's goodness, liberals have believed that human nature is generally good and more rational than irrational. Based on this evaluation, pre-twentieth-century liberalism was hopeful about the possibility of improving the quality of government and society.

This optimistic tone has partially given way in the literature of contemporary liberalism to a more pessimistic estimate of man and his chances for progress. The outlook which existed prior to World War I has been shattered by the international and domestic strife of this century, by the persistence of economic difficulties, and by the complex, technical nature of the problems which government must handle in today's world. Liberalism has not entirely lost its belief in man and in progress, but its skepticism has increased and it views the optimism of earlier liberal movements as unrealistic and largely irrelevant to the conditions of today's America.

The basic philosophy of twentieth-century liberalism also differs from that of the liberalism of the past. It is pragmatic and secular, placing its reliance on man and on his capacity to find through trial and error experimentation the means to solve his political, social, and economic problems. This has especially been the nature of recent reform movements; the New and Fair Deals of Presidents Roosevelt and Truman were both, for example, strongly pragmatic and secular.

Liberalism down through the early decades of the nineteenth century, however, was always connected with a religious outlook on the world. Its early exponents were ministers who had been influenced by the rationalism of the seventeenth and eighteenth centuries. Even Jefferson, an opponent of organized religion, frequently phrased his political thought in the language of eighteenth-century deism.

In these first two centuries of American history, liberalism was also closely associated with the philosophy of natural rights—with a belief in the existence of certain absolute rights possessed by each individual and derived from nature. The philosophy of natural rights was intimately related with a religious perspective, though one which emphasized reason rather than faith or revealed dogma. In eighteenth-century America, for example, the Congregationalism of John Wise, the Unitarian beliefs of Jonathan Mayhew, and the deism of Thomas Jefferson blended harmoniously with natural rights political philosophy.

The religious and natural rights orientation of American liberalism declined in importance in the nineteenth and early twentieth centuries and was slowly replaced by the secular and pragmatic liberalism of the present. Ironically, it is the conservative political thinker today who is most likely to recall the religious and natural rights beginnings of this nation's political and intellectual history; it is the liberal who is likely to ignore this tradition and to universalize the secular present into a general rule for liberalism. Although liberals have recently come to have more reservations about man's ability to solve his public problems, they have shown little or no inclination to return to the ideas of their religious and natural rights past.

Not only does the liberalism of the present differ from that which prevailed in earlier centuries in its estimation of man and its philosophy but it also has different ideals and different attitudes toward government. The liberalism of the seventeenth, eighteenth, and nineteenth centuries sought primarily to establish liberty for the members of the American nation, and it understood liberty to be the absence of governmental authority over man. The individual was considered free to the extent that his actions were unhindered by governmental controls.

American proponents of liberalism, until the end of the last century, followed the traditions of European liberalism which had arisen in the sixteenth and seventeenth centuries as a response to the dominant position of king and church. In the American colonies the demand for liberty advanced by liberals (and by many conservatives as well) was a demand to be free of British imperial rule and, in New England, the theocratic power of the Calvinist divines. But American liberals continued to define liberty in this negative sense even after independence had been won from Great Britain and the authority of Puritanism had been broken. Throughout most of the nineteenth century, liberals favored a policy of laissez-faire and looked upon each exercise of power by government as a diminution of the liberty of Americans.

This fear of government was especially pronounced in regard to the national government created by the Constitution of 1789. Liberals either opposed the ratification of the document because of its centralizing tendencies or were troubled by the possible consequences of this shift away from the states. During most of the nineteenth century, liberals opposed the exercise of positive authority by the central government except perhaps for the conduct of foreign affairs, which they considered its principal task. (America's geographic position and its policy of isolation kept even this function to a minimum.) Whatever domestic legislation was necessary—and the liberal bias in favor of laissez-faire did not admit much need—should be performed by those governments closest and presumably most responsive to the people—the state and local governments.

Toward the end of the nineteenth century, liberal political theorists introduced a new conception of the term liberty. Seeing the blighted human conditions brought on by a burgeoning industrial society, liberals found the old idea of liberty as the absence of governmental restraint inadequate to the needs of a new type of society. A man who was poor, uneducated, ill-housed, and subject to the fluctuations of the economic cycle could not be considered free though he lived in a nation whose government abided by the tenets of laissez-faire. True liberty, liberals began to contend, required the ability of a man to use his talents and energies in a constructive fashion—it meant the positive freedom to achieve and accomplish.

While twentieth-century liberalism has set as its principal goal the attainment of positive liberty for each member of society, it has not totally abandoned its dedication to the older idea of liberty. Indeed, liberalism in recent decades has championed the noneconomic liberties and rights contained in the Bill of Rights and in the Fourteenth and Fifteenth Amendments. But in matters of economic and social policy, liberals have given up the negative view of liberty and have advocated the need for governmental action to educate, house, and protect the welfare of the less successful members of the American society.

As a corollary to the goal of positive liberty, liberalism in this century has increasingly adopted the standard of equality as a proper end of public policy. Of course, American society and liberalism in particular have always held equality to be an important ideal. The legal principle of the equality of all men before the law and the statement in the Declaration of Independence that "all men are created equal" are the most obvious manifestations of this commitment to equality.

But the equality spoken of in the past was political, legal, and natural equality and was never understood to include economic or social affairs. Twentieth-century liberalism has tended to incorporate these latter areas into the meaning of equality and to advocate the adoption of public policies designed to reduce the social and economic inequalities that exist within American society. In the process of redefining the meaning of liberty, liberals have advocated a movement toward perfect social and economic equality, if not the actual attainment of this goal.

As liberalism in the twentieth century gradually accepted the ideals of positive liberty and equality as its main objectives, it also reconstructed its attitudes and beliefs about government. Positive liberty and equality required positive government. The older fear of government had to be replaced by a belief in its value, for only an active and energetic government could be expected to protect the welfare of the weaker members of society, liberate their energies, and achieve greater equality. By the time of the New Deal the remaining ties of American liberalism to its earlier limited government philosophy in economic and social matters had been severed, and it had fully accepted the wisdom of strong government.

In addition to this shift in ideas about government, twentieth-century American liberalism also reversed its position on the relative merits of the national as opposed to state and local governments. It abandoned its historic bias in favor of decentralization together with its dread of central authority and enthusiastically embraced the central government as the proper instrument by which to achieve its goal of positive liberty and equality. Since the 1930's liberals have looked upon the state and local governments as hopelessly outmoded institutions and have placed their expectations for reform on action by the national government.

The reasons for this theoretical change in liberalism are readily apparent. Action by the central government had the merit of establishing uniform national standards of public policy; reliance on state and local authorities would, on the contrary, produce uneven results with some areas adopting reforms and others rejecting change. Further, national policy, liberals maintained, would be less expensive to finance than action by the numerous state and local governments. Practical considerations also entered into the calculations of liberalism: the chances of attaining reform at the state and local level were far less promising than at the national level, since the national majority was more likely to be liberal than majorities in many of the smaller jurisdictions where conservative sentiment would succeed in blocking reform.

There is strong evidence, however, to support a belief that the romance between liberalism and Washington is now coming to an end. The domestic failings of the United States that came to light in the 1960's—poverty, racial discrimination, poor schools, deteriorated housing, to name just a few—exist despite a quarter-century of national reform legislation. Many liberals have come to the realization that not only has the size of the federal financial commitment been insufficient to meet the scope of domestic problems, but the local nature of these difficulties frustrates attempts to apply national solutions. The remedies proposed by these new liberals (and by some conservatives as well) are greater flexibility and decentralization of federal programs and the revitalization of state and local governments so that these institutions can be better prepared to play a more vigorous role in instituting social and economic reform.

Along with this new view of government and of the federal system, American liberalism in the twentieth century has drastically revised its evaluation of the system of separation of powers. The President has been raised to the central position of leadership in government by American liberals, who have maintained that the President should be the spokesman for the national majority and should provide the necessary moral and political leadership in the formulation of both international and domestic policy. Backed by the knowledge and expertise of the departments and agencies under his control, the President is expected to be the chief instrument for achieving the policy objectives of American liberalism.

Congress, to the contrary, has been an object of scorn to contemporary liberalism. Its conservative disposition (in large degree the product of its internal organization, which facilitates control by the most conservative rural legislators) has evoked a continual stream of liberal criticism. Rather than performing a positive role in promoting social and economic reform, Congress has devoted most of its energies to obstructing the reform programs of liberal Presidents. To alter this situation, liberals have advocated changes in the rules of the Congress so as to reduce the control of conservative forces in both houses. Abolition of the Senate filibuster, restricting the power of the House Rules Committee, and reforming the seniority system used to choose committee chairmen have been the main proposals advanced by liberals to achieve reduction in conservative power.

Since the early 1950's the United States Supreme Court has received the accolades of American liberalism. It has been praised for its numerous decisions upholding the claims of individuals and groups under the provisions of the Bill of Rights and the Fourteenth and Fifteenth Amendments to the Constitution. For its work in these areas the Court has been described by its admirers as a great institution of American democracy, and its power of judicial review has been defended because of its democratic nature. During the 1960's the Supreme Court reached a new peak of influence in the American governmental system, and at no time in its history had its prestige and popularity among American liberals been higher.

These views on the three branches of government have no special connection with any set of historic beliefs of American liberalism and in some respects run directly counter to what existed as the general trend of liberal thought. The ideas of liberalism on the executive and legislative branches reveal a particularly confused intellectual pattern. Throughout the colonial period and at least until the era of Jeffersonian democracy, liberalism looked with distrust upon the executive branch of government and considered the legislature the safest and most democratic institution of government. (Liberalism's acceptance of the legislature, however, was never total and uncritical; it accepted the separation of powers principle, for example, and rejected the parliamentary model of total legislative supremacy.)

After Jefferson, liberalism abandoned its support of the legislature but did not immediately adopt a belief in the virtue of a strong, popular President. It is true that liberals were enthusiastic supporters of President Jackson during the 1820's and 1830's and that Jackson was a strong President—strong at least by nineteenth-century standards—and he did see himself as the defender and interpreter of the interests of a national majority. Only Lincoln in a time of great domestic crisis surpassed Jackson as a powerful executive leader, but he did not have the undivided support of American liberals, many of whom were attracted to more militant opponents of slavery and the Confederacy. Jackson and Lincoln were, however, the exceptions to the general rule of weak and conservative Presidents in the nineteenth century, and American liberalism, with its deep belief in laissez-faire, did not emphasize the need for an energetic and popular chief executive.

It has only been in this century—especially since the time of Theodore Roosevelt—that liberalism has taken an unequivocal stand in favor of a forceful national executive. (Liberalism has also supported the development of strong governors at the state level and strong mayors in the larger cities of the nation.) Whether the unpopularity of Lyndon Johnson's Presidency and the Vietnam War among the liberals of the 1960's will permanently affect their thoughts on the nature of executive authority is a question that only the future can answer. These developments seem more likely to influence liberalism's attitudes toward executive power in foreign affairs than in domestic matters. Liberalism may well find itself in the uncomfortable intellectual position of advocating executive energy at home and greater legislative control and limitations on the President abroad.

Only on the subject of the judiciary has American liberalism maintained until recent decades a consistent intellectual posture. Since the adoption of the Constitution, liberals have looked on the courts with skeptical and even hostile eyes. The United States Supreme Court, its members appointed for life and possessing the important power of judicial review over actions of both the national and state governments, has been a favorite target of liberal criticism. Liberals have correctly understood that the Court was created to protect property rights against encroachments by popular majorities and have therefore opposed any broad assertion of the power of judicial review by the nation's highest tribunal.

In almost every period of American history, liberals have denounced important decisions of the Supreme Court and expressed disapproval of the conservative and undemocratic character of the Supreme Court. The anti-Federalists opposed the creation of a national judiciary, and the Jeffersonians and Jacksonians engaged in a series of conflicts with John Marshall and his Supreme Court. In the 1850's the abolitionists and other liberal opponents of slavery attacked the Court for its pro-Southern position, and at the turn of the twentieth century both the populists and the progressives criticized the Court and offered proposals to limit its powers. Perhaps the clearest example of liberalism's aversion to the Supreme Court was the attempt by President Franklin Roosevelt to "pack" the Court in 1937. After the Court had declared major parts of his New Deal legislative program unconstitutional, President Roosevelt, in the wake of his sweeping victory in the 1936 election, asked—unsuccessfully—that Congress give him the authority to appoint up to six additional members to the nation's highest tribunal. Only in the past two decades, as the Supreme Court moved from the defense of property rights to the protection of civil liberties and civil rights, have American liberals ended their traditional opposition to the Court and to judicial review. Criticism has given way to acclaim, and charges that the judiciary is conservative and undemocratic have been replaced by approbation for its democratic and educational function within the American governmental system.

A final source of confusion about the nature of American liberalism is to be found in the area of foreign affairs. It is commonly believed that liberalism is associated with internationalism, with a belief in America's necessary and desirable connection with the nations and events of the world. This understanding ignores the historic reality that from the time of the founding of the United States until well into the twentieth century this nation maintained a policy of isolation from world affairs. Reinforced by the facts of geography and the difficulties of communication, American liberals (and conservatives) favored a policy of creating no "entangling alliances" with foreign nations and limiting the scope of America's international contacts. A broad agreement existed that the United States should cultivate its own garden and avoid corrupting the American Eden by associating with the evils of the Old World.

Since World War I this nation has, of course, gradually turned away from its deliberate isolation and embarked on a new policy of internationalism, but it would be an oversimplification to see this change as exclusively the product of liberalism. Certainly the bulk of liberal opinion has favored internationalism, and the most important architects of this policy have been liberal Democratic Presidents—Woodrow Wilson, Franklin Roosevelt, and Harry Truman. But prominent Republican statesmen have also contributed much to America's new internationalism; the policies of Secretaries of State Charles Evans Hughes and Henry L. Stimson (later Secretary of War under President Franklin Roosevelt) can be cited as cases in point.

Yet liberalism in this century has not been fully committed to internationalism; some liberals have continued to defend a modified type of isolationism. They have accurately perceived the inherent contradiction between domestic liberalism and internationalism. During the New Deal, for example, some of President Roosevelt's most ardent domestic reformers counseled isolation. They feared that attempts to plan America's economy would be upset by foreign involvements, and they realized that a policy of internationalism would only detract from the energies and revenue available for domestic reform. An important source of liberal opposition to the Vietnam War in the 1960's was the belief that domestic reform should be given priority and that this nation could not solve the problems of its urban areas while it was engaged in the conduct of large-scale military and technical programs in Southeast Asia.

It should also be pointed out that there has been a geographic character to liberalism's international theories. Liberalism has been far more sympathetic to contact with European nations than with the countries of Asia. The economic, cultural, and intellectual bonds which exist between Europe and the United States—factors largely absent in the case of the Far East—are the obvious bases for liberalism's European orientation. (Conservatives, on the contrary, have been less isolationist in regard to Asia and more inclined to resist European involvements.) The entire question of internationalism versus isolationism in the twentieth century thus defies any simple generalizations along liberal-conservative lines and has, therefore, largely been omitted from this book's analysis of American liberal political thought.

If much that passes for liberalism today lacks the elements of tradition and historic continuity, must the student of American political theory conclude that liberalism is merely the politics of maneuver and tactic? Are there no enduring values which have motivated the thoughts and actions of American liberals throughout this nation's history? A liberal politics that is mere opportunism and that lacks at least some degree of tradition and continuity weakens both its moral standing and political strength in the community and allows its conservative opposition the opportunity to establish itself as the political movement of principle.

It is impossible to deny that many of the doctrines associated with liberalism are of an ephemeral nature and that to a considerable extent the ideas of liberalism have been shaped by the hard realities of practical politics. Nonetheless, it is still possible to discover some beliefs and values that have been held in common by liberals throughout the course of American political history. These common ideas are not to be found in the various programs advanced by liberalism or in the changing support it has given to different institutions of government. Rather they can only be elicited from an investigation of the basic assumptions and values which have guided the thoughts and actions of American liberals.

The central concept which binds together all of American liberalism is its individualism. Since colonial times liberalism has always had as its primary concern the welfare of the individual. Its ideas and actions have been molded by liberalism's search for programs designed to protect and promote this interest. Liberalism's individualism explains, for example, its often contradictory views on the proper role for government. Until the close of the nineteenth century when this nation lost its predominantly rural and agricultural character, liberalism believed that a laissez-faire philosophy would permit the maximum economic and personal development of the individual. With the advent of an urban industrial society in this century, liberalism found the old laissez-faire approach unsuited to the welfare of most individuals. Revealing its nondogmatic, pragmatic temper, liberalism turned to a theory of positive government as the best means to achieve its traditional ideal of individual fulfillment.

This concern for the individual is, perhaps, the principal item that distinguishes American liberalism from its conservative opposition.

American conservatism has raised institutions such as the church or abstract forces such as Providence and tradition to a position of primacy in its philosophy, and most important, it has stressed the fundamental nature of property rights and has placed this interest above the needs of the individual.

American liberalism has not rejected or even been hostile to church, Providence, tradition, or property, but it has never been prepared to elevate them to a status superior to that of the individual. It has been out of this concern for the individual, for example, that liberalism since the time of Roger Williams in the early seventeenth century has insisted upon the separation of church and state. Liberals have feared that cooperation between church and state would threaten the freedom and independence of the individual. Just as the power of the state must be limited and confined to its proper sphere of action, so also the church should deal only with spiritual matters. While the state must avoid hostility toward religion, it should provide no direct assistance or support. Only by following this policy of neutrality, liberalism has contended, can the sanctity of the individual in society be guaranteed.

One of the frequent contentions of conservatives is that man's will should be subordinated to the will of Providence and that social, economic, and political change should result only from the intervention of divine forces. According to this conservative belief finite man can only err when he places his understanding of human needs above that of God's. This religious viewpoint presented by some conservatives stands in direct opposition to the outlook of liberalism. Without denying the existence of God or His role in human affairs, American liberalism has seen man as a free agent possessing the intellectual ability to shape and control his life on earth.

In the same fashion liberalism has refused to worship at the shrine of tradition—a center frequented by most conservatives. While recognizing the contributions of the past, liberalism rejects the notion that the values of the past are infallible guides to present actions and that man should surrender his judgment to the wisdom and practices of the past. The attitude of liberalism toward the Constitution illustrates this point of view. Since the adoption of the Constitution, liberalism has accepted it as the basic instrument of government for the American nation. It has not, however, agreed that the specific interpretations of the Constitution that have been made in past ages must bind other generations. The Constitution should serve as a framework for the political system, but the general provisions of the document should be interpreted in light of the problems and knowledge of the present. The individual thus maintains his supremacy while still operating within the broad boundaries of a constitutional system of government.

Perhaps the greatest amount of confusion exists about the beliefs of American liberalism on the subject of private property. Conservatives have often considered property to be the principal interest to be defended in society and have criticized liberalism for its supposed hostility to property rights. But American liberalism has never opposed private property. On the contrary, it has accepted its existence as a positive good and has advocated policies designed to create a wider distribution of property within society. Unless this strong bias in favor of property is fully appreciated, the entire character of American liberalism will be misunderstood. Yet liberalism has never been willing to consider property to be more important than the individual. Abraham Lincoln best summarized the beliefs of liberalism toward property and the individual when, in describing the program of the new Republican Party, he wrote: "Republicans . . . are both for the *man* and the *dollar*; but in cases of conflict, the man *before* the dollar."

This emphasis on man expressed by Lincoln lies at the heart of liberalism's special role in championing the rights of the individual. From Roger Williams to the Supreme Court of Chief Justice Earl Warren, liberalism has been the most persistent advocate and defender of man's noneconomic liberties. Prior to the adoption of the Constitution, liberalism phrased its belief in the language of natural rights philosophy. The rights of the individual were natural rights—man's inheritance from nature. Throughout the colonial period liberalism interposed the natural rights of the individual against the arbitrary authority of state and church.

Arguing from natural rights had, however, one serious weakness— it lacked any objective definition of rights and relied entirely on subjective assertions of their existence and content. The decision at the end of the eighteenth century to establish the written Constitution eliminated this basic difficulty. Natural rights became more specific civil, constitutional protections. With the adoption of the Bill of Rights and, following the Civil War, the Fourteenth and Fifteenth Amendments, liberalism could turn to a body of written statements as a basis for defining the rights of the individual. In this century and more particularly in the post-World War II period, liberalism has made the enforcement of these constitutional guarantees one of the principal tenets of its political philosophy.

Along with its staunch support for individualism, American liberalism has also stressed the idea of an open society as a fundamental aspect of its political creed. Throughout the course of American history, liberal political thinkers have attacked all artificially created institutions and practices that have impeded the natural social and economic mobility produced by the differences in talents possessed by individual men. By eliminating man-made barriers that protected the vested interests of some while denying success to others, American liberalism has hoped to create a new type of social system in this nation. It has proposed an open society, a system based on individual merit and ability and not on privilege.

Criticism of privilege and defense of individual talent is a thread that runs through the entire history of American liberalism. The targets of criticism have varied from period to period. In the seventeenth century it was privilege possessed by the established churches and their clergy, aristocratic pretensions that a minority hoped to transfer from Europe to the New World, and the legal system which in parts of America gave some recognition to the claims of aristocracy. It was Jefferson who at the end of the eighteenth century spoke out against these artificial privileges and who so eloquently advanced the idea of an American aristocracy based not on birth but on talent and virtue.

Liberalism's struggle against vested privilege continued in the nineteenth century. The Jacksonians warred against the economic aristocracy—symbolized by the Bank of the United States—which had been created by their conservative predecessors. In mid-century, liberalism turned its attention to that most evil of caste systems, slavery, and succeeded in destroying at least its legal basis. Toward the close of the nineteenth century, liberalism began its long conflict with America's privileged economic elite which had been formed in the wake of the rapid industrialization of the post-Civil War period. In this century, liberalism continued its struggle with the "economic royalists," but it also recognized the existence of other forms of artificial status. It found evidence within American Protestantism of religious prejudice directed at the newly arrived Catholic and Jewish minorities. Most recently, liberalism has centered its criticisms on the legal, economic, and social barriers based on the standard of race that prevent the Negro minority from having more complete access to this nation's generally open social system.

To a considerable extent the United States has achieved the liberal vision of an open society. Viewed either historically or relative to the contemporary world, America has moved further in this direction than any comparable country in the world. Obstacle after obstacle has been swept aside in the nation's movement toward the goal of an open society. By the turn of the eighteenth century, America's militant republicanism uprooted the lingering traces of aristocracy based on birth. Liberalism's opposition to economic privilege has helped to create the broad degree of economic democracy which exists in modern America's increasingly middle-class society. Finally, privilege based on religion has diminished to the point where its presence is extremely difficult to detect and document.

The principal instrument responsible for the emergence of this open society is America's public school system. The policy of free public education for all children, first advocated by Jefferson, was actually created in New England in the early nineteenth century. This system gradually spread to the entire nation and today includes education for at least twelve years. It has largely been the public education system that has equipped each new generation of Americans—many of them recently arrived from Europe—with the intellectual skills necessary to take advantage of the social and economic opportunities existing in the nation.

Of course, racial barriers continue to block the more complete attainment of the ideal of the open society, and it is too soon to predict whether American society will succeed or fail in its attempt to eliminate these obstacles. It can only be said that, for the first time in its history, the nation is beginning to grapple with the full scope of its racial inequities. But even if the United States is successful in its quest for great racial justice, this will not mean that the goal of a completely open society has been reached. For the open society is an ideal, always to be sought after and never fully to be attained. It is a vision that the social conscience of each generation can redefine, pointing out new injustices and proposing plans for their solution.

Individualism and the open society stand, then, as the two enduring beliefs of American liberalism. Its other ideas have changed from period to period, as liberalism has attempted to discover more effective means to fulfill its deep commitment to individualism and the open society. Liberalism thus contains the elements of both change and stability— of pragmatic movement at the surface and of continuity and tradition in its fundamental values and ideas.

The dual emphasis on individualism and the open society constitutes the most significant contribution of liberalism to both the American and the Western political experience. Liberalism's acceptance of these doctrines sharply distinguishes it from its conservative opposition in the United States, for conservatism has either rejected or resisted individualism and the open society. Further, American liberalism has had an impact outside of this nation. Europe, and indeed much of the twentieth-century world, has increasingly been affected by the basic principles of American liberalism. While individualism is a concept drawn from the European political tradition, the idea of an open society is uniquely American. The growing concern for individual welfare and the demand for individual rights and a social and economic system that rejects artificial barriers of caste and class are evidence of the worldwide influence of American liberal political thought.

In conclusion, it is necessary to introduce a note of warning. American liberalism has been subject to a growing amount of criticism from spokesmen for extremist politics in this country. Its policies and principles have been derided both by the Old Right and in recent years by the New Left. These criticisms, coming at a time when serious domestic and international problems confront the United States, have placed American liberalism on the defensive. Liberalism has come to question whether its programs and principles are relevant to the contemporary world and to wonder if the future does not belong to the more militant and doctrinaire political creeds.

An examination of America's liberal experience should dispel such doubts. Liberalism's continuing ability to suggest new ideas to meet new problems while maintaining its allegiance to certain principles establishes a presumption in favor of liberalism's value and relevance. Only if American liberalism suffers a severe crisis of confidence can the criticisms of its enemies come true. A mature liberalism, secure in its sense of history, can continue to serve and lead America in these troubled times.

I

From the Colonies
to the Revolution

American liberal political thought throughout the eighteenth century was dominated by the ideas of seventeenth-century England. The major theorists, Jonathan Mayhew, Thomas Paine, and Thomas Jefferson, each had absorbed the natural rights philosophy of English liberalism, being particularly influenced by the thought of John Locke, whose political ideas were singularly well suited to the needs of a colonial people struggling to assert their independence.

America also produced a body of liberal political thought that did not draw its inspiration from Locke and English liberalism but was rooted in the harsh soil of the early New England settlements and colonies. The political thought of Roger Williams, though steeped in the religious and political conflicts of early seventeenth-century England, best illustrates this indigenous brand of American liberalism. Williams came to America to escape Anglican persecution of Puritanism only to find himself a dissenter within the Puritan majority of Massachusetts Bay. Not long after his arrival in the New World, Williams found it necessary to raise the issue of church and state with the Puritan authorities, thus importing to the colonies a controversy then raging in England. In the course of his debate with the Puritan leaders—most notably with John Cotton—Williams developed a number of daring and original political ideas which were the product of his experience in America: popular sovereignty, religious freedom, and the separation of church and state. Not content with abstract speculation, Williams applied these principles to the governmental systems created in the settlements which were eventually to become Rhode Island.

In *The Bloudy Tenent of Persecution*, Williams stated his belief in the idea of popular sovereignty. More than a century before Rousseau, Williams maintained that "the Sovereigne, originall, and foundation of civill power lies in the people." Viewing government as an artificial institution created by social compact, Williams recognized no restriction on the authority of the people to establish the type of government they believed most suited to their needs. Although Williams was a man primarily concerned with religious problems and believed that government was an "Ordinance of God," it was man and not God who created government and determined its form.

The issue which stood at the center of much of Williams' thought was that of the relationship between church and state. In *The Bloudy Tenent* he defended both the separation of church and state and the idea of religious freedom. Williams believed that church and state were concerned with different spheres. The church is a spiritual body interested only in the souls of men, while the state is a secular institution designed to maintain the civil peace and order. The state needs no assistance from the church to fulfill its function, and the church ought to rely solely on spiritual means in the saving of souls.

Williams' arguments in behalf of religious freedom are closely related to his belief in the separation of church and state and are cast in a predominantly religious mold. He viewed persecution for religious belief as contrary to the teachings of Jesus Christ who came to save and not to destroy men. God desired not persecution but freedom of religious conscience. Errors should be combated only by spiritual weapons and not by coercion. God desired true believers, Williams claimed, not hypocrites whose beliefs were compelled by the power of religious and secular authorities. Finally, Williams advanced a political argument in favor of religious freedom: it contributes to the peace and the good order of the community, whereas persecution weakens civil stability and creates disrespect and lawlessness.

The early Rhode Island settlements put into practice Williams' beliefs in popular sovereignty, separation of church and state, and religious freedom. The governments of these small communities were established by a covenant of the people based on the principle of majority rule operating in either a representative or a town meeting form of democracy. Some of the later settlements provided for a form of initiative, referendum, and recall. The terms for elected offices were short and the suffrage based on some standard of land ownership. This restriction, however, had a minimal effect on voting because of the liberal policy of granting land to all new settlers. Under the leadership of Williams, Rhode Island established a clear separation between church and state and extended the right of religious freedom to all who lived within its boundaries. During Williams' term as president of the colony, Jews arrived in Rhode Island, and several years later a number of the much despised Quakers settled in the area.

The concern that motivated all of Williams' political thought was the desire to protect the purity of religion from the corrupting inroads of civil power. By basing government on the authority of the people and establishing both the separation of church and state and the freedom of conscience, Williams hoped to achieve this religious objective. A century later American liberalism again advocated these doctrines, but its purposes were secular and its philosophy was not Christianity but natural rights. Jefferson, for example, argued for separation out of fear that the church would corrupt government, and he maintained that freedom of religion was a natural right of man.

The first signs of the secularization of American liberalism and the growing dominance of natural rights philosophy are shown in the political writing of the New England Congregational minister John Wise. Wise wrote *A Vindication of the Government of New England Churches* for theological reasons: he desired to defend the congregational system against an attempt to reduce the extent of local control over these churches. What is remarkable about this work is that Wise did not wish to establish the validity of the congregational form of church organization on the basis of scriptural authority but rather relied on purely political writings to prove his argument. Though Wise did, on occasion, cite religious authority, he gave primary emphasis to natural law political philosophy. "The spectacle of a Puritan minister examining 'the Light of Nature' to discover that democracy was the form of government most favored by the precepts of natural law, then grounding his case for democracy in the church on 'the near affinity our constitution holds' with political democracy, was truly astonishing. . . ."[1]

John Wise had read widely in the political philosophy of Europe; his writing is filled with reference to ancient, medieval, and sixteenth- and seventeenth-century authors. The source of Wise's natural law philosophy was not John Locke, as with mid- and late-eighteenth-century American liberal theorists, but the great German natural law jurist Samuel von Pufendorf (1632–1694). Pufendorf published his famous study *De jure naturae et gentium* in 1672, and it was printed in English translation in 1703. It is uncertain whether Wise read the Latin or the English edition, but his intellectual debt to Pufendorf is obvious and frankly admitted: "I shall principally take Baron Puffendorff for my chief guide and spokesman." Wise was apparently unaware of Locke's *Second Treatise of Civil Government* (1690), for his *Vindication* makes no reference to Locke or his political writings.

[1] Clinton Rossiter, *Seedtime of the Republic* (New York: Harcourt, Brace and Company, 1953), p. 212.

The political ideas of John Wise show the decline of Puritan ortho-doxy in early eighteenth-century America and the growing secularization of society. They further reveal the increasing appeal of democratic political thought, for Wise was fully committed to democracy in both church and state. His conception of democracy, however, was that of direct citizen participation for, like his contemporaries, he had no real comprehension of a representative form of government. Wise held up as models the two forms of democracy he knew best—congregationalism in church organization and the town meeting in government.

The clergy continued to play the leading role in the formulation of American liberal political doctrine almost to the eve of the Revolution-ary War. Jonathan Mayhew was the last of the great colonial liberal ministers, and his thought reveals the ambivalence of mid-eighteenth-century American thought—its religious past and its growing secular orientation. Clinton Rossiter has accurately described Mayhew's political philosophy as "an agreeable synthesis of Locke and St. Paul."[2] Although he had read widely in British political thought of the seventeenth century, Mayhew continued to rely on scriptural authority to support his political ideas.

Mayhew's religion was neither the dour authoritarianism of American Calvinism nor the hierarchical ceremonial religion of Anglicanism. Rather, Mayhew can be viewed as an early founder of New England Unitarianism in that his theology emphasized man's reason and freedom and the moral truths of early Christianity. The essential qualities of Mayhew's religious beliefs—its optimism and stress on reason and freedom—are also found in his political thought, which closely followed the doctrines of seventeenth-century English liberalism. The direct impact of John Locke's political philosophy is especially apparent in all of Mayhew's sermons and writings. His thought, like that of Locke, is based on a generally benevolent view of human nature and on a belief in man's reasonableness. Further, the ideas of both men are strongly individualistic and fully in the natural rights tradition of political thought.

The importance of Mayhew's political thought lies not in its origin-ality but in its application of Locke to mid-eighteenth-century America. Mayhew was one of the earliest and most prominent colonial proponents of Locke's political ideas, though he was unable completely to free his thinking from religious considerations, as Jefferson did a generation later. Most important, Mayhew was perhaps the first colonial leader to

2 *Ibid.*, p. 237.

declare his support for the right to resist tyrannical government. His belief was founded on the medieval and Lockean concept of the fiduciary nature of government—that government exercises authority in trust for the people. Its only legitimate purpose, to Mayhew as to Locke, was to promote "the common good and safety of society." When government fails in its trust, the people then possess the right and the duty to resist the exercise of wrongful authority. Despite Mayhew's religious orientation he refused to accept the idea that God sanctified all the acts of government. "Rulers have no authority from God to do mischief," he insisted. "It is blasphemy to call tyrants and oppressors God's ministers."

Although Mayhew advocated the right to resist illegal authority and hinted at the need for American independence, it was not until after 1765, when the conflict between the colonies and Great Britain sharpened, that ideas of resistance and independence gained increasing acceptance in America. No man did more to spread these ideas during the early months of the Revolutionary War than Thomas Paine. His popular pamphlet *Common Sense* savagely criticized the British governmental system, denied the advantages to America of reconciliation with the mother country, and played upon the growing feeling of American nationalism in counseling resistance and independence.

Common Sense, while primarily an agitational tract, also has consequence as a statement of political theory. For the most part Paine agreed with the principle tenets of the natural rights philosophy which dominated seventeenth- and eighteenth-century thought. He justified American independence, for example, in terms of its accord with nature—"a government of our own is our natural right," he declared.

Paine's significance as a political thinker must principally be ascribed to his role as a popularizer of thought and not to his originality. Nevertheless, there are several views set forth in *Common Sense* that are unusual and interesting. For one thing, Paine, unlike most followers of Locke and British liberalism, did not assume a particularly benevolent view of human nature. In the opening pages of the essay, Paine repeatedly emphasized the shortcomings of mankind and stated his conviction that society and government are institutions which allow men to overcome their natural deficiencies. Carefully distinguishing between the two, Paine maintained that society exists in order to help men fulfill their desires while government serves to control their vices.

Paine agreed with the proponents of British liberalism that government is an artificial creation and that security is its major purpose.

But, unlike the Lockeans, he opposed the separation of powers and favored a simpler, more directly democratic form of government. "I draw my idea of the form of government from a principle in nature which no art can overturn, viz. that the more simple any thing is, the less liable it is to be disordered, and the easier repaired when disordered."

It was on the basis of this belief that Paine subjected the English system to a withering criticism for its complexity and lack of responsibility to the public. Paine's insistence on simplicity and responsiveness in government provided perhaps the earliest American defense of this more radical view of democracy and established the intellectual foundation upon which later thinkers and political movements could build their ideas. Both the Jacksonian and the populist movements of the nineteenth century, for example, developed democratic views similar to those of Paine.

The high-water mark in the influence of seventeenth-century British liberalism in America was reached with the writing of the Declaration of Independence. The Declaration is more than a propaganda tract designed to justify the political and legal act of separation; it is also an important statement of the political theory that motivated the colonial patriots during this period of revolution. Condensed into a relatively few paragraphs are all of the major tenets of Lockean liberalism: an optimistic view of human nature, individualism, a belief in natural law and inalienable rights, limited government created by the consent of the governed, and the right to resist and to replace governments which act illegally.

The Declaration of Independence sets forth both the causes and the justification for America's right to rebel against Great Britain, but this right was carefully circumscribed and makes the Declaration the most moderate of revolutionary statements. It acknowledges the basically conservative quality of human nature—that men are more likely to endure evils than act to remove them. Further, the Declaration requires that the government which is to be overturned must have engaged in "a long train of abuses" intended to subject the people to despotism. Revolutions can be neither legal nor moral if they are entered into for "light and transient causes." Finally, the entire right of revolution is qualified by an appeal to the prudence of men; the abstract right to rebel must be examined and limited in the light of experience and tradition.

The Declaration was principally the creation of Thomas Jefferson, and the document reveals much about its author's political thought. It shows how deeply Jefferson had absorbed the political ideas of seventeenth-century English liberalism and particularly the thought of John Locke. Some observers have attempted to refute this understanding of Jefferson by pointing to his substitution of the word "happiness" for Locke's "property" in his listing of man's inalienable rights. Jefferson did not, however, mean to exclude property as a fundamental right, for he carefully stated that "life, liberty, and the pursuit of happiness" were only among, and not a full enumeration of, man's inalienable rights. Jefferson did intend to expand the rights of man by including the phrase about happiness in the Declaration, but nothing in the document or in any of his other writings indicates any departure from the bias in favor of property rights which he inherited from Locke and the other seventeenth-century Whig political theorists.

Jefferson's draft of the Declaration of Independence adds one important dimension to his political thought—his opposition to slavery. In listing the charges against King George, Jefferson included the monarch's support of slavery and the slave trade, and he condemned these practices with strong and certain language. It is clear from Jefferson's draft that he intended to give a universal meaning to his statement of the inalienable rights of man, for he described King George's support of slavery as a "cruel war against human nature itself" and a violation of man's "most sacred rights of life and liberty."

1. WILLIAMS

Religious Freedom

Roger Williams (1603–1683) was born in London, England, educated at Cambridge, and ordained as a Protestant minister in 1628 or 1629. Persecution of Puritans was on the increase in England at this time, and when Williams received a call to preach in the Massachusetts Bay colony, he accepted and sailed for the New World in 1630. Not long after his arrival, Williams got into difficulty with the Puritan leadership because of his open criticism of the prevailing political and religious system. He left Massachusetts Bay for a time to live and preach with the Separatists at Plymouth but soon returned to Salem. Once again his activities engendered the wrath of the Puritan establishment and he was banished from the colony. Williams led his followers from Massachusetts Bay, and they created the first Rhode Island settlements at Providence in 1636. By 1643 four settlements existed in the area, but internal divisions and harassment from Massachusetts Bay made manifest the need for a charter. Williams sailed to England and in 1644 obtained a charter for the Providence Plantations in the Narragansett Bay.

It was at this time that Williams took to pamphleteering to defend the liberal political and religious order he had founded in Rhode Island. The Preface and several of the most important chapters of Williams' most famous and significant work, *The Bloudy Tenent of Persecution for Cause of Conscience* (1644), are included in the following selection.* The arguments in this work are presented as a dialogue between Truth and Peace. Williams later served a term as president of the new colony and remained active in governmental affairs until his death in 1683.

PREFACE

First, That the blood of so many hundred thousand soules of *Protestants* and *Papists*, spilt in the *Wars* of *present* and *former Ages*,

* *The Complete Writings of Roger Williams*, III (New York: Russell and Russell, Inc., 1963), pp. 3–4, 62–64, 126–28, 146–47, 217–19, 247–50.

for their respective *Consciences*, is not *required* nor *accepted* by *Jesus Christ* the *Prince* of *Peace*.

Secondly, Pregnant *Scriptures* and *Arguments* are throughout the Worke proposed against the *Doctrine* of *persecution* for *cause* of *Conscience*.

Thirdly, Satisfactorie Answers are given to *Scriptures*, and objections produced by Mr. *Calvin, Beza,* Mr. *Cotton,* and the Ministers of the New English Churches and others former and later, tending to prove the *Doctrine of persecution* for cause of *Conscience*.

Fourthly, The *Doctrine of persecution* for cause of *Conscience,* is proved guilty of all the *blood* of the *Soules* crying for *vengeance* under the *Altar*.

Fifthly, All *Civill States* with their *Officers* of *justice* in their respective *constitutions* and *administrations* are proved *essentially Civill,* and therefore not *Judges, Governours* or *Defendours* of the *Spirituall* or *Christian state* and *Worship*.

Sixtly, It is the will and command of *God,* that (since the comming of his Sonne the *Lord Jesus*) a *permission* of the most *Paganish, Jewish, Turkish,* or *Antichristian consciences* and *worships,* bee granted to *all* men in all *Nations* and *Countries:* and they are onely to bee *fought* against with that *Sword* which is only (in *Soule matters*) *able* to *conquer,* to wit, the *Sword of Gods Spirit,* the *Word* of *God*.

Seventhly, The *state* of the Land of *Israel,* the *Kings* and *people* thereof in *Peace* & *War,* is proved *figurative* and *ceremoniall,* and no *patterne* nor *president* for any *Kingdome* or *civill state* in the *world* to follow.

Eightly, *God* requireth not an *uniformity* of *Religion* to be *inacted* and *inforced* in any *civill state*; which inforced *uniformity* (sooner or later) is the greatest occasion of *civill Warre, ravishing* of *conscience, persecution* of *Christ Jesus* in his servants, and of the *hypocrisie* and *destruction* of *millions* of *souls*.

Ninthly, In holding an inforced *uniformity* of *Religion* in a *civill state,* wee must necessarily *disclaime* our desires and hopes of the *Jewes conversion* to *Christ*.

Tenthly, An inforced *uniformity* of *Religion* throughout a *Nation* or *civill state,* confounds the *Civill* and *Religious,* denies the principles of Christianity and civility, and that *Jesus Christ* is come in the Flesh.

Eleventhly, The permission of other *consciences* and *worships* then a state professeth, only can (according to God) procure a firme and lasting *peace*, (good *assurance* being taken according to the *wisedome* of the *civill state* for *uniformity* of *civill obedience* from all sorts.)

Twelfthly, lastly, true *civility* and *Christianity* may both flourish in a *state* or *Kingdome*, notwithstanding the *permission* of divers and contrary *consciences*, either of *Jew* or *Gentile*.

CHAPTER III

Truth. In the Answer Mr. Cotton first layes downe severall *distinctions* and *conclusions* of his owne, tending to prove persecution.

Secondly, *Answers* to the *Scriptures*, and *Arguments* proposed against *persecution*.

Peace. The first distinction is this: By persecution for cause of Conscience, "I conceive you meane either for professing some point of *doctrine* which you beleeve in *conscience* to be the *truth*, or for *practising* some worke which you beleeve in *conscience* to be a *religious* dutie."

Truth. I acknowledge that to molest any person, *Jew* or *Gentile*, for either professing *doctrine*, or practising *worship* meerly *religious* or spirituall, it is to persecute him, and such a person (what ever his *doctrine* or *practice* be true or *false*) suffereth persecution for *conscience*.

But withall I desire it may bee well observed, that this *distinction* is not full and complete: For beside this that a man may be persecuted because he holdeth or practiseth what he beleeves in *conscience* to be a *Truth*, (as *Daniel* did, for which he was cast into the *Lyons* den, *Dan*. 6.) and many thousands of *Christians*, because they durst not cease to *preach* and *practise* what they beleeved was by *God* commanded, as the *Apostles* answered (*Acts* 4. & 5.) I say besides this a man may also be persecuted, because hee dares not be *constrained* to yeeld obedience to such *doctrines* and *worships* as are by men invented and appointed. So the three famous *Jewes* were cast down into the fiery furnace for refusing to fall downe (in a *non-conformity* to the whole conforming world) before the golden *Image*, Dan. 3. 21. So thousands of *Christs witnesses* (and of late in those bloudy *Marian* dayes) have rather chose to yeeld their *bodies* to all sorts of *torments*, then to subscribe to *doctrines*, or practise *worships*, unto which the States and Times (as *Nabuchadnezzar* to his golden *Image*) have compelled and urged them.

A chaste *wife* will not onely abhorre to be restrained from her *husbands bed*, as adulterous and polluted, but also abhor (if not much more) to bee constrained to the *bed* of a *stranger*. And what is abominable in *corporall*, is much more loathsome in *spirituall whoredome* and defilement.

The Spouse of *Christ Jesus* who could not finde her soules beloved in the *wayes* of his *worship* and *Ministery*, (*Cant.* 1. 3. and 5. Chapters) abhorred to turne aside to other *Flockes*, *Worships*, &c. and to imbrace the bosome of a false *Christ*, *Cant.* 1. 8.

CHAPTER XXXIV

Peace. But it is said, be it granted that in a *common plague* or *infection* none are smitten and dye but such as are appointed, yet it is not only every mans duty, but the common duty of the Magistrate to prevent *infection*, and to preserve the *common health* of the place; likewise though the number of the *Elect* be sure, and *God* knowes who are His, yet hath He appointed meanes for their *preservation* from *perdition*, and from *infection*, and therefore the *Angel* is blamed for suffering *Balaams* doctrine, and *Jesabel* to seduce Christ Jesus His servants, *Rev.* 2. *Tit.* 3. 10. *Rom.* 16. 17.

Truth. I answer, Let that Scripture and that of *Titus* reject an *Hereticke*, and *Rom.* 16. 17. avoid them that are *contentious*, &c. let them, and all of like nature be examined, and it will appeare that the great and good *Physitian Christ Jesus*, the *Head* of the *Body*, and *King* of the *Church* hath not been unfaithfull in providing spirituall *antidotes* and *preservatives* against the spirituall *sicknesses*, *sores*, *weaknesses*, *dangers* of his *Church* and people; but he never appointed the *civill sword* for either *antidote* or *remedy*, as an *addition* to those *spiritualls*, which he hath left with his *wife*, his *Church* or People.

Hence how great is the *bondage*, the *captivity* of Gods owne People to *Babylonish* or *confused mixtures* in Worship, and unto worldly and earthly policies to uphold *State Religions* or *Worships*, since that which is written to the *Angel* and *Church* at *Pergamus*, shall be interpreted as sent to the Governour and City of *Pergamus*, and that which is sent to *Titus*, and the Church of Christ at *Creet* must be delivered to the civill officers and City thereof.

But as the *Civill Magistrate* hath his charge of the *bodies* and *goods* of the *subject:* So have the *spirituall Officers*, *Governours* and *overseers* of *Christs City* or *Kingdome*, the charge of their *souls*, and *soule safety;* Hence that charge of *Paul* to *Tim.* 1 *Tim.* 5. 20. Them that sinne *rebuke* before all, that others may learne to *fear.* This is in the Church of Christ a spirituall meanes for the *healing* of a *soule* that hath sinned, or taken *infection*, and for the preventing of the infecting of others, that others may learne to feare, &c.

CHAPTER XLIV

Peace. The next Scripture produced against such Persecution, is 2 *Cor.* 10. 4. The *weapons* of our *warfare* are not *carnall*, but mighty through *God* to the pulling down of strong holds, casting down *imaginations*, and every high thing that exalteth it selfe against the *knowledge of God*, and bringing into *captivity* every thought to the obedience of *Christ*, and having in a readinesse to avenge all *disobedience*, &c.

Unto which it is answered, "When *Paul* saith, The *weapons* of our *warfare* are not *carnall*, but *spirituall:* he denieth not *civill* weapons of *Justice* to the *civill Magistrate*, Rom. 13., but only to *Church-officers:* and yet the *weapons* of *Church officers* he acknowledgeth to be such, as though they be *spirituall*, yet are ready to take *vengeance* on all *disobedience*, 2 Cor. 10. 6. which hath reference, amongst other *Ordinances*, to the censures of the *Church* against *scandalous offenders*.

Truth. I acknowledge that herein the Spirit of *God* denieth not *civill weapons* of *justice* to the *Civill Magistrate*, which the Scripture he quotes, *Rom.* 13. abundantly testifies.

Yet withall I must aske, why he here affirmeth the Apostle denies not *civill weapons* of Justice to the *civill Magistrate?* of which there is no question, unlesse that (according to his scope of proving *persecution* for *conscience*) he intends withall, that the *Apostle* denies not *civill weapons* of *justice* to the Civill *Magistrate* in *Spirituall* and *Religious* causes: The contrary whereunto (the Lord assisting) I shall evince, both from this very Scripture, and his owne observation, and lastly by that 13 of the Romanes, by himselfe quoted.

First then from this *Scripture* and his owne *Observation:* The *weapons* of *Church officers* (saith he) are such, which though they be *spirituall*, are ready to take vengeance on all *disobedience*; which hath reference (saith he) amongst other Ordinances, to the Censures of the *Church* against scandalous offenders.

I hence observe, that there being in this Scripture held forth a two-fold state, a *Civill state* and a *Spirituall*, *Civill officers* and *spirituall*, *civill weapons* and *spirituall weapons*, *civill vengeance* and *punishment*, and a *spirituall vengeance* and *punishment:* although the *Spirit* speakes not here expressly of *Civill Magistrates* and their *civill weapons*, yet these States being of different Natures and Considerations, as far differing as *Spirit* from *Flesh*, I first observe, that *Civill weapons* are most improper and unfitting in matters of the *Spirituall state* and *kingdome*, though in the *Civill state* most proper and sutable.

CHAPTER LXXX

Peace. Yea but (say they) the *godly* will not persist in *Heresie* or turbulent *Schisme*, when they are convinced in *Conscience*, &c.

Truth. Sweet *Truth*, if the Civill Court and *Magistracy* must judge (as before I have written) and those Civill Courts are as lawfull, consisting of *naturall men* as of *godly* persons, then what *consequences* necessarily will follow, I have before mentioned. And I adde, according to this *conclusion* it must follow, that, if the most *godly* persons yeeld not to once or twice *Admonition* (as is maintained by the *Answerer*) they must necessarily be esteemed *obstinate* persons, for if they were *godly* (saith he) they would yeeld. Must it not then be said (as it was by one, passing sentence of *Banishment* upon some, whose godlinesse was acknowledged) that he that commanded the *Judge* not to respect the poore in the cause of *judgement*, commands him not to respect the holy or the godly person?

Hence I could name the place and time when a *godly* man, a most desirable person for his trade, &c. (yet something different in *conscience*) propounded his willingnesse and desire to come to dwell in a certaine *Towne* in *New England*; it was answered by the Chiefe of the place, This man differs from us, and wee desire not to be troubled. So that in conclusion (for no other reason in the world) the poore man, though godly, usefull and peaceable, could not be admitted to a Civill Being and Habitation on the Common Earth in that Wildernesse amongst them.

The latter part of the Answer concerning the *Hereticke* or obstinate person to be excommunicated, and the *scandalous offender* to be punished in the *Commonweale*, which neither of both come neere our *Question:* I have spoken [of] I feare too largely already.

Peace. Mr *Cotton* concludes with a confident perswasion of having removed the grounds of that great *errour, viz.* that persons are not to be persecuted for cause of *conscience*.

Truth. And I beleeve (deare Peace) it shall appear to them that (with feare and trembling at the word of the Lord) examine these passages, that the charge of *errour* reboundeth backe[,] even such an *errour*, as may well bee called the *bloody tenent*, so directly contradicting the *spirit* and *minde* and *practice* of the *Prince* of *Peace*; so deeply guilty of the *blood* of soules compelled and forced to *Hypocrisie* in a *spirituall* and *soule rape*; so deeply guilty of the *blood* of the *Soules* under the *Altar*, persecuted in all *ages* for the *cause* of *Conscience*, and so destructive to the *civill peace* and *welfare* of all *Kingdomes*, *Countries*, and *Commonwealths*.

CHAPTER XCII

Peace. The 4. head is, The proper meanes of both these Powers to attaine their ends.

"First, the proper meanes whereby the Civill Power may and should attaine its end, are onely Politicall, and principally these Five.

"First the erecting and establishing what forme of Civill Government may seeme in wisedome most meet, according to generall rules of the Word, and state of the people.

"Secondly, the making, publishing, and establishing of wholesome Civill Lawes, not onely such as concerne Civill Justice, but also the free passage of true Religion: for, outward Civill Peace ariseth and is maintained from them both, from the latter as well as from the former:

"Civill peace cannot stand intire, where Religion is corrupted, 2 *Chron.* 15. 3. 5. 6. *Judg.* 8. And yet such Lawes, though conversant about Religion, may still be counted Civill Lawes, as on the contrary, an Oath doth still remaine Religious, though conversant about Civill matters.

"Thirdly, Election and appointment of Civill officers, to see execution of those Lawes.

"Fourthly, Civill Punishments and Rewards, of Transgressors and Observers of these Lawes.

"Fifthly, taking up Armes against the Enemies of Civill Peace.

"Secondly, the meanes whereby the Church may and should attaine her ends, are only ecclesiasticall, which are chiefly five.

"First, setting up that forme of Church Government only, of which Christ hath given them a pattern in his Word.

"Secondly, acknowledging and admitting of no Lawgiver in the Church, but Christ, and the publishing of his Lawes.

"Thirdly, Electing and ordaining of such officers onely, as Christ hath appointed in his Word.

"Fourthly, to receive into their fellowship them that are approved, and inflicting Spirituall censures against them that offend.

"Fifthly, Prayer and patience in suffering any evill from them that be without, who disturbe their peace.

"So that Magistrates, as Magistrates, have no power of setting up the Forme of Church Government, electing Church officers, punishing with Church censures, but to see that the Church doth her duty herein. And on the other side, the Churches as Churches, have no power (though as members of the Commonweale they may have power) of erecting or altering formes of Civill Government, electing of Civill officers, inflicting Civill punishments (no not on persons excommunicate) as by deposing Magistrates from their Civill Authoritie, or withdrawing the hearts of the people against them, to their Lawes, no more then to discharge wives, or children, or servants, from due obedience to their husbands, parents, or masters: or by taking up armes against their Magistrates, though he persecute them for Conscience: for though members of Churches who are publique officers also of the Civill State, may suppresse by force the violence of Usurpers, as *Jehoiada* did *Athaliah*, yet this they doe not as members of the Church, but as officers of the Civill State."

Truth. Here are divers considerable *passages* which I shall briefly examine, so far as concernes our *controversie.*

First, whereas they say, that the *Civill Power* may erect and establish what *forme* of *civill Government* may seemc in *wisedome* most meet, I acknowledge the *proposition* to be most true, both in it self, and also considered with the end of it, that a *civill Government* is an *Ordinance* of *God*, to conserve the *civill peace* of people, so farre as concernes their *Bodies* and *Goods*, as formerly hath beene said.

But from this *Grant* I infer, (as before hath been touched) that the *Soveraigne, originall*, and *foundation* of *civill power* lies in the *people*, (whom they must needs meane by the *civill power* distinct from the *Government* set up.) And if so, that a People may erect and establish what *forme* of *Government* seemes to them most meete for their *civill condition:* It is evident that such *Governments* as are by them erected and established, have no more *power*, nor for no longer time, then the *civill power* or people consenting and agreeing shall betrust them with. This is cleere not only in *Reafon*, but in the experience of all *commonweales*, where the people are not deprived of their *naturall freedome* by the power of *Tyrants.*

And if so, that the Magistrates receive their power of governing the Church, from the People; undeniably it followes, that a *people*, as a *people*, naturally considered (of what *Nature* or *Nation* soever in *Europe, Asia, Africa* or *America*) have fundamentally and originally, as men, a power to governe the *Church*, to see her doe her *duty*, to correct her, to redresse, reforme, establish, &c. And if this be not to pull *God* and *Christ*, and *Spirit* out of *Heaven*, and subject them unto *naturall*, sinfull, inconstant men, and so consequently to *Sathan* himselfe, by whom all *peoples* naturally are guided, let *Heaven* and *Earth* judge.

Peace. It cannot by their owne *Grant* be denied, but that the *wildest Indians* in *America* ought (and in their kind and severall degrees doe) to agree upon some *formes* of *Government*, some more *civill*, compact in Townes, &c. some lesse. As also that their *civill* and *earthly Governments* be as lawfull and true as any *Governments* in the *World*, and therefore consequently their *Governors* are *Keepers* of the *Church* or both *Tables*, (if any Church of Christ should arise or be amongst them:) and therefore lastly, (if *Christ* have betrusted and charged the *civill* Power with his *Church*) they must judge according to their *Indian* or *American consciences*, for other *consciences* it cannot be supposed they should have.

2. WISE

Colonial Democracy

John Wise (1652–1725), a Congregational clergyman, was born in Roxbury, Massachusetts, attended the free schools in that town, and was graduated from Harvard College in 1673. He spent most of his adult life as minister in Chebacco, a part of the parish of Ipswich, Massachusetts. *A Vindication of the Government of New England Churches* was the second of two pamphlets Wise published between 1710 and 1717 designed to counter a plan for church reorganization proposed by Increase Mather and other conservative members of the Massachusetts clergy. The plan would have reduced the independence of individual churches by placing some church activities in the hands of organized ministerial groups. Largely because of the ideas contained in *A Vindication*, from which this selection* is taken, American historian Moses Coit Tyler referred to Wise as "the first great American democrat."

* (Boston: Printed and sold by John Boyle, 1772), pp. 22–27, 29–35, 37, 41, 44–46.

I shall disclose several principles of natural knowledge; plainly discovering the law of nature; or the true sentiments of natural reason, with respect to man's being and government. And in this essay I shall peculiarly confine the discourse to two heads, *viz.*

Of the natural (in distinction from the civil), and then,
Of the civil being of man. And I shall principally take Baron *Puffendorff* for my chief guide and spokesman.

I shall consider man in a state of natural being, as a freeborn subject under the crown of heaven, and owing homage to none but God himself. It is certain civil government in general, is a very admirable result of providence, and an incomparable benefit to mankind, yet must needs be acknowledged to be the effect of human free-compacts and not of divine institution; it is the produce of man's reason, of human and rational combinations, and not from any direct orders of infinite wisdom, in any positive law wherein is drawn up this or that scheme of civil government. Government (says Lord Warrington) is necessary—in that no society of men can subsist without it; and that particular form of government is necessary which best suits the temper and inclination of a people. Nothing can be God's ordinance but what he has particularly declared to be such; there is no particular form of civil government described in God's word, neither does nature prompt it. The government of the *Jews* was changed five times. Government is not formed by nature, as other births or productions; if it were, it would be the same in all countries; because nature keeps the same method, in the same thing, in all climates. If a common-wealth be changed into a monarchy, is it nature that forms and brings forth the monarch? Or if a royal family be wholly extinct (as in *Noah*'s case, being not heir apparent from descent from *Adam*) is it nature that must go to work (with the king's bees, who themselves alone preserve the royal race in that empire) to breed a monarch before the people can have a king, or a government to be set over them? And thus we must leave the kings to resolve which is their best title to their crowns, whether natural right, or the constitution of government settled by human compacts, under the direction and conduct of reason. But to proceed under the head of a state of natural being, I shall more distinctly explain the state of human nature in its original capacity, as man is placed on earth by his Maker, and clothed with many investitures, and immunities which properly belong to man separately considered. As,

The prime immunity in man's state, is that he is most properly the subject of the law of nature. He is the favorite animal on earth; in that this part of God's image, *viz.* reason is congenate with his nature, wherein by a law immutable, enstamped upon his frame, God has provided a rule for men in all their actions, obliging each one to the performance of that which is right, not only as to justice, but likewise as to all other moral virtues, the which is nothing but the dictate of right reason founded in the soul of man. Molloy, DeMao, Praef. That which is to be drawn from man's reason, flowing from the true current of that faculty, when unperverted, may be said to be the law of nature, on which account, the Holy Scriptures declare it written on men's hearts. For being endowed with a soul, you may know from yourself, how, and what you ought to act Rom. 2. 14. *These having not a law, are a law to themselves.* So that the meaning is, when we acknowledge the law of nature to be the dictate of right reason, we must mean that the understanding of man is endowed with such a power, as to be able, from the contemplation of human condition to discover a necessity of living agreeably with this law; and likewise to find out some principle, by which the precepts of it, may be clearly and solidly demonstrated. The way to discover the law of nature in our own state, is by a narrow watch, and accurate contemplation of our natural condition, and propensions. Others say this is the way to find out the law of nature. . . . If a man any way doubts, whether what he is going to do to another man be agreeable to the law of nature, then let him suppose himself to be in that other man's room, and by this rule effectually executed. A man must be a very dull scholar to nature not to make proficiency in the knowledge of her laws. But more particularly in pursuing our condition for the discovery of the law of nature, this is very obvious to view, *viz.*

A principle of self-love, and self-preservation, is very predominant in every man's being
A sociable disposition
An affection or love to mankind in general

And to give such sentiments the force of a law, we must suppose a God who takes care of all mankind, and has thus obliged each one, as a subject of higher principles of being, than mere instincts. For that all law properly considered, supposes a capable subject and a superior power, and the law of God which is binding, is published by the dictates of right reason as other ways: Therefore says *Plutarch, to follow God and obey reason is the same thing.* But moreover that God has established the law of nature, as the general rule of government, is further illustrable from the many sanctions in providence, and from the peace and guilt of conscience in them that either obey, or violate the law of nature. But moreover, the foundation of the law of nature with relation to government, may be thus discovered. . . . Man is a creature extremely desirous of his own preservation; of himself he is plainly exposed to many wants, unable to secure his own safety, and maintenance without assistance of his fellows; and he is also able of returning kindness by the furtherance of mutual good; but yet man is often found to be malicious; insolent, and easily provoked, and as powerful in effecting mischief, as he is ready in designing it. Now that such a creature may be preserved, it is necessary that he be sociable; that is, that he be capable and disposed to unite himself to those of his own species, and to regulate himself towards them, that they may have no fair reason to do him harm; but rather incline to promote his interests, and secure his rights and concerns. This then is a fundamental law of nature, that every man as far as in him lies, do maintain a sociableness with others, agreeable with the main end and disposition of human nature in general. For this is very apparent, that reason and society render man the most potent of all creatures. And finally, from the principles of sociableness it follows as a fundamental law of nature, that man is not so wedded to his own interest, but that he can make the common good the mark of his aim. And hence he becomes capacitated to enter into a civil state by the law of nature; for without this property in nature, *viz.* Sociableness, which is for cementing of parts, every government would soon moulder and dissolve.

The second great immunity of man is an original liberty enstamped upon his rational nature. He that intrudes upon this liberty, violates the law of nature. In this discourse I shall waive the consideration of man's moral turpitude, but shall view him physically as a creature which God has made and furnished essentially with many ennobling immunities, which render him the most august animal in the world, and still, whatever has happened since his creation, he remains at the upper end of nature, and as such is a creature of a very noble character. For as to his dominion, the whole frame of the lower part of the universe is devoted to his use, and at his command; and his liberty under the conduct of right reason, is equal with his trust. Which liberty may be briefly considered, internally as to his mind, and externally as to his person.

The native liberty of man's nature implies, a faculty of doing or omitting things according to the direction of his judgment. But in a more special meaning, this liberty does not consist in a loose and ungovernable freedom, or in an unbounded license of acting. Such license is disagreeing with the condition and dignity of man, and would make man of a lower and meaner constitution than brute creatures; who in all their liberties are kept under a better and more rational government, by their instincts. Therefore, as *Plutarch* says, *Those persons only who live in obedience to reason, are worthy to be accounted free: They alone live as they will, who have learned what they ought to will.* So that the true natural liberty of man, such as really and truly agrees to him, must be understood, as he is guided and restrained by the ties of reason, and laws of nature; all the rest is brutal, if not worse.

Man's external personal, natural liberty, antecedent to all human parts, or alliances, must also be considered. And so every man must be conceived to be perfectly in his own power and disposal, and not to be controlled by the authority of any other. And thus every man, must be acknowledged equal to every man, since all subjection and all command are equally banished on both sides; and considering all men thus at liberty, every man, has a prerogative to judge for himself, *viz.* What shall be most for his behoof, happiness and well-being.

The third capital immunity belonging to man's nature, is an equality amongst men; which is not to be denied by the law of nature, till man has resigned himself with all his rights for the sake of a civil state; and then his personal liberty and equality is to be cherished, and preserved to the highest degree, as will consist with all just distinctions amongst men of honor, and shall be agreeable to the public good. For man has a high valuation of himself, and the passion seems to lay its first foundation (not in pride, but) really in the high and admirable frame and constitution of human nature. . . .

To consider man in a civil state of being; wherein we shall observe the great difference between a natural, and political state; for in the latter state many great disproportions appear, or at least many obvious distinctions are soon made amongst men; which doctrine is to be laid open under a few heads.

Every man considered in a natural state, must be allowed to be free, and at his own disposal; yet to suit man's inclinations to society; and in a peculiar manner to gratify the necessity he is in of public rule and order, he is impelled to enter into a civil community; and divests himself of his natural freedom, and puts himself under government; which amongst other things comprehends the power of life and death over him; together with authority to enjoin him some things to which he has an utter aversion, and to prohibit him other things, for which he may have as strong an inclination; so that he may be often under this authority, obliged to sacrifice his private, for the public good. So that though man is inclined to society, yet he is driven to a combination by great necessity. For that the true and leading cause of forming governments, and yielding up natural liberty, and throwing man's equality into a common pile to be new cast by the rules of fellowship; was really and truly to guard themselves against the injuries men were liable to interchangeably; for none so good to man, as man, and yet none a greater enemy. . . .

Let us conceive in our mind a multitude of men, all naturally free and equal; going about voluntarily, to erect themselves into a new commonwealth. Now their condition being such, to bring themselves into a politic body, they must needs enter into divers covenants.

They must interchangeably each man covenant to join in one lasting society, that they may be capable to concert the measures of their safety, by a public vote.

A vote or decree must then nextly pass to set up some particular species of government over them. And if they are joined in their first compact upon absolute terms to stand to the decision of the first vote concerning the species of government; Then all are bound by the majority to acquiesce in that particular form thereby settled, though their own private opinion, incline them to some other model.

After a decree has specified the particular form of government, then there will be need of a new covenant, whereby those on whom sovereignty is conferred, engage to take care of the common peace, and welfare. And the subjects on the other hand, to yield them faithful obedience. In which covenant is included that submission and union of wills, by which a state may be conceived to be but one person. So that the most proper definition of a civil state, is this, *viz*. A civil state is a compound moral person. Whose will (united by those covenants before passed) is the will of all; to the end it may use, and apply the strength and riches of private persons towards maintaining the common peace, security, and well-being of all, which may be conceived as though the whole state was now become but one man. . . .

The forms of a regular state are three only, which forms arise from

the proper and particular subject, in which the supreme power resides.
As,

A democracy, which is when the sovereign power is lodged in a
council consisting of all the members, and where every member has
the privilege of a vote. This form of government, appears in the greatest
part of the world to have been the most ancient. For that reason seems
to show it to be most probable, that when men (being originally in a
condition of natural freedom and equality) had thoughts of joining in
a civil body, would without question be inclined to administer their
common affairs, by their common judgment, and so must necessarily
to gratify that inclination establish a democracy; neither can it be
rationally imagined, that fathers of families being yet free and independent, should in a moment, or little time take off their long delight
in governing their own affairs, and devolve all upon some single
sovereign commander; for that it seems to have been thought more
equitable, that what belonged to all should be managed by all, when all
had entered by compact into one community. . . .

The second species of regular government, is an aristocracy; and
this is said then to be constituted when the people, or assembly united
by a first covenant, and having thereby cast themselves into the first
rudiment of a state; do then by common decree devolve the sovereign
power, in a council consisting of some select members; and these
having accepted of the designation, are then properly invested with
sovereign command; and then an aristocracy is formed.

The third species of a regular government, is a monarch which is
settled when the sovereign power is conferred on some one worthy
person. It differs from the former, because a monarch who is but one
person in natural, as well as in moral account, and so is furnished with
an immediate power of exercising sovereign command in all instances
of government; but the forenamed must needs have particular time
and place assigned; but the power and authority is equal in each.

Mixt governments, which are various and of divers kinds (not now
to be enumerated) yet possibly the fairest in the world is that which
has a regular monarchy; settled upon a noble democracy as its basis.
And each part of the government is so adjusted by pacts and laws
that render the whole constitution an *elysium*. It is said of the British
empire, that it is such a monarchy, as that by the necessary subordinate
concurrence of the lords and commons, in the making and repealing
all statutes or acts of parliament; it hath the main advantages of an
aristocracy, and of a democracy, and yet free from the disadvantages

and evils of either. It is such a monarchy, as by most admirable temperament affords very much to the industry, liberty, and happiness of the
subject, and reserves enough for the majesty and prerogative of any
king, who will own his people as subjects, not as slaves. It is a kingdom,
that of all the kingdoms of the world, is most like the kingdom of Jesus
Christ, whose yoke is easy, and burden light. . . .

. . . I shall now proceed to inquire, whether any of the aforesaid
species of regular, unmixt governments, can with any good shew of
reason be predictable of the churches of Christ on earth. . . .

A democracy. This is a form of government, which the light of nature
does highly value, and often directs to, as most agreeable to the just
and natural prerogatives of human beings. This was of great account,
in the early times of the world. And not only so, but upon the experience
of several thousand years, after the world had been tumbled and tost
from one species of government to another, at a great expense of
blood and treasure, many of the wise nations of the world have sheltered
themselves under it again; or at least have blendished, and balanced
their governments with it. . . .

How can it consist with the honorable terms man holds upon here
on earth; that the best sort of men that we can find in the world; such
men as are adorned with a double set of ennobling immunities, the
first from nature, the other from grace; that these men when they enter
into charter-party to manage a trade from heaven, must *ipso facto* be
clapt under a government, that is arbitrary and dispotic; yea that
carries the plain symptoms of a tyranny in it, when the light of nature
knows of a better species, and frequently has made use of it? It wants
no farther demonstration, for it's most apparent, that nature is so much
mistress of herself, that man in a natural state of being, is under God
the first subject of all power, and therefore can make his own choice,
and by deliberate compacts, settles his own conditions for the government of himself in a civil state of being; and when a government so
settled shall throw itself from its foundations, or the subjects of sovereign
power shall subvert or confound the constitution, they then degrade
themselves; and so all power returns again to the people, who are the
first owners. And what! Is man become so unfortunate, degraded and
debased, as to be without all power in settling a government over
himself, relating to the matters of his eternal well-being? Or when he
comes back to a fathers house, must he fall into the captivity of a meer
passive being, and be put under such tutors, as can easily turn tyrants
over him, and no relief left for him in his own hands; this is certainly

most repugnant to the light of nature, and very disagreeable with the liberty and free genius of a gospel state. Nay, in a word, if the government of the churches be settled by God, either in the hands of a church monarch, or aristocracy, and the people are no ways the subject of church power: Nay, if they are not under Christ, the fountain of power; then the reformation so called, is but a mere cheat, a schism, and notorious rebellion; neither is there room for the least palliation, or shadow of excuse, for the reformers in renouncing their obedience to their public governors. . . .

But to wind up the whole discourse in a few words, . . .

Three particulars; or so many golden maxims, securing the honor of congregational churches.

Particular 1. That the people or fraternity under the gospel, are the first subjects of power; or else religion sinks the dignity of human nature into a baser capacity with relation to ecclesiastical, than it is in, in a natural state of being with relation to civil government.

Particular 2. That a democracy in church or state, is a very honorable and regular government according to the dictates of right reason. And therefore,

Particular 3. That these churches of New England, in their ancient constitution of church order; it being a democracy, are manifestly justified and defended by the law and light of nature. . . .

3. MAYHEW

The Right of Resistance

Jonathan Mayhew (1720–1766), a native of Chilmark, Martha's Vineyard, was graduated from Harvard College and immediately entered the Congregational ministry. From 1747 until his death, nineteen years later, Mayhew served as minister at Boston's famed West Church. Both a theological and a political liberal, Mayhew rejected the orthodox Calvinist doctrines of predestination and total depravity and helped lay the foundation for American Unitarianism. Politically, Mayhew was a persistent opponent of British encroachments on American liberties. The following selection* is taken from his 1750 sermon "A Discourse Concerning Unlimited Submission and Non-Resistance to the Higher Powers."

It is evident that the affairs of civil government may properly fall under a moral and religious consideration, at least so far forth as it relates to the general nature and end of magistracy, and to the grounds and extent of that submission which persons of a private character ought to yield to those who are vested with authority. This must be allowed by all who acknowledge the divine original of Christianity. For, although there be a sense, and a very plain and important sense, in which Christ's kingdom is not of this world, his inspired apostles have, nevertheless, laid down some general principles concerning the office of civil rulers, and the duty of subjects, together with the reason and obligation of that duty. And from hence it follows, that it is proper for all who acknowledge the authority of Jesus Christ, and the inspiration of his apostles, to endeavor to understand what is in fact the doctrine which they have delivered concerning this matter. It is the duty of Christian magistrates to inform themselves what it is which their religion teaches concerning the nature and design of their office. And it is equally the duty of all Christian people to inform themselves what it is which their religion teaches concerning that subjection which they owe to the higher powers. It is for these reasons that I have attempted to examine into the Scripture account of this matter, in order to lay it before you with the same freedom which I constantly use with relation to other doctrines and precepts of Christianity; not doubting but you will judge upon everything offered to your consideration with the same spirit of freedom and liberty with which it is spoken. . . .

The apostle's doctrine, [St. Paul's] in the passage thus explained, concerning the office of civil rulers, and the duty of subjects, may be summed up in the following observations, viz.:

That the end of magistracy is the good of civil society, *as such.*

That civil rulers, *as such,* are the ordinance and ministers of God; it being by his permission and providence that any bear rule, and agreeable to his will that there should be *some persons* vested with authority in society, for the well-being of it.

That which is here said concerning civil rulers extends to all of them in common. It relates indifferently to monarchical, republican, and

---

* John Wingate Thornton, ed., *The Pulpit of the American Revolution* (Boston: Gould and Lincoln, 1860), pp. 53–54, 60–67, 69–71, 77–79.

aristocratical government, and to all other forms which truly answer
the sole end of government—the happiness of society; and to all the
different degrees of authority in any particular state; to inferior officers
no less than to the supreme.

That disobedience to civil rulers in the due exercise of their authority
is not merely a political sin, but a heinous office against God and religion.

That the true ground and reason of our obligation to be subject to
the higher powers is, the usefulness of magistracy (when properly
expressed) to human society, and its subserviency to the general welfare.

That obedience to civil rulers is here equally required under all forms
of government which answer the sole end of all government—the good
of society; and to every degree of authority, in any state, whether
supreme or subordinate. From whence it follows—

That if unlimited obedience and non-resistance be here required as a
duty under any one form of government, it is also required as a duty
under all other forms, and as a duty to subordinate rulers as well as
to the supreme.

And, lastly, that those civil rulers to whom the apostle enjoins
subjection are the persons *in possession; the powers that be;* those who
are actually vested with authority.

There is one very important and interesting point which remains to
be inquired into, namely, the *extent* of that subjection to the higher
powers which is here enjoined as a duty upon all Christians. Some have
thought it warrantable and glorious to disobey the civil powers in
certain circumstances, and in cases of very great and general oppression,
when humble remonstrances fail of having any effect; and, when the
public welfare cannot be otherwise provided for and secured, to rise
unanimously even against the sovereign himself, in order to redress
their grievances; to vindicate their natural and legal rights; to break
the yoke of tyranny, and free themselves and posterity from inglorious
servitude and ruin. It is upon this principle that many royal oppressors
have been driven from their thrones into banishment, and many slain
by the hands of their subjects. It was upon this principle that Tarquin
was expelled from Rome, and Julius Caesar, the conqueror of the world
and the tyrant of his country, cut off in the senate-house. It was upon
this principle that King Charles I. was beheaded before his own
banqueting-house. It was upon this principle that King James II. was
made to fly that country which he aimed at enslaving; and upon this
principle was that revolution brought about which has been so fruitful
of happy consequences to Great Britain. But, in opposition to this

principle, it has often been asserted that the Scripture in general, and the passage under consideration in particular, makes all resistance to princes a crime, in any case whatever. If they turn tyrants, and become the common oppressors of those whose welfare they ought to regard with a paternal affection, we must not pretend to right ourselves, unless it be by prayers, and tears, and humble entreaties. And if these methods fail of procuring redress, we must not have recourse to any other, but all suffer ourselves to be robbed and butchered at the pleasure of the "Lord's anointed," lest we should incur the sin of rebellion and the punishment of damnation!—for he has God's authority and commission to bear him out in the worst of crimes so far that he may not be withstood or controlled. Now, whether we are obliged to yield such an absolute submission to our prince, or whether disobedience and resistance may not be justifiable in some cases, notwithstanding anything in the passage before us, is an inquiry in which we all are concerned; and this is the inquiry which is the main design of the present discourse.

Now, there does not seem to be any necessity of supposing that an absolute, unlimited obedience, whether active or passive, is here enjoined, merely for this reason—that the precept is delivered in absolute terms, without any exception or limitation expressly mentioned. We are enjoined to be "subject to the higher powers"; and to be "subject for conscience' sake." And because these expressions are absolute and unlimited, or, more properly, general, some have inferred that the subjection required in them must be absolute and unlimited also,—at least so far forth as to make passive obedience and non-resistance a duty in all cases whatever, if not active obedience likewise;—though, by the way, there is here no distinction made betwixt active and passive obedience; and if either of them be required in an unlimited sense, the other must be required in the same sense also, by virtue of the present argument, because the expressions are equally absolute with respect to both. But that unlimited obedience of any sort cannot be argued merely from the indefinite expressions in which obedience is enjoined, appears from hence, that expressions of the same nature frequently occur in Scripture, upon which it is confessed on all hands that no such absolute and unlimited sense ought to be put. For example: "Love not the world, neither the things that are in the world," "Lay not up for yourselves treasures upon earth," "Take therefore no thought for the morrow," are precepts expressed in at least equally absolute and unlimited terms; but it is generally allowed that they are to be understood with certain restrictions and limitations; some degree of love to the world and the things of it being allowable. . . .

But, to instance in some Scripture precepts which are more directly to the point in hand: Children are commanded to obey their parents, and servants their masters, in as absolute and unlimited terms as subjects are here commanded to obey their civil rulers. Thus this same apostle: "Children, obey your parents in the Lord; for this is right. Honor thy father and mother, which is the first commandment with promise. Servants, be obedient to them that are your masters according to the flesh, with fear and trembling, with singleness of your heart, as unto Christ." Thus, also, wives are commanded to be obedient to their husbands: "Wives, submit yourselves unto your own husbands, as unto the Lord; for the husband is head of the wife, even as Christ is the head of the church. Therefore, as the church is subject unto Christ, so let the wives be to their own husbands in everything." In all these cases, submission is required in terms at least as absolute and universal as are ever used with respect to rulers and subjects. But who supposes that the apostle ever intended to teach that children, servants, and wives, should, in all cases whatever, obey their parents, masters and husbands respectively, never making any opposition to their will, even although they should require them to break the commandments of God, or should causelessly make an attempt upon their lives? No one puts such a sense upon these expressions, however absolute and unlimited. Why, then, should it be supposed that the apostle designed to teach universal obedience, whether active or passive, to the higher powers, merely because his precepts are delivered in absolute and unlimited terms? And if this be a good argument in one case, why is it not in others also? If it be said that resistance and disobedience to the higher powers is here said positively to be a sin, so also is the disobedience of children to parents, servants to masters, and wives to husbands, in other places of Scripture. But the question still remains, whether, in all these cases, there be not some exceptions. In the three latter it is allowed there are; and from hence it follows, that barely the use of absolute expressions is no proof that obedience to civil rulers is in all cases a duty, or resistance in all cases a sin. I should not have thought it worth while to take any notice of this argument, had it not been much insisted upon by some of the advocates for passive obedience and non-resistance; for it is in itself perfectly trifling, and rendered considerable only by the stress that has been laid upon it for want of better.

There is, indeed, one passage in the New Testament where it may seem, at first view, that an unlimited submission to civil rulers is enjoined: "Submit yourselves to every ordinance of man for the Lord's sake." To *every ordinance of man*. However, this expression is no stronger than that before taken notice of with relation to the duty of wives: "So let the wives be subject to their own husbands *in everything*." But the true solution of this difficulty (if it be one) is this: By "every ordinance of man" is not meant every command of the civil magistrate without exception, but every order of magistrates appointed by man, whether superior or inferior; for so the apostle explains himself in the very next words: "Whether it be to the king as supreme, or to governors, as unto them that are sent," etc. But although the apostle had not subjoined any such explanation, the reason of the thing itself would have obliged us to limit the expression "every ordinance of man" to such human ordinances and commands as are not inconsistent with the ordinances and commands of God, the Supreme Lawgiver, or with any other higher and antecedent obligations. . . .

And if we attend to the nature of the argument with which the apostle here enforces the duty of submission to the higher powers, we shall find it to be such a one as concludes not in favor of submission to all who bear the title of rulers in common, but only to those who actually perform the duty of rulers by exercising a reasonable and just authority for the good of human society. This is a point which it will be proper to enlarge upon, because the question before us turns very much upon the truth or falsehood of this position. It is obvious, then, in general, that the civil rulers whom the apostle here speaks of, and obedience to whom he presses upon Christians as a duty, are good rulers, such as are, in the exercise of their office and power, benefactors to society. Such they are described to be throughout this passage. Thus, it is said that they are not a terror to good works, but to the evil; that they are God's ministers for good; revengers to execute wrath upon him that doeth evil; and that they attend continually upon this very thing. St. Peter gives the same account of rulers: They are "for a praise to them that do well, and the punishment of evil doers." It is manifest that this character and description of rulers agrees only to such as are rulers in fact, as well as in name; to such as govern well, and act agreeably to their office. And the apostle's argument for submission to rulers is wholly built and grounded upon a presumption that they do in fact answer this character, and is of no force at all upon supposition of the contrary. If rulers are a terror to good works, and not to the evil; if they are not ministers for good to society, but for evil and distress, by violence and oppression; if they execute wrath upon sober, peaceable persons, who do their duty as members of society, and suffer rich and honorable knaves to escape with impunity; if, instead of attending continually upon the good work of advancing the public welfare, they attend continually upon the gratification of their own lust and pride and ambition, to the destruction of the public welfare;—if this be the case, it is plain that the apostle's argument for submission does not reach them; they are not the same, but different persons from those whom he characterizes, and who must be obeyed, according to his reasoning. . . .

. . . If those who bear the title of civil rulers do not perform the duty of civil rulers, but act directly counter to the sole end and design of their office; if they injure and oppress their subjects, instead of defending their rights and doing them good, they have not the least pretense to be honored, obeyed, and rewarded, according to the apostle's argument. For his reasoning, in order to show the duty of subjection to the higher powers, is, as was before observed, built wholly upon the supposition that they do, in fact, perform the duty of rulers.

Thus, upon a careful review of the apostle's reasoning in this passage, it appears that his arguments to enforce submission are of such a nature as to conclude only in favor of submission to such rulers as he himself describes; *i.e.*, such as rule for the good of society, which is the only end of their institution. Common tyrants and public oppressors are not entitled to obedience from their subjects by virtue of anything here laid down by the inspired apostle.

I now add, further, that the apostle's argument is so far from proving it to be the duty of people to obey and submit to such rulers as act in contradiction to the public good, and so to the design of their office, that it proves the direct contrary. For, please to observe that if the end of all civil government be the good of society; if this be the thing that is aimed at in constituting civil rulers; and if the motive and argument for submission to government be taken from the apparent usefulness of civil authority,—it follows, that when no such good end can be answered by submission, there remains no argument or motive to enforce it; and if, instead of this good end's being brought about by submission, a contrary end is brought about, and the ruin and misery of society effected by it, here is a plain and positive reason against submission in all such cases, should they ever happen. And therefore, in such cases, a regard to the public welfare ought to make us withhold from our rulers that obedience and submission which it would otherwise be our duty to render to them. If it be our duty, for example, to obey our king merely for this reason, that he rules for the public welfare (which is the only argument the apostle makes use of), it follows, by a parity of reason, that when he turns tyrant, and makes his subjects his prey to devour and destroy, instead of his charge to defend and cherish, we are bound to throw off our allegiance to him, and to resist; and that according to the tenor of the apostle's argument in this passage. Not to discontinue our allegiance in this case would be to join with the sovereign in promoting the slavery and misery of that society, the welfare of which we ourselves, as well as our sovereign, are indispensably obliged to secure and promote, as far as in us lies. It is true the apostle puts no case of such a tyrannical prince; but, by his grounding his argument for submission wholly upon the good of civil society, it is plain he implicitly authorizes, and even requires us to make resistance, whenever this shall be necessary to the public safety and happiness. . . .

4. PAINE

Independence—A Natural Right

Thomas Paine (1737–1809), political pamphleteer and revolutionary agitator, was born in Thetford, England, into a poor Quaker-Anglican family. He received little formal education and left home at the age of nineteen. Between 1756 and 1774 Paine engaged in a variety of pursuits—sailor, teacher, corset maker, grocer, tobacconist, and exciseman—with little economic or personal success. In 1774 he met Benjamin Franklin in London, and with Franklin's encouragement he sailed to America in October of that year. After arriving in Philadelphia, Paine turned to journalism. On January 10, 1776, his most famous and influential pamphlet, *Common Sense*, portions of which are presented in the following selection,* was published anonymously. The 47-page work cost two shillings and sold approximately 120,000 copies in the first three months after its appearance. Following

* William M. Van der Weyde, ed., *The Life and Works of Thomas Paine*, II (New Rochelle, N.Y.: Thomas Paine National Historical Association, 1925), pp. 97–104, 122–27, 129–31, 146.

the outbreak of the war, Paine enlisted in the American army and continued to publish a series of pamphlets called *Crisis* which supported the independence movement. The conditions of peace were not well suited to Paine's temperament, and in 1787 he returned to Europe to begin a fifteen-year period of revolutionary activity in England and France. Between 1791 and 1792 Paine published *The Rights of Man*, a reply to Edmund Burke's criticism of the French Revolution. The work was banned in England, and Paine was tried *in absentia* for treason and punished by being outlawed from the country. Meanwhile in France, Paine had been given French citizenship and elected to the national Convention, where he sat as a member of the Gironde group. With the rise to power of Robespierre, Paine was deprived of these rights and imprisoned in December, 1793. He was released eleven months later, following the fall of Robespierre, with his citizenship and Convention seat restored. Paine remained in France and between 1794 and 1796 published *The Age of Reason*, an attack on Christianity and a defense of deism. Finally, in October, 1802, Paine returned to the United States and spent the last seven years of his life at Bordentown, New Jersey, and New Rochelle, New York, in isolation, poverty, and declining health.

ON THE ORIGIN AND DESIGN OF GOVERNMENT IN GENERAL, WITH CONCISE REMARKS ON THE ENGLISH CONSTITUTION

Some writers have so confounded society with government, as to leave little or no distinction between them; whereas they are not only different, but have different origins. Society is produced by our wants and government by our wickedness; the former promotes our happiness *positively* by uniting our affections, the latter *negatively* by restraining our vices. The one encourages intercourse, the other creates distinctions. The first is a patron, the last a punisher.

Society in every state is a blessing, but government, even in its best state, is but a necessary evil; in its worst state an intolerable one: for when we suffer, or are exposed to the same miseries *by a government*, which we might expect in a country *without government*, our calamity is heightened by reflecting that we furnish the means by which we suffer. Government, like dress, is the badge of lost innocence; the palaces of kings are built upon the ruins of the bowers of paradise. For were the impulses of conscience clear, uniform and irresistibly obeyed, man would need no other law-giver; but that not being the case, he finds it necessary to surrender up a part of his property to furnish means for the protection of the rest; and this he is induced to do by the same prudence which in every other case advises him, out of two evils to choose the least. Wherefore, security being the true design and end of government, it unanswerably follows that whatever form thereof appears most likely to ensure it to us, with the least expense and greatest benefit, is preferable to all others.

In order to gain a clear and just idea of the design and end of government, let us suppose a small number of persons settled in some sequestered part of the earth, unconnected with the rest; they will then represent the first peopling of any country, or of the world. In this state of natural liberty, society will be their first thought. A thousand motives will excite them thereto; the strength of one man is so unequal to his wants, and his mind so unfitted for perpetual solitude, that he is soon obliged to seek assistance and relief of another, who in his turn requires the same. Four or five united would be able to raise a tolerable dwelling in the midst of a wilderness, but one man might labor out the common period of life without accomplishing any thing; when he had felled his timber he could not remove it, nor erect it after it was removed; hunger in the mean time would urge him to quit his work, and every different want would call him a different way. Disease, nay even misfortune, would be death; for though neither might be mortal, yet either would disable him from living, and reduce him to a state in which he might rather be said to perish than to die.

Thus necessity, like a gravitating power, would soon form our newly arrived emigrants into society, the reciprocal blessings of which would supercede, and render the obligations of law and government unnecessary while they remained perfectly just to each other; but as nothing but Heaven is impregnable to vice, it will unavoidably happen that in proportion as they surmount the first difficulties of emigration, which bound them together in a common cause, they will begin to relax in their duty and attachment to each other: and this remissness will point out the necessity of establishing some form of government to supply the defect of moral virtue.

Some convenient tree will afford them a State House, under the branches of which the whole colony may assemble to deliberate on public matters. It is more than probable that their first laws will have the title only of regulations and be enforced by no other penalty than public disesteem. In this first parliament every man by natural right will have a seat.

But as the colony increases, the public concerns will increase likewise, and the distance at which the members may be separated, will render it too inconvenient for all of them to meet on every occasion as at first, when their number was small, their habitations near, and the public concerns few and trifling. This will point out the convenience of their consenting to leave the legislative part to be managed by a select number chosen from the whole body, who are supposed to have the same concerns at stake which those have who appointed them, and who will act in the same manner as the whole body would act were they present. If the colony continue increasing, it will become necessary to augment the number of representatives, and that the interest of every part of the colony may be attended to, it will be found best to divide the whole into convenient parts, each part sending its proper number: and that the *elected* might never form to themselves an interest separate from the *electors*, prudence will point out the propriety of having elections often: because as the *elected* might by that means return and mix again with the general body of the *electors* in a few months, their fidelity to the public will be secured by the prudent reflection of not making a rod for themselves. And as this frequent interchange will establish a common interest with every part of the community, they will mutually and naturally support each other, and on this, (not on the unmeaning name of king,) depends the *strength of government, and the happiness of the governed.*

Here then is the origin and rise of government; namely, a mode rendered necessary by the inability of moral virtue to govern the world; here too is the design and end of government, viz. freedom and security. And however our eyes may be dazzled with show, or our ears deceived by sound; however prejudice may warp our wills, or interest darken our understanding, the simple voice of nature and reason will say, 'tis right.

I draw my idea of the form of government from a principle in nature which no art can overturn, viz. that the more simple any thing is, the less liable it is to be disordered, and the easier repaired when disordered; and with this maxim in view I offer a few remarks on the so much boasted Constitution of England. That it was noble for the dark and slavish times in which it was erected, is granted. When the world was overrun with tyranny the least remove therefrom was a glorious rescue. But that it is imperfect, subject to convulsions, and incapable of producing what it seems to promise, is easily demonstrated.

Absolute governments, (though the disgrace of human nature) have this advantage with them, they are simple; if the people suffer, they know the head from which their suffering springs; know likewise the remedy; and are not bewildered by a variety of causes and cures.

But the Constitution of England is so exceedingly complex, that the nation may suffer for years together without being able to discover in which part the fault lies; some will say in one and some in another, and every political physician will advise a different medicine.

I know it is difficult to get over local or long standing prejudices, yet if we will suffer ourselves to examine the component parts of the English Constitution, we shall find them to be the base remains of two ancient tyrannies, compounded with some new Republican materials.

First.—The remains of monarchical tyranny in the person of the king.

Secondly.—The remains of aristocratical tyranny in the persons of the peers.

Thirdly.—The new Republican materials, in the persons of the Commons, on whose virtue depends the freedom of England.

The two first, by being hereditary, are independent of the people; wherefore in a *constitutional sense* they contribute nothing towards the freedom of the State.

To say that the Constitution of England is an *union* of three powers, reciprocally *checking* each other, is farcical; either the words have no meaning, or they are flat contradictions.

To say that the Commons is a check upon the king, presupposes two things.

First.—That the king is not to be trusted without being looked after; or in other words, that a thirst for absolute power is the natural disease of monarchy.

Secondly.—That the Commons, by being appointed for that purpose, are either wiser or more worthy of confidence than the crown.

But as the same constitution which gives the Commons a power to check the king by withholding the supplies, gives afterwards the king a power to check the Commons, by empowering him to reject their other bills; it again supposes that the king is wiser than those whom it has already supposed to be wiser than him. A mere absurdity!

There is something exceedingly ridiculous in the composition of monarchy; it first excludes a man from the means of information, yet empowers him to act in cases where the highest judgment is required. The state of a king shuts him from the world, yet the business of a king requires him to know it thoroughly; wherefore the different parts, by unnaturally opposing and destroying each other, prove the whole character to be absurd and useless. . . .

THOUGHTS ON THE PRESENT STATE OF
AMERICAN AFFAIRS

In the following pages I offer nothing more than simple facts, plain arguments, and common sense: and have no other preliminaries to settle with the reader, than that he will divest himself of prejudice and prepossession, and suffer his reason and his feelings to determine for themselves: that he will put on, or rather that he will not put off, the true character of a man, and generously enlarge his views beyond the present day.

Volumes have been written on the subject of the struggle between England and America. Men of all ranks have embarked in the controversy, from different motives, and with various designs; but all have been ineffectual, and the period of debate is closed. Arms as the last resource decide the contest; the appeal was the choice of the king, and the continent has accepted the challenge. . . .

The sun never shone on a cause of greater worth. 'Tis not the affair of a city, a county, a province, or a kingdom; but of a continent—of at least one eighth part of the habitable globe. 'Tis not the concern of a day, a year, or an age; posterity are virtually involved in the contest, and will be more or less affected even to the end of time, by the proceedings now. Now is the seed-time of continental union, faith and honor. The least fracture now will be like a name engraved with the point of a pin on the tender rind of a young oak; the wound would enlarge with the tree, and posterity read it in full grown characters. . . .

As much has been said of the advantages of reconciliation, which, like an agreeable dream, has passed away and left us as we were, it is but right that we should examine the contrary side of the argument, and inquire into some of the many material injuries which these colonies sustain, and always will sustain, by being connected with and dependent on Great Britain. To examine that connection and dependence, on the principles of nature and common sense, to see what we have to trust to, if separated, and what we are to expect, if dependent.

I have heard it asserted by some, that as America has flourished under her former connection with Great Britain, the same connection is necessary towards her future happiness, and will always have the same effect. Nothing can be more fallacious than this kind of argument. We may as well assert that because a child has thrived upon milk, that it is never to have meat, or that the first twenty years of our lives is to become a precedent for the next twenty. But even this is admitting more than is true; for I answer roundly, that America would have flourished as much, and probably much more, had no European power taken any notice of her. The commerce by which she hath enriched herself are the necessaries of life, and will always have a market while eating is the custom of Europe.

But she has protected us, say some. That she hath engrossed us is true, and defended the continent at our expense as well as her own, is admitted; and she would have defended Turkey from the same motive, *viz.* for the sake of trade and dominion.

Alas! we have been long led away by ancient prejudices and made large sacrifices to superstition. We have boasted the protection of Great Britain, without considering, that her motive was *interest* not *attachment;* and that she did not protect us from *our enemies* on *our account;* but from *her enemies* on *her own account*, from those who had no quarrel with us on any *other account*, and who will always be our enemies on the *same account*. Let Britain waive her pretensions to the continent, or the continent throw off the dependance, and we should be at peace with France and Spain, were they at war with Britain. The miseries of Hanover's last war ought to warn us against connections.

It hath lately been asserted in Parliament, that the colonies have no relation to each other but through the parent country, *i.e.* that Pennsylvania and the Jerseys, and so on for the rest, are sister colonies by the way of England; this is certainly a very round-about way of proving relationship, but it is the nearest and only true way of proving enmity (or enemyship, if I may so call it.) France and Spain never were, nor perhaps ever will be, our enemies as *Americans*, but as our being the *subjects of Great Britain*.

But Britain is the parent country, say some. Then the more shame upon her conduct. Even brutes do not devour their young, nor savages make war upon their families; wherefore, the assertion, if true, turns to her reproach; but it happens not to be true, or only partly so, and the phrase *parent* or *mother country* hath been jesuitically adopted by the king and his parasites, with a low papistical design of gaining an unfair bias on the credulous weakness of our minds. Europe, and not England, is the parent country of America. This new world hath been the asylum for the persecuted lovers of civil and religious liberty from *every part* of Europe. Hither have they fled, not from the tender embraces of the mother, but from the cruelty of the monster; and it is so far true of England, that the same tyranny which drove the first emigrants from home, pursues their descendants still. . . .

Much hath been said of the united strength of Britain and the colonies, that in conjunction they might bid defiance to the world. But this is mere presumption; the fate of war is uncertain, neither do the expressions mean any thing; for this continent would never suffer itself to be drained of inhabitants, to support the British arms in either Asia, Africa or Europe.

Besides, what have we to do with setting the world at defiance? Our plan is commerce, and that, well attended to, will secure us the peace and friendship of all Europe; because it is the interest of all Europe to have America a free port. Her trade will always be a protection, and her barrenness of gold and silver secure her from invaders.

I challenge the warmest advocate for reconciliation to show a single advantage that this continent can reap by being connected with Great Britain. I repeat the challenge; not a single advantage is derived. Our corn will fetch its price in any market in Europe, and our imported goods must be paid for buy them where we will.

But the injuries and disadvantages which we sustain by that connection, are without number; and our duty to mankind at large, as well as to ourselves, instruct us to renounce the alliance: because, any submission to, or dependence on, Great Britain, tends directly to involve this continent in European wars and quarrels, and set us at variance with nations who would otherwise seek our friendship, and against whom we have neither anger nor complaint. As Europe is our market for trade, we ought to form no partial connection with any part of it. It is the true interest of America to steer clear of European contentions, which she never can do, while, by her dependence on Britain, she is made the make-weight in the scale of British politics.

Europe is too thickly planted with kingdoms to be long at peace, and whenever a war breaks out between England and any foreign power, the trade of America goes to ruin, *because of her connection with Britain*. The next war may not turn out like the last, and should it not, the advocates for reconciliation now will be wishing for separation then, because neutrality in that case would be a safer convoy than a man of war. Every thing that is right or reasonable pleads for separation. The blood of the slain, the weeping voice of nature cries, 'TIS TIME TO PART. Even the distance at which the Almighty hath placed England and America is a strong and natural proof that the authority of the one over the other, was never the design of heaven. The time likewise at which the continent was discovered, adds weight to the argument, and the manner in which it was peopled, encreases the force of it. The Reformation was preceded by the discovery of America: As if the

Almighty graciously meant to open a sanctuary to the persecuted in future years, when home should afford neither friendship nor safety. . . .

A government of our own is our natural right: and when a man seriously reflects on the precariousness of human affairs, he will become convinced, that it is infinitely wiser and safer, to form a Constitution of our own in a cool deliberate manner, while we have it in our power, than to trust such an interesting event to time and chance. . . .

5. JEFFERSON
The Declaration of Independence

Thomas Jefferson (1743–1826) was born in Albemarle County, then the Virginia frontier. He received a classical education from private tutors and in 1760 entered the College of William and Mary, from which he was graduated two years later. Jefferson read law for five years under the guidance of George Wythe, perhaps the most famous lawyer of his time. Admitted to the bar in 1767, he practiced until the outbreak of the Revolutionary War, when he abandoned this career forever. Jefferson served in the Virginia House of Burgesses from 1769 to 1775 and, because of his strong opposition to British imperial policy, gained a reputation as a colonial patriot. It was thus natural that Virginia should choose him as a delegate to the Continental Congress. Jefferson served during the summer and autumn of 1775 and again after May, 1776. It was during this latter period that Jefferson worked as a member of the five-man committee that drafted the Declaration of Independence. He left Congress in the fall of 1776 and returned to Virginia, where he was promptly chosen to sit in the state House of Delegates. His record of achievements between October, 1776, and June, 1779, is impressive. He introduced the bill which abolished entail in the state and was an active member of the committee which revised Virginia's criminal code. His proposal to outlaw primogeniture was eventually enacted in 1785, and his bill for establishing religious freedom was adopted in 1786. Jefferson's educational reforms, however, were not adopted, a fact which was a lifelong disappointment to him. Elected to two terms as governor of Virginia in 1779 and 1780, he resigned in 1781 during a period of British invasion of the state and retired to private life in a condition of some disgrace. But by June, 1783, his popularity had recovered sufficiently for him to be elected a delegate to

Congress. His impressive service in that body led to an appointment in the diplomatic field in May, 1784. Jefferson spent the next five years in France as a commercial commissioner and minister. Upon his return to America at the end of 1789, Jefferson accepted President Washington's appointment as the new nation's first Secretary of State. He held that position for three years, despite continuing differences with Washington's Secretary of the Treasury, Alexander Hamilton. Jefferson expected that his second retirement from public life at the close of 1793 would be permanent, but he was nominated for President by the Republican opposition in 1796 and was only narrowly defeated by John Adams. He served as Vice President from 1797 to 1801, when he became President in an election decided by the House of Representatives. He retired from public life in 1809, disillusioned by his experience as President, and returned to his beloved Monticello, where he spent the remaining seventeen years of his life rarely traveling more than a few miles away from his home.

This selection* is Jefferson's rough draft of the Declaration of Independence. It served as the model upon which all subsequent changes were made. The most important of these was the deletion by Congress of Jefferson's remarks about slavery. The underlining indicates items eliminated in the final draft of the Declaration; the words and phrases in the margin indicate material included in the final document.

When in the course of human events it becomes necessary for one people to dissolve the political bands which have connected them with another, and to assume among the powers of the earth the separate & equal station to which the laws of nature and of nature's God entitle them, a decent respect to the opinions of mankind requires that they should declare the causes which impel them to the separation.

We hold these truths to be self-evident: that all men are created equal; that they are endowed by their creator with inherent and   certain inalienable rights; that among these are life, liberty, & the pursuit of happiness: that to secure these rights, governments are instituted among men, deriving their just powers from the consent ot the governed; that whenever any form of government becomes destructive of these ends, it is the right of the people to alter or abolish it, & to institute new government, laying it's foundation on such principles, & organizing it's powers in such form, as to them shall seem most likely to effect their safety & happiness. Prudence indeed will dictate that governments long established should not be changed for light & transient causes;

* Paul L. Ford, ed., *The Works of Thomas Jefferson*, I (New York: G. P. Putnam's Sons, 1904), pp. 35–42.

and accordingly all experience hath shown that mankind are more disposed to suffer while evils are sufferable, than to right themselves by abolishing the forms to which they are accustomed. But when a long train of abuses & usurpations begun at a distinguished period and pursuing invariably the same object, evinces a design to reduce them under absolute despotism, it is their right, it is their duty to throw off such government, & to provide new guards for their future security. Such has been the patient sufferance of these colonies; & such is now
alter   the necessity which constrains them to expunge their former systems of government. The history of the present king of Great Britain
repeated   is a history of unremitting injuries & usurpations, among which appears no solitary fact to contradict the uniform tenor of
all having   the rest but all have in direct object the establishment of an absolute tyranny over these states. To prove this let facts be submitted to a candid world for the truth of which we pledge a faith yet unsullied by falsehood.

He has refused his assent to laws the most wholesome & necessary for the public good.

He has forbidden his governors to pass laws of immediate & pressing importance, unless suspended in their operation till his assent should be obtained; & when so suspended, he has utterly neglected to attend to them.

He has refused to pass other laws for the accommodation of large districts of people, unless those people would relinquish the right of representation in the legislature, a right inestimable to them, & formidable to tyrants only.

He has called together legislative bodies at places unusual, uncomfortable, and distant from the depository of their public records, for the sole purpose of fatiguing them into compliance with his measures.

He has dissolved representative houses repeatedly & continually for opposing with manly firmness his invasions on the rights of the people.

He has refused for a long time after such dissolutions to cause others to be elected, whereby the legislative powers, incapable of anihilation, have returned to the people at large for their exercise, the state remaining in the meantime exposed to all the dangers of invasion from without & convulsions within.

He has endeavored to prevent the population of these states; for that purpose obstructing the laws for naturalization of foreigners, refusing to pass others to encourage their migrations hither, & raising the conditions of new appropriations of lands.

He has <u>suffered</u> the administration of justice ^{obstructed} <u>totally to cease in some of these states</u> refusing his assent ^{by} to laws for establishing judiciary powers.

He has made <u>our</u> judges dependant on his will alone, for the tenure of their offices, & the amount & paiment of their salaries.

He has erected a multitude of new offices <u>by a self assumed power</u> and sent hither swarms of new officers to harass our people and eat out their substance.

He has kept among us in times of peace standing armies <u>and ships of war</u> without the consent of our legislatures.

He has affected to render the military independant of, & superior to the civil power.

He has combined with others to subject us to a jurisdiction foreign to our constitutions & unacknowledged by our laws, giving his assent to their acts of pretended legislation for quartering large bodies of armed troops among us; for protecting them by a mock-trial from punishment for any murders which they should commit on the inhabitants of these states; for cutting off our trade with all parts of the world; for imposing taxes on us without our consent; for depriving ^{in many cases} us [ ] of the benefits of trial by jury; for transporting us beyond seas to be tried for pretended offences; for abolishing the free system of English laws in a neighboring province, establishing therein an arbitrary government, and enlarging it's boundaries, so as to render it at once an example and fit instrument for introducing the same ^{colonies} absolute rule into these <u>states</u>; for taking away our charters, abolishing our most valuable laws, and altering fundamentally the forms of our governments; for suspending our own legislatures, & declaring themselves invested with power to legislate for us in all cases whatsoever.

^{by declaring us out of his protection, and waging war against us.} He has abdicated government here <u>withdrawing his governors</u>, and declaring us out of his allegiance & protection.

He has plundered our seas, ravaged our coasts, burnt our towns, & destroyed the lives of our people.

He is at this time transporting large armies of foreign mercenaries to compleat the works of death, desolation & tyranny already begun with circumstances of cruelty and perfidy [ ] unworthy the ^{scarcely paralleled in the most barbarous ages, &} head of a civilized nation.

He has constrained our fellow citizens taken captive on ^{totally}

the high seas to bear arms against their country, to become the executioners of their friends & brethren, or to fall themselves by their hands.

He has [ ] endeavored to bring on the inhabitants of our frontiers the merciless Indian savages, whose known rule of warfare is an undistinguished destruction of all ages, sexes, & conditions of existence. <small>excited domestic insurrection among us, & has</small>

He has incited treasonable insurrections of our fellow-citizens, with the allurements of forfeiture & confiscation of our property.

He has waged cruel war against human nature itself, violating it's most sacred rights of life and liberty in the persons of a distant people who never offended him, captivating & carrying them into slavery in another hemisphere, or to incur miserable death in their transportation thither. This piratical warfare, the opprobium of INFIDEL powers, is the warfare of the CHRISTIAN king of Great Britain. Determined to keep open a market where MEN should be bought & sold, he has prostituted his negative for suppressing every legislative attempt to prohibit or to restrain this execrable commerce. And that this assemblage of horrors might want no fact of distinguished die, he is now exciting those very people to rise in arms among us, and to purchase that liberty of which he has deprived them, by murdering the people on whom he also obtruded them: thus paying off former crimes committed against the LIBERTIES of one people, with crimes which he urges them to commit against the LIVES of another.

In every stage of these oppressions we have petitioned for redress in the most humble terms: our repeated petitions have been answered only by repeated injuries.

A prince whose character is thus marked by every act which may define a tyrant is unfit to be the ruler of a [ ] people who mean to be free. Future ages will scarcely believe that the hardiness of one man adventured, within the short compass of twelve years only, to lay a foundation so broad & so undisguised for tyranny over a people fostered & fixed in principles of freedom. <small>free</small>

Nor have we been wanting in attention to our British brethren. We have warned them from time to time of attempts by their legislature to extend a jurisdiction over these our states. We have reminded them of the circumstances of our emigration & settlement here, no one of which could warrant so strange a pretension: that these were effected at the expense of our own blood & treasure, unassisted by the wealth or the strength of Great Britain: that in constituting indeed our several forms of <small>an unwarrantable us</small>

government, we had adopted one common king, thereby laying a foundation for perpetual league & amity with them: but that submission to their parliament was no part of our constitution, nor ever in idea,

have

and we have

conjured them by

if history may be credited: and, we [ ] appealed to their native justice and magnanimity as well as to the ties of our common kindred to disavow these usurpations which were likely to interrupt our connection and correspondence.   *would inevitably*

They too have been deaf to the voice of justice & of consanguinity, and when occasions have been given them, by the regular course of their laws, of removing from their councils the disturbers of our harmony, they have, by their free election, re-established them in power. At this very time too they are permitting their chief magistrate to send over not only soldiers of our common blood, but Scotch & foreign mercenaries to invade & destroy us. These facts have given the last stab to agonizing affection, and manly spirit bids us to renounce forever these unfeeling brethren. We must endeavor to forget our former love for them, and hold them as we hold the rest of mankind, enemies in war, in peace friends. We might have been a free and a great people together; but a communication of grandeur & of freedom it seems is below their dignity. Be it so, since they will have it. The road to happiness & to glory is open to us too. We will tread it apart from them, and acquiesce in the necessity which denounces   *We must therefore*

our eternal separation [ ]!

and hold them as we hold the rest of mankind, enemies in war, in peace friends.

We therefore the representatives of the United States of America in General Congress assembled do in the name & by authority of the good people of these states reject & renounce all allegiance & subjection to the kings of Great Britain & all others who may hereafter claim by, through or under them: we utterly dissolve all political connection which may heretofore have subsisted between us & the people or

We therefore the representatives of the United States of America in General Congress assembled, appealing to the supreme judge of the world for the rectitude of our intentions, do in the name, & by the authority of the good people of these colonies, solemnly publish & declare that these united colonies are & of right ought to be free & independent states; that they are absolved from all allegiance to the British parliament of Great Britain: & <u>finally we do assert & declare these colonies to be free & independent states</u>, & that as free & independent states, they have full power to levy war, conclude peace, contract alliances, establish commerce, & to do all other acts & things which independent states may of right do.

And for the support of this declaration we mutually pledge to each other our lives, our fortunes, & our sacred honor.

crown, and that all political connection between them & the state of Great Britain is, & ought to be, totally dissolved; & that as free & independent states they have full power to levy war, conclude peace, contract alliances, establish commerce & to do all other acts & things which independent states may of right do.

And for the support of this declaration, with a firm reliance on the protection of divine providence we mutually pledge to each other our lives, our fortunes, & our sacred honor.

II

Anti-Federalism and Jeffersonian Democracy

The Constitution of 1787 represents the greatest triumph of conservative Federalist political thought. But that document was adopted only after an intense debate against determined opposition. Many of the opponents were obscure local and state political figures whose prestige and intellect were no match for the many prominent supporters of the Constitution. The ranks of the anti-Federalists, however, did contain important and articulate spokesmen. Several delegates to the Constitutional Convention campaigned against adoption: Elbridge Gerry in Massachusetts, Robert Yates and John Lansing in New York, Luther Martin in Maryland, and the influential George Mason in Virginia. Other anti-Federalist leaders included Governor George Clinton of New York, and Patrick Henry and Richard Henry Lee of Virginia.

The anti-Federalists produced several political works of significance: perhaps the most balanced and reasoned argument against the Constitution was presented by Richard Henry Lee in a series of essays entitled *Letters of the Federal Farmer to the Republican*. Lee acknowledged that the Articles of Confederation contained defects, that several state governments were badly administered, and that there was a general need for stronger government in the country. He also expressed anxiety that some debtor groups were seeking to destroy the rights of creditors. But Lee feared that this slight threat to stability was being used by "young visionary men" and "aristocrats" to justify drastic alterations in the existing constitutional order, and he did not believe that the situation was sufficiently grave to warrant the changes proposed by the new Constitution.

The major criticisms levied by Lee at the Constitution were typical of those made by the anti-Federalists. First, he pointed to the consolidating purpose of the document and warned of the dangerous consequences which were likely to follow from the adoption of such a system, and second, he and the anti-Federalists criticized the proposed Constitution for not containing a Bill of Rights—an omission the Federalists agreed to correct immediately upon the ratification of the document.

There can be little doubt that Thomas Jefferson is looked upon by most Americans and by many foreign observers of this nation as perhaps the principal expounder of American liberalism. There is, however, considerable misunderstanding of Jefferson as a person and as a political thinker. He is mistakenly thought to have had highly abstract interests, to be more European in character than American. Such a view fails to consider his deep involvement in the mechanical and agricultural arts and his near-compulsive need to document the affairs of Monticello. It ignores also Jefferson's failure to attempt a single comprehensive statement of his political and philosophical ideas; the substance of his thought can be obtained only from a reading of his many essays, letters, and public papers. Finally, the belief that Jefferson was primarily a theoretician is belied by his willingness to alter his opinions and practices when new facts and conditions mandated change.

This is not to say that Jefferson was a pragmatist who believed only in the importance of results rather than theory. On the contrary, he was deeply concerned with ideas, but not with achieving total consistency. The theoretical quality of Jefferson's mind was tempered by a nondogmatic, scientific spirit: theory and fact were joined in a relationship of mutual dependence.

Considerable public confusion also abounds over the precise nature of Jefferson's political, economic, and social thought. This is caused in part by the many and scattered sources of his ideas and by his occasional change of mind. But the confusion results primarily from the misuse of Jefferson's ideas by public officials and ideological defenders of particular political creeds. Jefferson's words are frequently quoted out of the contexts of source, time, and situation so as to ascribe to him thoughts that are either incorrect or misleading.

An accurate understanding of Jefferson's political ideas must begin with his view of human nature—the foundation upon which his philosophy is constructed. Mirroring the generally optimistic outlook of the Enlightenment, Jefferson believed not that men were angels but that they were reasonable and that in an age of increasing education and scientific knowledge their rationality could be expected to grow. It followed, therefore, that government could be safely based on the consent of the people. Indeed, Jefferson believed that this was the only legal and moral principle which could justify the exercise of governmental authority.

While Jefferson spoke out in defense of man's rationality and urged the necessity of government by the consent of the governed, he also expressed fear that the power of government might be abused by public officials. In his *Notes on Virginia*, Jefferson warned of the danger of an "elective despotism," and he continually stated his fear of arbitrary acts by agents of the people. Thus, a belief in government based on consent and a fear of the agents of the people are the two dominant themes which run through Jefferson's political writings. He viewed the problem of statecraft as that of creating consent while at the same time limiting the discretion inherent in any system of delegated authority.

The fundamental principle Jefferson favored in order to obtain consent was majority rule. He considered this principle to be the very definition of republicanism, and he criticized all forms of government that fell short of this standard. Jefferson believed that to implement majority rule the legislature should be the primary institution of government since it was closest to the people and hence the least dangerous center of authority. Jefferson was most distrustful of the judiciary because he believed that it was the branch of government least responsive to the people. Finally, he was also suspicious of the executive branch of government. In his drafts for a Virginia constitution, Jefferson denied the governor a veto power and provided for the election of the executive by the state legislature. As President, Jefferson revealed his mistrust of strong executive power by preferring to work through his party leaders in the Congress rather than assert his own authority as an independent national leader.

Jefferson's advocacy of majority rule had other important consequences for his political thought. It led him to propose that the suffrage be expanded to include all those who "fight or pay" and to condemn malapportioned legislative districts. In addition, his search for true republican government caused him to accept the idea that the majority of one age should not be permitted to bind future generations to its decisions. "The earth belongs in usufruct to the living," Jefferson insisted; "the dead have no rights." He envisioned an ongoing democratic revolution in which the laws and constitutions created by one generation would be revised every nineteen years—the life-span Jefferson calculated for the majority of a given generation.

But Jefferson's acceptance of majority rule must be considered in connection with other aspects of his political thought. He did not, for one thing, believe that the majority should be a source of strong government. "I own I am not a friend of very energetic government," Jefferson wrote James Madison in December, 1787, revealing his bias in favor of laissez-faire—placing maximum reliance on individual initiative.

Further, Jefferson placed limitations on the exercise of power by the majority. In his first Inaugural Address he stated that the majority must recognize and respect the rights of the minority: "Though the will of the majority is in all cases to prevail, that will to be rightful must be reasonable; that the minority possess their equal rights, which equal law must protect, and to violate would be oppression."

This appeal to the majority to act reasonably was in the nature of a moral command and lacked any definite means of enforcement. A far more important source of limitation on the majority was Jefferson's theory of natural rights, which he so eloquently set forth in the Declaration of Independence and which he continued to assert throughout his life. No government, republican or nonrepublican, had the moral or legal power to infringe man's inalienable natural rights.

Not content with this appeal to nature for the protection of the individual against the authority of government, Jefferson also insisted that the people should have a written statement of rights against government: "a bill of rights is what the people are entitled to against every government on earth." It should be noted that Jefferson's belief in the necessity of a written bill of rights and in the inviolable character of natural rights was motivated primarily by fear that public officials would abuse the power entrusted to them and not by fear of the people. Repeatedly in his writings Jefferson stated his confidence in the virtue of the American people and his distrust of men who exercise the power of government.

Jefferson's suspicion of public officials had important consequences for his political theory. His ideal form of government was the New England town meeting, in which the power of government remained in the hands of the people and no delegation of authority was required. Jefferson recognized, however, that direct democracy was impossible except in very small territorial units, and he acknowledged the necessity of a representative system of government beyond the town level. But representation required methods for controlling the propensity of officials to abuse their trust, and Jefferson proposed a number of devices to achieve this end. Short terms of office would both keep government responsive to the majority and permit the rapid removal from office of men who misused their authority. The localism present in Jefferson's thought is understandable in large measure by his fear of delegated power. His plan for the creation of local wards was designed to keep government close to the people so that they would best be able to scrutinize the affairs of their agents. (Jefferson's localism had a moral purpose as well. Men who conducted their own public affairs would be both better citizens and more virtuous individuals, and local government provides more opportunity for direct participation than does government at a higher and more distant level.)

Somewhat paradoxically, in light of his support for majority rule and his belief in the primacy of the legislature, Jefferson favored government based on the separation of powers system. His reasons for accepting separation of powers, however, differed from the reasons given by most of its supporters. The Federalists, for example, stressed separation as a means of controlling the people; Jefferson, on the contrary, saw it as a method of controlling the rulers. His drafts for a Virginia constitution made in 1776 and 1783 and his thoughts given in *Notes on Virginia* reveal his acceptance of the separation of powers system. Further, Jefferson never expressed criticism of its use in the American national Constitution.

Summarizing Jefferson's political thought gives to his ideas a rigidity and speculative quality which is not especially justified. While there are many ideas which he persistently expounded during his long life, it is also important to appreciate the more flexible aspect of Jefferson's mind. Throughout most of his writing, for example, Jefferson stressed the advantages of local government and evidenced no particular interest or concern with the legal question of sovereignty. But after the passage of the Alien and Sedition Acts by the Federalists in 1798, he sharply altered the character of his thought to meet the crisis. In the Kentucky Resolutions Jefferson maintained that the Constitution was a compact among the states which gave only delegated powers to the central government and reserved the remaining authority to the states and the people. The Alien and Sedition Acts were not based on any legitimate delegation and hence violated the terms of the compact. Further, Jefferson outlined a plan of individual and combined action by the states to nullify these laws. The Kentucky Resolutions provided a theoretical foundation for the Southern political theorists of the mid-nineteenth century, though Jefferson's states' rights phase is hardly representative of his political thought.

Jefferson's conduct as President also shows that he was prepared to sacrifice intellectual consistency when practical demands made such a departure desirable. Thus his theoretical commitment to the idea of a weak executive did not prevent him from using the power of his office to purchase the Louisiana Territory from Napoleon in 1803. In so doing, Jefferson contributed significantly to the development of a strong national executive.

But the flexible nature of Jefferson's mind is, perhaps, best illustrated by his attitude toward the national Constitution. There were many features of the document to which he objected because they were removed from the true republican principle of majority rule. He did, however, insist upon the adoption of a bill of rights and would have preferred changes to have been made in the Constitution so that it would be more in accord with republicanism. In spite of his criticisms, Jefferson gave his support to the adoption of the Constitution and had no qualms about participating in the government after its ratification.

The nondoctrinaire quality of Jefferson's thought is clearly shown in his views on economic issues. Reflecting his own rural life and preferences, Jefferson initially favored an agrarian economic system for America. Manufacturing would be left to the workshops of Europe, and this country would trade its agricultural produce for its few industrial needs. Jefferson's economic ideas were primarily based on moral considerations: he believed that virtue was more likely to flourish in a rural civilization than in one composed of large cities containing great masses of people.

But international conditions at the close of the eighteenth century and during his years as President convinced Jefferson of the need to abandon the ideal of an agrarian America. While he still expressed dislike of cities, he now spoke favorably of the development of manufacturing—of placing industry and agriculture on an equal plane of importance—and he offered the goal of a self-sufficient America free from dependence on the factories of Europe.

The major objective of Jefferson's social thought was to create through a weak decentralized government an open society in which each individual was free to develop his own talents and moral virtue. Consequently, Jefferson opposed all government actions that extended favors and protection to the few—laws that interfered with the workings of an open society. Primogeniture, entail, the union of church and state, and the Hamiltonian economic program were all examples of unfair privilege that worked against the welfare of the American society.

Jefferson revealed his antagonism to the social system of Europe and the intensity of his own vision of America's uniqueness in his discussion of aristocracy with John Adams. His aristocracy was not that of birth and wealth but the natural aristocracy of talent and virtue. Its origins were not in the artificial guarantees of government but in a public educational system which trained young men to the limit of their abilities—a system which would extend from the local ward primary schools to the university at the state level. Jefferson fervently believed in public education and in its potential for creating an entirely new social order in this nation. Commenting to John Adams on his defeated educational plan for Virginia, he wrote: "Worth and genius would thus have been sought out from every condition of life, and completely prepared by education for defeating the competition of wealth and birth for public trusts."

Much of Jefferson's thought seem remote to the needs of the twentieth century and far different from the liberalism associated with contemporary America. His staunch individualism and his agrarian localism are aspects of a vanished world; his belief in natural rights and in the growing rationality of man seems almost naïve to a far more skeptical world. But Jefferson's vital importance remains, not in the specifics of his thought but rather in his "imperishable faith expressed in imperishable rhetoric." It is not his means but his end— "the pursuit of happiness"—which is lasting, his belief in the importance of people, his "sense of values."[1] Jefferson's thought continues to serve as a standard by which we evaluate our current political behavior.

Nothing so provoked the minds and emotions of Jeffersonians as John Marshall's Supreme Court. Appointed Chief Justice during the closing hours of the Adams administration in 1801, Marshall remained on the Supreme Court until his death in 1835 and continued to interpret the Constitution according to good Federalist principles though his party had long since disappeared from America's political scene. During his long years of service the "Great" Chief Justice established the Supreme Court as a vital part of the American governmental system by asserting the Court's power to review the actions of both the national and state governments. Further, in a long series of cases Marshall developed a set of precedents which stated a broad construction of national powers and a corresponding narrower view of state authority.

Jefferson was highly critical of Marshall's constitutional ideas, which ran directly counter to his own republican beliefs. The most effective rebuttals to Marshall's thought, however, were made by two of Jefferson's intellectual supporters—John Gibson of the Pennsylvania

---

[1] Richard Hofstadter, *The American Political Tradition* (New York: Vintage Books, 1954), p. 43.

Supreme Court and John Taylor, a leading Virginia political personality of the period.

In a dissenting opinion in the 1825 case of *Eakin* v. *Raub*, Gibson responded directly to Marshall's opinion in *Marbury* v. *Madison* that claimed for the Court the right to review acts of Congress. (At the close of his opinion Gibson accepted the necessity of Court review of actions of state legislatures.) Most important, Gibson rejected Marshall's questionable contention that: "It is, emphatically, the province and duty of the judicial department, to say what the law is" in cases in which a statute is said to contravene the Constitution. The right to construe the Constitution as the fundamental written law belongs to the legislature, Gibson insisted: the courts possess only the authority to interpret the laws enacted by the legislature.

Chief Justice Marshall's opinion in *McCulloch* v. *Maryland* caused John Taylor of Caroline to write a long systematic analysis of the many issues raised by the case. Much of Taylor's *Construction Construed and Constitutions Vindicated* is devoted to a criticism of the Second Bank of the United States and to Marshall's interpretation of the "necessary and proper" clause. Taylor looked upon the Bank as a perversion of the true end of government, which was the satisfaction of the welfare of all citizens. The Bank served to advance only the interests of a privileged minority and hence was contrary to the purposes of both good government and the national Constitution. Marshall's defense of the Bank violated these standards and, in addition, extended the legislative power of Congress far beyond what had been intended by the framers of the Constitution. The utility of that document would be vindicated, Taylor maintained, when the false constitutional doctrines of John Marshall were abandoned and the country returned to true republican principles.

Taylor also devoted considerable space in his *Construction Construed and Constitutions Vindicated* to the issue of judicial review. Fully revealing the Jeffersonian distrust of the judiciary, he rejected the idea that any such authority was granted or intended by the Constitution. Marshall's assertion that the Supreme Court possessed judicial review violated two main principles of the Constitution—the doctrine of checks and balances and the doctrine of dual sovereignty. The checks and balances system was designed to prevent any one branch of government at either the state or the federal level from gaining supremacy over the other two branches. The dual sovereignty of state and nation attempted to guarantee that neither government within the federal system could gain ascendancy over the other. Under the leadership of John Marshall, Taylor maintained, the Supreme Court had violated both of these fundamental principles by claiming the right to review the laws of Congress and the actions of state legislatures and state courts. Rather than a government of limits and divisions, the Supreme Court had turned the American constitutional system into one of national sovereignty and judicial supremacy.

Taylor has been called "the philosopher of Jeffersonian democracy," and in some respects this is an accurate statement. Not only did Taylor and Jefferson fear judicial power; they also opposed the Hamiltonian–Federalist economic program because of their belief in a weak central government and laissez-faire. But there were important differences between the two men which refute the notion that Taylor was a complete disciple of Jefferson. Taylor extended his belief in the sanctity of private property to include the ownership of slaves, whereas Jefferson opposed slavery. Further, Taylor stressed state sovereignty; Jefferson was primarily a believer in local government. A precursor of John C. Calhoun and the Southern states' rights school of thought, Taylor was as much the representative of the decline of Jeffersonian democracy as he was its leading proponent.

6. LEE

Criticism of the Constitution

Richard Henry Lee (1732–1794) was born in Westmoreland County, Virginia, and devoted his entire adult life to public service. He served in the Virginia House of Burgesses and, after 1764, led the opposition to British imperial policies. In March of 1773 Lee, along with Patrick Henry and Thomas Jefferson, originated the plan to establish intercolonial committees of correspondence. As a Virginia delegate to the Continental Congress, he introduced the resolutions that called for American independence from Great Britain and led to the writing of the Declaration of Independence. A signer of that document, he subsequently played an influential role in the Continental Congress in developing support for confederation, though he had only a small part in writing the Articles of Confederation. He served as a member of the Virginia House of Delegates from 1780 until 1784, when he was chosen to be a delegate to the Congress of the Articles of Confederation. He later served as president of that body for a year term. While recognizing the deficiencies of the Articles, Lee opposed all proposals to extend the powers of Congress. He declined to serve as a delegate to the Philadelphia Convention and later set forth his opposition to the Constitution in his *Letters of the Federal Farmer to the Republican*. The following selection* is taken from the first two of these letters. Lee went on to hold a seat in the new Senate until ill health forced his retirement in 1792. He devoted most of his energies in the Senate to the adoption of the Bill of Rights, and many of his proposals became part of the first ten amendments to the Constitution. Lee died in his Westmoreland County home in 1794.

---

* Paul L. Ford, ed., *Pamphlets on the Constitution of the United States* (Brooklyn: n.p., 1888), pp. 283, 288–92.

LETTER I

October 8th, 1787.

Dear Sir,

My letters to you last winter, on the subject of a well-balanced national government for the United States, were the result of free enquiry; when I passed from that subject to enquiries relative to our commerce, revenues, past administration, etc. I anticipated the anxieties I feel, on carefully examining the plan of government proposed by the convention. It appears to be a plan retaining some federal features; but to be the first important step, and to aim strongly to one consolidated government of the United States. It leaves the powers of government, and the representation of the people, so unnaturally divided between the general and state governments, that the operations of our system must be very uncertain. My uniform federal attachments, and the interest I have in the protection of property, and a steady execution of the laws, will convince you, that, if I am under any bias at all, it is in favor of any general system which shall promise those advantages. The instability of our laws increases my wishes for firm and steady government; but then, I can consent to no government, which, in my opinion, is not calculated equally to preserve the rights of all orders of men in the community. My object has been to join with those who have endeavored to supply the defects in the forms of our governments by a steady and proper administration of them. Though I have long apprehended that fraudulent debtors, and embarrassed men, on the one hand, and men, on the other, unfriendly to republican equality, would produce an uneasiness among the people, and prepare the way, not for cool and deliberate reforms in the governments, but for changes calculated to promote the interests of particular orders of men. Acquit me, sir, of any agency in the formation of the new system; I shall be satisfied with seeing, if it shall be adopted, a prudent administration. Indeed I am so much convinced of the truth of Pope's maxim, that "That which is best administered is best," that I am much inclined to subscribe to it from experience. I am not disposed to unreasonably contend about forms. I know our situation is critical, and it behooves us to make the best of it. A federal government of some sort is necessary. We have suffered the present to languish; and whether the confederation was capable or not originally of answering any valuable purposes, it is now but of little importance. I will pass by the men, and states, who have been particularly instrumental in preparing the way for a change, and, perhaps, for governments not very favorable to the people at large. A constitution is now presented which we may reject, or which we may accept with or without amendments; and to which point we ought to direct our exertions is the question. To determine this question, with propriety, we must attentively examine the system itself, and the probable consequences of either step. This I shall endeavor to do, so far as I am able, with candor and fairness; and leave you to decide upon the propriety of my opinions, the weight of my reasons, and how far my conclusions are well drawn. Whatever may be the conduct of others, on the present occasion, I do not mean, hastily and positively to decide on the merits of the constitution proposed. I shall be open to conviction and always disposed to adopt that which, all things considered, shall appear to me to be most for the happiness of the community. It must be granted, that if men hastily and blindly adopt a system of government, they will as hastily and as blindly be led to alter or abolish it; and changes must ensue, one after another, till the peaceable and better part of the community will grow weary with changes, tumults and disorders, and be disposed to accept any government, however despotic, that shall promise stability and firmness.

The first principal question that occurs, is, Whether, considering our situation, we ought to precipitate the adoption of the proposed constitution? If we remain cool and temperate, we are in no immediate danger of any commotions; we are in a state of perfect peace, and in no danger of invasions; the state governments are in the full exercise of their powers; and our governments answer all present exigencies, except the regulation of trade, securing credit, in some cases, and providing for the interest, in some instances, of the public debts; and whether we adopt a change three or nine months hence, can make but little odds with the private circumstances of individuals; their happiness and prosperity, after all, depend principally upon their own exertions. We are hardly recovered from a long and distressing war: The farmers, fishmen, etc. have not yet fully repaired the waste made by it. Industry and frugality are again assuming their proper station. Private debts are lessened, and public debts incurred by the war have been, by various ways, diminished; and the public lands have now become a productive source for diminishing them much more. I know uneasy men, who with very much to precipitate, do not admit all these facts; but they are facts well known to all men who are thoroughly informed in the affairs of this country. It must, however, be admitted, that our federal system is defective, and that some of the state governments are not well administered; but, then, we impute to the defects in our governments many evils and embarrassments which are most clearly the result of the late war. We must allow men to conduct on the present occasion, as on all similar ones. They will urge a thousand pretenses to answer their purposes on both sides. When we want a man to change his condition, we describe it as miserable, wretched, and despised; and draw a pleading picture of that which we would have him assume. And when we wish the contrary, we reverse our descriptions. Whenever a clamor is raised, and idle men get to work, it is highly necessary to examine facts carefully, and without unreasonably suspecting men of falsehood, to examine and inquire attentively, under what impressions they act. It is too often the case in political concerns, that men state facts not as they are, but as they wish them to be; and almost every man, by calling to mind past scenes, will find this to be true.

Nothing by the passions of ambitious, impatient, or disorderly men, I conceive, will plunge us into commotions, if time should be taken fully to examine and consider the system proposed. Men who feel easy in their circumstances, and such as are not sanguine in their expectations relative to the consequences of the proposed change, will remain quiet under the existing governments. Many commercial and monied men, who are uneasy, not without just cause, ought to be respected; and, by no means, unreasonably disappointed in their expectations and hopes; but as to those who expect employments under the new constitution; as to those weak and ardent men who always expect to be gainers by revolutions and whose lot it generally is to get out of one difficulty into another, they are very little to be regarded: and as to those who designedly avail themselves of this weakness and ardor, they are to be despised. It is natural for men, who wish to hasten the adoption of a measure, to tell us, now is the crisis—now is the critical moment which must be seized, or all will be lost: and to shut the door against free enquiry, whenever conscious the thing presented has defects in it, which time and investigation will probably discover. This has been the custom of tyrants and their dependents in all ages. If it is true, what has been so often said, that the people of this country cannot change their condition for the worse, I presume it still behooves them to endeavor deliberately to change it for the better. The fickle and ardent, in any community, are the proper tools for establishing despotic government. But it is deliberate and thinking men, who must establish and secure governments on free principles. Before they decide on the plan proposed, they will inquire whether it will probably be a blessing or a curse to this people.

The present moment discovers a new face in our affairs. Our object has been all along, to reform our federal systems, and to strengthen our governments—to establish peace, order and justice in the community—but a new object now presents. The plan of government now proposed is evidently calculated totally to change, in time, our condition as a people. Instead of being thirteen republics, under a federal head, it is clearly designed to made us one consolidated government. Of this, I think, I shall fully convince you, in my following letters on this subject. This consolidation of the states has been the object of several men in this country for some time past. Whether such a change can ever be effected in any manner; whether it can be effected without convulsions and civil wars; whether such a change will not totally destroy the liberties of this country—time only can determine. . . .

Your's Etc.
The Federal Farmer

LETTER II

October 9, 1787

Dear Sir,

The essential parts of a free and good government are a full and equal representation of the people in the legislature, and the jury trial of the vicinage in the administration of justice—a full and equal representation, is that which possesses the same interests, feelings, opinions, and views the people themselves would were they all assembled —a fair representation, therefore, should be so regulated that every order of men in the community, according to the common course of elections, can have a share in it—in order to allow professional men, merchants, traders, farmers, mechanics, etc. to bring a just proportion of their best informed men respectively into the legislature, the representation must be considerably numerous—We have about 200 state senators in the United States, and a less number than that of federal representatives cannot, clearly, be a full representation of this people, in the affairs of internal taxation and police, were there but one legislature for the whole union. The representation cannot be equal, or the situation of the people proper for one government only if the extreme parts of the society cannot be represented as fully as the central—It is apparently impracticable that this should be the case in this extensive country—it would be impossible to collect a representation of the parts of the country five, six, and seven hundred miles from the seat of government.

Under one general government alone, there could be but one judiciary, one supreme and a proper number of inferior courts. I think it would be totally impracticable in this case to preserve a due administration of justice, and the real benefits of the jury trial of the vicinage—there are now supreme courts in each state in the union and a great number of county and other courts subordinate to each supreme court—most of these supreme and inferior courts are itinerant, and hold their sessions in different parts every year of their respective states, counties and districts—with all these moving courts, our citizens, from the vast extent of the country must travel very considerable distances from home to find the place where justice is administered. I am not for bringing justice so near to individuals as to afford them any temptation to engage in law suits; though I think it one of the greatest benefits in a good government, that each citizen should find a court of justice within a reasonable distance, perhaps, within a day's travel of his home; so that, without great inconveniences and enormous expenses, he may have the advantages of his witnesses and jury—it would be impracticable to derive these advantages from one judiciary—the one supreme court at most could only set in the center of the union, and move once a year into the center of the eastern and southern extremes of it—and, in this case, each citizen, on an average would travel 150 or 200 miles to find this court—that, however, inferior courts might be properly placed in the different counties, and districts of the union, the appellate jurisdiction would be intolerable and expensive.

If it were possible to consolidate the states, and preserve the features of a free government, still it is evident that the middle states, the parts of the union, about the seat of government, would enjoy great advantages, while the remote states would experience the many inconveniences of remote provinces. Wealth, offices, and the benefits of government would collect in the center: and the extreme states, and their principal towns, become much less important.

There are other considerations which tend to prove that the idea of one consolidated whole, on free principles, is ill-founded—the laws of a free government rest on the confidence of the people and operate gently—and never can extend their influence very far—if they are executed on free principles, about the center, where the benefits of the government induce the people to support it voluntarily; yet they must be executed on the principles of fear and force in the extremes—This has been the case with every extensive republic of which we have any accurate account.

There are certain inalienable and fundamental rights, which in forming the social compact, ought to be explicitly ascertained and fixed—a free and enlightened people, in forming this compact, will not resign all their rights to those who govern, and they will fix limits to their legislators and rulers, which will soon be plainly seen by those who are governed, as well as by those who govern: and the latter will know they cannot be passed unperceived by the former, and without giving a general alarm—These rights should be made the bases of every constitution; and if a people be so situated, or have such different opinions that they cannot agree in ascertaining and fixing them, it is a very strong argument against their attempting to form one entire society, to live under one system of laws only—I confess, I never thought the people of these states differed essentially in these respects; they having derived all these rights from one common source, the British systems; and having in the formation of their state constitutions, discovered that their ideas relative to these rights are very similar. However, it is now said that the states differ so essentially in these respects, and even in the important article of the trial by jury, that when assembled in convention, they can agree to no words by which to establish that trial, or by which to ascertain and establish many other of these rights, as fundamental articles in the social compact. If so, we proceed to consolidate the states on no solid basis whatever.

But I do not pay much regard to the reasons given for not bottoming the new constitution on a better bill of rights. I still believe a complete federal bill of rights to be very practicable. Nevertheless I acknowledge the proceedings of the convention furnish my mind with many new and strong reasons, against a complete consolidation of the states. They tend to convince me, that it cannot be carried with propriety very far—that the convention has gone much farther in one respect than it found it practicable to go in another; that is, they propose to lodge in the general government very extensive powers—*powers* nearly, if not altogether, complete and unlimited, over the purse and the sword. But, in its organization, they furnish the strongest proof that the proper limbs, or parts of a government, to support and execute those powers on proper principles (or in which they can be falsely lodged) cannot be formed. These powers must be lodged somewhere in every society;

but then they should be lodged where the strength and guardians of the people are collected. They can be wielded, or safely used, in a free country only by an able executive and judiciary, a respectable senate, and a secure, full, and equal representation of the people. I think the principles I have premised or brought into view, are well founded—I think they will not be denied by any fair reasoner. It is in connection with these, and other solid principles, we are to examine the constitution. It is not a few democratic phrases, or a few well formed features, that will prove its merits; or a few small omissions that will produce its rejection among men of sense; they will inquire what are the essential powers in a community, and what are nominal ones; where and how the essential powers shall be lodged to secure government, and to secure true liberty.

In examining the proposed constitution carefully, we must clearly perceive an unnatural separation of these powers from the substantial representation of the people. The state governments will exist, with all their governors, senators, representatives, officers and expenses; in these will be nineteen-twentieths of the representatives of the people; they will have a near connection, and their members an immediate intercourse with the people; and the probability is, that the state governments will possess the confidence of the people, and be considered generally as their immediate guardians.

The general government will consist of a new species of executive, a small senate, and a very small house of representatives. As many citizens will be more than three hundred miles from the seat of this government as will be nearer to it, its judges and officers cannot be very numerous, without making our governments very expensive. Thus will stand the state and the general governments, should the constitution be adopted without any alterations in their organization; but as to powers, the general government will possess all essential ones, at least on paper, and those of the states a mere shadow of power. And therefore, unless the people shall make some great exertions to restore to the state governments their powers in matters of internal police; as the powers to lay and collect, exclusively, internal taxes, to govern the militia, and to hold the decisions of their own judicial courts upon their own laws final, the balance cannot possibly continue long; but the state governments must be annihilated, or continue to exist for no purpose. . . .

Your's Etc.
The Federal Farmer

7. JEFFERSON
Notes on Virginia

Notes on Virginia is Jefferson's only full-length scholarly book. It was written in response to a series of questions about the state posed by the French legation in Philadelphia. A first draft of the study was completed in December, 1781, and extensive revisions were made over the next few years. Jefferson circulated copies of his *Notes* to close friends but never intended it for public release, largely because of his hostile remarks on the Virginia constitution of 1776 and on the subject of slavery. But after an unauthorized version of the *Notes* was printed in France in 1785, Jefferson reluctantly agreed to publish an approved edition. The following selection* covers his views on the Virginia constitution and on political economy.

QUERY XIII
The Constitution of the State and its several charters?

. . . This constitution was formed when we were new and unexperienced in the science of government. It was the first, too, which was formed in the whole United States. No wonder then that time and trial have discovered very capital defects in it.

1. The majority of the men in the State, who pay and fight for its support, are unrepresented in the legislature, the roll of freeholders entitled to vote not including generally the half of those on the roll of the militia, or of the tax-gatherers.

2. Among those who share the representation, the shares are very unequal. Thus the county of Warwick, with only one hundred fighting men, has an equal representation with the county of Loudon, which has one thousand seven hundred and forty-six. So that every man in Warwick has as much influence in the government as seventeen men in Loudon. . . .

It will appear at once that nineteen thousand men, living below

* *Notes on the State of Virginia* (Boston: Printed by David Carlisle, 1801), pp. 158, 171–75, 243–45.

the falls of the rivers, possess half the senate, and want four members only of possessing a majority of the house of delegates; a want more than supplied by the vicinity of their situation to the seat of government, and of course the greater degree of convenience and punctuality with which their members may and will attend in the legislature. These nineteen thousand, therefore, living in one part of the country, give law to upwards of thirty thousand living in another, and appoint all their chief officers, executive and judiciary. From the difference of their situation and circumstances, their interests will often be very different.

3. The senate is, by its constitution, too homogenous with the house of delegates. Being chosen by the same electors, at the same time, and out of the same subjects, the choice falls of course on men of the same description. The purpose of establishing different houses of legislation is to introduce the influence of different interests or different principles. Thus in Great Britain it is said their constitution relies on the house of commons for honesty, and the lords for wisdom; which would be a rational reliance, if honesty were to be bought with money, and if wisdom were hereditary. In some of the American States, the delegates and senators are so chosen, as that the first represent the persons, and the second the property of the State. But with us, wealth and wisdom have equal chance for admission into both houses. We do not, therefore, derive from the separation of our legislature into two houses, those benefits which a proper complication of principles are capable of producing, and those which alone can compensate the evils which may be produced by their dissensions.

4. All the powers of government, legislative, executive, and judiciary, result to the legislative body. The concentrating these in the same hands is precisely the definition of despotic government. It will be no alleviation that these powers will be exercised by a plurality of hands, and not by a single one. One hundred and seventy-three despots would surely be as oppressive as one. Let those who doubt it turn their eyes on the republic of Venice. As little will it avail us that they are chosen by ourselves. An *elective despotism* was not the government we fought for, but one which should not only be founded on free principles, but in which the powers of government should be so divided and balanced among several bodies of magistracy, as that no one could transcend their legal limits, without being effectually checked and restrained by the others. For this reason that convention which passed the ordinance of government, laid its foundation on this basis, that the

legislative, executive, and judiciary departments should be separate and distinct, so that no person should exercise the powers of more than one of them at the same time. But no barrier was provided between these several powers. The judiciary and executive members were left dependent on the legislative, for their subsistence in office, and some of them for their continuance in it. If, therefore, the legislature assumes executive and judiciary powers, no opposition is likely to be made; nor, if made, can it be effectual; because in that case they may put their proceedings into the form of an act of assembly, which will render them obligatory on the other branches. . . .

QUERY XIX

The present state of manufactures, commerce, interior and exterior trade?

We never had an interior trade of any importance. Our exterior commerce has suffered very much from the beginning of the present contest. During this time we have manufactured within our families the most necessary articles of clothing. Those of cotton will bear some comparison with the same kinds of manufacture in Europe; but those of wool, flax and hemp are very coarse, unsightly, and unpleasant; and such is our attachment to agriculture, and such our preference for foreign manufactures, that be it wise or unwise, our people will certainly return as soon as they can, to the raising raw materials, and exchanging them for finer manufactures than they are able to execute themselves.

The political economists of Europe have established it as a principle, that every State should endeavor to manufacture for itself; and this principle, like many others, we transfer to America, without calculating the difference of circumstance which should often produce a difference of result. In Europe the lands are either cultivated, or locked up against the cultivator. Manufacture must therefore be resorted to of necessity not of choice, to support the surplus of their people. But we have an immensity of land courting the industry of the husbandman. Is it best then that all our citizens should be employed in its improvement, or that one half should be called off from that to exercise manufactures and handicraft arts for the other? Those who labor in the earth are the chosen people of God, if ever He had a chosen people, whose breasts He has made His peculiar deposit for substantial and genuine virtue. It is the focus in which he keeps alive that sacred fire, which otherwise might escape from the face of the earth. Corruption of morals in the mass of cultivators is a phenomenon of which no age nor nation has furnished an example. It is the mark set on those, who, not looking up to heaven, to their own soil and industry, as does the husbandman, for their subsistence, depend for it on casualties and caprice of customers. Dependence begets subservience and venality, suffocates the germ of virtue, and prepares fit tools for the designs of ambition. This, the natural progress and consequence of the arts, has sometimes perhaps been retarded by accidental circumstances; but, generally speaking, the proportion which the aggregate of the other classes of citizens bears in any State to that of its husbandmen, is the proportion of its unsound to its healthy parts, and is a good enough barometer whereby to measure its degree of corruption. While we have land to labor then, let us never wish to see our citizens occupied at a workbench, or twirling a distaff. Carpenters, masons, smiths, are wanting in husbandry; but, for the general operations of manufacture, let our workshops remain in Europe. It is better to carry provisions and materials to workmen there, than bring them to the provisions and materials, and with them their manners and principles. The loss by the transportation of commodities across the Atlantic will be made up in happiness and permanence of government. The mobs of great cities add just so much to the support of pure government, as sores do to the strength of the human body. It is the manners and spirit of a people which preserve a republic in vigor. A degeneracy in these is a canker which soon eats to the heart of its laws and constitution.

8. JEFFERSON

An Evaluation of the New Constitution

Jefferson served as American minister to France for five years during the 1780's. It was in Paris that he first read a draft of the new Constitution. In a letter of December 20, 1787, to James Madison,* Jefferson stated his thoughts on the proposed document.

* Paul L. Ford, ed., *The Works of Thomas Jefferson*, V (New York: G. P. Putnam's Sons, 1904), pp. 370–75.

Dear Sir,

. . . The season admitting only of operations in the Cabinet, and these being in a great measure secret, I have little to fill a letter. I will therefore make up the deficiency by adding a few words on the Constitution proposed by our Convention. I like much the general idea of framing a government which should go on of itself peaceably, without needing continual recurrence to the state legislatures. I like the organization of the government into Legislative, Judiciary & Executive. I like the power given the Legislature to levy taxes, and for that reason solely approve of the greater house being chosen by the people directly. For tho' I think a house chosen by them will be very illy qualified to legislate for the Union, for foreign nations &c. yet this evil does not weight against the good of preserving inviolate the fundamental principle that the people are not to be taxed but by representatives chosen immediately by themselves. I am captivated by the compromise of the opposite claims of the great & little states, of the latter to equal, and the former to proportional influence. I am much pleased too with the substitution of the method of voting by persons, instead of that of voting by states: and I like the negative given to the Executive with a third of either house, though I should have liked it better had the Judiciary been associated for that purpose, or invested with a similar and separate power. There are other good things of less moment. I will now add what I do not like. First the omission of a bill of rights providing clearly & without the aid of sophisms for freedom of religion, freedom of the press, protection against standing armies, restrictions against monopolies, the eternal & unremitting force of the habeas corpus laws, and trials by jury in all matters of fact triable by the laws of the land & not by the law of nations. To say, as Mr. Wilson does that a bill of rights was not necessary because all is reserved in the case of the general government which is not given, while in the particular ones all is given which is not reserved, might do for the audience to whom it was addressed, but is surely a *gratis dictum*, opposed by strong inferences from the body of the instrument, as well as from the omission of the clause of our present confederation which had declared that in express terms. It was a hard conclusion to say because there has been no uniformity among the states as to the cases triable by jury, because some have been so incautious as to abandon this mode of trial, therefore the more prudent states shall be reduced to the same level of calamity. It would have been much more just & wise to have concluded the other way that as most of the states had judiciously preserved this palladium, those who had wandered should be brought back to it, and to have established general right instead of general wrong. Let me add that a bill of rights is what the people are entitled to against every government on earth, general or particular, & what no just government should refuse, or rest on inferences. The second feature I dislike, and greatly dislike, is the abandonment in every instance of the necessity of rotation in office, and most particularly in the case of the President. Experience concurs with reason in concluding that the first magistrate will always be re-elected if the Constitution permits it. He is then an officer for life. This once observed, it becomes of so much consequence to certain nations to have a friend or a foe at the head of our affairs that they will interfere with money & with arms. A Galloman or an Angloman will be supported by the nation he befriends. If once elected, and at a second or third election out voted by one or two votes, he will pretend false votes, foul play, hold possession of the reins of government, be supported by the States voting for him, especially if they are the central ones lying in a compact body themselves & separating their opponents: and they will be aided by one nation of Europe, while the majority are aided by another. The election of a President of America some years hence will be much more interesting to certain nations of Europe than ever the election of a king of Poland was. Reflect on all the instances in history antient & modern, of elective monarchies, and say if they do not give foundation for my fears. The Roman emperors, the popes, while they were of any importance, the German emperors till they became hereditary in practice, the kings of Poland, the Deys of the Ottoman dependances. It may be said that if elections are to be attended with these disorders, the seldomer they are renewed the better. But experience shews that the only way to prevent disorder is to render them uninteresting by frequent changes. An incapacity to be elected a second time would have been the only effectual preventative. The power of removing him every fourth year by the vote of the people is a power which will not be exercised. The king of Poland is removeable every day by the Diet, yet he is never removed.—Smaller objections are the Appeal in fact as well as law, and the binding all persons Legislative Executive & Judiciary by oath to maintain that constitution. I do not pretend to decide what would be the best method of procuring the establishment of the manifold good things in this constitution, and of getting rid of the bad. Whether by adopting it in hopes of future amendment, or, after it has been duly weighed & canvassed by the people, after seeing the parts they generally dislike, & those they generally approve, to say to them "We see now what you wish. Send together your deputies again, let them frame a constitution for you omitting what you have condemned, & establishing the powers you approve. Even these will be a great addition to the energy of your government."—At all events I hope you will not be discouraged from other trials, if the present one should fail of its full effect.—I have thus told you freely what I like & dislike: merely as a matter of curiosity, for I know your own judgment has been formed on all these points after having heard everything which could be urged on them. I own I am not a friend to a very energetic government. It is always oppressive. The late rebellion in Massachusetts has given more alarm than I think it should have done. Calculate that one rebellion in 13 states in the course of 11 years, is but one for each state in a century & a half. No country should be so long without one. Nor will any degree of power in the hands of government prevent insurrections. France, with all it's despotism, and two or three hundred thousand men always in arms has had three insurrections in the three years I have been here in every one of which greater numbers were engaged than in Massachusetts & a great deal more blood was spilt. In Turkey, which Montesquieu supposes more despotic, insurrections are the events of every day. In England, where the hand of power is lighter than here, but heavier than with us they happen every half dozen years. Compare again the ferocious depredations of their insurgents with the order, the moderation & the almost self extinguishment of ours.—After all, it is my principle that the will of the majority should always prevail. If they approve the proposed Convention in all it's parts, I shall concur in it chearfully, in hopes that they will amend it whenever they shall find it work wrong. I think our governments will remain virtuous for many centuries; as long as they are chiefly agricultural; and this will be as long as there shall be vacant lands in any part of America. When they get piled upon one another in large cities, as in Europe, they will become corrupt as in Europe. Above all things I hope the education of the common people will be attended to; convinced that on their good sense we may rely with the most security for the preservation of a due degree of liberty. I have tired you by this time with my disquisitions & will therefore only add assurances of the sincerity of those sentiments of esteem & attachment with which I am Dear Sir your affectionate friend & servant.

P. S. The instability of our laws is really an immense evil. I think it would be well to provide in our constitutions that there shall always be a twelve-month between the ingrossing a bill & passing it: that it should then be offered to it's passage without changing a word: and that if circumstances should be thought to require a speedier passage, it should take two thirds of both houses instead of a bare majority.

9. JEFFERSON

The Earth Belongs to the Living

In a letter to James Madison, dated September 6, 1789,* Jefferson, writing from Paris, discussed at length the question of whether one generation has a right to bind another to its decisions.

DEAR SIR,—I sit down to write to you without knowing by what occasion I shall send my letter. I do it because a subject comes into my head which I would wish to develope a little more than is practicable in the hurry of the moment of making up general despatches.

The question Whether one generation of men has a right to bind another, seems never to have been started either on this or our side of the water. Yet it is a question of such consequences as not only to merit decision, but place also, among the fundamental principles of every government. The course of reflection in which we are immersed here on the elementary principles of society has presented this question to my mind; and that no such obligation can be transmitted I think very capable of proof. I set out on this ground which I suppose to be self evident, "*that the earth belongs in usufruct to the living;*" that the dead have neither powers nor rights over it. The portion occupied by any individual ceases to be his when himself ceases to be, and reverts to the society. If the society has formed no rules for the appropriation of its lands in severalty, it will be taken by the first occupants. These will generally be the wife and children of the decedent. If they have

* Paul L. Ford, ed., *The Works of Thomas Jefferson,* VI (New York: G. P. Putnam's Sons, 1904), pp. 3–11.

formed rules of appropriation, those rules may give it to the wife and children, or to some one of them, or to the legatee of the deceased. So they may give it to his creditor. But the child, the legatee or creditor takes it, not by any natural right, but by a law of the society of which they are members, and to which they are subject. Then no man can by *natural right* oblige the lands he occupied, or the persons who succeed him in that occupation, to the paiment of debts contracted by him. For if he could, he might during his own life, eat up the usufruct of the lands for several generations to come, and then the lands would belong to the dead, and not to the living, which would be reverse of our principle. What is true of every member of the society individually, is true of them all collectively, since the rights of the whole can be no more than the sum of the rights of individuals. To keep our ideas clear when applying them to a multitude, let us suppose a whole generation of men to be born on the same day, to attain mature age on the same day, and to die on the same day, leaving a succeeding generation in the moment of attaining their mature age all together. Let the ripe age be supposed of 21. years, and their period of life 34. years more, that being the average term given by the bills of mortality to persons who have already attained 21. years of age. Each successive generation would, in this way, come on and go off the stage at a fixed moment, as individuals do now. Then I say the earth belongs to each of these generations during it's course, fully, and in their own right. The 2d. generation receives it clear of the debts and incumbrances of the 1st., the 3d. of the 2d. and so on. For if the 1st. could charge it with a debt, then the earth would belong to the dead and not the living generation. Then no generation can contract debts greater than may be paid during the course of it's own existence. At 21. years of age they may bind themselves and their lands for 34. years to come: at 22. for 33: at 23 for 32. and at 54 for one year only; because these are the terms of life which remain to them at those respective epochs. But a material difference must be noted between the succession of an individual and that of a whole generation. Individuals are parts only of a society, subject to the laws of a whole. These laws may appropriate the portion of land occupied by a decedent to his creditor rather than to any other, or to his child, on condition he satisfies his creditor. But when a whole generation, that is, the whole society dies, as in the case we have supposed, and another generation or society succeeds, this forms a whole, and there is no superior who can give their territory to a third society, who may have lent money to their predecessors beyond their faculty of paying.

What is true of a generation all arriving to self-government on the same day, and dying all on the same day, is true of those on a constant course of decay and renewal, with this only difference. A generation coming in and going out entirè, as in the first case, would have a right in the 1st year of their self dominion to contract a debt for 33. years, in the 10th. for 24., in the 20th. for 14., in the 30th. for 4., whereas generations changing daily, by daily deaths and births, have one constant term beginning at the date of their contract, and ending when a majority of those of full age at that date shall be dead. The length of that term may be estimated from the tables of mortality, corrected by the circumstances of climate, occupation &c. peculiar to the country of the contractors. . . .

I suppose that the received opinion, that the public debts of one generation devolve on the next, has been suggested by our seeing habitually in private life that he who succeeds to lands is required to pay the debts of his ancestor or testator, without considering that this requisition is municipal only, not moral, flowing from the will of the society which has found it convenient to appropriate the lands become vacant by the death of their occupant on the condition of a paiment of his debts; but that between society and society, or generation and generation there is no municipal obligation, no umpire but the law of nature. We seem not to have perceived that, by the law of nature, one generation is to another as one independant nation to another.

The interest of the national debt of France being in fact but a two thousandth part of it's rent-roll, the paiment of it is practicable enough; and so becomes a question merely of honor or expediency. But with respect to future debts; would it not be wise and just for that nation to declare in the constitution they are forming that neither the legislature, nor the nation itself can validly contract more debt, than they may pay within their own age, or within the term of 19. years? And that all future contracts shall be deemed void as to what shall remain unpaid at the end of 19. years from their date? This would put the lenders, and the borrowers also, on their guard. By reducing too the faculty of borrowing within its natural limits, it would bridle the spirit of war, to which too free a course has been procured by the inattention of money lenders to this law of nature, that succeeding generations are not responsible for the preceding.

On similar ground it may be proved, that no society can make a perpetual constitution, or even a perpetual law. The earth belongs always to the living generation. They may manage it then, and what proceeds from it, as they please, during their usufruct. They are masters too of their own persons, and consequently may govern them as they please. But persons and property make the sum of the objects of government. The constitution and the laws of their predecessors extinguished them, in their natural course, with those whose will gave them being. This could preserve that being till it ceased to be itself, and no longer. Every constitution, then, and every law, naturally expires at the end of 19. years. If it be enforced longer, it is an act of force and not of right.

It may be said that the succeeding generation exercising in fact the power of repeal, this leaves them as free as if the constitution or law had been expressly limited to 19. years only. In the first place, this objection admits the right, in proposing an equivalent. But the power of repeal is not an equivalent. It might be indeed if every form of government were so perfectly contrived that the will of the majority could always be obtained fairly and without impediment. But this is true of no form. The people cannot assemble themselves; their representation is unequal and vicious. Various checks are opposed to every legislative proposition. Factions get possession of the public councils. Bribery corrupts them. Personal interests lead them astray from the general interests of their constituents; and other impediments arise so as to prove to every practical man that a law of limited duration is much more manageable than one which needs a repeal.

This principle that the earth belongs to the living and not to the dead is of very extensive application and consequences in every country, and most especially in France. It enters into the resolution of the questions Whether the nation may change the descent of lands holden in tail? Whether they may change the appropriation of lands given antiently to the church, to hospitals, colleges, orders of chivalry, and otherwise in perpetuity? whether they may abolish the charges and privileges attached on lands, including the whole catalogue ecclesiastical and feudal? it goes to hereditary offices, authorities and jurisdictions; to hereditary orders, distinctions and appellations; to perpetual monopolies in commerce, the arts or sciences; with a long train of *et ceteras:* and it renders the question of reimbursement a question of generosity and not of right. In all these cases the legislature of the day could authorize such appropriations and establishments for their own time, but no longer; and the present holders, even where they or their ancestors have purchased, are in the case of *bona fide* purchasers of what the seller had no right to convey.

Turn this subject in your mind, my Dear Sir, and particularly as to the power of contracting debts, and develope it with that perspicuity and cogent logic which is so peculiarly yours. Your station in the councils of our country gives you an opportunity of producing it to public consideration, of forcing it into discussion. At first blush it may be rallied as a theoretical speculation; but examination will prove it to be solid and salutary. It would furnish matter for a fine preamble to our first law for appropriating the public revenue; and it will exclude, at the threshold of our new government the contagious and ruinous errors of this quarter of the globe, which have armed despots with means not sanctioned by nature for binding in chains their fellow-men. We have already given, in example one effectual check to the Dog of war, by transferring the power of letting him loose from the executive to the Legislative body, from those who are to spend to those who are to pay. I should be pleased to see this second obstacle held out by us also in the first instance. No nation can make a declaration against the validity of long-contracted debts so disinterestedly as we, since we do not owe a shilling which may not be paid with ease principal and interest, within the time of our own lives. . . . I write you no news, because when an occasion occurs I shall write a separate letter for that.

10. JEFFERSON
The Kentucky Resolutions

In June and July, 1798, the Federalist-controlled Congress passed four laws known as the Alien and Sedition Acts. The Republicans were outraged, but they also realized that the laws were politically unpopular and they began a campaign of criticism against them. Jefferson was Vice President at the time and chose not to oppose the Alien and Sedition Acts publicly. He secretly worked against them, however, and prepared the initial draft of the

Kentucky Resolutions,* which were adopted by the legislature of that commonwealth in November, 1798.

Resolved, that the several States composing the United States of America, are not united on the principles of unlimited submission to their General Government; but that by compact under the style and title of a Constitution for the United States and of amendments thereto, they constituted a General Government for special purposes, delegated to that Government certain definite powers, reserving each State to itself, the residuary mass of right to their own self Government; and that whensoever the General Government assumes undelegated powers, its acts are unauthoritative, void, and of no force: That to this compact each State acceded as a State, and is an integral party, its co-States forming as to itself, the other party: That the Government created by this compact was not made the exclusive or final *judge* of the extent of the powers delegated to itself; since that would have made its discretion, and not the Constitution, the measure of its powers; but that as in all other cases of compact among parties having no common Judge, each party has an equal right to judge for itself, as well of infractions as of the mode and measure of redress.

II. Resolved, that the Constitution of the United States having delegated to Congress a power to punish treason, counterfeiting the securities and current coin of the United States, piracies and felonies committed on the High Seas, and offenses against the laws of nations, and no other crimes whatever, and it being true as a general principle, and one of the amendments to the Constitution having also declared, "that the powers not delegated to the United States by the Constitution, nor prohibited by it to the States, are reserved to the States respectively, or to the people," therefore also the same act of Congress passed on the 14th day of July, 1798, and entitled "An act in addition to the act entitled an act for the punishment of certain crimes against the United States" as also the act passed by them on the 27th day of June, 1798, entitled "An act to punish frauds committed on the Bank of the United States" (and all other of their acts which assume to create, define, or punish crimes other than those enumerated in the Constitution) are altogether void and of no force, and that the power to create, define, and punish such other crimes is reserved, and of right appertains solely and exclusively to the respective States, each within its own Territory.

*Nathaniel S. Shaler, *Kentucky: A Pioneer Commonwealth* (Boston: Houghton, Mifflin and Company, 1885), pp. 409–16.

III. Resolved, that it is true as a general principle, and is also expressly declared by one of the amendments to the Constitution that "the powers not delegated to the United States by the Constitution, nor prohibited by it to the States, are reserved to the States respectively or to the people;" and that no power over the freedom of religion, freedom of speech, or freedom of the press being delegated to the United States by the Constitution, nor prohibited by it to the States, all lawful powers respecting the same did of right remain, and were reserved to the States, or to the people: That thus was manifested their determination to retain to themselves the right of judging how far the licentiousness of speech and of the press may be abridged without lessening their useful freedom, and how far those abuses which cannot be separated from their use, should be tolerated rather than the use be destroyed; and thus also they guarded against all abridgement by the United States of the freedom of religious opinions and exercises, and retained to themselves the right of protecting the same, as this state by a Law passed on the general demand of its Citizens, had already protected them from all human restraint or interference: And that in addition to this general principle and express declaration, another and more special provision has been made by one of the amendments to the Constitution which expressly declares, that "Congress shall make no law respecting an Establishment of religion, or prohibiting the free exercise thereof, or abridging the freedom of speech, or the press," thereby guarding in the same sentence, and under the same words, the freedom of religion, of speech, and of the press, insomuch, that whatever violates either, throws down the sanctuary which covers the others, and that libels, falsehoods, and defamation, equally with heresy and false religion, are withheld from the cognizance of federal tribunals. That therefore the act of the Congress of the United States passed on the 14th day of July 1798, entitled "An act in addition to the act for the punishment of certain crimes against the United States," which does abridge the freedom of the press, is not law, but is altogether void and of no effect.

IV. Resolved, that alien friends are under the jurisdiction and protection of the laws of the State wherein they are; that no power over them has been delegated to the United States, nor prohibited to the individual States distinct from their power over citizens; and it being true as a general principle, and one of the amendments to the Constitution having also declared, that "the powers not delegated to the United States by the Constitution nor prohibited by it to the States are reserved to the States respectively or to the people," the act of the Congress of the United States passed on the 22d day of June, 1798, entitled "An act concerning aliens," which assumes power over alien friends not delegated by the Constitution, is not law, but is altogether void and of no force.

V. Resolved, that in addition to the general principle as well as the express declaration, that powers not delegated are reserved, another and more special provision inserted in the Constitution from abundant caution has declared, "that the *migration* or importation of such persons as any of the States now existing shall think proper to admit, shall not be prohibited by the Congress prior to the year 1808." That this Commonwealth does admit the migration of alien friends described as the subject of the said act concerning aliens; that a provision against prohibiting their migration, is a provision against all acts equivalent thereto, or it would be nugatory; that to remove them when migrated is equivalent to a prohibition of their migration, and is therefore contrary to the said provision of the Constitution and void.

VI. Resolved, that the imprisonment of a person under the protection of the Laws of this Commonwealth on his failure to obey the simple *order* of the President to depart out of the United States, as is undertaken by the said act entitled "An act concerning Aliens," is contrary to the Constitution, one amendment to which has provided, that "no person shall be deprived of liberty without due process of law," and that another having provided "that in all criminal prosecutions, the accused shall enjoy the right to a public trial by an impartial jury, to be informed of the nature and cause of the accusation, to be confronted with the witnesses against him, to have compulsory process for obtaining witnesses in his favour, and to have the assistance of counsel for his defence," the same act undertaking to authorize the President to remove a person out of the United States who is under the protection of the Law, on his own suspicion, without accusation, without jury, without public trial, without confrontation of the witnesses against him, without having witnesses in his favour, without defence, without counsel, is contrary to these provisions also of the Constitution, is therefore not law but utterly void and of no force.

That transferring the power of judging any person who is under the protection of the laws, from the Courts to the President of the United States, as is undertaken by the same act concerning Aliens, is against the article of the Constitution which provides, that "the judicial power of the United States shall be vested in Courts, the Judges of which shall hold their offices during good behaviour," and that the said act is void for that reason also; and it is further to be noted, that this transfer of Judiciary power is to that magistrate of the General Government who already possesses all the Executive, and a qualified negative in all the Legislative powers.

VII. Resolved, that the construction applied by the General Government (as is evinced by sundry of their proceedings) to those parts of the Constitution of the United States which delegate to Congress a power to lay and collect taxes, duties, imposts, and excises; to pay the debts, and provide for the common defence, and general welfare of the United States, and to make all laws which shall be necessary and proper for carrying into execution the powers vested by the Constitution in the Government of the United States, or any department thereof, goes to the destruction of all the limits prescribed to their power by the Constitution—That words meant by that instrument to be subsiduary only to the execution of the limited powers, ought not to be so construed as themselves to give unlimited powers, nor a part so to be taken, as to destroy the whole residue of the instrument: That the proceedings of the General Government under colour of these articles, will be a fit and necessary subject for revisal and correction at a time of greater tranquility, while those specified in the preceding resolutions call for immediate redress.

VIII. Resolved, that the preceeding Resolutions be transmitted to the Senators and Representatives in Congress from this Commonwealth, who are hereby enjoined to present the same to their respective Houses, and to use their best endeavours to procure at the next session of Congress, a repeal of the aforesaid unconstitutional and obnoxious acts.

IX. Resolved lastly, that the Governor of this Commonwealth be, and is hereby authorised and requested to communicate the preceding Resolutions to the Legislatures of the several States, to assure them that this Commonwealth considers Union for specified National purposes, and particularly for those specified in their late Federal Compact, to be friendly to the peace, happiness, and prosperity of all the States: that faithful to that compact, according to the plain intent and meaning in which it was understood and acceded to by the several parties, it is sincerely anxious for its preservation: that it does also believe, that to take from the States all the powers of self government, and transfer them to a general and consolidated Government, without regard to the special delegations and reservations solemnly agreed to

in that compact, is not for the peace, happiness, or prosperity of these States: And that therefore, this Commonwealth is determined, as it doubts not its co-States are, tamely to submit to undelegated & consequently unlimited powers in no man or body of men on earth: that if the acts before specified should stand, these conclusions would flow from them; that the General Government may place any act they think proper on the list of crimes & punish it themselves, whether enumerated or not enumerated by the Constitution as cognizable by them: that they may transfer its cognizance to the President or any other person, who may himself be the accuser, counsel, judge, and jury, whose *suspicions* may be the evidence, his order the sentence, his officer the executioner, and his breast the sole record of the transaction: that a very numerous and valuable description of the inhabitants of these States, being by this precedent reduced as outlaws to the absolute dominion of one man and the barrier of the Constitution thus swept away from us all, no rampart now remains against the passions and the power of a majority of Congress, to protect from a like exportation or other more grievous punishment the minority of the same body, the Legislatures, Judges, Governors, & Counsellors of the States, nor their other peaceable inhabitants who may venture to reclaim the constitutional rights & liberties of the States & people, or who for other causes, good or bad, may be obnoxious to the views or marked by the suspicions of the President, or be thought dangerous to his or their elections or other interests public or personal: that the friendless alien has indeed been selected as the safest subject of a first experiment: but the citizen will soon follow, or rather has already followed; for, already has a Sedition Act marked him as its prey: that these and successive acts of the same character, unless arrested on the threshold, may tend to drive these States into revolution and blood, and will furnish new calumnies against Republic Governments, and new pretexts for those who wish it to be believed, that man cannot be governed but by a rod of iron: that it would be a dangerous delusion were a confidence in the men of our choice to silence our fears for the safety of our rights: that confidence is every where the parent of despotism: free government is founded in jealousy and not in confidence; it is jealousy and not confidence which prescribes limited Constitutions to bind down those whom we are obliged to trust with power: that our Constitution has accordingly fixed the limits to which and no further our confidence may go; and let the honest advocate of confidence read the Alien and Sedition Acts, and say if the Constitution has not been wise in fixing limits to the Government it created, and whether we should be wise in destroying those limits? Let him say what the Government is if it be not a tyranny, which the men of our choice have conferred on the President, and the President of our choice has assented to and accepted over the friendly strangers, to whom the mild spirit of our Country and its laws had pledged hospitality and protection: that the men of our choice have more respected the bare suspicions of the President than the solid rights of innocence, the claims of justification, the sacred force of truth, and the forms & substance of law and justice. In questions of power then let no more be heard of confidence in man, but bind him down from mischief by the chains of the Constitution. That this Commonwealth does therefore call on its co-States for an expression of their sentiments on the acts concerning Aliens, and for the punishment of certain crimes herein before specified, plainly declaring whether these acts are or are not authorized by the Federal Compact? And it doubts not that their sense will be so announced as to prove their attachment unaltered to limited Government, whether general or particular, and that the rights and liberties of their co-States will be exposed to no dangers by remaining embarked on a common bottom with their own: That they will concur with this Commonwealth in considering the said acts as so palpably against the Constitution as to amount to an undisguised declaration, that the Compact is not meant to be the measure of the powers of the General Government, but that it will proceed in the exercise over these States of all powers whatsoever: That they will view this as seizing the rights of the States and consolidating them in the hands of the General Government with a power assumed to bind the States (not merely in cases made federal) but in all cases whatsoever, by laws made, not with their consent, but by others against their consent: That this would be to surrender the form of Government we have chosen, and to live under one deriving its powers from its own will, and not from our authority; and that the co-States recurring to their natural right in cases not made federal, will concur in declaring these acts void and of no force, and will each unite with this Commonwealth in requesting their repeal at the next session of Congress.

11. JEFFERSON
First Inaugural Address

Jefferson was narrowly defeated for the Presidency by John Adams in 1796. Four years later he gained that high office, though only after the House of Representatives had ended the electoral college tie between Jefferson and Aaron Burr. On the morning of March 4, 1801, Jefferson walked from his boardinghouse to the Capitol to take the oath of office and to deliver his Inaugural Address.* It was a time of international tension and furious domestic political strife. In his first Inaugural, Jefferson presented his basic political beliefs and sought to allay the fears of some Federalists that a pro-French American Jacobin had taken office.

FRIENDS AND FELLOW CITIZENS:

Called upon to undertake the duties of the first Executive office of our country, I avail myself of the presence of that portion of my fellow citizens which is here assembled to express my grateful thanks for the favor with which they have been pleased to look towards me, to declare a sincere consciousness that the task is above my talents, and that I approach it with those anxious and awful presentments, which the greatness of the charge, and the weakness of my powers so justly inspire.

A rising nation spreads over a wide and fruitful land, traversing all the seas with the rich productions of their industry, engaged in commerce with nations who feel power and forget right, advancing rapidly to destinies beyond the reach of the mortal eye; when I contemplate these transcendent objects, and see the honor, the happiness, and the hopes of this beloved country committed to the issues and the auspices of this day, I shrink from the contemplation, and humble myself before the magnitude of the undertaking.

Utterly indeed should I despair, did not the presence of many whom I here see, remind me, that in the other high authorities provided by our

*Paul L. Ford, ed., *The Works of Thomas Jefferson*, IX (New York: G. P. Putnam's Sons, 1905), pp. 193–200.

constitution, I shall find resources of wisdom, of virtue, and of zeal, on which to rely under all difficulties.

To you then, gentlemen who are charged with the sovereign functions of legislation and to those associated with you, I look with encouragement for that guidance and support which may enable us to steer with safety, the vessel in which we are all enbarked admidst the conflicting elements of a troubled sea.

During the contest of opinion through which we have passed, the animation of discussions and of exertions, has sometimes worn an aspect which might impose on strangers unused to think freely, and to speak and to write what they think.

But this being now decided by the voice of the nation, announced according to the rules of the constitution, all will of course arrange themselves under the will of the law, and unite in common efforts for the common good. All too will bear in mind this sacred principle that though the will of the Majority is in all cases to prevail, that will, to be rightful, must be reasonable: that the Minority possess their equal rights, which equal laws must protect, and to violate would be oppression.

Let us then, fellow citizens, unite with one heart and one mind; let us restore to social intercourse that harmony and affection, without which Liberty, and even Life itself, are but dreary things.

And let us reflect that having banished from our land that religious intolerance under which mankind so long bled and suffered we have yet gained little, if we countenance a political intolerance as despotic, as wicked, and capable of as bitter and bloody persecutions.

During the throes and convulsions of the ancient world, during the agonizing spasms of infuriated man, seeking through blood and slaughter his long lost liberty, it was not wonderful that the agitation of the billows should reach even this distant and peaceful shore: that this should be more felt and feared by some, and less by others, and should divide opinions as to measures of safety.

But every difference of opinion is not a difference of principle. We have called, by different names, brethren of the same principle. We are all republicans: we are all federalists.

If there be any among us who wish to dissolve this union, or to change its republican form, let them stand undisturbed, as monuments of the safety with which error of opinion may be tolerated where reason is left free to combat it.

I know indeed that some honest men have feared that a republican government cannot be strong; that this government is not strong enough. But would the honest patriot, in the full tide of successful experiment abandon a government which so far kept us free and firm on the theoretic and visionary fear that this government, the world's best hope may, by possibility, want energy to preserve itself?

I trust not. I believe this, on the contrary, the strongest government on earth.

I believe it the only one where every man, at the call of the law, would fly to the standard of the law; would meet invasions of public order, as his own personal concern.

Some times it is said that Man cannot be trusted with the government of himself.—Can he then be trusted with the government of others? Or have we found angels in the form of kings to govern him?—Let History answer this question.

Let us then pursue with courage and confidence our own federal and republican principles, our attachment to Union and Representative government.

Kindly separated by nature, and a wide ocean, from the exterminating havoc of one quarter of the globe;

Too high-minded to endure the degradations of the others;

Possessing a chosen country, with room enough for all descendants to the 100th and 1,000th generation;

Entertaining a due sense of our equal right, to the industry, to honor and confidence from our fellow-citizens resulting not from birth, but from our actions and their sense of them, enlightened by a benign religion, professed indeed and practiced in various forms, yet all of them inculcating honesty, truth, temperance, gratitude, and the love of man, acknowledging and adoring an overruling providence, which by all it's dispensations prove that it delights in the happiness of man here, and his greater happiness hereafter;

With all these blessings, what more is necessary to make us a happy and prosperous people? Still one thing more, fellow citizens—a wise and frugal government, which shall restrain men from injuring one another, shall leave them otherwise free to regulate their own pursuits of industry and improvement, and shall not take from the mouth of labor the bread it has earned.

This is the sum of good government, and this is necessary to close the circle of our felicities.

About to enter fellow citizens on the exercise of duties, which comprehend everything dear and valuable to you, it is proper you should understand what I deem the essential principle of this government and consequently those which ought to shape its administration.

I will compress them in the narrowest compass they will bear, stating the general principle, but not all its limitations.

Equal and exact justice to all men, of whatever state or persuasion, religion, or political:

Peace, commerce, and honest friendship with all nations, entangling alliances with none:

The support of the State governments in all their rights, as the most competent administrations for our domestic concerns, and the surest bulwarks against antirepublican tendencies:

The preservation of the General government, in its whole constitutional vigor, as the sheet anchor of our peace at home, and safety abroad.

A jealous care of the right of election by the people, a mild and safe corrective of abuses, which are lopped by the sword of revolution, where peaceable remedies are unprovided.

Absolute acquiescence in the decisions of the Majority—the vital principle of republics, from which is no appeal but to force, the vital principle and immediate parent of despotism.

A well disciplined militia, our best reliance in peace, and for the first moments of war, till regulars may relieve them: The Supremacy of the Civil over Military authority:

Economy in public expense, that labor may be lightly burthened:

The honest paiment of our debts and sacred preservation of the public faith:

Encouragement of Agriculture, and of Commerce as it's handmaid:

The diffusion of information, and arraignment of all abuses at the bar of the public reason:

Freedom of Religion, freedom of the press, and freedom of person under the protection of the Habeas corpus: And trial by juries, impartially selected.

These Principles form the bright constellation which has gone before us, and guided our steps, thro' an age of Revolution and Reformation: The wisdom of our Sages, and blood of our Heroes, have been devoted to their attainment: they should be the Creed of our political faith, the Text of civic instruction, the Touchstone by which to try the services of those we trust; and should we wander from them, in moments of error or alarm, let us hasten to retrace our steps and to regain the road which alone leads to Peace, Liberty and Safety.

I repair then, fellow citizens to the post which you have assigned me.

With experience enough in subordinate stations to know the difficulties of this the greatest of all, I have learnt to expect that it will rarely fall to the lot of imperfect man to retire from this station with the reputation and favor which bring him into it.

Without pretensions to that high confidence you reposed in our first and greatest revolutionary character whose preeminent services had entitled him to the first place in his country's love, and had destined for him the fairest page in the volume of faithful history, I ask so much confidence only as may give firmness and effect to the legal administration of your affairs.

I shall often go wrong thro' defect of judgment: when right, I shall often be thought wrong by those whose positions will not command a view of the whole ground.

I ask your indulgence for my own errors, which will never be intentional: and your support against the errors of others who may condemn what they would not if seen in all it's parts.

The approbation implied by your suffrage, is a great consolation to me for the past: and my future solicitude will be to retain the good opinion of those who have bestowed it in advance, to conciliate that of others, by doing them all the good in my power, and to be instrumental to the happiness and freedom of all.

Relying then on the patronage of your good will, I advance with obedience to the work, ready to retire from it whenever you become sensible how much better choice it is in your power to make.

And may that infinite power which rules the destinies of the universe lead our councils to what is best, and give them a favorable issue for your peace and prosperity.

12. JEFFERSON
A Natural Aristocracy

Following their retirement from public life, Jefferson and John Adams, longtime political enemies, engaged in a friendly exchange of letters on topics of mutual interest. A letter dated October 28, 1813,* sets forth Jefferson's thoughts on the subject of aristocracy.

DEAR SIR,—According to the reservation between us, of taking up one of the subjects of our correspondence at a time, I turn to your letters of August the 16th and September the 2d. . . .

. . . I agree with you that there is a natural aristocracy among men. The grounds of this are virtue and talents. Formerly, bodily powers gave place among the *aristoi*. But since the invention of gunpowder has armed the weak as well as the strong with missile death, bodily strength, like beauty, good humor, politeness and other accomplishments, has become but an auxiliary ground for distinction. There is also an artificial aristocracy, founded on wealth and birth, without either virtue or talents; for with these it would belong to the first class. The natural aristocracy I consider as the most precious gift of nature, for the instruction, the trusts, and government of society. And indeed, it would have been inconsistent in creation to have formed man for the social state, and not to have provided virtue and wisdom enough to manage the concerns of the society. May we not even say, that that form of government is the best, which provides the most effectually for a pure selection of these natural *aristoi* into the offices of government? The artificial aristocracy is a mischievous ingredient in government, and provision should be made to prevent its ascendancy. On the question, what is the best provision, you and I differ; but we differ as rational friends, using the free exercise of our own reason, and mutually indulging its errors. You think it best to put the *pseudo-aristoi* into a

*Paul L. Ford, ed., *The Works of Thomas Jefferson*, XI (New York: G. P. Putnam's Sons, 1905), pp. 341–50.

separate chamber of legislation, where they may be hindered from doing mischief by their co-ordinate branches, and where, also, they may be a protection to wealth against the Agrarian and plundering enterprises of the majority of the people. I think that to give them power in order to prevent them from doing mischief, is arming them for it, and increasing instead of remedying the evil. For if the co-ordinate branches can arrest their action, so may they that of the co-ordinates. Mischief may be done negatively as well as positively. Of this, a cabal in the Senate of the United States has furnished many proofs. Nor do I believe them necessary to protect the wealthy; because enough of these will find their way into every branch of the legislation, to protect themselves. From fifteen to twenty legislatures of our own, in action for thirty years past, have proved that no fears of an equalization of property are to be apprehended from them. I think the best remedy is exactly that provided by all our constitutions, to leave to the citizens the free election and separation of the *aristoi* from the *pseudo-aristoi*, of the wheat from the chaff. In general they will elect the really good and wise. In some instances, wealth may corrupt, and birth blind them; but not in sufficient degree to endanger the society.

It is probable that our difference of opinion may, in some measure, be produced by a difference of character in those among whom we live. From what I have seen of Massachusetts and Connecticut myself, and still more from what I have heard, and the character given of the former by yourself, who know them so much better, there seems to be in those two states a traditionary reverence for certain families, which has rendered the offices of the government nearly hereditary in those families. I presume that from an early period of your history, members of those families happening to possess virtue and talents, have honestly exercised them for the good of the people, and by their services have endeared their names to them. In coupling Connecticut with you, I mean it politically only, not morally. For having made the Bible the common law of their land, they seemed to have modeled their morality on the story of Jacob and Laban. But although this hereditary succession to office with you, may, in some degree, be founded in real family merit, yet in a much higher degree, it has proceeded from your strict alliance of Church and State. These families are canonised in the eyes of the people on common principles, "you tickle me, and I will tickle you." In Virginia we have nothing of this. Our clergy, before the revolution, having been secured against rivalship by fixed salaries, did not give themselves the trouble of acquiring influence over the people. Of wealth, there were great accumulations in particular families, handed down from generation to generation, under the English law of entails. But the only object of ambition for the wealthy was a seat in the King's Council. All their court then was paid to the crown and its creatures; and they Philipised in all collisions between the King and the people. Hence they were unpopular; and that unpopularity continues attached to their names. A Randolph, a Carter, or a Burwell must have great personal superiority over a common competitor to be elected by the people even at this day. At the first session of our legislature after the Declaration of Independence, we passed a law abolishing entails. And this was followed by one abolishing the privilege of primogeniture, and dividing the lands of intestates equally among all their children, or other representatives. These laws, drawn by myself, laid the ax to the foot of pseudo-aristocracy. And had another which I prepared been adopted by the legislature, our work would have been complete. It was a bill for the more general diffusion of learning. This proposed to divide every county into wards of five or six miles square, like your townships; to establish in each ward a free school for reading, writing and common arithmetic; to provide for the annual selection of the best subjects from these schools, who might receive, at the public expense, a higher degree of education at a district school; and from these district schools to select a certain number of the most promising subjects, to be completed at an University, where all the useful sciences should be taught. Worth and genius would thus have been sought out from every condition of life, and completely prepared by education for defeating the competition of wealth and birth for public trusts. My proposition had, for a further object, to impart to these wards those portions of self-government for which they are best qualified, by confiding to them the care of their poor, their roads, police, elections, the nomination of jurors, administration of justice in small cases, elementary exercises of militia; in short, to have made them little republics, with a warden at the head of each, for all those concerns which, being under their eye, they would better manage than the larger republics of the county or State. A general call of ward meetings by their wardens on the same day through the State, would at any time produce the genuine sense of the people on any required point, and would enable the State to act in mass, as your people have so often done, and with so much effect by their town meetings. The law for religious freedom, which made a part of this system, having put down the aristocracy of the clergy, and restored to the citizen the freedom of the mind, and those of entails and descents nurturing an equality of condition among them, this on education would have raised the mass of the people to the high ground of moral respectability necessary to their own safety, and to orderly government; and would have completed the great object of qualifying them to select the veritable *aristoi*, for the trusts of government, to the exclusion of the pseudalists; . . . Although this law has not yet been acted on but in a small and inefficient degree, it is still considered as before the legislature, with other bills of the revised code, not yet taken up, and I have great hope that some patriotic spirit will, at a favorable moment, call it up, and make it the key-stone of the arch of our government.

With respect to aristocracy, we should further consider, that before the establishment of the American States, nothing was known to history but the man of the old world, crowded within limits either small or overcharged, and steeped in the vices which that situation generates. A government adapted to such men would be one thing; but a very different one, that for the man of these States. Here every one may have land to labor for himself, if he chooses; or, preferring the exercise of any other industry, may exact for it such compensation as not only to afford a comfortable subsistence, but wherewith to provide for a cessation from labor in old age. Every one, by his property, or by his satisfactory situation, is interested in the support of law and order. And such men may safely and advantageously reserve to themselves a wholesome control over their public affairs, and a degree of freedom, which, in the hands of the *canaille* of the cities of Europe, would be instantly perverted to the demolition and destruction of everything public and private. The history of the last twenty-five years of France, and of the last forty years in America, nay of its last two hundred years, proves the truth of both parts of this observation.

But even in Europe a change has sensibly taken place in the mind of man. Science has liberated the ideas of those who read and reflect, and the American example has kindled feelings of right in the people. An insurrection has consequently begun, of science, talents, and courage, against rank and birth, which have fallen into contempt. It has failed in its first effort, because the mobs of the cities, the instrument used for its accomplishment, debased by ignorance, poverty and vice, could not be restrained to rational action. But the world will recover from the panic of this first catastrophe. Science is progressive, and talents and enterprise on the alert. Resort may be had to the people of the country, a more governable power from their principles and subordination; and rank, and birth, and tinsel-aristocracy will finally shrink into insignificance, even there. This, however, we have no right to meddle with. It suffices for us, if the moral and physical condition of our own citizens qualifies them to select the able and good for the direction of their government, with a recurrence of elections at such short periods as will enable them to displace an unfaithful servant, before the mischief he meditates may be irremediable.

I have thus stated my opinion on a point on which we differ, not with a view to controversy, for we are both too old to change opinions which are the result of a long life of inquiry and reflection; but on the suggestions of a former letter of yours, that we ought not to die before we have explained ourselves to each other. We acted in perfect harmony, through a long and perilous contest for our liberty and independence. A constitution has been acquired, which, though neither of us thinks perfect yet both consider as competent to render our fellow citizens the happiest and the securest on whom the sun has ever shone. If we do not think exactly alike as to its imperfections, it matters little to our country, which, after devoting to it long lives of disinterested labor, we have delivered over to our successors in life, who will be able to take care of it and of themselves.

Of the pamphlet on aristocracy which has been sent to you, or who may be its author, I have heard nothing but through your letter. If the person you suspect, it may be known from the quaint, mystical, and hyperbolical ideas, involved in affected, newfangled and pedantic terms which stamp his writings. Whatever it be, I hope your quiet is not to be affected at this day by the rudeness or intemperance of scribblers; but that you may continue in tranquility to live and to rejoice in the prosperity of our country, until it shall be your own wish to take your seat among the *aristoi* who have gone before you. Ever and affectionately yours.

13. JEFFERSON

A Criticism of Judicial Review

Jefferson became increasingly disturbed during the early years of the nineteenth century by the growing power of the Supreme Court under the leadership of Chief Justice John Marshall and by specific decisions of the Court. In a letter dated June 11, 1815,* to W. H. Torrance, Jefferson stated his thoughts on the subject of constitutional interpretation.

SIR,

. . . The second question, whether the judges are invested with exclusive authority to decide on the constitutionality of a law, has been heretofore a subject of consideration with me in the exercise of official duties. Certainly there is not a word in the constitution which has given that power to them more than to the executive or legislative branches. Questions of property, of character and of crime being ascribed to the judges, through a definite course of legal proceeding, laws involving such questions belong, of course, to them; and as they decide on them ultimately and without appeal, they of course decide *for themselves*. The constitutional validity of the law or laws again prescribing executive action, and to be administered by that branch ultimately and without appeal, the executive must decide for *themselves* also, whether, under the constitution, they are valid or not. So also as to laws governing the proceedings of the legislature, that body must judge *for itself* the constitutionality of the law, and equally without appeal or control from its co-ordinate branches. And, in general, that branch which is to act ultimately, and without appeal, on any law, is the rightful expositor of the validity of the law, uncontrolled by the opinions of the other co-ordinate authorities. It may be said that contradictory decisions may arise in such case, and produce inconvenience. This is possible, and is a necessary failing in all human proceed-

* Paul L. Ford, ed., *The Works of Thomas Jefferson*, XI (New York: G. P. Putnam's Sons, 1905), pp. 473–75.

ings. Yet the prudence of the public functionaries, and authority of public opinion, will generally produce accommodation. Such an instance of difference occurred between the judges of England (in the time of Lord Holt) and the House of Commons, but the prudence of those bodies prevented inconvenience from it. So in the cases of Duane and of William Smith of South Carolina, whose characters of citizenship stood precisely on the same ground, the judges in a question of *meum* and *tuum* which came before them, decided that Duane was not a citizen; and in a question of membership, the House of Representatives, under the same words of the same provision, adjudged William Smith to be a citizen. Yet no inconvenience has ensued from these contradictory decisions. This is what I believe myself to be sound. But there is another opinion entertained by some men of such judgment and information as to lessen my confidence in my own. That is, that the legislature alone is the exclusive expounder of the sense of the constitution, in every part of it whatever. And they allege in its support, that this branch has authority to impeach and punish a member of either of the others acting contrary to its declaration of the sense of the constitution. It may indeed be answered, that an act may still be valid although the party is punished for it, right or wrong. However, this opinion which ascribes exclusive exposition to the legislature, merits respect for its safety, there being in the body of the nation a control over them, which, if expressed by rejection on the subsequent exercise of their elective franchise, enlists public opinion against their exposition, and encourages a judge or executive on a future occasion to adhere to their former opinion. Between these two doctrines, every one has a right to choose, and I know of no third meriting any respect.

I have thus, Sir, frankly, without the honor of your acquaintance, confided to you my opinion; trusting assuredly that no use will be made of it which shall commit me to the contentions of the newspapers. From that field of disquietude my age asks exemption, and permission to enjoy the privileged tranquility of a private and unmeddling citizen. In this confidence accept the assurances of my respect and consideration.

14. JEFFERSON
Economic Views—1816

In his *Notes on Virginia* Jefferson had defended the idea of an agrarian nonindustrial America. He continued to be identified with this viewpoint, though events changed his mind about its desirability. To refute his earlier position, Jefferson wrote a letter, dated January 9, 1816,* to his friend Benjamin Austin.

DEAR SIR,—

. . . You tell me I am quoted by those who wish to continue our dependence on England for manufactures. There was a time when I might have been so quoted with more candor, but within the thirty years which have since elapsed, how are circumstances changed! We were then in peace. Our independent place among nations was acknowledged. A commerce which offered the raw material in exchange for the same material after receiving the last touch of industry, was worthy of welcome to all nations. It was expected that those especially to whom manufacturing industry was important, would cherish the friendship of such customers by every favor, by every inducement, and particularly cultivate their peace by every act of justice and friendship. Under this prospect the question seemed legitimate, whether, with such an immensity of unimproved land, courting the hand of husbandry, the industry of agriculture, or that of manufactures, would add most to the national wealth? And the doubt was entertained on this consideration chiefly, that to the labor of the husbandman a vast addition is made by the spontaneous energies of the earth on which it is employed: for one grain of wheat committed to the earth, she renders twenty, thirty, and even fifty fold, whereas to the labor of the manufacturer nothing is added. Pounds of flax, in his hands, yield, on the contrary, but pennyweights of lace. This exchange, too, laborious as it

---

* Paul L. Ford, ed., *The Works of Thomas Jefferson*, XI (New York: G. P. Putnam's Sons, 1905), pp. 502–5.

might seem, what a field did it promise for the occupations of the ocean; what a nursery for that class of citizens who were to exercise and maintain our equal rights on that element? This was the state of things in 1785, when the *Notes on Virginia* were first printed; when, the ocean being open to all nations, and their common right in it acknowledged and exercised under regulations sanctioned by the assent and usage of all, it was thought that the doubt might claim some consideration. But who in 1785 could foresee the rapid depravity which was to render the close of that century the disgrace of the history of man? Who could have imagined that the two most distinguished in the rank of nations, for science and civilization, would have suddenly descended from that honorable eminence, and setting at defiance all those moral laws established by the Author of nature between nation and nation, as between man and man, would cover earth and sea with robberies and piracies, merely because strong enough to do it with temporal impunity; and that under this disbandment of nations from social order, we should have been despoiled of a thousand ships, and have thousands of our citizens reduced to Algerine slavery. Yet all this has taken place. One of these nations interdicted to our vessels all harbors of the globe without having first proceeded to some one of hers, there paid a tribute proportioned to the cargo, and obtained her license to proceed to the port of destination. The other declared them to be lawful prize if they had touched at the port or been visited by a ship of the enemy nation. Thus were we completely excluded from the ocean. Compare this state of things with that of '85, and say whether an opinion founded in the circumstances of that day can be fairly applied to those of the present. We have experienced what we did not then believe, that there exists both profligacy and power enough to exclude us from the field of interchange with other nations: that to be independent for the comforts of life we must fabricate them ourselves. We must now place the manufacturer by the side of the agriculturist. The former question is suppressed, or rather assumes a new form. Shall we make our own comforts, or go without them, at the will of a foreign nation? He, therefore, who is now against domestic manu-facture, must be for reducing us either to dependence on that foreign nation, or to be clothed in skins, and to live like wild beasts in dens and caverns. I am not one of these; experience has taught me that manufactures are now as necessary to our independence as to our comfort; and if those who quote me as of a different opinion, will keep pace with me in purchasing nothing foreign where an equivalent of domestic fabric can be obtained, without regard to difference of price, it will not be our fault if we do not soon have a supply at home equal to our demand, and wrest that weapon of distress from the hand which has wielded it. If it shall be proposed to go beyond our own supply, the question of '85 will then recur, will our *surplus* labor be then most beneficially employed in the culture of the earth, or in the fabrications of art? We have time yet for consideration, before that question will press upon us; and the maxim to be applied will depend on the circumstances which shall then exist; for in so complicated a science as political economy, no one axiom can be laid down as wise and expedient for all times and circumstances, and for their contraries. Inattention to this is what has called for this explanation, which reflection would have rendered unnecessary with the candid, while nothing will do it with those who use the former opinion only as a stalking horse, to cover their disloyal propensities to keep us in eternal vassalage to a foreign and unfriendly people. . . .

15. JEFFERSON
Political Philosophy—1816

Jefferson had long been a critic of the Virginia constitution of 1776. In his *Notes on Virginia* and again a decade later he had unsuccessfully urged constitutional reform. When a strong movement for change arose in the western part of the state in 1816 under the leadership of Samuel Kercheval, Jefferson agreed to lend his support to the campaign and wrote two letters on political theory to Kercheval, asking that they be kept secret. But Kercheval realized their political importance and soon made them public. The first and most significant of the two letters, dated July 12, 1816,* contains an especially important statement of Jefferson's political thought.

SIR,—I duly received your favor of June the 13th, with the copy of the letters on the calling a convention, on which you are pleased to ask

* Paul L. Ford, ed., *The Works of Thomas Jefferson*, XII (New York: G. P. Putnam's Sons, 1905), pp. 3–15.

my opinion. I have not been in the habit of mysterious reserve on any subject, nor of buttoning up my opinions within my own doublet. On the contrary, while in public service especially, I thought the public entitled to frankness, and intimately to know whom they employed. But I am now retired: I resign myself, as a passenger, with confidence to those at present at the helm, and ask but for rest, peace and good will. The question you propose, on equal representation, has become a party one, in which I wish to take no public share. Yet, if it be asked for your own satisfaction only, and not to be quoted before the public, I have no motive to withhold it, and the less from you, as it coincides with your own. At the birth of our republic, I committed that opinion to the world, in the draught of a constitution annexed to the *Notes on Virginia*, in which a provision was inserted for a representation permanently equal. The infancy of the subject at that moment, and our inexperience of self-government, occasioned gross departures in that draught from genuine republican canons. In truth, the abuses of monarchy had so much filled all the space of political contemplation, that we imagined everything republican which was not monarchy. We had not yet penetrated to the mother principle, that "governments are republican only in proportion as they embody the will of their people, and execute it." Hence, our first constitutions had really no leading principles in them. But experience and reflection have but more and more confirmed me in the particular importance of the equal representation then proposed. On that point, then, I am entirely in sentiment with your letters; and only lament that a copy-right of your pamphlet prevents their appearance in the newspapers, where alone they would be generally read, and produce general effect. The present vacancy too, of other matter, would give them place in every paper, and bring the question home to every man's conscience.

But inequality of representation in both Houses of our legislature, is not the only republican heresy in this first essay of our revolutionary patriots at forming a constitution. For let it be agreed that a government is republican in proportion as every member composing it has his equal voice in the direction of its concerns (not indeed in person, which would be impracticable beyond the limits of a city, or small township, but) by representatives chosen by himself, and responsible to him at short periods, and let us bring to the test of this canon every branch of our constitution.

In the legislature, the House of Representatives is chosen by less than half the people, and not at all in proportion to those who do choose. The Senate are still more disproportionate, and for long terms of irresponsibility. In the Executive, the Governor is entirely independent of the choice of the people, and of their control; his Council equally so, and at best but a fifth wheel to a wagon. In the Judiciary, the judges of the highest courts are dependent on none but themselves. In England, where judges were named and removable at the will of an hereditary executive, from which branch most misrule was feared, and has flowed, it was a great point gained, by fixing them for life, to make them independent of that executive. But in a government founded on the public will, this principle operates in an opposite direction, and against that will. There, too, they were still removable on a concurrence of the executive and legislative branches. But we have made them independent of the nation itself. They are irremovable, but by their own body, for any depravities of conduct, and even by their own body for the imbecilities of dotage. The justices of the inferior courts are self-chosen, are for life, and perpetuate their own body in succession for ever, so that a faction once possessing themselves of the bench of a county, can never be broken up, but hold their county in chains, forever indissoluble. Yet these justices are the real executive as well as judiciary, in all our minor and most ordinary concerns. They tax us at will; fill the office of sheriff, the most important of all the executive officers of the county; name nearly all our military leaders, which leaders, once named, are removable but by themselves. The juries, our judges of all fact, and of law when they choose it, are not selected by the people, nor amenable to them. They are chosen by an officer named by the court and executive. Chosen, did I say? Picked up by the sheriff from the loungings of the court yard, after everything respectable has retired from it. Where then is our republicanism to be found? Not in our constitution certainly, but merely in the spirit of our people. That would oblige even a despot to govern us republicanly. Owing to this spirit, and to nothing in the form of our constitution, all things have gone well. But this fact, so triumphantly misquoted by the enemies of reformation, is not the fruit of our constitution, but has prevailed in spite of it. Our functionaries have done well, because generally honest men. If any were not so, they feared to show it.

But it will be said, it is easier to find faults than to amend them. I do not think their amendment so difficult as is pretended. Only lay down true principles, and adhere to them inflexibly. Do not be frightened into their surrender by the alarms of the timid, or the croakings of wealth against the ascendency of the people. If experience be called for, appeal to that of our fifteen or twenty governments for forty years, and show me where the people have done half the mischief in these forty years, that a single despot would have done in a single year; or show half the riots and rebellions, the crimes and the punishments, which have taken place in any single nation, under kingly government, during the same period. The true foundation of republican government is the equal right of every citizen, in his person and property, and in their management. Try by this, as a tally, every provision of our constitution, and see if it hangs directly on the will of the people. Reduce your legislature to a convenient number for full, but orderly discussion. Let every man who fights or pays, exercise his just and equal right in their election. Submit them to approbation or rejection at short intervals. Let the executive be chosen in the same way, and for the same term, by those whose agent he is to be; and leave no screen of a council behind which to skulk from responsibility. It has been thought that the people are not competent electors of judges *learned in the law.* But I do not know that this is true, and, if doubtful, we should follow principle. In this, as in many other elections, they would be guided by reputation, which would not err oftener, perhaps, than the present mode of appointment. In one State of the Union, at least, it has long been tried, and with the most satisfactory success. The judges of Connecticut have been chosen by the people every six months, for nearly two centuries, and I believe there has hardly ever been an instance of change; so powerful is the curb of incessant responsibility. If prejudice, however, derived from a monarchical institution, is still to prevail against the vital elective principle of our own, and if the existing example among ourselves of periodical election of judges by the people be still mistrusted, let us at least not adopt the evil, and reject the good, of the English precedent; let us retain amovability on the concurrence of the executive and legislative branches, and nomination by the executive function. Nomination to office is an executive function. To give it to the legislature, as we do, is a violation of the principle of the separation of powers. It swerves the members from correctness, by temptations to intrigue for office themselves, and to a corrupt barter of votes; and destroys responsibility by dividing it among a multitude. By leaving nomination in its proper place, among executive functions, the principle of the distribution of power is preserved, and responsibility weighs with its heaviest force on a single head.

The organization of our county administrations may be thought more difficult. But follow principle, and the knot unties itself. Divide the counties into wards of such size as that every citizen can attend, when called on, and act in person. Ascribe to them the government of their wards in all things relating to themselves exclusively. A justice, chosen by themselves, in each, a constable, a military company, a patrol, a school, the care of their own poor, their own portion of the public roads, the choice of one or more jurors to serve in some court, and the delivery, within their own wards, of their own votes for all elective officers of higher sphere, will relieve the county administration of nearly all its business, will have it better done, and by making every citizen an acting mèmber of the government, and in the offices nearest and most interesting to him, will attach him by his strongest feelings to the independence of his country, and its republican constitution. The justices thus chosen by every ward, would constitute the county court, would do its judiciary business, direct roads and bridges, levy county and poor rates, and administer all the matters of common interest to the whole country. These wards, called townships in New England, are the vital principle of their governments, and have proved themselves the wisest invention ever devised by the wit of man for the perfect exercise of self-government, and for its preservation. We should thus marshal our government into, 1, the general federal republic, for all concerns foreign and federal; 2, that of the State, for what relates to our own citizens exclusively; 3, the county republics, for the duties and concerns of the county; and 4, the ward republics, for the small, and yet numerous and interesting concerns of the neighborhood; and in government, as well as in every other business of life, it is by division and subdivision of duties alone, that all matters, great and small, can be managed to perfection. And the whole is cemented by giving to every citizen, personally, a part in the administration of the public affairs.

The sum of these amendments is, 1. General Suffrage. 2. Equal representation in the legislature. 3. An executive chosen by the people. 4. Judges elective or amovable. 5. Justices, jurors, and sheriffs elective. 6. Ward divisions. And 7. Periodical amendments of the constitution.

I have thrown out these as loose heads of amendment, for consideration and correction; and their object is to secure self-government by the republicanism of our constitution, as well as by the spirit of the people; and to nourish and perpetuate that spirit. I am not among those who fear the people. They, and not the rich, are our dependence for continued freedom. And to preserve their independence, we must not let our rulers load us with perpetual debt. We must make our election between *economy and liberty*, or *profusion and servitude*. If we run into such debts, as that we must be taxed in our meat and in our drink, in our necessaries and our comforts, in our labors and our amusements, for our callings and our creeds, as the people of England are, our people, like them, must come to labor sixteen hours in the twenty-four, give the earnings of fifteen of these to the government for their debts and daily expenses; and the sixteenth being insufficient to afford us bread, we must live, as they now do, on oatmeal and potatoes; have no time to think, no means of calling the mismanagers to account; but be glad to obtain subsistence by hiring ourselves to rivet their chains on the necks of our fellow-sufferers. Our landholders, too, like theirs, retaining indeed the title and stewardship of estates called theirs, but held really in trust for the treasury, must wander, like theirs, in foreign countries, and be contented with penury, obscurity, exile, and the glory of the nation. This example reads to us the salutary lesson, that private fortunes are destroyed by public as well as by private extravagance. And this is the tendency of all human governments. A departure from principle in one instance becomes a precedent for a second; that second for a third; and so on, till the bulk of the society is reduced to be mere automatons of misery, and to have no sensibilities left but for sinning and suffering. Then begins, indeed, the *bellum omnium in omnia*, which some philosophers observing to be so general in this world, have mistaken it for the natural, instead of the abusive state of man. And the fore horse of this frightful team is public debt. Taxation follows that, and in its train wretchedness and oppression.

Some men look at constitutions with sanctimonious reverence, and deem them like the arc of the covenant, too sacred to be touched. They ascribe to the men of the preceding age a wisdom more than human, and suppose what they did to be beyond amendment. I knew that age well; I belonged to it, and labored with it. It deserved well of its country. It was very like the present, but without the experience of the present; and forty years of experience in government is worth a century of book-reading; and this they would say themselves, were they to rise from the dead. I am certainly not an advocate for frequent and untried changes in laws and constitutions. I think moderate imperfections had better be borne with; because, when once known, we accommodate ourselves to them, and find practical means of correcting their ill effects. But I know also, that laws and institutions must go hand in hand with the progress of the human mind. As that becomes more developed, more enlightened, as new discoveries are made, new truths disclosed, and manners and opinions change with the change of circumstances, institutions must advance also, and keep pace with the times. We might as well require a man to wear still the coat which fitted him when a boy, as civilized society to remain ever under the regimen of their barbarous ancestors. It is this preposterous idea which has lately deluged Europe in blood. Their monarchs, instead of wisely yielding to the gradual change of circumstances, of favoring progressive accommodation to progressive improvement, have clung to old abuses, entrenched themselves behind steady habits, and obliged their subjects to seek through blood and violence rash and ruinous innovations, which, had they been referred to the peaceful deliberations and collected wisdom of the nation, would have been put into acceptable and salutary forms. Let us follow no such examples, nor weakly believe that one generation is not as capable as another of taking care of itself, and of ordering its own affairs. Let us, as our sister States have done, avail ourselves of our reason and experience, to correct the crude essays of our first and unexperienced, although wise, virtuous, and well-meaning councils. And lastly, let us provide in our constitution for its revision at stated periods. What these periods should be, nature herself indicates. By the European tables of mortality, of the adults living at any one moment of time, a majority will be dead in about nineteen years. At the end of that period, then, a new majority is come into place; or, in other words, a new generation. Each generation is as independent as the one preceding, as that was of all which had gone before. It has then, like them, a right to choose for itself the form of government it believes most promotive of its own happiness; consequently, to accommodate to the circumstances in which it finds itself, that received from its predecessors; and it is for the peace and good of mankind that a solemn opportunity of doing this every nineteen or twenty years, should be provided by the constitution; so that it may be handed on, with periodical repairs, from generation to generation, to the end of time, if anything human can so long endure. It is now forty years since the constitution of Virginia was formed. The same tables inform us, that, within that period, two-thirds of the adults then living are now dead. Have then the remaining third, even if they had the wish, the right to hold in obedience to their will, and to laws heretofore made by them, the other two-thirds, who, with themselves, compose the present mass of adults? If they have not, who has? The dead? But the dead have no rights. They are nothing; and nothing cannot own something. Where there is no substance, there can be no accident. This corporeal globe, and everything upon it, belong to its present corporeal inhabitants, during their generation. They alone have a right to direct what is the concern of themselves alone, and to declare the law of that direction; and this declaration can only be made by their majority. That majority, then, has a right to depute representatives to a convention, and to make the constitution what they think will be the best for themselves. But how collect their voice? This is the real difficulty. If invited by private authority, or county or district meetings, these divisions are so large that few will attend; and their voice will be imperfectly, or falsely pronounced. Here, then, would be one of the advantages of the ward divisions I have proposed. The mayor of every ward, on a question like the present, would call his ward together, take the simple yea or nay of its members, convey these to the county court, who would hand on those of all its wards to the proper general authority; and the voice of the whole people would be thus fairly, fully, and peaceably expressed, discussed, and decided by the common reason of the society. If this avenue be shut to the call of sufferance, it will make itself heard through that of force, and we shall go on, as other nations are doing, in the endless circle of oppression, rebellion, reformation; and oppression, rebellion, reformation, again; and so on forever.

These, Sir, are my opinions of the governments we see among men, and of the principles by which alone we may prevent our own falling into the same dreadful track. I have given them at greater length than your letter called for. But I cannot say things by halves; and I confide them to your honor, so to use them as to preserve me from the gridiron of the public papers. If you shall approve and enforce them, as you have done that of equal representation, they may do some good. If not, keep them to yourself as the effusions of withered age and useless time. I shall, with not the less truth, assure you of my great respect and consideration.

16.   GIBSON

Attack on Judicial Review

John Bannister Gibson (1780–1853) served several terms in the Pennsylvania legislature before his appointment in 1813 as a state district court judge. Three years later he was elevated to the state supreme court, and in 1827 the governor appointed him chief justice of that court. Although considered by President Jackson in 1830 as a possible nominee to fill a vacancy on the United States Supreme Court, Gibson was passed over in favor of another Pennsylvanian, Henry Baldwin. Gibson continued his service on the Pennsylvania supreme court until his death in 1853. His dissenting opinion in the obscure and unimportant case of *Eakin* v. *Raub** stands as the most reasoned reply to Chief Justice Marshall's opinion in *Marbury* v. *Madison.* Two decades later Gibson gave his reluctant approval to judicial review because the Pennsylvania Constitutional Convention of 1838 had "sanctioned the pretensions of the courts to deal freely with the acts of the legislature; and from experience of the necessity of the case" (*Norris* v. *Clymer,* 2 Pa. 277 [1845]).

. . . I am aware, that a right to declare all unconstitutional acts void . . . is generally held as a professional dogma; but, I apprehend, rather as a matter of faith than of reason. I admit that I once embraced the same doctrine, but without examination, and I shall therefore state the arguments that impelled me to abandon it, with great respect for those by whom it is still maintained. But I may premise, that it is not a little remarkable, that although the right in question has all along been claimed by the judiciary, no judge has ventured to discuss it, except Chief Justice Marshall . . . and if the argument of a jurist so distinguished for the strength of his ratiocinative powers be found inconclusive, it may fairly be set down to the weakness of the position which he attempts to defend. . . .

. . . [T]he constitution is said to be a law of superior obligation; and consequently, that if it were to come into collision with an act of the

* 12 Sergeant and Rawle 330, 344–56 (1825).

legislature, the latter would have to give way. This is conceded. But it is a fallacy, to suppose, that they can come into collision *before the judiciary*. . . .

The constitution and the *right* of the legislature to pass the act, may be in collision. But is that a legitimate subject for judicial determination? If it be, the judiciary must be a peculiar organ, to revise the proceedings of the legislature, and to correct its mistakes; and in what part of the constitution are we to look for this proud pre-eminence? Viewing the matter in the opposite direction, what would be thought of an act of assembly in which it should be declared that the Supreme Court had, in a particular case, put a wrong construction on the constitution of the *United States*, and that the judgment should therefore be reversed. It would doubtless be thought a usurpation of judicial power. But it is by no means clear, that to declare a law void which has been enacted according to the forms prescribed in the constitution, is not a usurpation of legislative power. It is an act of sovereignty; and sovereignty and legislative power are said by Sir William *Blackstone* to be convertible terms. It is the business of the judiciary, to interpret the laws, not scan the authority of the lawgiver; and without the latter, it cannot take cognisance of a collision between a law and the constitution. So that to affirm that the judiciary has a right to judge of the existence of such collision, is to take for granted the thing to be proved. . . .

But it has been said to be emphatically the business of the judiciary to ascertain and pronounce what the law is; and that this necessarily involves a consideration of the constitution. It does so: but how far? If the judiciary will inquire into anything beside the form of enactment, where shall it stop? There must be some point of limitation to such an inquiry; for no one will pretend, that a judge would be justifiable in calling for the election returns, or scrutinizing the qualifications of those who composed the legislature.

. . . [I]n theory, all the organs of the government are of equal capacity; or, if not equal, each must be supposed to have superior capacity only for those things which peculiarly belong to it; and, as legislation peculiarly involves the consideration of those limitations which are put on the law-making power, and the interpretation of the laws when made, involves only the construction of the laws themselves, it follows that the construction of the constitution in this particular belongs to the legislature, which ought therefore to be taken to have superior capacity to judge of the constitutionality of its own acts. . . .

Everyone knows how seldom men think exactly alike on ordinary subjects; and a government constructed on the principle of assent by all its parts, would be inadequate to the most simple operations. The notion of a complication of counter checks has been carried to an extent in theory, of which the framers of the constitution never dreamt. When the entire sovereignty was separated into its elementary parts, and distributed to the appropriate branches, all things incident to the exercise of its powers was committed to each branch exclusively. The negative which each part of the legislature may exercise, in regard to the acts of the other, was thought sufficient to prevent material infractions of the restraints which were put on the power of the whole; for, had it been intended to interpose the judiciary as an additional barrier, the matter would surely not have been left in doubt. The judges would not have been left to stand on the insecure and ever shifting ground of public opinion as to constructive powers; they would have been placed on the impregnable ground of an express grant. They would not have been compelled to resort to the debates in the convention, or the opinion that was generally entertained at the time. A constitution, or a statute, is supposed to contain the whole will of the body from which it emanated; and I would just as soon resort to the debates in the legislature for the construction of an act of assembly, as to the debates in the convention for the construction of the constitution.

The power is said to be restricted to cases that are free from doubt or difficulty. But the abstract existence of a power cannot depend on the clearness or obscurity of the case in which it is to be exercised; for that is a consideration that cannot present itself, before the question of the existence of the power shall have been determined; and, if its existence be conceded, no considerations of policy arising from the obscurity of the particular case, ought to influence the exercise of it. . . . To say, therefore, that the power is to be exercised but in perfectly clear cases, is to betray a doubt of the propriety of exercising it at all. Were the same caution used in judging of the existence of the power that is inculcated as to the exercise of it, the profession would perhaps arrive at a different conclusion. . . .

But the judges are sworn to support the constitution, and are they not bound by it as the law of the land? . . . The oath to support the constitution is not peculiar to the judges, but is taken indiscriminately by every officer of the government, and is designed rather as a test of the political principles of the man, than to bind the officer in the discharge of his duty: otherwise it were difficult to determine what operation it is to have in the case of a recorder of deeds, for instance, who, in the execution of his office, has nothing to do with the constitution. But granting it to relate to the official conduct of the judge, as well as every other officer, and not to his political principles, still it must be understood in reference to supporting the constitution, *only as far as that may be involved in his official duty*; and consequently, if his official duty does not comprehend an inquiry into the authority of the legislature, neither does his oath. . . .

But do not the judges do a *positive act* in violation of the constitution, when they give effect to an unconstitutional law? Not if the law has been passed according to the forms established in the constitution. The fallacy of the question is, in supposing that the judiciary adopts the act of the legislature as its own; whereas the enactment of a law and the interpretation of it are not concurrent acts, and as the judiciary is not required to concur in the enactment, neither is it in the breach of the constitution which may be the consequence of enactment; the fault is imputable to the legislature, and on it the responsibility exclusively rests. . . .

But it has been said, that this construction would deprive the citizen of the advantages which are peculiar to a written constitution, by at once declaring the power of the legislature in practice to be illimitable. . . .

I am of opinion that it rests with the people, in whom full and absolute sovereign power resides, to correct abuses in legislation, by instructing their representatives to repeal the obnoxious act. . . . It might, perhaps, have been better to vest the power in the judiciary; as it might be expected that its habits of deliberation, and the aid from the arguments of counsel, would more frequently lead to accurate conclusions. On the other hand, the judiciary is not infallible; and an error by it would admit of no remedy but a more distinct expression of the public will, through the extraordinary medium of a convention; whereas, an error by the legislature admits of a remedy by an exertion of the same will, in the ordinary exercise of the right of suffrage,—a mode better calculated to attain that end, without popular excitement. It may be said, the people would probably not notice an error of their representatives. But they would as probably do so, as notices of error of the judiciary; and, beside, it is a *postulate* in the theory of our government, and the very basis of the superstructure, that the people are wise, virtuous, and competent to manage their own affairs: and if they are not so, in fact, still every question of this sort must be determined according to the principles of the constitution, as it came from the hands of the framers, and the existence of a defect which was not foreseen, would not justify those who administer the government, in applying a corrective in practice, which can be provided only by convention. . . .

But in regard to an act of [a state] assembly, which is found to be in collision with the constitution, laws, or treaties of the *United States*, I take the duty of the judiciary to be exactly the reverse. By becoming parties to the federal constitution, the states have agreed to several limitations of their individual sovereignty, to enforce which, it was thought necessary to prevent them from giving effect to laws in violation of those limitations, through the instrumentality of their own judges. Accordingly, it is declared in the sixth article and second section of the federal constitution, that "This constitution, and the laws of the *United States* which shall be made in pursuance thereof, and all treaties which shall be made under the authority of the *United States*, shall be the *supreme* law of the land; and the *judges* in every *state* shall be BOUND thereby: anything in the *laws* or *constitution* of any *state* to the contrary notwithstanding."

17. TAYLOR
Defense of States' Rights

John Taylor (1753–1824), Virginia farmer, Revolutionary War officer, member of the Virginia House of Delegates, and three-time United States Senator, was also an important American political theorist. (He was commonly known as John Taylor of Caroline, after the Virginia county of his birth and residence.) Taylor was a close ally of Thomas Jefferson and strongly supported his successful quest for the Presidency in 1800. He played an important role in the writing of the Twelfth Amendment and continued his support for Administration policies throughout Jefferson's term in office. Taylor refused, however, to support Madison's nomination in 1808, preferring Monroe. Later he became a strong critic of the War of 1812. During these years he was associated with the largely Virginian group of political figures known as the Tertium Quid. The following selection is taken from *Construction*

*Construed and Constitutions Vindicated,** which was published in 1820 and inspired by his opposition to the decisions of Chief Justice Marshall. Taylor's other books include *Tyranny Unmasked* (1822), an attack on the protective tariff, and *New Views on the Constitution of the United States* (1823), his last published work.

. . . Previously to the union, the states were in the enjoyment of sovereignty or supremacy. Not having relinquished it by the union, in fact having then exercised it, there was no occasion, in declaring the supremacy of the constitution and laws made in pursuance thereof, to notice that portion of state supremacy, originally attached to, not severed from, and of course remaining with the powers not delegated to the federal government; whilst it was necessary to recognize that other portion of supremacy, attached to the special powers transferred from the states to the federal government. But, by recognizing the supremacy transferred, it was not intended to destroy the portion of supremacy not transferred. The supremacy retained, and a choice of means convenient or necessary for the execution of the powers reserved, was as indispensable an appendage of state rights, as of the limited powers delegated to congress. And in fact the unqualified supremacy, bestowed upon the constitution, is equally a guaranty of state and of federal powers, as is demonstrated by the positive limitation of the supremacy bestowed on federal laws, to such as were comformable to the restricted legislative power, created by the constitution. Suppose a state should declare war, tax imports, or regulate commerce; or, that congress should tax exports, alter the course of descents, or liberate the negroes; would these be questions of supremacy, unconnected with the powers actually delegated and reserved? If not, supremacy is limited by these powers, and cannot extend them. In like manner, neither the federal nor state courts, can under colour of supremacy, exceed its own sphere. If one should assume admiralty jurisdiction, and the other the distribution of intestates' estates, the party usurping could not constitutionally defend its usurpation under colour of supremacy. Unconstitutional judgments, like unconstitutional laws, are null and void, and both courts are mutually bound by their oaths to the constitution, and have a mutual right to resist and defeat, by every means in their power, unconstitutional laws, falling within their respective jurisdictions. Had an oath of loyalty, not to the constitution, but to the supremacy of one court, been imposed, it might have been

* (Richmond: Shepherd and Pollard, 1820), pp. 142–47, 159.

otherwise. An exclusive right in either to ascertain the extent of its own jurisdiction would leave its jurisdiction without limits, and the rights of neither judicial sphere can be defended against the other, except by using all the means it possesses; just, as a senate and house of representatives can only defend their respective constitutional rights. The supremacy of the constitution is not confined to any particular department or functionary, but extends to our entire system of political law. Under its protection, the federal senate has a right to defend itself against the house of representatives; and the federal judicial power against the federal legislative power; and if so, it seems impossible to doubt, that the same sanction invests the state and federal judicial powers with a mutual right of self defence, against the aggressions of each other.

I renounce the idea sometimes advanced, that the state governments ever were or continue to be, sovereign or unlimited. If the people are sovereign, their governments cannot also be sovereign. In the state constitutions, some limitations are to be found; in the federal constitution, they are infinitely more abundant and explicit. Whatever arguments can be urged against the sovereignty of state governments, stronger can be urged against the sovereignty of the federal government. Both governments are subjected to restrictions, and the power by which both were constituted has entrusted neither with an exclusive power of enforcing these restrictions upon the other, because it would have conceded its own supremacy by so doing, and parted with its inherent authority.

No derived power can be greater than the primitive power. No state, nor a majority of states, had any species of primitive sovereignty or supremacy over other states. Elections by states, therefore, cannot confer upon a majority of congress a supremacy never possessed by a majority of states, especially as from the form of the senate, the representatives of a minority of people may pass a law, and this representation of the minority might, if it possessed a legislative supremacy, exercise a sovereign power over the majority. If federal legislatures do not possess an absolute supremacy, federal judiciaries cannot possess it, since judgments cannot enforce that which is not law. In conformity with this reasoning, neither federal legislative majorities, nor a majority of the states, can amend the constitution, because it was a compact by which each state delegated for itself only limited powers to the federal government; attended by a supremacy not of any political sphere, but of the constitution, limited and confined to the powers delegated, and not extending to the portion of primitive state supremacy, never delegated. Thus it happened, that no state was bound by the constitution, until it had acceded individually to that compact. And hence it results, that the right of construing the constitution within their respective spheres, is mutual between the state and general governments, because the latter have no supremacy over the state powers retained, and the former no supremacy over the federal powers delegated, except that which provides the stipulated mode of amending the constitution.

It is objected, that if the supreme federal court do not possess an unlimited or unchecked supremacy in construing the constitution, clashing constructions will ensue. This is true; and yet it is not a good reason for overturning our system for dividing, limiting and checking power, if that system be a good one; and if it be even a bad one, the people only, and neither one of their departments separately, nor all united, can alter or amend it. The objection applies as strongly to the other departments of our government, as to the judicial. If the federal legislature and executive do not possess an absolute supremacy over the state legislatures and executives, clashing constitutional constructions will ensue. The jurisdiction of the federal judicial power is as expressly limited, as the legislative and executive federal powers. There is no judicial supremacy recognized in the supreme federal court, except that over inferior federal courts. And, if the supremacy of the constitution bestows upon any federal department a supremacy over the correspondent state department, it must bestow upon every federal department, a similar supremacy over the other correspondent state departments.

It is therefore obvious, that the subject proposed by the objection for consideration is, whether it is better to abandon our primary division of powers between the state and federal governments, to prevent clashing constructions; or to retain this chief security against a gradual introduction of oppression, trusting to the mutual prudence of these governments, and the supreme authority of the people, for meeting the inconvenience, as it appears. The greatest scope of human wisdom is, to compare evils and choose the least. I cannot discern the wisdom of one who cuts off his head, lest his face should be scratched occasionally as he journeys through life. Montesquieu has somewhere said, that when the savage of America wants fruit, he cuts down the tree to obtain it. Shall we act with still less foresight, by cutting down the division of power between the general and state governments, calculated to produce the fruit of moderation in both, that one may cram us with the fruits of supremacy? . . .

The mutuality of the right of construction in the several departments of the state and federal governments, was the reason, which suggested the section of the constitution of the United States requiring that, "the senators and representatives in congress, and the members of the several *state legislatures*, and all *executive and judicial officers, both of the United States, and of the several states*, shall be bound, by oath or affirmation, to support the constitution." The mutuality of the oath, by imposing a common duty, implies a common right; because the duty cannot be discharged, except by exercising the right of construction. To impose the duty by the highest sanction, and yet to have impliedly designed that its performance should be rendered null and void, by a constructive supremacy in one political sphere over the others, would amount to the same thing, as if the oath had been, that the enumerated spheres should be subordinate to one, invested with a supremacy over the rest. Would this latter have been equivalent to the actual oath? If not, can a construction by which it is substantially enforced, be correct? By the actual oath, the constitution, in conformity with its great principle of a division and co-ordinateness of powers between the state and general governments, divides also its confidence for its own preservation. The same confidence is divided by the special powers invested in the states and in the general government for its execution. If the oath binds the federal judicial power to disregard a mandate from a state judicial power, prohibiting the exercise of its constitutional powers; it also binds the judicial power of a state, to disregard a similar mandate from the judicial power of the union; and compels both to protect the officers and individuals upon whom their respective jurisdictions may operate: otherwise, one jurisdiction may supersede the other. This would be certainly a greater evil, than even a necessity for a reference to the people to settle a collision.

If a greater sphere of action conferred supremacy according to the constitution of the union, and if the federal government possesses the greater sphere of action, (the positions upon which the court relies as justifying its decision,) where was the necessity for declaring the constitution and the laws made in pursuance thereof to be the *supreme law* of the land? The supremacy had passed, as the court asserts, attached to the greater sphere of action. If it was attached to this greater sphere of action, it is not bestowed by this clause; and yet this clause is referred to by the court, as auxiliary to their implied supremacy.

In the several mixtures of truth and error to be found in the opinion of the court, this has been managed with the most ingenuity. The supremacy expressed has been united with the supremacy implied, without any examination of the nature of the first, or of its great difference from the latter. A government of laws and not of men, is a definition of liberty; a government of men and not of laws, of despotism. The expressed supremacy asserts the first principle; the implied supremacy of the men composing the legislative or judicial federal departments, asserts the second. By blending them, their extreme contrariety is endeavoured to be obscured, and the clause conferring *supremacy on the constitution and the laws made in pursuance thereof*, is very ingeniously changed from a restriction, into an amplification of power. Yet it is under the supremacy conferred upon the constitution by this very clause, that the federal judicial sphere exercises a controul over the federal legislative sphere in the case of unconstitutional laws, because the difference between a supremacy of the constitution and a supremacy in congress, is manifest; whilst the same court insists upon a supremacy in congress over the powers reserved to the states, and denies to congress a supremacy over the powers delegated to itself. This seems to me to be obviously incorrect, because I consider the constitution to have derived from this clause an absolute supremacy for the preservation of the powers reserved to the states, as well as of those delegated to the general government; and not as bestowing on any one sphere, state or federal, an exclusive right to ascertain the extent of those powers; such a right being in fact a despotism of men.

Important as this subject is, to avoid prolixity, I shall overlook sundry features of the constitution, and only add a few observations to those already urged. A union of states clearly admits the sovereignty and equality of the parties uniting. A union does not, as a consequence of union, tacitly and impliedly, reduce these sovereign and equal parties to subordinate corporations; because in that case, they could not alter or dissolve the union, without the consent of the power, to which they would be subordinate. The federal government is allowed by the court to be limited. Can it be limited by a power subordinate to itself, or is it only limited by the didactick lessons of the constitution? The Federalist speaks of the jealousy which would arise between the federal and state governments, because they would be mutual checks upon each other, as co-ordinate powers always struggle for sovereignty; and of the great security for a free government, arising from this feature of the constitution. But a paramount or supreme power in congress obliterates this feature. And of what avail is a preceptive limitation, bereft of the co-ercive resource for its execution? If congress be a paramount or supreme judge of its own legislative power, its power is unlimited. We have no conception of an unlimited power, beyond one, limited only by its own will. If the jurisdiction of the supreme federal court is limited only by its own will, it is in like manner unlimited. Power can never be checked by itself, or by its own subordinate instrument. The constitution certainly intended to invest the legislative and judicial spheres of the federal and state governments, with distinct and independent objects of legislation and cognizance; but, these mutual rights however clear can never be preserved, if one party possesses a supremacy over the other, and the other, no power of resistance. . . .

Finally, it ought to be observed, that the constitution does not invest the federal court with any jurisdiction, in cases of collision between either the legislative or judicial powers of the state and federal governments; and as such a jurisdiction would be infinitely more important than any other with which it is endowed, the omission is not sufficiently accounted for by saying, either that the case was overlooked, as never likely to happen, or, that though its importance was foreseen as extremely probable, this important jurisdiction was bestowed by inference only, while cases of jurisdiction comparatively insignificant were minutely expressed. But the omission is well accounted for, if we consider the constitution as having contemplated the state and federal governments as its co-ordinate guardians, designed to check and balance each other; since, having established that primary and important principle by the division of powers between them, it would have been as obvious an inconsistency to have bestowed a power on the federal courts to settle collisions as to their mutual rights, as to have reserved the same supervising power to the state courts. . . .

III

Jacksonian
Democracy

The Constitution written in Philadelphia in 1787 and the constitutions produced at state conventions during the 1780's reveal the uncertainties and anxieties of the age. A new nation, struggling for survival, embarked on a course of self-government, but the course that was followed was a cautious one reflecting the precarious position of the new nation and the fear that excessive democracy would destroy its existence. At both national and state levels, constitutions were adopted that placed limitations on the powers of the majority. Property qualifications for voting, checks and balances, the electoral college, the legislative caucus, and an independent judiciary were among the most important devices designed to frustrate the power of the people.

But a greater degree of democracy was not to be denied to the people of the United States. In the years following the end of the War of 1812 the first strong demand for democratic reform arose in respect to the nature of the state constitutions. Six new states entering the Union between 1816 and 1821 adopted suffrage laws providing for universal white male suffrage. This movement spread eastward to the original thirteen states, and constitutional conventions were called in a number of them to consider proposals for democratic reform.

The specific issues varied from state to state, but property and democracy were the general subjects in each convention. Conservatives such as Joseph Story, John Adams, and Daniel Webster in Massachusetts, James Kent in New York, and John Marshall and John Randolph in Virginia spoke in defense of property rights. They argued, for example, in favor of the need to continue restrictions on voting for the upper house of the Massachusetts and New York legislatures and for the general freehold voting qualification in Virginia.

The proponents of the new democracy could claim few prominent members in their ranks, but they did have a number of articulate spokesmen for their cause. David Buel, Jr., in New York is a case in point. An obscure delegate from Rensselaer County, Buel presented an eloquent case for repeal of the property qualification for voting for state senators and effectively challenged the basic premise of James Kent's argument. Buel denied that the majority of people in the United States were hostile to the property rights of the minority as Kent had maintained. Kent had based his contention on a description of "the existing state of society in European kingdoms." But Buel asked, "Are arguments, drawn from the state of society in Europe, applicable to our situations?" He emphatically denied that they were. Land is more widely distributed in this nation than in the European kingdoms, and education has contributed to the greater virtue, intelligence, and love of freedom by Americans, he said. Buel, even in this early period of our history, saw the futility of applying European theories of class conflict to American society.

The pressure to change state government was, however, only the first phase of America's drive for democracy in the early nineteenth century. The most important part of this movement for democratic reform took place under the leadership of Andrew Jackson during his two terms as President (1829–37). Jackson, with the broad support of the nation's farmers and the growing number of workers in the larger cities, came to symbolize the new age of democracy.

The Jacksonian movement had few intellectuals to produce a body of political theory to justify its program. Several authors and critics of the period—Orestes A. Brownson and John L. O'Sullivan for example—attempted to perform this function, but their efforts were not as successful in capturing the essential ideas and spirit of the age as were the speeches and writings of Jackson himself and those of his most important and influential adviser, Roger B. Taney.

A good deal of confusion exists about the nature of Jacksonian democracy. Despite the tendency to interpret Jacksonianism as an early version of the New Deal, a close examination reveals more differences than similarities Both were against the excessive economic influence of a minority, and both movements sought to extend the power of the majority over government and the economy. The New Deal, however, attempted to secure control over powerful economic forces by the positive use of governmental power. It favored regulation of the economy and legislation that would protect and promote the welfare of the weaker, less successful members of the community. The Jacksonians had no such conception of government. They were far closer to the laissez-faire traditions of Jefferson than to the positive state theories of Franklin Roosevelt. The writings of Jackson and Taney continually stress the need to allow the operation of a free competitive capitalism and to eliminate any special rights given by government to a privileged minority.

Further, the Jacksonians were not strong believers in centralized government as were most New Dealers. Jackson, it is true, acted with dispatch against South Carolina's attempt at nullification in 1832. But this was based on his deep support for the Union and not on a belief in a powerful, positive national government. Jackson's writings repeatedly emphasize the desirability of handling domestic problems at the state level.

Finally, the New Deal, preoccupied with the economic problems of a terrible depression, was unconcerned with reforming the nation's political system so as to increase the people's power. The Jacksonians, on the contrary, imbued with an unquestioning faith in the virtue and ability of the common man, presented a broad program for political change. They failed to abolish the electoral college, but they were remarkably successful in achieving most of their other goals: the convention system for nominating public officials, the spoils system for office holding, the strong executive at both national and state levels to speak in behalf of the interests of the majority, and the direct election of judges and administrative officials in the executive branch of government. A century and a half later, the American governmental system still functions under the influence of the ideas and institutions of Jacksonian democracy.

18. BUEL

Expansion of the Voting Right

On August 28, 1821, a constitutional convention opened in Albany, New York. A call for the convention had been approved in a popular referendum earlier in the year. One of the major issues faced by the body was the question of whether a property qualification should be maintained for electing the state senate. The debate on the subject produced a clear confrontation between the defenders of property and the spokesmen of the new democracy. James Kent spoke brilliantly in favor of the voting restriction. The best reply to Kent was made in a speech by David Buel, Jr., delegate from Rensselaer County in upstate New York.* When the vote was taken, Buel's liberal position triumphed and this bastion of privilege was eliminated from New York's governmental system.

. . . The subject now before the committee, is thought by many gentlemen to be the most important that will fall under our deliberations. . . . The question whether it is safe and proper to extend the right of suffrage to other classes of our citizens, besides the landholders, is decided as I think, by the sober sense and deliberate acts of the great American people. To this authority I feel willing to bow. An examination of the constitutions of the different states, will show us that those enlightened bodies of statesmen and patriots who have from time to time been assembled for the grave and important purpose of forming and reforming the constitutions of the states—have sanctioned and established as a maxim, the opinion that there is no danger in confiding the most extensive right of suffrage to the intelligent population of these United States.

Of the twenty-four states which compose this union, twelve states

* Reports of the Proceedings and Debates of the Convention of 1821 (Albany: Printed and published by E. and E. Hosford, 1821), pp. 239 44.

require only a certain time of residence as a qualification to vote for all their elective officers—eight require in addition to residence the payment of taxes or the performance of militia duty—four states only *require* a freehold qualification, viz. New-York, North-Carolina, Virginia, and Rhode-Island. The distinction which the amendment of the gentleman from Albany proposes to continue, exists only in the constitution of this state, and in that of North-Carolina.

In some of the states, the possession of a freehold, constitutes one of several qualifications, either of which gives the right of suffrage; but in four only, is the exclusive right of voting for any department of the government confined to landholders.

The progressive extension of the right of suffrage by the reformations which have taken place in several of the state constitutions, adds to the force of the authority. By the original constitution of Maryland, (made in 1776,) a considerable property qualification was necessary to constitute an elector. By successive alterations in the years 1802, and 1810, the right has been extended to all the white citizens who have a permanent residence in the state. A similar alteration has been made in the constitution of South-Carolina; and by the recent reformations in the constitutions of Connecticut and Massachusetts, property qualifications in the electors have been abolished; the right is extended in the former almost to universal suffrage, and in the latter to all the citizens who pay taxes. It is not in the smaller states only, that these liberal principles respecting suffrage, have been adopted. The constitution of Pennsylvania, adopted in the year 1790, extends the right of suffrage to all the citizens who pay taxes, and to their sons between the age of twenty-one and twenty-two years.

That constitution was formed by men, distinguished for patriotism and talents. At the head of them, we find the name of Judge [James] Wilson, a distinguished statesman, and one of the founders of the constitution of the United States.

The constitution of Pennsylvania was formed on the broad principle of suffrage, which that distinguished man lays down in his writings. "That every citizen whose circumstances do not render him necessarily dependant on the will of another, should possess a vote in electing those, by whose conduct his property, his reputation, his liberty, and his life may be almost materially affected." This is the correct rule, and it has been adopted into the constitution of every state which has been formed since the government of the United States was organized. So universal an admission of the great principle of general suffrage, by the Conventions of discreet and sober minded men, who have been engaged in forming or amending the different constitutions, produces a strong conviction that the principle is safe and salutary.

It is said by those who contend that the right of voting for senators should be confined to the landholders, that the framers of our constitution were wise and practical men, and that they deemed this distinction essential to the security of the landed property; and that we have not encountered any evils from it during the forty years experience which we have had. To this I answer, that if the restriction of the right of suffrage has produced no positive evil, it cannot be shown to have produced any good results.

The qualifications for assembly voters, under the existing constitution, are as liberal as any which will probably be adopted by this Convention. Is it pretended that the assembly, during the forty-three years experience which we have enjoyed under our constitution, has been, in any respect, inferior to the senate? Has the senate, although elected exclusively by freeholders, been composed of men of more talents, or greater probity, than the assembly? Have the rights of property, generally, or of the landed interest in particular, been more vigilantly watched, and more carefully protected by the senate than by the assembly? I might appeal to the journals of the two houses, and to the recollections and information of the members of the committee on this subject; but it is unnecessary, as I understand the gentlemen who support the amendment, distinctly admit, that hitherto the assembly has been as safe a depository of the rights of the landed interest, as the senate. But it is supposed that the framers of our constitution must have had wise and cogent reasons for making such a distinction between the electors of the different branches of the government. May we not, however, without the least derogation from the wisdom and good intentions of the framers of our constitution, ascribe the provision in question to circumstances which then influenced them, but which no longer ought to have weight?

When our constitution was framed, the domain of the state was in the hands of a few. The proprietors of the great manors were almost the only men of great influence; and the landed property was deemed worthy of almost exclusive consideration. Before the revolution, freeholders only were allowed to exercise the right of suffrage. The notions of our ancestors, in regard to real property, were all derived from England. The feudal tenures were universally adopted. The law of primogeniture, by which estates descended to the eldest son, and the rule of descent by which the male branches inherited the paternal estate, to the exclusion of the female, entails, and many other provisions of feudal origin were in force. The tendency of this system, it is well understood, was to keep the lands of the state in few hands. But since that period, by the operation of wiser laws, and by the prevalence of juster principles, an entire revolution has taken place in regard to real property. Our laws for regulating descents, and for converting entailed estates into fee-simple, have gradually increased the number of land-holders: Our territory has been rapidly divided and subdivided: And although the landed interest is no longer controlled by the influence of a few great proprietors, its aggregate importance is vastly increased, and almost the whole community have become interested in its protection. In New-England, the inhabitants, from the earliest period, have enjoyed the system which we are progressively attaining to. There, the property of the soil has always been in the hands of the *many*. The great bulk of the population are farmers and freeholders, yet no provision is incorporated in their constitutions, excluding those who are not freeholders from a full participation in the right of suffrage. May we not trace the notions of the framers of our constitution, respecting the exclusive privilege of the freeholders, to the same source from whence they derived all their ideas of real property?

In England, from the earliest times, the superiority of the landed interest was maintained. To go no farther back than the Norman invasion, we find the domain of England parcelled out in great manors among the followers of the Conqueror. They and their descendants, for many years, were the only legislative and judiciary power in the kingdom. Their baronies gave them the right of legislation. It was a privilege annexed to the land which their vassals cultivated. Their vassals, in process of time, became freeholders, and formed the juries in the manor courts.

It was a long time before any other interests than that of the land-holders was attended to. For some hundred years, the great cities and boroughs were not considered worthy of being represented in the great councils of the kingdom. And although numerous great interests have since arisen, the house of peers and the knights of the shire, are still supposed to represent the landed interest exclusively. It was not surprising that the framers of our constitution, though they in the main aimed to establish our government on republican principles, should have adopted some of the notions which they inherited, with their domains, from their ancestors. The force of habit and prejudice which induced those illustrious men to incorporate in the constitution absurd provisions, will manifestly appear by adverting to a single instance of the application of the rule established by them, to determine the right of voting for senators and governor.

A man who is possessed of a piece of land worth $250 for his own life, or the life of another person, is a freeholder, and has the right to vote for governor and senators. But one who has an estate in ever so valuable a farm, for 999 years, or any other definite term, however long, is not a freeholder and cannot vote. The absurdity of the distinction, at this day, is so glaring as to require no comment. Yet there are numerous farmers, in different parts of the state, who are excluded from the right of suffrage on this absurd distinction between freehold and leasehold estates. No person will now pretend that a farmer who holds his land by a thousand years lease is less attached to the soil, or less likely to exercise the privilege of freeman discreetly, than a freeholder. We shall not, I trust, be accused of want of respect to settled institutions, if we expunge such glaring absurdities from our constitution. It is supposed however, by the honourable member before me [James Kent] that landed property will become insecure under the proposed extension of the right of suffrage, by the influx of a more dangerous population. That gentleman has drawn a picture from the existing state of society in European kingdoms, which would be indeed appalling, if we could suppose such a state of society could exist here. But are arguments, drawn from the state of society in Europe, applicable to our situation? . . .

It is conceded by my honourable friend, that the great landed estates must be cut up by the operation of our laws of descent; that we have already seen those laws effect a great change; and that it is the inevitable tendency of our rules of descent, to divide up our territory into farms of moderate size. The real property, therefore, will be in the hands of the *many*. But in England, and other European kingdoms, it is the policy of the aristocracy to keep the lands in few hands. The laws of primogeniture, the entailments and family settlements, all tend to give a confined direction to the course of descents. Hence we find in Europe, the landed estates possessed by a few rich men; and the great bulk of the population poor, and without that attachment to the government which is found among the owners of the soil. Hence, also, the poor envy and hate the rich, and mobs and insurrections sometimes render property insecure. Did I believe that our population would degenerate into such a state, I should, with the advocates for the amendment, hesitate in extending the right of suffrage; but I confess I have no such fears. I have heretofore had doubts respecting the safety of adopting the principles of a suffrage as extensive as that now contemplated. I have given to the subject the best reflection of which I am capable; and I have satisfied myself, that there is no danger in adopting those liberal principles which are incorporated in almost all the constitutions of these United States.

There are in my judgment, many circumstances which will forever preserve the people of this state from the vices and the degradation of European population, beside those which I have already taken notice of. The provision already made for the establishment of common schools, will, in a very few years, extend the benefit of education to all our citizens. The universal diffusion of information will forever distinguish our population from that of Europe. Virtue and intelligence are the true basis on which every republican government must rest. When these are lost, freedom will no longer exist. The diffusion of education is the only sure means of establishing these pillars of freedom. I rejoice in this view of the subject, that our common school fund will (if the report on the legislative department be adopted,) be consecrated by a constitutional provision; and I feel no apprehension, for myself, or my posterity, in confiding the right of suffrage to the great mass of such a population as I believe ours will always be. The farmers in this country will always out number all other portions of our population. Admitting that the increase of our cities, and especially of our commercial metropolis, will be as great as it has been hitherto; it is not to be doubted that the agricultural population will increase in the same proportion. The city population will never be able to depress that of the country. New-York has always contained about a tenth part of the population of the state, and will probably always bear a similar proportion. Can she, with such a population, under any circumstances, render the property of the vast population of the country insecure? It may be that mobs will occasionally be collected, and commit depredations in a great city; but, can the mobs traverse our immense territory, and invade the farms, and despoil the property of the landholders? And if such a state of things were possible, would a senate, elected by freeholders, afford any security? It is the regular administration of the laws by an independent judiciary, that renders property secure against private acts of violence. And there will always be a vast majority of our citizens interested in preventing legislative injustice.

But the gentleman who introduced the proposition now before the committee, has predicted dangers of another kind to the landed interest, if their exclusive right of electing the senate shall be taken away. He supposes, that combinations of other interests will be formed to depress the landholders, by charging them exclusively with the burthen of taxation.

I cannot entertain any apprehension that such a state of things will ever exist. Under any probable extension of the right of suffrage, the landed interest will, in my view of the subject, always maintain a vast preponderance of numbers and influence. From what combinations of other interests can danger arise? The mercantile and manufacturing interests are the only ones which can obtain a formidable influence. Are the owners of manufacturing establishments, scattered through the state, as they always must be, likely to enter into a confederacy with the merchants of the great cities, for the purpose of depressing the yoemanry and landholders of this great state? Has our past experience shewn any tendency in those two great interests, to unite in any project, especially for such an one as that which I have mentioned? We usually find the merchants and manufacturers acting as rivals to each other: but both feel a community of interest with the landholders; and it will ever be the interest of the farmers, as it ever has been, to foster and protect both the manufacturing and mercantile interests. The discussions which the tariff has undergone, both in and out of congress, have demonstrated the feelings of rivalship which exist between our manufacturers and our merchants. But who has ever heard, in this or any other country, of a combination of those two classes of men, to destroy the interest of the farmers? No other combination, then, can be imagined, but that of the poor against the rich. Can it be anticipated, that those who have no property can ever so successfully combine their efforts, as to have a majority in both branches of the legislature, unfriendly to the security of property?

One ground of the argument of gentlemen who support the amendment is, that the extension of the right of suffrage will give an undue influence to the rich over the persons who depend upon them for employment; but if the rich control the votes of the poor, the result cannot be unfavourable to the security of property. The supposition that, at some future day, when the poor shall become numerous, they may imitate the radicals of England, or the jacobins of France; that they may rise, in the majesty of their strength, and usurp the property of the landholders, is so unlikely to be realized, that we may dismiss all fear arising from that source. Before that can happen, wealth must lose all its influence; public morals must be destroyed; and the nature of our government changed, and it would be in vain to look to a senate, chosen by landholders, for security in a case of such extremity. I cannot but think, that all the dangers which it is predicted will flow from doing away the exclusive right of the landholders to elect the senators, are groundless.

I contend, that by the true principle of our government, property, as such, is not the basis of representation. Our community is an association of persons—of human beings—not a partnership founded on property. The declared object of the people of this state in associating, was, to "establish such a government as they deemed best calculated to secure the rights and liberties of the good people of the state, and most conducive to their happiness and safety." Property, it is admitted, is one of the rights to be protected and secured; and although the protection of life and liberty is the highest object of attention, it is certainly true, that the security of property is a most interesting and important object in every free government. Property is essential to our temporal happiness; and is necessarily one of the most interesting subjects of legislation. The desire of acquiring property is a universal passion. I readily give to property the important place which has been assigned to it by the honourable member from Albany [James Kent]. To property we are indebted for most of our comforts, and for much of our temporal happiness. The numerous religious, moral, and benevolent institutions which are every where established, owe their existence to wealth; and it is wealth which enables us to make those great internal improvements which we have undertaken. Property is only one of the incidental rights of the person who possesses it; and, as such, it must be made secure; but it does not follow, that it must therefore be represented specifically in any branch of the government. It ought, indeed, to have influence—and it will have, when properly enjoyed. So ought talents to have an influence. It is certainly as important to have men of good talents in your legislature, as to have men of property; but you surely would not set up men of talents as a separate order, and give them exclusive privileges.

The truth is, that both wealth and talents will ever have a great influence; and without the aid of exclusive privileges, you will find the influence of both wealth and talents predominant in our halls of legislation. . . .

19.   JACKSON

Popular Democracy

Andrew Jackson (1767–1845), seventh President of the United
States, was born in the small rural community of Waxhaw, South Carolina.
Although only a boy of nine when the Revolutionary War broke out, Jackson
nonetheless fought against the British and, at the age of fourteen, was the only
surviving member of a family that had been decimated by the war. Jackson
taught school for a short time, then read law in North Carolina before moving
west to the frontier settlement of Jonesboro, Tennessee, where he established
a successful legal practice. Jackson was a member of the convention that wrote
Tennessee's first constitution after its admission into the Union in 1796,
and he was elected as the state's first member of the House of Representatives.
He soon resigned this seat and was selected to represent Tennessee in the
United States Senate. In 1798 he again resigned this seat and returned to his
home state, where he was subsequently elected to a seat on the Tennessee
superior court. Jackson gained national fame during the War of 1812 for his
successful military campaign against the Creek Indians and for his defense of
New Orleans against the attacking British. In 1818 he led a controversial
expedition against hostile Indians along the Alabama-Florida border, and
after the purchase of Florida, President Monroe appointed him governor of
the new territory. In 1823, as a prelude to his bid for the Presidency the
following year, Jackson was again chosen to serve in the Senate. He received
the most popular votes of the four rivals in the election of 1824, but none of
the candidates obtained the necessary majority of electoral votes. Amid
anguished cries of "corruption" by the Jacksonians, the supporters of Henry
Clay in the House of Representatives united behind John Q. Adams to
elect him President. But the defeat was only a temporary setback, for Jackson
was elected President over Adams in the election of 1828.

This selection* is taken from Jackson's first Annual Message, which he
delivered to Congress on December 8, 1829.

---

* James D. Richardson, ed., *A Compilation of the Messages and Papers of the
Presidents, 1789–1897*, II (Washington: Government Printing Office, 1896), pp. 442,
447–49, 451–52.

Fellow-Citizens of the Senate and House of Representatives: It affords me pleasure to tender my friendly greetings to you on the occasion of your assembling at the seat of Government to enter upon the important duties to which you have been called by the voice of our countrymen. The task devolves on me, under a provision of the Constitution, to present to you, as the Federal Legislature of twenty-four sovereign States and 12,000,000 happy people, a view of our affairs, and to propose such measures as in the discharge of my official functions have suggested themselves as necessary to promote the objects of our Union.

In communicating with you for the first time it is to me a source of unfeigned satisfaction, calling for mutual gratulation and devout thanks to a benign Providence, that we are at peace with all mankind, and that our country exhibits the most cheering evidence of general welfare and progressive improvement. . . .

I consider it one of the most urgent of my duties to bring to your attention the propriety of amending that part of our Constitution which relates to the election of President and Vice-President. Our system of government was by its framers deemed an experiment, and they therefore consistently provided a mode of remedying its defects.

To the people belongs the rights of electing their Chief Magistrate; it was never designed that their choice should in any case be defeated, either by the intervention of electoral colleges or by the agency confided, under certain contingencies, to the House of Representatives. Experience proves that in proportion as agents to execute the will of the people are multiplied there is danger of their wishes being frustrated. Some may be unfaithful; all are liable to err. So far, therefore, as the people can with convenience speak, it is safer for them to express their own will.

The number of aspirants to the Presidency and the diversity of the interests which may influence their claims leave little reason to expect a choice in the first instance, and in that event the election must devolve on the House of Representatives, where it is obvious the will of the people may not be always ascertained, or, if ascertained, may not be regarded. From the mode of voting by States the choice is to be made by 24 votes, and it may often occur that one of these will be controlled by an individual Representative. Honors and offices are at the disposal of the successful candidate. Repeated ballotings may make it apparent that a single individual holds the cast in his hands. May he not be tempted to name his reward? But even without corruption, supposing the probity of the Representative to be proof against the powerful motives by which it may be assailed, the will of the people is still constantly liable to be misrepresented. One may err from ignorance of the wishes of his constituents; another from a conviction that it is his duty to be governed by his own judgment of the fitness of the candidates; finally, although all were inflexibly honest, all accurately informed of the wishes of their constituents, yet under the present mode of election a minority may often elect a President, and when this happens it may reasonably be expected that efforts will be made on the part of the majority to rectify this injurious operation of their institutions. But although no evil of this character should result from such a perversion of the first principle of our system—that the majority is to govern—it must be very certain that a President elected by a minority can not enjoy the confidence necessary to the successful discharge of his duties.

In this as in all other matters of public concern policy requires that as few impediments as possible should exist to the free operation of the public will. Let us, then, endeavor so to amend our system that the office of Chief Magistrate may not be conferred upon any citizen but in pursuance of a fair expression of the will of the majority.

I would therefore recommend such an amendment of the Constitution as may remove all intermediate agency in the election of the President and Vice-President. The mode may be so regulated as to preserve to each State its present relative weight in the election, and a failure in the first attempt may be provided for by confining the second to a choice between the two highest candidates. In connection with such an amendment it would seem advisable to limit the service of the Chief Magistrate to a single term of either four or six years. If, however, it should not be adopted, it is worthy of consideration whether a provision disqualifying for office the Representatives in Congress on whom such an election may have devolved would not be proper.

While members of Congress can be constitutionally appointed to offices of trust and profit it will be the practice, even under the most conscientious adherence to duty, to select them for such stations as they are believed to be better qualified to fill than other citizens; but the purity of our Government would doubtless be promoted by their exclusion from all appointments in the gift of the President, in whose election they may have been officially concerned. The nature of the judicial office and the necessity of securing in the Cabinet and in diplomatic stations of the highest rank the best talents and political experience should, perhaps, except these from the exclusion.

There are, perhaps, few men who can for any great length of time enjoy office and power without being more or less under the influence of feelings unfavorable to the faithful discharge of their public duties. Their integrity may be proof against improper considerations immediately addressed to themselves, but they are apt to acquire a habit of looking with indifference upon the public interests and of tolerating conduct from which an unpracticed man would revolt. Office is considered as a species of property, and government rather as a means of promoting individual interests than as an instrument created solely for the service of the people. Corruption in some and in others a perversion of correct feelings and principles divert government from its legitimate ends and make it an engine for the support of the few at the expense of the many. The duties of all public officers are, or at least admit of being made, so plain and simple that men of intelligence may readily qualify themselves for their performance; and I can not but believe that more is lost by the long continuance of men in office than is generally to be gained by their experience. I submit, therefore, to your consideration whether the efficiency of the Government would not be promoted and official industry and integrity better secured by a general extension of the law which limits appointments to four years.

In a country where offices are created solely for the benefit of the people no one man has any more intrinsic right to official station than another. Offices were not established to give support to particular men at the public expense. No individual wrong is, therefore, done by removal, since neither appointment to nor continuance in office, is matter of right. The incumbent became an officer with a view to public benefits, and when these require his removal they are not to be sacrificed to private interests. It is the people, and they alone, who have a right to complain when a bad officer is substituted for a good one. He who is removed has the same means of obtaining a living that are enjoyed by the millions who never held office. The proposed limitations would destroy the idea of property now so generally connected with official station, and although individual distress may be sometimes produced, it would, by promoting that rotation which constitutes a leading principle in the republican creed, give healthful action to the system. . . .

. . . [The] state of the finances exhibits the resources of the nation in an aspect highly flattering to its industry and auspicious of the ability of Government in a very short time to extinguish the public debt. When this shall be done our population will be relieved from a considerable portion of its present burthens, and will find not only new motives to patriotic affection, but additional means for the display of individual enterprise. The fiscal power of the States will also be increased, and may be more extensively exerted in favor of education and other public objects, while ample means will remain in the Federal Government to promote the general weal in all the modes permitted to its authority.

After the extinction of the public debt it is not probable that any adjustment of the tariff upon principles satisfactory to the people of the Union will until a remote period, if ever, leave the Government without a considerable surplus in the Treasury beyond what may be required for its current service. As, then, the period approaches when the application of the revenue to the payment of debt will cease, the disposition of the surplus will present a subject for the serious deliberation of Congress; and it may be fortunate for the country that it is yet to be decided. Considered in connection with the difficulties which have heretofore attended appropriations for purposes of internal improvement, and with those which this experience tells us will certainly arise whenever power over such subjects may be exercised by the General Government, it is hoped that it may lead to the adoption of some plan which will reconcile the diversified interests of the States and strengthen the bonds which unite them. Every member of the Union, in peace and in war, will be benefited by the improvement of inland navigation and the construction of highways in the several States. Let us, then, endeavor to attain this benefit in a mode which will be satisfactory to all. That hitherto adopted has by many of our fellow-citizens been deprecated as an infraction of the Constitution, while by others it has been viewed as inexpedient. All feel that it has been employed at the expense of harmony in the legislative councils.

To avoid these evils it appears to me that the most safe, just, and federal disposition which could be made of the surplus revenue would be its apportionment among the several States according to their ratio of representation, and should this measure not be found warranted by the Constitution that it would be expedient to propose to the States an amendment authorizing it. I regard an appeal to the source of power in cases of real doubt, and where its exercise is deemed indispensable to the general welfare, as among the most sacred of all our obligations. Upon this country more than any other has, in the providence of God, been cast the special guardianship of the great principle of adherence to written constitutions. If it fail here, all hope in regard to it will be extinguished. That this was intended to be a government of limited and specific, and not general, powers must be admitted by all, and it is our duty to preserve for it the character intended by its framers. If experience points out the necessity for an enlargement of these powers, let us apply for it to those for whose benefit it is to be exercised, and not undermine the whole system by a resort to over-strained constructions. The scheme has worked well. It has exceeded the hopes of those who devised it, and become an object of admiration to the world. We are responsible to our country and to the glorious cause of self-government for the preservation of so great a good. The great mass of legislation relating to our internal affairs was intended to be left where the Federal Convention found it—in the State govern-ments. Nothing is clearer, in my view, than that we are chiefly indebted for the success of the Constitution under which we are now acting to the watchful and auxiliary operation of the State authorities. This is not the reflection of a day, but belongs to the most deeply rooted convictions of my mind. I can not, therefore, too strongly or too earnestly, for my own sense of its importance, warn you against all encroachments upon the legitimate sphere of State sovereignty. Sus-tained by its healthful and invigorating influence the federal system can never fall. . . .

20. JACKSON
Veto of Privilege

The charter of the Second Bank of the United States was not due to expire until 1836, but in 1832 Henry Clay, leader of the National Republican Party, convinced the Bank president, Nicholas Biddle, that he should apply for recharter immediately. Clay had just received his party's Presidential nomination, and he believed that the Bank issue would win him the fall election. A bill to recharter the Bank passed the Congress on July 3, 1832, and was sent to President Jackson. A week later, on July 10, the President returned the bill to Congress with a veto message* that reveals Jackson's hostility to privilege and his belief in the virtue of the common man.

* James D. Richardson, ed., *A Compilation of the Messages and Papers of the Presidents, 1789–1897*, II (Washington: Government Printing Office, 1896), pp. 576–78, 590–91.

To the Senate: The bill "to modify and continue" the act entitled "An act to incorporate the subscribers to the Bank of the United States" was presented to me on the 4th July instant. Having considered it with that solemn regard to the principles of the Constitution which the day was calculated to inspire, and come to the conclusion that it ought not to become a law, I herewith return it to the Senate, in which it originated, with my objections.

A bank of the United States is in many respects convenient for the Government and useful to the people. Entertaining this opinion, and deeply impressed with the belief that some of the powers and privileges possessed by the existing bank are unauthorized by the Constitution, subversive of the rights of the States, and dangerous to the liberties of the people, I felt it my duty at an early period of my Administration to call the attention of Congress to the practicability of organizing an institution combining all its advantages and obviating these objections. I sincerely regret that in the act before me I can perceive none of those modifications of the bank charter which are necessary, in my opinion, to make it compatible with justice, with sound policy, or with the Constitution of our country.

The present corporate body, denominated the president, directors, and company of the Bank of the United States, will have existed at the time this act is intended to take effect twenty years. It enjoys an exclusive privilege of banking under the authority of the General Government, a monopoly of its favor and support, and, as a necessary consequence, almost a monopoly of the foreign and domestic exchange. The powers, privileges, and favors bestowed upon it in the original charter, by increasing the value of the stock far above its par value, operated as a gratuity of many millions to the stockholders.

An apology may be found for the failure to guard against this result in the consideration that the effect of the original act of incorporation could not be certainly foreseen at the time of its passage. The act before me proposes another gratuity to the holders of the same stock, and in many cases to the same men, of at least seven millions more. This donation finds no apology in any uncertainty as to the effect of the act. On all hands it is conceded that its passage will increase at least 20 or 30 per cent more the market price of the stock, subject to the payment of the annuity of $200,000 per year secured by the act, thus adding in a moment one-fourth to its par value. It is not our own citizens only who are to receive the bounty of our Government. More than eight millions of the stock of this bank are held by foreigners.

By this act the American Republic proposes virtually to make them a present of some millions of dollars. For these gratuities to foreigners and to some of our own opulent citizens the act secures no equivalent whatever. They are the certain gains of the present stockholders under the operation of this act, after making full allowance for the payment of the bonus.

Every monopoly and all exclusive privileges are granted at the expense of the public, which ought to receive a fair equivalent. The many millions which this act proposes to bestow on the stockholders of the existing bank must come directly or indirectly out of the earnings of the American people. It is due to them, therefore, if their Government sell monopolies and exclusive privileges, that they should at least exact for them as much as they are worth in open market. The value of the monopoly in this case may be correctly ascertained. The twenty-eight millions of stock would probably be at an advance of 50 per cent, and command in market at least $42,000,000, subject to the payment of the present bonus. The present value of the monopoly, therefore, is $17,000,000, and this the act proposes to sell for three millions, payable in fifteen annual installments of $200,000 each.

It is not conceivable how the present stockholders can have any claim to the special favor of the Government. The present corporation has enjoyed its monopoly during the period stipulated in the original contract. If we must have such a corporation, why should not the Government sell out the whole stock and thus secure to the people the full market value of the privileges granted? Why should not Congress create and sell twenty-eight millions of stock, incorporating the purchasers with all the powers and privileges secured in this act and putting the premium upon the sales into the Treasury?

But this act does not permit competition in the purchase of this monopoly. It seems to be predicated on the erroneous idea that the present stockholders have a prescriptive right not only to the favor but to the bounty of Government. It appears that more than a fourth part of the stock is held by foreigners and the residue is held by a few hundred of our own citizens, chiefly of the richest class. For their benefit does this act exclude the whole American people from competition in the purchase of this monopoly and dispose of it for many millions less than it is worth. This seems the less excusable because some of our citizens not now stockholders petitioned that the door of competition might be opened, and offered to take a charter on terms much more favorable to the Government and country.

But this proposition, although made by men whose aggregate wealth is believed to be equal to all the private stock in the existing bank, has been set aside, and the bounty of our Government is proposed to be again bestowed on the few who have been fortunate enough to secure the stock and at this moment wield the power of the existing institution. I can not perceive the justice or policy of this course. If our Government must sell monopolies, it would seem to be its duty to take nothing less than their full value, and if gratuities must be made once in fifteen or twenty years let them not be bestowed on the subjects of a foreign government nor upon a designated and favored class of men in our own country. It is but justice and good policy, as far as the nature of the case will admit, to confine our favors to our own fellow-citizens, and let each in his turn enjoy an opportunity to profit by our bounty. In the bearings of the act before me upon these points I find ample reasons why it should not become a law. . . .

It is to be regretted that the rich and powerful too often bend the acts of government to their selfish purposes. Distinctions in society will always exist under every just government. Equality of talents, of education, or of wealth can not be produced by human institutions. In the full enjoyment of the gifts of Heaven and the fruits of superior industry, economy, and virtue, every man is equally entitled to protection by law; but when the laws undertake to add to these natural and just advantages artificial distinctions, to grant titles, gratuities, and exclusive privileges, to make the rich richer and the potent more powerful, the humble members of society—the farmers, mechanics, and laborers—who have neither the time nor the means of securing like favors to themselves, have a right to complain of the injustice of their Government. There are no necessary evils in government. Its evils exist only in its abuses. If it would confine itself to equal protection, and, as Heaven does it rains, shower its favors alike on the high and the low, the rich and the poor, it would be an unqualified blessing. In the act before me there seems to be a wide and unnecessary departure from these just principles.

Nor is our Government to be maintained or our Union preserved by invasions of the rights and powers of the several States. In thus attempting to make our General Government strong we make it weak. Its true strength consists in leaving individuals and States as much as possible to themselves—in making itself felt, not in its power, but in its beneficence; not in its control, but in its protection; not in binding the States more closely to the center, but leaving each to move unobstructed in its proper orbit.

Experience should teach us wisdom. Most of the difficulties our Government now encounters and most of the dangers which impend over our Union have sprung from an abandonment of the legitimate objects of Government by our national legislation, and the adoption of such principles as are embodied in this act. Many of our rich men have not been content with equal protection and equal benefits, but have besought us to make them richer by act of Congress. By attempting to gratify their desires we have in the results of our legislation arrayed section against section, interest against interest, and man against man, in a fearful commotion which threatens to shake the foundations of our Union. It is time to pause in our career to review our principles, and if possible revive that devoted patriotism and spirit of compromise which distinguished the sages of the Revolution and the fathers of our Union. If we can not at once, in justice to interests vested under improvident legislation, make our Government what it ought to be, we can at least take a stand against all new grants of monopolies and exclusive privileges, against any prostitution of our Government to the advancement of the few at the expense of the many, and in favor of compromise and gradual reform in our code of laws and system of political economy.

I have now done my duty to my country. If sustained by my fellow-citizens, I shall be grateful and happy; if not, I shall find in the motives which impel me ample grounds for contentment and peace. In the difficulties which surround us and the dangers which threaten our institutions there is cause for neither dismay nor alarm. For relief and deliverance let us firmly rely on that kind Providence which I am sure watches with peculiar care over the destinies of our Republic, and on the intelligence and wisdom of our countrymen. Through *His* abundant goodness and *their* patriotic devotion our liberty and Union will be preserved.

21.   TANEY

Jacksonian Democracy in the Courts

Roger Brooke Taney (1777–1864) was born into the plantation aristocracy of Calvert County in southern Maryland. He received his education in local schools and at Dickenson College. Because he was a second son at a time of economic decline in agriculture, Taney prepared for a career in law. He engaged in private practice and served several terms in the Maryland legislature between 1799 and 1821. Taney's background was that of Roman Catholicism in religion, Tobacco and Slavery in economics, and Federalism in politics. Taney remained a devout Roman Catholic throughout his life, and while he personally came to oppose slavery, his deep roots in the plantation slave system obviously affected his unfortunate opinion in the Dred Scott case, 19 Howard 393 (1857). Politically he remained a Federalist until the dissolution of the party following the War of 1812. He became an early supporter of Andrew Jackson for the Presidency and eventually a member of the Democratic Party. Following Jackson's election in 1828, Taney remained in Maryland as the state's attorney general, but when the President reorganized his Cabinet in 1831 Taney accepted an appointment as Attorney General of the United States. The most important event of his brief tenure in this office was the struggle over the Second Bank of the United States. It was on Taney's advice that President Jackson vetoed the proposal to recharter the institution. In September, 1833, when Secretary of the Treasury William Duane refused to withdraw the government's deposits from the Bank as the President had ordered, Jackson replaced him with Taney, who acted immediately to execute the order. Jackson next nominated Taney as an Associate Justice of the United States Supreme Court, but the Senate never acted to confirm the appointment. Political conditions had changed by 1836, however, and when the President designated Taney to serve as Chief Justice, following the death of John Marshall, the Senate confirmed the nomination.

One of the first and most important disputes handled by the Taney Court was the case of *Charles River Bridge* v. *Warren Bridge*.* In 1785 the Massachusetts legislature granted a charter to the Charles River Bridge Company to build a toll bridge between Boston and Charlestown. In 1828 the legislature

* 11 Peters 420, 536, 543–44, 548–49, 550–53 (1837).

gave a similar right to the Warren Bridge Company, which constructed a bridge a short distance away from the original crossing. The new bridge company was allowed to charge tolls for a period of up to six years, when ownership of the structure was to pass to the state and the bridge be operated toll-free. The Charles River Bridge Company challenged the act of 1828 as an unconstitutional infringement on the contract rights given to it in 1785. Chief Justice Taney delivered the majority opinion of the Court.

The questions involved in this case are of the gravest character, and the court have given to them the most anxious and deliberate consideration. The value of the right claimed by the plaintiffs is large in amount, and many persons may no doubt be seriously affected in their pecuniary interests by any decision which the court may pronounce; and the questions which have been raised as to the power of the several States, in relation to the corporations they have chartered, are pregnant with important consequences; not only to the individuals who are concerned in the corporate franchises, but to the communities in which they exist. The court are fully sensible that it is their duty, in exercising the high powers conferred on them by the Constitution of the United States, to deal with these great and extensive interests with the utmost caution; guarding, as far as they have the power to do so, the rights of property, and at the same time carefully abstaining from any encroachment on the rights reserved to the States. . . .

This brings us to the Act of the Legislature of Massachusetts of 1785, by which the plaintiffs were incorporated by the name of "The Proprietors of the Charles River Bridge;" and it is here, and in the law of 1792, prolonging their charter, that we must look for the extent and nature of the franchise conferred upon the plaintiffs.

Much has been said in the argument of the principles of construction by which this law is to be expounded, and what undertakings, on the part of the State, may be implied. The court think there can be no serious difficulty on that head. It is the grant of certain franchises by the public to a private corporation, and in a matter where the public interest is concerned. The rule of construction in such cases is well settled, both in England, and by the decisions of our own tribunals. In 2 Barn. & Adol. 793, in the case of The Proprietors of the Stourbridge Canal v. Wheely et al., the court say, "the canal having been made under an act of Parliament, the rights of the plaintiffs are derived entirely from that act. This, like many other cases, is a bargain between a company of adventurers and the public, the terms of which are expressed in the statute; and the rule of construction in all such cases, is now fully established to be this—that any ambiguity in the terms of the contract, must operate against the adventurers, and in favor of the public, and the plaintiffs can claim nothing that is not clearly given them by the act." . . .

Adopting the rule of construction above stated as the settled one, we proceed to apply it to the charter of 1785, to the proprietors of the Charles River Bridge. This act of incorporation is in the usual form, and the privileges such as are commonly given to corporations of that kind. It confers on them the ordinary faculties of a corporation, for the purpose of building the bridge; and establishes certain rates of toll, which the company are authorized to take. This is the whole grant. There is no exclusive privilege given to them over the waters of Charles River, above or below their bridge. No right to erect another bridge themselves, nor to prevent other persons from erecting one. No engagement from the State that another shall not be erected, and no undertaking not to sanction competition, nor to make improvements that may diminish the amount of its income. Upon all these subjects the charter is silent, and nothing is said in it about a line of travel, so much insisted on in the argument, in which they are to have exclusive privileges. No words are used from which an intention to grant any of these rights can be inferred. If the plantiff is entitled to them, it must be implied simply from the nature of the grant, and cannot be inferred from the words by which the grant is made.

The relative position of the Warren Bridge has already been described. It does not interrupt the passage over the Charles River Bridge, nor make the way to it or from it less convenient. None of the faculties or franchises granted to that corporation have been revoked by the Legislature; and its right to take the tolls granted by the charter remains unaltered. In short, all the franchises and rights of property enumerated in the charter, and there mentioned to have been granted to it, remain unimpaired. But its income is destroyed by the Warren Bridge; which, being free, draws off the passengers and property which would have gone over it, and renders their franchise of no value. This is the gist of the complaint. For it is not pretended that the erection of the Warren Bridge would have done them any injury, or in any degree affected their right of property, if it had not diminished the amount of their tolls. In order, then, to entitle themselves to relief, it is necessary to show that the Legislature contracted not to do the act of which they complain; and that they impaired, or in other words violated, that contract, by the erection of the Warren Bridge.

The inquiry then is, does the charter contain such a contract on the part of the State? Is there any such stipulation to be found in that instrument? It must be admitted on all hands, that there is none—no words that even relate to another bridge, or to the diminution of their tolls, or to the line of travel. If a contract on that subject can be gathered from the charter, it must be by implication, and cannot be found in the words used. Can such an agreement be implied? The rule of construction before stated is an answer to the question. In charters of this description, no rights are taken from the public or given to the corporation, beyond those which the words of the charter, by their natural and proper construction, purport to convey. There are no words which import such a contract as the plaintiffs in error contend for, and none can be implied; ... The whole community are interested in this inquiry, and they have a right to require that the power of promoting their comfort and convenience, and of advancing the public prosperity, by providing safe, convenient, and cheap ways for the transportation of produce, and the purposes of travel, shall not be construed to have been surrendered or diminished by the State, unless it shall appear by plain words that it was intended to be done. . . .

Indeed, the practice and usage of almost every State in the Union, old enough to have commenced the work of internal improvement, is opposed to the doctrine contended for on the part of the plaintiffs in error. Turnpike roads have been made in succession, on the same line of travel; the latter ones interfering materially with the profits of the first. These corporations have, in some instances, been utterly ruined by the introduction of newer and better modes of transportation and traveling. In some cases railroads have rendered the turnpike roads on the same line of travel so entirely useless, that the franchise of the turnpike corporation is not worth preserving. Yet in none of these cases have the corporations supposed that their privileges were invaded, or any contract violated on the part of the State. Amid the multitude of cases which have occurred, and have been daily occurring for the last forty or fifty years, this is the first instance in which such an implied contract has been contended for, and this court called upon to infer it from an ordinary act of incorporation, containing nothing more than the usual stipulations and provisions to be found in every such law. The absence of any such controversy, when there must have been so many occasions to give rise to it, proves that neither States, individuals, nor corporations, ever imagined that such a contract could be implied from such charters. It shows that the men who voted for these laws never imagined that they were forming such a contract; and if we maintain that they have made it, we must create it by legal fiction, in opposition to the truth of the fact, and the obvious intention of the party. We cannot deal thus with the rights reserved to the States; and by legal intendments and mere technical reasoning take away from them any portion of that power over their own internal police and improvement, which is so necessary to their well being and prosperity.

And what would be the fruits of this doctrine of implied contracts on the part of the States, and of property in a line of travel by a corporation, if it should now be sanctioned by this court? To what results would it lead us? If it is to be found in the charter to this bridge, the same process of reasoning must discover it in the various acts which have been passed within the last forty years, for turnpike companies. And what is to be the extent of the privileges of exclusion on the different sides of the road? The counsel who have so ably argued this case, have not attempted to define it by any certain boundaries. How far must the new improvement be distant from the old one? How near may you approach without invading its rights in the privileged line? If this court should establish the principles now contended for, what is to become of the numerous railroads established on the same line of travel with turnpike companies; and which have rendered the franchises of the turnpike corporations of no value? Let it once be understood that such charters carry with them these implied contracts, and give this unknown and undefined property in a line of traveling, and you will soon find the old turnpike corporations awakening from their sleep, and calling upon this court to put down the improvements which have taken their place. The millions of property which have been invested in railroads and canals, upon lines of travel which had been before occupied by turnpike corporations, will be put in jeopardy. We shall be thrown back to the improvements of the last century, and obliged to stand still until the claims of the old turnpike corporations shall be satisfied, and they shall consent to permit these States to avail themselves of the lights of modern science, and to partake of the benefit of those improvements which are now adding to the wealth and prosperity, and the convenience and comfort, of every other part of the civilized world. Nor is this all. This court will find itself compelled to fix, by some arbitrary rule, the width of this new kind of property in a line of travel; for if such a right of property exists, we have no lights to guide us in marking out its extent, unless, indeed, we resort to the old feudal grants, and to the exclusive rights of ferries, by prescription, between towns; and are prepared to decide that when a turnpike road from one town to another had been made, no railroad or canal, between these two points, could afterwards be established. This court are not prepared to sanction principles which must lead to such results. . . .

IV

Freedom
and the Union

In the three decades before the outbreak of the Civil War a national debate continued over the issue of slavery and the related topic of the nature of the American Union. Intellectual spokesmen for the South defended the moral, economic, and legal validity of the slave system and advanced a theory of the Union that emphasized state sovereignty and the rights of nullification and secession. Northern liberal thought on the slavery and sovereignty problems did not have the same consistency as Southern conservatism. The political ideas of William Lloyd Garrison, Henry David Thoreau, and Abraham Lincoln reveal the differences and, indeed, contradictions within Northern liberalism. Garrison and Thoreau, for example, opposed slavery on moral grounds, whereas Lincoln stressed economic reasons. Thoreau stated a theory of individual sovereignty, Lincoln developed a nationalist interpretation of sovereignty in answer to the states' rights argument of the South, and Garrison expressed his hostility to the entire matter.

Garrison, the most important and perhaps the most militant of the abolitionist leaders, based his antagonism to slavery on moral and religious grounds. Slavery, he argued, violated the natural rights of each man to "life, liberty, and the pursuit of happiness"—rights which had been recognized in the American Declaration of Independence; all laws that approved of man's ownership of man violated these God-given natural rights and were thereby null and void. His program to end slavery was simple and uncompromising: immediate abolition with no compensation to the slaveholders.

Garrison had no interest in the legal issue of sovereignty or in the preservation of the Union if its destruction was necessary to end slavery. He looked upon the entire American constitutional system as a prop to defend slavery, and he once denounced the Constitution as "a covenant with death and agreement with hell."

Vilified in the South and attacked by many Northerners, Garrison nonetheless continued his moral crusade against slavery for more than thirty years. He deliberately ignored all political and legal realities and fulfilled the standards he had set for himself in the first issue of *The Liberator*, on January 1, 1831:

> I will be harsh as truth, and as uncompromising as justice. On this
> subject, I do not wish to think, or speak, or write, with moderation. . . .
> I am in earnest—I will not equivocate—I will not excuse—I will not retreat
> a single inch—AND I WILL BE HEARD.

Henry David Thoreau's opposition to slavery was based on a well-
reasoned political philosophy, which was set forth in his 1849 essay
"Civil Disobedience." At the basis of his philosophy was a fierce individualism—a belief not in the sovereignty of state or nation but of the
individual conscience. Thoreau's ideal was a society in which each man is
left free to seek his own moral perfection by following the demands of his
own conscience. Under such conditions the conflicts and tensions
ordinarily found in society would vanish, and man, who is the creator
of all progress in civilization, would be free to make his maximum
contribution to this forward movement.

Thoreau looked upon government as a hindrance to both personal
and cultural improvement, and he accepted the traditional liberal
belief that the existence of government is a sign of man's moral failings.
When men have become morally perfect, the need for government
will disappear, Thoreau believed. The opening sentences of "Civil
Disobedience" state his basic philosophy:

> I heartily accept the motto—"That government is best which governs
> least;" and I should like to see it acted up to more rapidly and system-
> atically. Carried out, it finally amounts to this, which also I believe,—
> "That government is best which governs not at all;" and when men are
> prepared for it, that will be the kind of government which they will have.

Under most circumstances Thoreau was prepared to support the
demands placed upon him by government. He did this out of a desire
to be a "good neighbor" and because the majority had the physical
force to back its will. But Thoreau did not mean to indicate by his
obedience that he desired the services of government or that the
majority was right in its decision. On the contrary, he believed that
each person should be his own government and that rule by the majority
was merely a practical operating principle and not an indication of truth.

Thoreau's great importance to political theory and to the contemporary world rests, of course, on the doctrine of civil disobedience—
the right, the duty, of the individual to disobey acts of government
that violate his conscience. On the few matters of great moral urgency
that may arise during the lifetime of an individual, Thoreau insisted
that a man must not surrender his perception of truth to that of the

majority. Slavery was one of these vital issues, and Thoreau counseled disobedience and enumerated a number of techniques designed to undermine the authority of government and contribute to its moral conversion.

Thoreau's method of civil disobedience constitutes a significant contribution to political thought, but the doctrine is not without its intellectual and practical problems. Is conscience a sufficient standard for disobeying lawful acts of government? What conditions must guide the practitioners of civil disobedience? Is civil disobedience acceptable in all circumstances? May not the doctrine contribute to a general disrespect for the rule of law and dangerously weaken the fabric of society? Questions such as these must be carefully analyzed before Thoreau's ideas can be incorporated into the main body of liberal political thought.

Abraham Lincoln's opposition to slavery was based on ideas far different from those of Garrison and Thoreau. Lincoln was neither an abolitionist nor a proponent of individual sovereignty. His opposition, while more complex than that of the abolitionists, was no less real, and it motivated his thoughts and actions throughout his public life.

Perhaps the most important of Lincoln's reasons for opposing slavery was his fear, common in the Midwest of the 1840's and 1850's, that slavery would extend into free soil territory and unfairly compete with the farmers of these areas. Lincoln therefore argued that slavery should not be permitted to expand into new sections of the nation but no attempt should be made to disturb its presence in those states in which it already existed. In his Peoria speech of October 16, 1854, Lincoln denounced the Kansas–Nebraska Act, which repealed the Missouri Compromise and permitted the residents of these two areas to determine the status of slavery.

While Lincoln continued to rest his opposition to slavery on economic grounds, a stronger sense of moral criticism entered his thoughts in the late 1850's. He expressed deep concern for the worsening condition of the Negro in both the North and the South, and he attacked those who, like Senator Stephen Douglas, sought to limit the moral principles of the Declaration of Independence to the white man. "I had thought," Lincoln said in his Springfield speech of June 26, 1857, "that the Declaration of Independence contemplated the progressive improvement in the condition of all men everywhere."

Lincoln was fundamentally a disciple of Jefferson in his political thinking. In an April 6, 1859, letter to a group of Boston Republicans, he stated his conviction that the "principles of Jefferson are the definitions and axioms of free society," and he struck out at those in the United States who would replace "the principles of free government" with those of "classification, caste, and legitimacy." Summarizing his views on the incompatibility of freedom and slavery, Lincoln declared that "he who would *be* no slave, must consent to *have* no slave. Those who deny freedom to others, deserve it not for themselves; and, under a just God, can not long retain it."

It is certainly possible to point to shortcomings in Lincoln's political thought. In his comments on equality, for example, he was careful to indicate that he supported political, legal, and economic equality and not equality in social relations between the races. (It must be said, however, that many of his statements condemning the idea of social equality were said during the heat of political campaigns in which Lincoln was forced to defend himself against charges that he was too strong a supporter of the Negro.) Further indication that Lincoln shared the prejudices of the white majority of the time is shown by his discussion of the possibility of returning the Negro to Africa. Colonization interested Lincoln, as it did many Americans in the period before the Civil War, and while he favored it in the abstract, Lincoln came to look upon it as a practical impossibility.

Finally, it is possible to criticize Lincoln for placing the slavery question in a position subordinate to that of saving the Union. Throughout his public life he repeatedly made clear his dedication to this goal. In his October, 1854, Peoria speech, for example, Lincoln declared: "Much as I hate slavery, I would consent to the extension of it rather than see the Union dissolve, just as I would consent to any great evil to avoid a greater one."

To support his policy of placing primary emphasis on saving the Union, Lincoln developed a strongly nationalist interpretation of sovereignty. In his first Inaugural Address, given on March 4, 1861, Lincoln stated his conviction that the Union was superior even to the Constitution and he denied that a state could legally leave the Union. Lincoln considered violent attempts to destroy the Union as unlawful insurrections against the rightful authority of the United States government. Acting on the premise that the Union was superior to the Constitution, he took actions of doubtful constitutionality during the Civil War in order to save the Union. Lincoln's policy was eventually successful, and in the course of preserving the Union, he also abolished slavery in the United States by issuing the Emancipation Proclamation on January 1, 1863.

22. GARRISON

The Immorality of Slavery

William Lloyd Garrison (1805–1879) was a native of Newbury-port, Massachusetts. He received little formal education but did serve an apprenticeship in a newspaper office and went on to edit several small Massachusetts papers. His interest in the slavery question dates to about 1829, the year in which he made his first public attack on that institution. For the next three decades Garrison devoted most of his time and effort to the cause of immediate abolition of slavery. He lectured widely, founded the abolitionist journal *The Liberator* in 1830, and in 1831 helped organize the New England Anti-Slave Society. Two years later Garrison was one of approximately fifty delegates who met in Philadelphia to create the American Anti-Slave Society. Its "Declaration of Sentiments"* on December 6, 1833, was largely written by Garrison, who went on to serve as the society's president from 1843 to 1865.

The Convention assembled in the city of Philadelphia, to organize a National Anti-Slavery Society, promptly seize the opportunity to promulgate the following Declaration of Sentiments, as cherished by them in relation to the enslavement of one-sixth portion of the American people.

More than fifty-seven years have elapsed, since a band of patriots convened in this place, to devise measures for the deliverance of this country from a foreign yoke. The corner-stone upon which they founded the Temple of Freedom was broadly this—"That all men are created equal; that they are endowed by their Creator with certain inalienable rights; that among these are life, LIBERTY, and the pursuit of happiness." At the sound of their trumpet-call, three millions of people rose up as

---

* *Selections from the Writings and Speeches of William Lloyd Garrison* (Boston: R. F. Wallcut, 1852), pp. 66–71.

from the sleep of death, and rushed to the strife of blood; deeming it more glorious to die instantly as freemen, than desirable to live one hour as slaves. They were few in number—poor in resources; but the honest conviction that Truth, Justice and Right were on their side, made them invincible.

We have met together for the achievement of an enterprise, without which that of our fathers is incomplete; and which, for its magnitude, solemnity, and probable results upon the destiny of the world, as far transcends theirs as moral truth does physical force.

In purity of motive, in earnestness of zeal, in decision of purpose, in intrepidity of action, in steadfastness of faith, in sincerity of spirit, we would not be inferior to them.

Their principles led them to wage war against their oppressors, and to spill human blood like water, in order to be free. Ours forbid the doing of evil that good may come, and lead us to reject, and to entreat the oppressed to reject, the use of all carnal weapons for deliverance from bondage; relying solely upon those which are spiritual, and mighty through God to the pulling down of strongholds.

Their measures were physical resistance—the marshalling in arms— the hostile array—the mortal encounter. Ours shall be such only as the opposition of moral purity to moral corruption—the destruction of error by the potency of truth—the overthrow of prejudice by the power of love—and the abolition of slavery by the spirit of repentance.

Their grievances, great as they were, were trifling in comparison with the wrongs and sufferings of those for whom we plead. Our fathers were never slaves—never bought and sold like cattle—never shut out from the light of knowledge and religion—never subjected to the lash of brutal task-masters.

But those, for whose emancipation we are striving—constituting at the present time at least one-sixth part of our countrymen—are recognized by law, and treated by their fellow-beings, as marketable commodities, as goods and chattels, as brute beasts; are plundered daily of the fruits of their toil without redress; really enjoy no constitutional nor legal protection from licentious and murderous outrages upon their persons; and are ruthlessly torn asunder—the tender babe from the arms of its frantic mother—the heart-broken wife from her weeping husband—at the caprice or pleasure of irresponsible tyrants. For the crime of having a dark complexion, they suffer the pangs of hunger, the infliction of stripes, the ignominy of brutal servitude. They are kept in heathenish darkness by laws expressly enacted to make their instruction a criminal offence.

These are the prominent circumstances in the condition of more than two millions of our people, the proof of which may be found in thousands of indisputable facts, and in the laws of the slaveholding States.

Hence we maintain—that, in view of the civil and religious privileges of this nation, the guilt of its oppression is unequalled by any other on the face of the earth; and, therefore, that it is bound to repent instantly, to undo the heavy burdens, and to let the oppressed go free.

We further maintain—that no man has a right to enslave or imbrute his brother—to hold or acknowledge him, for one moment, as a piece of merchandize—to keep back his hire by fraud—or to brutalize his mind, by denying him the means of intellectual, social and moral improvement.

The right to enjoy liberty is inalienable. To invade it is to usurp the prerogative of Jehovah. Every man has a right to his own body—to the products of his own labor—to the protection of law—and to the common advantages of society. It is piracy to buy or steal a native African, and subject him to servitude. Surely, the sin is as great to enslave an American as an African.

Therefore we believe and affirm—that there is no difference, in principle, between the African slave trade and American slavery:

That every American citizen, who detains a human being in involuntary bondage as his property, is, according to Scripture, (Ex. xxi. 16,) a man-stealer:

That the slaves ought instantly to be set free, and brought under the protection of law:

That if they had lived from the time of Pharaoh down to the present period, and had been entailed through successive generations, their right to be free could never have been alienated, but their claims would have constantly risen in solemnity:

That all those laws which are now in force, admitting the right of slavery, are therefore, before God, utterly null and void; being an audacious usurpation of the Divine prerogative, a daring infringement on the law of nature, a base overthrow of the very foundations of the social compact, a complete extinction of all the relations, endearments and obligations of mankind, and a presumptuous transgression of all the holy commandments; and that therefore they ought instantly to be abrogated.

We further believe and affirm—that all persons of color, who possess the qualifications which are demanded of others, ought to be admitted forthwith to the enjoyment of the same privileges, and the exercise of the same prerogatives, as others; and that the paths of preferment, of wealth, and of intelligence, should be opened as widely to them as to persons of a white complexion.

We maintain that no compensation should be given to the planters emancipating their slaves:

Because it would be a surrender of the great fundamental principle, that man cannot hold property in man:

Because slavery is a crime, and therefore is not an article to be sold:

Because the holders of slaves are not the just proprietors of what they claim; freeing the slaves is not depriving them of property, but restoring to its rightful owner; it is not wronging the master, but righting the slave—restoring him to himself:

Because immediate and general emancipation would only destroy nominal, not real property; it would not amputate a limb or break a bone of the slaves, but by infusing motives into their breasts, would make them doubly valuable to the masters as free laborers; and

Because, if compensation is to be given at all, it should be given to the outraged and guiltless slaves, and not to those who have plundered and abused them.

We regard as delusive, cruel and dangerous, any scheme of expatriation which pretends to aid, either directly or indirectly, in the emancipation of the slaves, or to be a substitute for the immediate and total abolition of slavery.

We fully and unanimously recognize the sovereignty of each State, to legislate exclusively on the subject of the slavery which is tolerated within its limits; we concede that Congress, under the present national compact, has no right to interfere with any of the slave States, in relation to this momentous subject:

But we maintain that Congress has a right, and is solemnly bound, to suppress the domestic slave trade between the several States, and to abolish slavery in those portions of our territory which the Constitution has placed under its exclusive jurisdiction.

We also maintain that there are, at the present time, the highest obligations resting upon the people of the free States to remove slavery by moral and political action, as prescribed in the Constitution of the United States. They are now living under a pledge of their tremendous physical force, to fasten the galling fetters of tyranny upon the limbs of millions in the Southern States; they are liable to be called at any moment to suppress a general insurrection of the slaves; they authorize the slave owners to vote for three-fifths of his slaves as property, and thus enable him to perpetuate his oppression; they support a standing army at the South for its protection; and they seize the slave, who has escaped into their territories, and send him back to be tortured by an enraged master or a brutal driver. This relation to slavery is criminal, and full of danger: IT MUST BE BROKEN UP.

These are our views and principles—these our designs and measures. With entire confidence in the overruling justice of God, we plant ourselves upon the Declaration of our Independence and the truths of Divine Revelation, as upon the Everlasting Rock.

We shall organize Anti-Slavery Societies, if possible, in every city, town and village in our land.

We shall send forth agents to lift up the voice of remonstrance, of warning, of entreaty, and of rebuke.

We shall circulate, unsparingly and extensively, anti-slavery tracts and periodicals.

We shall enlist the pulpit and the press in the cause of the suffering and the dumb.

We shall aim at a purification of the churches from all participation in the guilt of slavery.

We shall encourage the labor of freemen rather than that of slaves, by giving a preference to their productions: and

We shall spare no exertions nor means to bring the whole nation to speedy repentance.

Our trust for victory is solely in God. We may be personally defeated, but our principles never! Truth, Justice, Reason, Humanity, must and will gloriously triumph. Already a host is coming up to the help of the Lord against the mighty, and the prospect before us is full of encouragement.

Submitting this Declaration to the candid examination of the people of this country, and of the friends of liberty throughout the world, we hereby affix our signatures to it; pledging ourselves that, under the guidance and by the help of Almighty God, we will do all that in us lies, consistently with this Declaration of our principles, to overthrow the most execrable system of slavery that has ever been witnessed upon earth; to deliver our land from its deadliest curse; to wipe out the foulest stain which rests upon our national escutcheon; and to secure to the colored population of the United States, all the rights and privileges which belong to them as men, and as Americans—come what may to our persons, our interests, or our reputation—whether we live to witness the triumph of Liberty, Justice and Humanity or perish untimely as martyrs in this great, benevolent, and holy cause.

23. THOREAU
The Sovereign Individual

Henry David Thoreau (1817–1862), essayist, poet, naturalist, transcendentalist philosopher, was born in Concord, Massachusetts, and attended Concord Academy and Harvard College. Thoreau was little interested in politics and had little sympathy for the political reformers of his day. His primary concern was with nature and philosophical contemplation. Thoreau's two years at Walden Pond and his major published work, *Walden*, illustrate these interests. But he became deeply upset by the issue of slavery, and from 1852 until 1860, when illness prevented him from continuing his efforts, Thoreau wrote and lectured on the subject. He strongly defended the activities of his friend John Brown, including Brown's use of violence. His essay "Civil Disobedience," from which this selection is taken, was first published in 1849 and is Thoreau's only major statement of political thought. It was prompted by his arrest during the summer of 1845 for nonpayment of a poll tax—a levy Thoreau refused to pay as a protest against slavery and the Mexican War.

I heartily accept the motto,—"That government is best which governs least;" and I should like to see it acted up to more rapidly and systematically. Carried out, it finally amounts to this, which also I believe,—"That government is best which governs not at all;" and when men are prepared for it, that will be the kind of government which they will have. Government is at best but an expedient; but most governments are usually, and all governments are sometimes, inexpedient. The objections which have been brought against a standing army, and they are many and weighty, and deserve to prevail, may also at last be brought against a standing government. The standing army is only an arm of the standing government. The government itself, which is only the mode which the people have chosen to execute their will, is equally liable to be abused and perverted before the people can act through it. Witness the present Mexican war, the work of comparatively a few individuals using the standing government as their tool; for, in the outset, the people would not have consented to this measure.

This American government,—what is it but a tradition, though a recent one, endeavoring to transmit itself unimpaired to posterity, but each instant losing some of its integrity? It has not the vitality and force of a single living man; for a single man can bend it to his will. It is a sort of wooden gun to the people themselves. But it is not the less necessary for this; for the people must have some complicated machinery or other, and hear its din, to satisfy that idea of government which they have. Governments show thus how successfully men can be imposed on, even impose on themselves, for their own advantage. It is excellent, we must all allow. Yet this government never of itself furthered any enterprise, but by the alacrity with which it got out of its way. *It* does not keep the country free. *It* does not settle the West. *It* does not educate. The character inherent in the American people has done all that has been accomplished; and it would have done somewhat more, if the government had not sometimes got in its way. For government is an expedient by which men would fain succeed in letting one another alone; and, as has been said, when it is most expedient, the governed are most let alone by it. Trade and commerce, if they were not made of India-rubber, would never manage to bounce over the obstacles which legislators are continually putting in their way; and, if one were to judge these men wholly by the effects of their actions and not partly by their intentions, they would deserve to be classed and punished with those mischievous persons who put obstructions on the railroads.

But, to speak practically and as a citizen, unlike those who call themselves no-government men, I ask for, not at once no government, but *at once* a better government. Let every man make known what kind of government would command his respect, and that will be one step toward obtaining it.

After all, the practical reason why, when the power is once in the hands of the people, a majority are permitted, and for a long period continue, to rule is not because they are most likely to be in the right, nor because this seems fairest to the minority, but because they are physically the strongest. But a government in which the majority rule in all cases cannot be based on justice, even as far as men understand it.

Can there not be a government in which majorities do not virtually decide right and wrong, but conscience?—in which majorities decide only those questions to which the rule of expediency is applicable? Must the citizen ever for a moment, or in the least degree, resign his conscience to the legislator? Why has every man a conscience, then? I think that we should be men first, and subjects afterward. It is not desirable to cultivate a respect for the law, so much as for the right. The only obligation which I have a right to assume is to do at any time what I think right. It is truly enough said, that a corporation has no conscience; but a corporation of conscientious men is a corporation *with* a conscience. Law never made men a whit more just; and, by means of their respect for it, even the well-disposed are daily made the agents of injustice. . . .

How does it become a man to behave toward this American government to-day? I answer, that he cannot without disgrace be associated with it. I cannot for an instant recognize that political organization as *my* government which is the *slave's* government also.

All men recognize the right of revolution; that is, the right to refuse allegiance to, and to resist, the government, when its tyranny or its inefficiency are great and unendurable. But almost all say that such is not the case now. But such was the case, they think, in the Revolution of '75. If one were to tell me that this was a bad government because it taxed certain foreign commodities brought to its ports, it is most probable that I should not make an ado about it, for I can do without them. All machines have their friction; and possibly this does enough good to counterbalance the evil. At any rate, it is a great evil to make a stir about it. But when the friction comes to have its machine, and oppression and robbery are organized, I say, let us not have such a machine any longer. In other words, when a sixth of the population of a nation which has undertaken to be the refuge of liberty are slaves, and a whole country is unjustly overrun and conquered by a foreign army, and subjected to military law, I think that it is not too soon for honest men to rebel and revolutionize. What makes this duty the more urgent is the fact that the country so overrun is not our own, but ours is the invading army. . . .

The broadest and most prevalent error requires the most disinterested virtue to sustain it. The slight reproach to which the virtue of patriotism is commonly liable, the noble are most likely to incur. Those who, while they disapprove of the character and measures of a government, yield to it their allegiance and support are undoubtedly its most conscientious supporters, and so frequently the most serious obstacles to reform. Some are petitioning the state to dissolve the Union, to disregard the requisitions of the President. Why do they not dissolve it themselves,—the union between themselves and the state,—and refuse to pay their quota into its treasury? Do not they stand in the same relation to the state that the state does to the Union? And have not the same reasons prevented the state from resisting the Union which have prevented them from resisting the state?

How can a man be satisfied to entertain an opinion merely, and enjoy *it*? Is there any enjoyment in it, if his opinion is that he is aggrieved? If you are cheated out of a single dollar by your neighbor, you do not rest satisfied with knowing that you are cheated, or with saying that you are cheated, or even with petitioning him to pay you your due; but you take effectual steps at once to obtain the full amount, and see that you are never cheated again. Action from principle, the perception and the performance of right, changes things and relations; it is essentially revolutionary, and does not consist wholly with anything which was. It not only divides states and churches, it divides families; ay, it divides the *individual*, separating the diabolical in him from the divine.

Unjust laws exist: shall we be content to obey them, or shall we endeavor to amend them, and obey them until we have succeeded, or shall we transgress them at once? Men generally, under such a government as this, think that they ought to wait until they have persuaded the majority to alter them. They think that, if they should resist, the remedy would be worse than the evil. But it is the fault of the government itself that the remedy *is* worse than the evil. *It* makes it worse. Why is it not more apt to anticipate and provide for reform? Why does it not cherish its wise minority? Why does it cry and resist before it is hurt? Why does it not encourage its citizens to be on the alert to point out its faults, and *do* better than it would have them? Why does it always crucify Christ, and excommunicate Copernicus and Luther, and pronounce Washington and Franklin rebels?

One would think, that a deliberate and practical denial of its authority was the only offense never contemplated by government; else, why has it not assigned its definite, its suitable and proportionate penalty? If a man who has no property refuses but once to earn nine shillings for the state, he is put in prison for a period unlimited by any law that I know, and determined only by the discretion of those who placed him there;

but if he should steal ninety times nine shillings from the state, he is soon permitted to go at large again.

If the injustice is part of the necessary friction of the machine of government, let it go, let it go: perchance it will wear smooth,—certainly the machine will wear out. If the injustice has a spring, or a pulley, or a rope, or a crank, exclusively for itself, then perhaps you may consider whether the remedy will not be worse than the evil; but if it is of such a nature that it requires you to be the agent of injustice to another, then, I say, break the law. Let your life be a counter friction to stop the machine. What I have to do is to see, at any rate, that I do not lend myself to the wrong which I condemn.

As for adopting the ways which the state has provided for remedying the evil, I know not of such ways. They take too much time, and a man's life will be gone. I have other affairs to attend to. I came into this world, not chiefly to make this a good place to live in, but to live in it, be it good or bad. A man has not everything to do, but something; and because he cannot do *everything*, it is not necessary that he should do *something* wrong. It is not my business to be petitioning the Governor or the Legislature any more than it is theirs to petition me; and if they should not hear my petition, what should I do then? But in this case the state has provided no way: its very Constitution is the evil. This may seem to be harsh and stubborn and unconciliatory; but it is to treat with the utmost kindness and consideration the only spirit that can appreciate or deserves it. So is all change for the better, like birth and death, which convulse the body.

I do not hesitate to say, that those who call themselves Abolitionists should at once effectually withdraw their support, both in person and property, from the government of Massachusetts and not wait till they constitute a majority of one, before they suffer the right to prevail through them. I think that it is enough if they have God on their side, without waiting for that other one. Moreover, any man more right than his neighbors constitutes a majority of one already.

I meet this American government, or its representative, the state government, directly, and face to face, once a year—no more—in the person of its tax-gatherer; this is the only mode in which a man situated as I am necessarily meets it; and it then says distinctly, Recognize me; and the simplest, most effectual, and, in the present posture of affairs, the indispensablest mode of treating with it on this head, of expressing your little satisfaction with and love for it, is to deny it then. My civil neighbor, the tax-gatherer, is the very man I have to deal with,—for it is, after all, with men and not with parchment that I quarrel,—and he has voluntarily chosen to be an agent of the government. How shall he ever know well what he is and does as an officer of the government, or as a man, until he is obliged to consider whether he shall treat me, his neighbor, for whom he has respect, as a neighbor and well-disposed man, or as a maniac and disturber of the peace, and see if he can get over this obstruction to his neighborliness without a ruder and more impetuous thought or speech corresponding with his action. I know this well, that if one thousand, if one hundred, if ten men whom I could name,—if ten *honest* men only,—ay, if *one* HONEST man, in this State of Massachusetts, *ceasing to hold slaves*, were actually to withdraw from this copartnership, and be locked up in the county jail therefor, it would be the abolition of slavery in America. For it matters not how small the beginning may seem to be: what is once well done is done forever. But we love better to talk about it: that we say is our mission. Reform keeps many scores of newspapers in its service, but not one man. If my esteemed neighbor, the State's ambassador, who will devote his days to the settlement of the question of human rights in the Council Chamber, instead of being threatened with the prisons of Carolina, were to sit down the prisoner of Massachusetts, that State which is so anxious to foist the sin of slavery upon her sister,—though at present she can discover only an act of inhospitality to be the ground of a quarrel with her,—the Legislature would not wholly waive the subject the following winter.

Under a government which imprisons any unjustly, the true place for a just man is also a prison. The proper place to-day, the only place which Massachusetts has provided for her freer and less desponding spirits, is in her prisons, to be put out and locked out of the State by her own act, as they have already put themselves out by their principles. It is there that the fugitive slave, and the Mexican prisoner on parole, and the Indian come to plead the wrongs of his race should find them; on that separate, but more free and honorable ground, where the State places those who are not *with* her, but *against* her,—the only house in a slave State in which a free man can abide with honor. If any think that their influence would be lost there, and their voices no longer afflict the ear of the State, that they would not be as an enemy within its walls, they do not know by how much truth is stronger than error, nor how much more eloquently and effectively he can combat injustice who has experienced a little in his own person. Cast your whole vote, not a strip of paper merely, but your whole influence. A minority is powerless while it conforms to the majority; it is not even a minority then; but it is irresistible when it clogs by its whole weight. If the alternative is to keep all just men in prison, or give up war and slavery, the State will not hesitate which to choose. If a thousand men were not to pay their tax-bills this year, that would not be a violent and bloody measure, as it would be to pay them, and enable the State to commit violence and shed innocent blood. This is, in fact, the definition of a peaceable revolution, if any such is possible. If the tax-gatherer, or any other public officer, asks me, as one has done, "But what shall I do?" my answer is, "If you really wish to do anything, resign your office." When the subject has refused allegiance, and the officer has resigned his office, then the revolution is accomplished. But even suppose blood should flow. Is there not a sort of blood shed when the conscience is wounded? Through this wound a man's real manhood and immortality flow out, and he bleeds to an everlasting death. I see this blood flowing now.

I have contemplated the imprisonment of the offender, rather than the seizure of his goods,—though both will serve the same purpose,— because they who assert the purest right, and consequently are most dangerous to a corrupt State, commonly have not spent much time in accumulating property. To such the State renders comparatively small service, and a slight tax is wont to appear exorbitant, particularly if they are obliged to earn it by special labor with their hands. If there were one who lived wholly without the use of money, the State itself would hesitate to demand it of him. But the rich man—not to make any invidious comparison—is always sold to the institution which makes him rich. Absolutely speaking, the more money, the less virtue; for money comes between a man and his objects, and obtains them for him; and it was certainly no great virtue to obtain it. It puts to rest many questions which he would otherwise be taxed to answer; while the only new question which it puts is the hard but superfluous one, how to spend it. Thus his moral ground is taken from under his feet. The opportunities of living are diminished in proportion as what are called the "means" are increased. The best thing a man can do for his culture when he is rich is to endeavor to carry out those schemes which he entertained when he was poor. Christ answered the Herodians according to their condition. "Show me the tribute-money," said he;— and one took a penny out of his pocket;—if you use money which has the image of Cæsar on it and which he has made current and valuable, that is, *if you are men of the State*, and gladly enjoy the advantages of

Cæsar's government, then pay him back some of his own when he demands it. "Render therefore to Cæsar that which is Cæsar's, and to God those things which are God's,"—leaving them no wiser than before as to which was which; for they did not wish to know.

When I converse with the freest of my neighbors, I perceive that, whatever they may say about the magnitude and seriousness of the question, and their regard for the public tranquillity, the long and the short of the matter is, that they cannot spare the protection of the existing government, and they dread the consequences to their property and families of disobedience to it. For my own part, I should not like to think that I ever rely on the protection of the State. But, if I deny the authority of the State when it presents its tax-bill, it will soon take and waste all my property, and so harass me and my children without end. This is hard. This makes it impossible for a man to live honestly, and at the same time comfortably, in outward respects. It will not be worth the while to accumulate property; that would be sure to go again. You must hire or squat somewhere, and raise but a small crop, and eat that soon. You must live within yourself, and depend upon yourself always tucked up and ready for a start, and not have many affairs. A man may grow rich in Turkey even, if he will be in all respects a good subject of the Turkish government. Confucius said: "If a state is governed by the principles of reason, poverty and misery are subjects of shame; if a state is not governed by the principles of reason, riches and honors are the subjects of shame." No: until I want the protection of Massachusetts to be extended to me in some distant Southern port, where my liberty is endangered, or until I am bent solely on building up an estate at home by peaceful enterprise, I can afford to refuse allegiance to Massachusetts, and her right to my property and life. It costs me less in every sense to incur the penalty of disobedience to the State than it would to obey. I should feel as if I were worth less in that case.

Some years ago, the State met me in behalf of the Church, and commanded me to pay a certain sum toward the support of a clergyman whose preaching my father attended, but never I myself. "Pay," it said, "or be locked up in the jail." I declined to pay. But, unfortunately, another man saw fit to pay it. I did not see why the schoolmaster should be taxed to support the priest, and not the priest the schoolmaster; for I was not the State's schoolmaster, but I supported myself by voluntary subscription. I did not see why the lyceum should not present its tax-bill, and have the State to back its demand, as well as the

Church. However, at the request of the selectmen, I condescended to make some such statement as this in writing:—"Know all men by these presents, that I, Henry Thoreau, do not wish to be regarded as a member of any incorporated society which I have not joined." This I gave to the town clerk; and he has it. The State, having thus learned that I did not wish to be regarded as a member of that church, has never made a like demand on me since; though it said that it must adhere to its original presumption that time. If I had known how to name them, I should then have signed off in detail from all the societies which I never signed on to; but I did not know where to find a complete list.

I have paid no poll-tax for six years. I was put into a jail once on this account, for one night; and, as I stood considering the walls of solid stone, two or three feet thick, the door of wood and iron, a foot thick, and the iron grating which strained the light, I could not help being struck with the foolishness of that institution which treated me as if I were mere flesh and blood and bones, to be locked up. I wondered that it should have concluded at length that this was the best use it could put me to, and had never thought to avail itself of my services in some way. I saw that, if there was a wall of stone between me and my townsmen, there was a still more difficult one to climb or break through before they could get to be as free as I was. I did not for a moment feel confined, and the walls seemed a great waste of stone and mortar. I felt as if I alone of all my townsmen had paid my tax. They plainly did not know how to treat me, but behaved like persons who are underbred. In every threat and in every compliment there was a blunder; for they thought that my chief desire was to stand the other side of that stone wall. I could not but smile to see how industriously they locked the door on my meditations, which followed them out again without let or hindrance, and *they* were really all that was dangerous. As they could not reach me, they had resolved to punish my body; just as boys, if they cannot come at some person against whom they have a spite, will abuse his dog. I saw that the State was half-witted, that it was timid as a lone woman with her silver spoons, and that it did not know its friends from its foes, and I lost all my remaining respect for it, and pitied it.

Thus the State never intentionally confronts a man's sense, intellectual or moral, but only his body, his senses. It is not armed with superior wit or honesty, but with superior physical strength. I was not born to be forced. I will breathe after my own fashion. Let us see who is the strongest. What force has a multitude? They only can force me who obey a higher law than I. They force me to become like themselves. I do not hear of *men* being *forced* to live this way or that by masses of men. What sort of life were that to live? When I meet a government which says to me, "Your money or your life," why should I be in haste to give it my money? It may be in a great strait, and not know what to do: I cannot help that. It must help itself; do as I do. It is not worth the while to snivel about it. I am not responsible for the successful working of the machinery of society. I am not the son of the engineer. I perceive that, when an acorn and a chestnut fall side by side, the one does not remain inert to make way for the other, but both obey their own laws, and spring and grow and flourish as best they can, till one, perchance, overshadows and destroys the other. If a plant cannot live according to its nature, it dies; and so a man. . . .

When I came out of prison,—for some one interfered, and paid that tax,—I did not perceive that great changes had taken place on the common, such as he observed who went in a youth and emerged a tottering and gray-headed man; and yet a change had to my eyes come over the scene,—the town, and State, and country,—greater than any that mere time could effect. I saw yet more distinctly the State in which I lived. I saw to what extent the people among whom I lived could be trusted as good neighbors and friends; that their friendship was for summer weather only; that they did not greatly propose to do right; that they were a distinct race from me by their prejudices and super-stitions, as the Chinamen and Malays are; that in their sacrifices to humanity they ran no risks, not even to their property; that after all they were not so noble but they treated the thief as he had treated them, and hoped, by a certain outward observance and a few prayers, and by walking in a particular straight though useless path from time to time, to save their souls. This may be to judge my neighbors harshly; for I believe that many of them are not aware that they have such an institution as the jail in their village. . . .

I have never declined paying the highway tax, because I am as desirous of being a good neighbor as I am of being a bad subject; and as for supporting schools, I am doing my part to educate my fellow-countrymen now. It is for no particular item in the tax-bill that I refuse to pay it. I simply wish to refuse allegiance to the State, to withdraw and stand aloof from it effectually. I do not care to trace the course of my dollar, if I could, till it buys a man or a musket to shoot with,—the dollar is innocent,—but I am concerned to trace the effects of my allegiance. In fact, I quietly declare war with the State, after my fashion, though I will still make what use and get what advantage of her I can, as is usual in such cases.

If others pay the tax which is demanded of me, from a sympathy with the State, they do but what they have already done in their own case, or rather they abet injustice to a greater extent than the State requires. If they pay the tax from a mistaken interest in the individual taxed, to save his property, or prevent his going to jail, it is because they have not considered wisely how far they let their private feelings interfere with the public good.

This, then, is my position at present. But one cannot be too much on his guard in such a case, lest his action be biased by obstinacy or an undue regard for the opinions of men. Let him see that he does only what belongs to himself and to the hour. . . .

I do not wish to quarrel with any man or nation. I do not wish to split hairs, to make fine distinctions, or set myself up as better than my neighbors. I seek rather, I may say, even an excuse for conforming to the laws of the land. I am but too ready to conform to them. Indeed, I have reason to suspect myself on this head; and each year, as the tax-gatherer comes round, I find myself disposed to review the acts and position of the general and State governments, and the spirit of the people, to discover a pretext for conformity.

> "We must affect our country as our parents,
>   And if at any time we alienate
>   Our love or industry from doing it honor,
>   We must respect effects and teach the soul
>   Matter of conscience and religion,
>   And not desire of rule or benefit."

I believe that the State will soon be able to take all my work of this sort out of my hands, and then I shall be no better a patriot that my fellow-countrymen. Seen from a lower point of view, the Constitution, with all its faults, is very good; the law and the courts are very respectable; even this State and this American government are, in many respects, very admirable, and rare things, to be thankful for, such as a great many have described them; but seen from a point of view a little higher, they are what I have described them; seen from a higher still, and the highest, who shall say what they are, or that they are worth looking at or thinking of at all?

However, the government does not concern me much, and I shall bestow the fewest possible thoughts on it. It is not many moments that I live under a government, even in this world. If a man is thought-free, fancy-free, imagination-free, that which *is not* never for a long time appearing *to be* to him, unwise rulers or reformers cannot fatally interrupt him.

I know that most men think differently from myself; but those whose lives are by profession devoted to the study of these or kindred subjects content me as little as any. Statesmen and legislators, standing so completely within the institution, never distinctly and nakedly behold it. They speak of moving society, but have no resting-place without it. They may be men of a certain experience and discrimination, and have no doubt invented ingenious and even useful systems, for which we sincerely thank them; but all their wit and usefulness lie within certain not very wide limits. They are wont to forget that the world is not governed by policy and expediency. . . .

The authority of government, even such as I am willing to submit to,—for I will cheerfully obey those who know and can do better than I, and in many things even those who neither know nor can do so well,—is still an impure one: to be strictly just, it must have the sanction and consent of the governed. It can have no pure right over my person and property but what I concede to it. The progress from an absolute to a limited monarchy, from a limited monarchy to a democracy, is a progress toward a true respect for the individual. Even the Chinese philosopher was wise enough to regard the individual as the basis of the empire. Is a democracy, such as we know it, the last improvement possible in government? Is it not possible to take a step further towards recognizing and organizing the rights of man? There will never be a really free and enlightened State until the State comes to recognize the individual as a higher and independent power, from which all its own power and authority are derived, and treats him accordingly. I please myself with imagining a State at last which can afford to be just to all men, and to treat the individual with respect as a neighbor; which even would not think it inconsistent with its own repose if a few were to live aloof from it, not meddling with it, nor embraced by it, who fulfilled all the duties of neighbors and fellow-men. A State which bore this kind of fruit, and suffered it to drop off as fast as it ripened, would prepare the way for a still more perfect and glorious State, which also I have imagined, but not yet anywhere seen.

24.   LINCOLN

Opposition to Slavery

Abraham Lincoln (1809–1865), the sixteenth President of the United States, was born in a log cabin in an area of Hardin (presently Larue) County, Kentucky, known as Sinking Spring Farm. His personal struggle from this obscure and humble beginning to the Presidency is a familiar part of American folk history and requires no retelling. A general survey of Lincoln's political career is useful, however, for the light it casts on Lincoln's political thinking. Lincoln served from 1834 to 1841 as a Whig member of the Illinois state legislature. He expressed his opposition to slavery but also condemned the activities of the abolitionists. Lincoln served one term in the United States House of Representatives (1847–49) as the lone Whig from Illinois. During his brief career in the House, Lincoln spoke out against the Mexican War, supported the Wilmot Proviso and introduced a bill for gradual and compensated abolition in the District of Columbia. He was a member of the Whig convention of 1848 and a proponent of Zachary Taylor's nomination. He campaigned actively for Taylor during the fall of 1848 and then returned to Springfield, Illinois, to resume his private legal career. By 1856 Lincoln had clearly identified himself as a supporter of the newly formed Republican Party and soon became a leader of the Illinois organization. He was unsuccessful in his bid for election to the United States Senate in 1858, but the publicity and popularity which he received in his contest with the Democratic nominee, Stephen A. Douglas, led to his nomination for President by the Republican Party in 1860. Lincoln perfectly suited the needs of his party at this time. He was an opponent of slavery but not identified with radical abolition; he had never been associated with the antiforeign Know-Nothing movement; and his personality was able to arouse the enthusiasm and support of the divided members of the Republican convention.

The following selection* is taken from Lincoln's Peoria, Illinois, speech of October 16, 1854. The address is partly a response to the remarks made by Senator Douglas on the slavery question two weeks earlier at Springfield. The Peoria speech is important because it is one of the first complete statements of Lincoln's views on slavery.

* Roy P. Basler, ed., *The Collected Works of Abraham Lincoln*, II (New Brunswick: Rutgers University Press, 1953), pp. 255–56, 263–66, 270–71, 276.

. . . I think, and I shall try to show, that it [repeal of the Missouri Compromise] is wrong; wrong in its direct effect, letting slavery into Kansas and Nebraska—and wrong in its prospective principle, allowing it to spread to every other part of the wide world, where men can be found inclined to take it.

This *declared* indifference, but as I must think, covert *real* zeal for the spread of slavery, I can not but hate. I hate it because of the monstrous injustice of slavery itself. I hate it because it deprives our republican example of its just influence in the world—enables the enemies of free institutions, with plausibility, to taunt us as hypocrites—causes the real friends of freedom to doubt our sincerity, and especially because it forces so many really good men amongst ourselves into an open war with the very fundamental principles of civil liberty—criticising the Declaration of Independence, and insisting that there is no right principle of action but *self-interest*.

Before proceeding, let me say I think I have no prejudice against the Southern people. They are just what we would be in their situation. If slavery did not now exist amongst them, they would not introduce it. If it did now exist amongst us, we should not instantly give it up. This I believe of the masses north and south. Doubtless there are individuals, on both sides, who would not hold slaves under any circumstances; and others who would gladly introduce slavery anew, if it were out of existence. We know that some southern men do free their slaves, go north, and become tip-top abolitionists; while some northern ones go south, and become most cruel slave-masters.

When southern people tell us they are no more responsible for the origin of slavery, than we; I acknowledge the fact. When it is said that the institution exists; and that it is very difficult to get rid of it, in any satisfactory way, I can understand and appreciate the saying. I surely will not blame them for not doing what I should not know how to do myself. If all earthly power were given me, I should not know what to do, as to the existing institution. My first impulse would be to free all the slaves, and send them to Liberia,—to their own native land. But a moment's reflection would convince me, that whatever of high hope, (as I think there is) there may be in this, in the long run, its sudden execution is impossible. If they were all landed there in a day, they would all perish in the next ten days; and there are not surplus shipping and surplus money enough in the world to carry them there in many times ten days. What then? Free them all, and keep them among us as underlings? Is it quite certain that this betters their condition? I think

I would not hold one in slavery, at any rate; yet the point is not clear enough for me to denounce people upon. What next? Free them, and make them politically and socially, our equals? My own feelings will not admit of this; and if mine would, we well know that those of the great mass of white people will not. Whether this feeling accords with justice and sound judgment, is not the sole question, if indeed, it is any part of it. A universal feeling, whether well or ill-founded, can not be safely disregarded. We can not, then, make them equals. It does seem to me that systems of gradual emancipation might be adopted; but for their tardiness in this, I will not undertake to judge our brethren of the south.

When they remind us of their constitutional rights, I acknowledge them, not grudgingly, but fully, and fairly; and I would give them any legislation for the reclaiming of their fugitives, which should not, in its stringency, be more likely to carry a free man into slavery, than our ordinary criminal laws are to hang an innocent one.

But all this; to my judgment, furnishes no more excuse for permitting slavery to go into our own free territory, than it would for reviving the African slave trade by law. The law which forbids the bringing of slaves *from* Africa; and that which has so long forbid the taking them *to* Nebraska, can hardly be distinguished on any moral principle; and the repeal of the former could find quite as plausible excuses as that of the latter. . . .

. . . . [W]e know the opening of new countries to slavery, tends to the perpetuation of the institution, and so does KEEP men in slavery who otherwise would be free. This result we do not FEEL like favoring, and we are under no legal obligation to suppress our feelings in this respect.

Equal justice to the south, it is said, requires us to consent to the extending of slavery to new countries. That is to say, inasmuch as you do not object to my taking my hog to Nebraska, therefore I must not object to you taking your slave. Now, I admit this is perfectly logical, if there is no difference between hogs and negroes. But while you thus require me to deny the humanity of the negro, I wish to ask whether you of the south yourselves, have ever been willing to do as much? It is kindly provided that of all those who come into the world, only a small percentage are natural tyrants. That percentage is no larger in the slave States than in the free. The great majority, south as well as north, have human sympathies, of which they can no more divest themselves than they can of their sensibility to physical pain. These sympathies in the bosoms of the southern people, manifest in many ways, their sense of the wrong of slavery, and their consciousness that, after all, there is humanity in the negro. If they deny this, let me address them a few plain questions. In 1820 you joined the north, almost unanimously, in declaring the African slave trade piracy, and in annexing to it the punishment of death. Why did you do this? If you did not feel that it was wrong, why did you join in providing that men should be hung for it? The practice was no more than bringing wild negroes from Africa, to sell to such as would buy them. But you never thought of hanging men for catching and selling wild horses, wild buffaloes or wild bears.

Again, you have amongst you, a sneaking individual, of the class of native tyrants, known as the "SLAVE-DEALER." He watches your necessities, and crawls up to buy your slave, at a speculating price. If you cannot help it, you sell to him; but if you can help it, you drive him from your door. You despise him utterly. You do not recognize him as a friend, or even as an honest man. Your children must not play with his; they may rollick freely with the little negroes, but not with the "slave-dealers" children. If you are obliged to deal with him, you try to get through the job without so much as touching him. It is common with you to join hands with the men you meet; but with the slave dealer you avoid the ceremony—instinctively shrinking from the snaky contact. If he grows rich and retires from business, you still remember him, and still keep up the ban of non-intercourse upon him and his family. Now why is this? You do not so treat the man who deals in corn, cattle or tobacco.

And yet again; there are in the United States and territories, including the District of Columbia, 433,643 free blacks. At $500 per head they are worth over two hundred millions of dollars. How comes this vast amount of property to be running about without owners? We do not see free horses or free cattle running at large. How is this? All these free blacks are the descendants of slaves, or have been slaves themselves, and they would be slaves now, but for SOMETHING which has operated on their white owners, inducing them, at vast pecuniary sacrifices, to liberate them. What is that SOMETHING? Is there any mistaking it? In all these cases it is your sense of justice, and human sympathy, continually telling you, that the poor negro has some natural right to himself—that those who deny it, and make mere merchandise of him, deserve kickings, contempt and death.

And now, why will you ask us to deny the humanity of the slave?

and estimate him only as the equal of the hog? Why ask us to do what you will not do yourselves? Why ask us to do for *nothing*, what two hundred million of dollars could not induce you to do?

But one great argument in the support of the repeal of the Missouri Compromise, is still to come. That argument is "the sacred right of self government." It seems our distinguished Senator has found great difficulty in getting his antagonists, even in the Senate to meet him fairly on this argument—some poet has said

> "Fools rush in where angels fear to tread."

At the hazzard of being thought one of the fools of this quotation, I meet that argument—I rush in, I take that bull by the horns.

I trust I understand, and truly estimate the right of self-government. My faith in the proposition that each man should do precisely as he pleases with all which is exclusively his own, lies at the foundation of the sense of justice there is in me. I extend the principles to communities of men, as well as to individuals. I so extend it, because it is politically wise, as well as naturally just: politically wise, in saving us from broils about matters which do not concern us. Here, or at Washington, I would not trouble myself with the oyster laws of Virginia, or the cranberry laws of Indiana.

The doctrine of self government is right—absolutely and eternally right—but it has no just application, as here attempted. Or perhaps I should rather say that whether it has such just application depends upon whether a negro is *not* or *is* a man. If he is *not* a man, why in that case, he who *is* a man may, as a matter of self-government, do just as he pleases with him. But if the negro *is* a man, is it not to that extent, a total destruction of self-government, to say that he too shall not govern *himself*? When the white man governs himself that is self-government; but when he governs himself, and also governs *another* man, that is *more* than self-government—that is despotism. If the negro is a *man*, why then my ancient faith teaches me that "all men are created equal;" and that there can be no moral right in connection with one man's making a slave of another.

Judge Douglas frequently, with bitter irony and sarcasm, paraphrases our argument by saying "The white people of Nebraska are good enough to govern themselves, *but they are not good enough to govern a few miserable negroes*!!"

Well I doubt not that the people of Nebraska are, and will continue to be as good as the average of people elsewhere. I do not say the contrary. What I do say is, that no man is good enough to govern another man, *without that other's consent*. I say this is the leading principle—the sheet anchor of American republicanism. Our Declaration of Independence says:

"We hold these truths to be self evident: that all men are created equal; that they are endowed by their Creator with certain inalienable rights; that among these are life, liberty and the pursuit of happiness. That to secure these rights, governments are instituted among men, DERIVING THEIR JUST POWERS FROM THE CONSENT OF THE GOVERNED."

I have quoted so much at this time merely to show that according to our ancient faith, the just powers of governments are derived from the consent of the governed. Now the relation of masters and slaves is, PRO TANTO, a total violation of this principle. The master not only governs the slave without his consent; but he governs him by a set of rules altogether different from those which he prescribes for himself. Allow ALL the governed an equal voice in the government, and that, and that only is self government.

Let it not be said I am contending for the establishment of political and social equality between the whites and blacks. I have already said the contrary. I am not now combating the argument of NECESSITY, arising from the fact that the blacks are already amongst us; but I am combating what is set up as MORAL argument for allowing them to be taken where they have never yet been—arguing against the EXTENSION of a bad thing, which where it already exists, we must of necessity, manage as we best can. . . .

But Nebraska is urged as a great Union-saving measure. Well I too, go for saving the Union. Much as I hate slavery, I would consent to the extension of it rather than see the Union dissolved, just as I would consent to any GREAT evil, to avoid a GREATER one. But when I go to Union saving, I must believe, at least, that the means I employ has some adaptation to the end. To my mind, Nebraska has no such adaptation.

> "It hath no relish of salvation in it."

It is an aggravation, rather, of the only one thing which ever endangers the Union. When it came upon us, all was peace and quiet. The nation was looking to the forming of new bonds of Union; and a long course of peace and prosperity seemed to lie before us. In the whole range of possibility, there scarcely appears to me to have been any thing, out of which the slavery agitation could have been revived, except the very project of repealing the Missouri compromise. Every inch of territory we owned, already had a definite settlement of the slavery question, and by which, all parties were pledged to abide. Indeed, there was no uninhabited country on the continent, which we could acquire; if we except some extreme northern regions, which are wholly out of the question. In this state of case, the genius of Discord himself, could scarcely have invented a way of again getting [setting?] us by the ears, but by turning back and destroying the peace measures of the past. The councils of that genius seem to have prevailed, the Missouri compromise was repealed; and here we are, in the midst of a new slavery agitation, such, I think, as we have never seen before. Who is responsible for this? Is it those who resist the measure; or those who, causelessly, brought it forward, and pressed it through, having reason to know, and, in fact, knowing it must and would be so resisted? It could not but be expected by its author, that it would be looked upon as a measure for the extension of slavery, aggravated by a gross breach of faith. Argue as you will, and long as you will, this is the naked FRONT and ASPECT, of the measure. And in this aspect, it could not but produce agitation. Slavery is founded in the selfishness of man's nature—opposition to it, is [in?] his love of justice. These principles are an eternal antagonism; and when brought into collision so fiercely, as slavery extension brings them, shocks, and throes, and convulsions must ceaselessly follow. Repeal the Missouri compromise—repeal all compromises—repeal the declaration of independence—repeal all past history, you still can not repeal human nature. It still will be the abundance of man's heart, that slavery extension is wrong; and out of the abundance of his heart, his mouth will continue to speak. . . .

Our republican robe is soiled, and trailed in the dust. Let us repurify it. Let us turn and wash it white, in the spirit, if not the blood, of the Revolution. Let us turn slavery from its claims of "moral right," back upon its existing legal rights, and its arguments of "necessity." Let us return it to the position our fathers gave it; and there let it rest in peace. Let us re-adopt the Declaration of Independence, and with it, the practices, and policy, which harmonize with it. Let north and south—let all Americans—let all lovers of liberty everywhere—join in the great and good work. If we do this, we shall not only have saved the Union; but we shall have so saved it, as to make, and to keep it, forever worthy of the saving. We shall have so saved it, that the succeeding millions of free happy people, the world over, shall rise up, and call us blessed, to the latest generations. . . .

25. LINCOLN
On Dred Scott

In March, 1857, the Supreme Court handed down its decision in the Dred Scott case, and an intense national debate followed. Perhaps the most celebrated parts of the debate were the speeches given by Illinois Senator Stephen A. Douglas and Abraham Lincoln. On June 12, 1857, in Springfield, Illinois, Douglas defended the Court's decision. Two weeks later, on June 26, 1857, speaking in the same Hall of Representatives, Lincoln responded to Douglas and expressed his thoughts on the Dred Scott decision.*

. . . And now as to the Dred Scott decision. That decision declares two propositions—first, that a negro cannot sue in the U.S. Courts; and secondly, that Congress cannot prohibit slavery in the Territories. It was made by a divided court—dividing differently on the different points. Judge Douglas does not discuss the merits of the decision; and, in that respect, I shall follow his example, believing I could no more improve on McLean and Curtis, than he could on Taney.

He denounces all who question the correctness of that decision, as offering violent resistance to it. But who resists it? Who has, in spite of the decision, declared Dred Scott free, and resisted the authority of his master over him?

Judicial decisions have two uses—first, to absolutely determine the case decided, and secondly, to indicate to the public how other similar cases will be decided when they arise. For the latter use, they are called "precedents" and "authorities."

We believe, as much as Judge Douglas, (perhaps more) in obedience to, and respect for the judicial department of government. We think its decisions on Constitutional questions, when fully settled, should control, not only the particular cases decided, but the general policy of the country, subject to be disturbed only by amendments of the

* Roy P. Basler, ed., *The Collected Works of Abraham Lincoln*, II (New Brunswick: Rutgers University Press, 1953), pp. 400–1, 403–10.

Constitution as provided in that instrument itself. More than this would be revolution. But we think the Dred Scott decision is erroneous. We know the court that made it, has often over-ruled its own decisions, and we shall do what we can to have it to over-rule this. We offer no *resistance* to it.

Judicial decisions are of greater or less authority as precedents, according to circumstances. That this should be so, accords both with common sense, and the customary understanding of the legal profession.

If this important decision had been made by the unanimous concurrence of the judges, and without any apparent partisan bias, and in accordance with legal public expectation, and with the steady practice of the departments throughout our history, and had been in no part, based on assumed historical facts which are not really true; or, if wanting in some of these, it had been before the court more than once, and had there been affirmed and re-affirmed through a course of years, it then might be, perhaps would be, factious, nay, even revolutionary, to not acquiesce in it as a precedent.

But when, as it is true we find it wanting in all these claims to the public confidence, it is not resistance, it is not factious, it is not even disrespectful, to treat it as not having yet quite established a settled doctrine for the country. . . .

I have said, in substance, that the Dred Scott decision was, in part; based on assumed historical facts which were not really true; and I ought not to leave the subject without giving some reasons for saying this; I therefore give an instance or two, which I think fully sustain me. Chief Justice Taney, in delivering the opinion of the majority of the Court, insists at great length that negroes were no part of the people who made, or for whom was made, the Declaration of Independence, or the Constitution of the United States.

On the contrary, Judge Curtis, in his dissenting opinion, shows that in five of the then thirteen states, to wit, New Hampshire, Massachusetts, New York, New Jersey and North Carolina, free negroes were voters, and, in proportion to their numbers, had the same part in making the Constitution that the white people had. He shows this with so much particularity as to leave no doubt of its truth; and, as a sort of conclusion on that point, holds the following language:

"The Constitution was ordained and established by the people of the United States, through the action, in each State, of those persons who were qualified by its laws to act thereon in behalf of themselves and all other citizens of the State. In some of the States, as we have seen, colored persons were among those qualified by law to act on the subject. These colored persons were not only included in the body of 'the people of the United States,' by whom the Constitution was ordained and established; but in at least five of the States they had the power to act, and, doubtless, did act, by their suffrages, upon the question of its adoption."

Again, Chief Justice Taney says: "It is difficult, at this day to realize the state of public opinion in relation to that unfortunate race, which prevailed in the civilized and enlightened portions of the world at the time of the Declaration of Independence, and when the Constitution of the United States was framed and adopted." And again, after quoting from the Declaration, he says: "The general words above quoted would seem to include the whole human family, and if they were used in a similar instrument at this day, would be so understood."

In these the Chief Justice does not directly assert, but plainly assumes, as a fact, that the public estimate of the black man is more favorable *now* than it was in the days of the Revolution. This assumption is a mistake. In some trifling particulars, the condition of that race has been ameliorated; but, as a whole, in this country, the change between then and now is decidedly the other way; and their ultimate destiny has never appeared so hopeless as in the last three or four years. In two of the five States—New Jersey and North Carolina—that then gave the free negro the right of voting, the right has since been taken away; and in a third—New York—it has been greatly abridged; while it has not been extended, so far as I know, to a single additional State, though the number of the States has more than doubled. In those days, as I understand, masters could, at their own pleasure, emancipate their slaves; but since then, such legal restraints have been made upon emancipation, as to amount almost to prohibition. In those days, Legislatures held the unquestioned power to abolish slavery in their respective States; but now it is becoming quite fashionable for State Constitutions to withhold that power from the Legislatures. In those days, by common consent, the spread of the black man's bondage to new countries was prohibited; but now, Congress decides that it *will* not continue the prohibition, and the Supreme Court decides that it *could* not if it would. In those days, our Declaration of Independence was held sacred by all, and thought to include all; but now, to aid in making the bondage of the negro universal and eternal, it is assailed, and sneered at, and construed, and hawked at, and torn, till, if its framers could rise from their graves, they could not at all recognize it.

All the powers of earth seem rapidly combining against him. Mammon is after him; ambition follows, and philosophy follows, and the Theology of the day is fast joining the cry. They have him in his prison house; they have searched his person, and left no prying instrument with him. One after another they have closed the heavy iron doors upon him, and now they have him, as it were, bolted in with a lock of a hundred keys, which can never be unlocked without the concurrence of every key; the keys in the hands of a hundred different men, and they scattered to a hundred different and distant places; and they stand musing as to what invention, in all the dominions of mind and matter, can be produced to make the impossibility of his escape more complete than it is.

It is grossly incorrect to say or assume, that the public estimate of the negro is more favorable now than it was at the origin of the government. . . .

There is a natural disgust in the minds of nearly all white people, to the idea of an indiscriminate amalgamation of the white and black races; and Judge Douglas evidently is basing his chief hope, upon the chances of being able to appropriate the benefit of this disgust to himself. If he can, by much drumming and repeating, fasten the odium of that idea upon his adversaries, he thinks he can struggle through the storm. He therefore clings to this hope, as a drowning man to the last plank. He makes an occasion for lugging it in from the opposition to the Dred Scott decision. He finds the Republicans insisting that the Declaration of Independence includes ALL men, black as well as white; and forthwith he boldly denies that it includes negroes at all, and proceeds to argue gravely that all who contend it does, do so only because they want to vote, and eat, and sleep, and marry with negroes! He will have it that they cannot be consistent else. Now I protest against that counterfeit logic which concludes that, because I do not want a black woman for a *slave* I must necessarily want her for a *wife*. I need not have her for either, I can just leave her alone. In some respects she certainly is not my equal; but in her natural right to eat the bread she earns with her own hands without asking leave of any one else, she is my equal, and the equal of all others.

Chief Justice Taney, in his opinion in the Dred Scott case, admits that the language of the Declaration is broad enough to include the whole human family, but he and Judge Douglas argue that the authors of that instrument did not intend to include negroes, by the fact that they did not at once, actually place them on an equality with the whites. Now this grave argument comes to just nothing at all, by the other fact, that they did not at once, *or ever afterwards*, actually place all white people on an equality with one or another. And this is the staple argument of both the Chief Justice and the Senator, for doing this obvious violence to the plain unmistakable language of the Declaration. I think the authors of that notable instrument intended to include *all* men, but they did not intend to declare all men equal *in all respects*. They did not mean to say all were equal in color, size, intellect, moral developments, or social capacity. They defined with tolerable distinctness, in what respects they did consider all men created equal— equal in "certain inalienable rights, among which are life, liberty, and the pursuit of happiness." This they said, and this meant. They did not mean to assert the obvious untruth, that all were then actually enjoying that equality, nor yet, that they were about to confer it immediately upon them. In fact they had no power to confer such a boon. They meant simply to declare the *right*, so that the *enforcement* of it might follow as fast as circumstances should permit. They meant to set up a standard maxim for free society, which should be familiar to all, and revered by all; constantly looked to, constantly labored for, and even though never perfectly attained, constantly approximated, and thereby constantly spreading and deepening its influence, and augmenting the happiness and value of life to all people of all colors everywhere. The assertion that "all men are created equal" was of no practical use in effecting our separation from Great Britain; and it was placed in the Declaration, not for that, but for future use. Its authors meant it to be, thank God, it is now proving itself, a stumbling block to those who in after times might seek to turn a free people back into the hateful paths of despotism. They knew the proneness of prosperity to breed tyrants, and they meant when such should re-appear in this fair land and commence their vocation they should find left for them at least one hard nut to crack.

I have now briefly expressed my view of the *meaning* and *objects* of that part of the Declaration of Independence which declares that "all men are created equal."

Now let us hear Judge Douglas' view of the same subject, as I find it in the printed report of his late speech. Here it is:

"No man can vindicate the character, motives and conduct of the signers of the Declaration of Independence, except upon the hypothesis that they referred to the white race alone, and not to the African, when they declared all men to have been created equal—that they were speaking of British subjects on this continent being equal to British subjects born and residing in Great Britain—that they were entitled to the same inalienable rights, and among them were enumerated life, liberty and the pursuit of happiness. The Declaration was adopted for the purpose of justifying the colonists in the eyes of the civilized world in withdrawing their allegiance from the British crown, and dissolving their connection with the mother country."

My good friends, read that carefully over some leisure hour, and ponder well upon it—see what a mere wreck—mangled ruin—it makes of our once glorious Declaration.

"They were speaking of British subjects on this continent being equal to British subjects born and residing in Great Britain!" Why, according to this, not only negroes but white people outside of Great Britain and America are not spoken of in that instrument. The English, Irish and Scotch, along with white Americans, were included to be sure, but the French, Germans and other white people of the world are all gone to pot along with the Judge's inferior races.

I had thought the Declaration promised something better than the condition of British subjects; but no, it only meant that we should be *equal* to them in their own oppressed and *unequal* condition. According to that, it gave no promise that having kicked off the King and Lords of Great Britain, we should not at once be saddled with a King and Lords of our own.

I had thought the Declaration contemplated the progressive improvement in the condition of all men everywhere; but no, it merely "was adopted for the purpose of justifying the colonists in the eyes of the civilized world in withdrawing their allegiance from the British crown, and dissolving their connection with the mother country." Why, that object having been effected some eighty years ago, the Declaration is of no practical use now—mere rubbish—old wadding left to rot on the battle-field after the victory is won.

I understand you are preparing to celebrate the "Fourth," tomorrow week. What for? The doings of that day had no reference to the present: and quite half of you are not even descendants of those who were referred to at that day. But I suppose you will celebrate; and will even go so far as to read the Declaration. Suppose after you read it once in the old fashioned way, you read it once more with Judge Douglas' version. It will then run thus: "We hold these truths to be self-evident that all British subjects who were on this continent eighty-one years ago, were created equal to all British subjects born and *then* residing in Great Britain."

And now I appeal to all—to Democrats as well as others,—are you really willing that the Declaration shall be thus frittered away?—thus left no more at most, than an interesting memorial of the dead past? thus shorn of its vitality, and practical value; and left without the *germ* or even the *suggestion* of the individual rights of man in it?

But Judge Douglas is especially horrified at the thought of the mixing blood by the white and black races: agreed for once—a thousand times agreed. There are white men enough to marry all the white women, and black men enough to marry all the black women; and so let them be married. On this point we fully agree with the Judge; and when he shall show that his policy is better adapted to prevent amalgamation than ours we shall drop ours, and adopt his. Let us see. In 1850 there were in the United States, 405,751 mulattoes. Very few of these are the offspring of whites and *free* blacks; nearly all have sprung from black *slaves* and white masters. A separation of the races is the only perfect preventive of amalgamation but as an immediate separation is impossible the next best thing is to *keep* them apart *where* they are not already together. If white and black people never get together in Kansas, they will never mix blood in Kansas. That is at least one self-evident truth. A few free colored persons may get into the free States, in any event; but their number is too insignificant to amount to much in the way of mixing blood. In 1850 there were in the free states, 56,649 mulattoes; but for the most part they were not born there— they came from the slave States, ready made up. In the same year the slave States had 348,874 mulattoes all of home production. The proportion of free mulattoes to free blacks—the only colored classes in the free states—is much greater in the slave than in the free states. It is worthy of note too, that among the free states those which make the colored man the nearest to equal the white, have, proportionably the fewest mulattoes the least of amalgamation. In New Hampshire, the State which goes farthest towards equality between the races, there are just 184 Mulattoes while there are in Virginia—how many do you think? 79,775, being 23,126 more than in all the free States together. . . .

I have said that the separation of the races is the only perfect preventive of amalgamation. I have no right to say all the members of the Republican party are in favor of this, nor to say that as a party they are in favor of it. There is nothing in their platform directly on the subject. But I can say a very large proportion of its members are for it, and that the chief plank in their platform—opposition to the spread of slavery—is most favorable to that separation.

Such separation, if ever effected at all, must be effected by colonization; and no political party, as such, is now doing anything directly for colonization. Party operations at present only favor or retard colonization incidentally. The enterprise is a difficult one; but "when there is a will there is a way;" and what colonization needs most is a hearty will. Will springs from the two elements of moral sense and self-interest. Let us be brought to believe it is morally right, and, at the same time, favorable to, or, at least, not against, our interest, to transfer the African to his native clime, and we shall find a way to do it, however great the task may be. The children of Israel, to such numbers as to include four hundred thousand fighting men, went out of Egyptian bondage in a body.

How differently the respective courses of the Democratic and Republican parties incidentally bear on the question of forming a will—a public sentiment—for colonization, is easy to see. The Republicans inculcate, with whatever of ability they can, that the negro is a man; that his bondage is cruelly wrong, and that the field of his oppression ought not to be enlarged. The Democrats deny his manhood; deny, or dwarf to insignificance, the wrong of his bondage; so far as possible, crush all sympathy for him, and cultivate and excite hatred and disgust against him; compliment themselves as Union-savers for doing so; and call the indefinite outspreading of his bondage "a sacred right of self-government."

The plainest print cannot be read through a gold eagle; and it will be ever hard to find many men who will send a slave to Liberia, and pay his passage while they can send him to a new country, Kansas for instance, and sell him for fifteen hundred dollars, and the rise.

26.   LINCOLN

Republicans—"The Party of the Man"

Although Stephen A. Douglas defeated him in the 1858 election for the United States Senate seat from Illinois, Lincoln had made an impressive showing against the nation's most prominent Democrat, and his popularity among the nation's Republicans increased. A group of Boston party leaders requested Lincoln's presence at a Jefferson birthday celebration in their city, but he was unable to make the journey. In a letter from Springfield, dated April 6, 1859,* Lincoln expressed his regrets and went on to comment on Jefferson and his philosophical relationship to the existing Democratic and Republican parties.

Gentlemen

Your kind note inviting me to attend a Festival in Boston, on the 13th. Inst. in honor of the birth-day of Thomas Jefferson, was duly received. My engagements are such that I can not attend.

Bearing in mind that about seventy years ago, two great political parties were first formed in this country, that Thomas Jefferson was the head of one of them, and Boston the head-quarters of the other, it is both curious and interesting that those supposed to descend politically from the party opposed to Jefferson, should now be celebrating his birth-day in their own original seat of empire, while those claiming political descent from him have nearly ceased to breathe his name everywhere.

Remembering too, that the Jefferson party was formed upon their supposed superior devotion to the *personal* rights of men, holding the rights of *property* to be secondary only, and greatly inferior, and then assuming that the so-called democracy of to-day, are the Jefferson, and their opponents, the anti-Jefferson party, it will be equally interesting to note how completely the two have changed hands as to the principle upon which they were originally supposed to be divided.

* Roy P. Basler, ed., *The Collected Works of Abraham Lincoln*, III (New Brunswick: Rutgers University Press, 1953), pp. 374–76.

The democracy of to-day holds the *liberty* of one man to be absolutely nothing, when in conflict with another man's right of *property*. Republicans, on the contrary, are both for the *man* and the *dollar*; but in cases of conflict, the man *before* the dollar.

I remember once being much amused at seeing two partially intoxicated men engage in a fight with their great-coats on, which fight, after a long, and rather harmless contest, ended in each having fought himself *out* of his own coat, and *into* that of the other. If the two leading parties of this day are really identical with the two in the days of Jefferson and Adams, they have performed about the same feat as the two drunken men.

But soberly, it is now no child's play to save the principles of Jefferson from total overthrow in this nation.

One would start with great confidence that he could convince any sane child that the simpler propositions of Euclid are true; but, nevertheless, he would fail, utterly, with one who would deny the definitions and axioms. The principles of Jefferson are the definitions and axioms of free society. And yet they are denied, and evaded, with no small show of success. One dashingly calls them "glittering generalities"; and still others insidiously argue that they apply only to "superior races."

These expressions, differing in form, are identical in object and effect —the supplanting the principles of free government, and restoring those of classification, caste, and legitimacy. They would delight a convocation of crowned heads, plotting against the people. They are the van-guard— the miners, and sappers—of returning despotism. We must repulse them, or they will subjugate us.

This is a world of compensations; and he who would *be* no slave, must consent to *have* no slave. Those who deny freedom to others, deserve it not for themselves; and, under a just God, can not long retain it.

All honor to Jefferson—to the man who, in the concrete pressure of a struggle for national independence by a single people, had the coolness, forecast, and capacity to introduce into a merely revolutionary document, an absolute truth, applicable to all men and all times, and so to enbalm it there, that to-day, and in all coming days, it shall be a rebuke and a stumbling-block to the very harbingers of re-appearing tyranny and oppression.

Your obedient servant,
A. Lincoln

27. LINCOLN
First Inaugural Address

In the four-way contest for the Presidency in the election of 1860 Lincoln polled only 40 percent of the total popular vote but won a clear majority in the electoral college. The South had often warned that the election of a "Black Republican" would mean the end of the Union, and four days after Lincoln's election South Carolina passed an ordinance of secession. By March 4, 1861, when Lincoln was inaugurated, Mississippi, Florida, Alabama, Georgia, Louisiana, and Texas had also withdrawn from the Union, and the opening shots of the Civil War were soon to be exchanged. Though somber in tone, Lincoln's Inaugural Address* still offered the hope that peace and union were possible. But Lincoln also made clear his duty to maintain the Union, and he stated a novel argument to support his contention that the Union of States was indissoluble.

Fellow citizens of the United States:

In compliance with a custom as old as the government itself, I appear before you to address you briefly, and to take, in your presence, the oath prescribed by the Constitution of the United States, to be taken by the President "before he enters on the execution of his office."

I do not consider it necessary, at present, for me to discuss those matters of administration about which there is no special anxiety, or excitement.

Apprehension seems to exist among the people of the Southern States, that by the accession of a Republican Administration, their property, and their peace, and personal security, are to be endangered. There has never been any reasonable cause for such apprehension. Indeed, the most ample evidence to the contrary has all the while existed, and been open to their inspection. It is found in nearly all the published speeches of him who now addresses you. I do but quote from one of

* Roy P. Basler, ed., *The Collected Works of Abraham Lincoln*, IV (New Brunswick: Rutgers University Press, 1953), pp. 262–66, 268–71.

those speeches when I declare that "I have no purpose, directly or indirectly, to interfere with the institution of slavery in the States where it exists. I believe I have no lawful right to do so, and I have no inclination to do so." Those who nominated and elected me did so with full knowledge that I had made this, and many similar declarations, and had never recanted them. . . .

I now reiterate these sentiments: and in doing so, I only press upon the public attention the most conclusive evidence of which the case is susceptible, that the property, peace and security of no section are to be in anywise endangered by the now incoming Administration. I add too, that all the protection which, consistently with the Constitution and the laws, can be given, will be cheerfully given to all the States when lawfully demanded, for whatever cause—as cheerfully to one section, as to another. . . .

It is seventy-two years since the first inauguration of a President under our national Constitution. During that period fifteen different and greatly distinguished citizens, have, in succession, administered the executive branch of the government. They have conducted it through many perils; and, generally, with great success. Yet, with all this scope for precedent, I now enter upon the same task for the brief constitutional term of four years, under great and peculiar difficulty. A disruption of the Federal Union heretofore only menaced, is now formidably attempted.

I hold, that in contemplation of universal law, and of the Constitution, the Union of these States is perpetual. Perpetuity is implied, if not expressed, in the fundamental law of all national governments. It is safe to assert that no government proper, ever had a provision in its organic law for its own termination. Continue to execute all the express provisions of our national Constitution, and the Union will endure forever—it being impossible to destroy it, except by some action not provided for in the instrument itself.

Again, if the United States be not a government proper, but an association of States in the nature of contract merely, can it, as a contract, be peaceably unmade, by less than all the parties who made it? One party to a contract may violate it—break it, so to speak; but does it not require all to lawfully rescind it?

Descending from these general principles, we find the proposition that, in legal contemplation, the Union is perpetual, confirmed by the history of the Union itself. The Union is much older than the Constitution. It was formed in fact, by the Articles of Association in 1774.

It was matured and continued by the Declaration of Independence in 1776. It was further matured and the faith of all the then thirteen States expressly plighted and engaged that it should be perpetual, by the Articles of Confederation in 1778. And finally, in 1787, one of the declared objects for ordaining and establishing the Constitution, was *"to form a more perfect union."*

But if destruction of the Union, by one, or by a part only, of the States, be lawfully possible, the Union is *less* perfect than before the Constitution, having lost the vital element of perpetuity.

It follows from these views that no State, upon its own mere motion, can lawfully get out of the Union,—that *resolves* and *ordinances* to that effect are legally void; and that acts of violence, within any State or States, against the authority of the United States, are insurrectionary or revolutionary, according to circumstances.

I therefore consider that, in view of the Constitution and the laws, the Union is unbroken; and, to the extent of my ability, I shall take care, as the Constitution itself expressly enjoins upon me, that the laws of the Union be faithfully executed in all the States. Doing this I deem to be only a simple duty on my part; and I shall perform it, so far as practicable, unless my rightful masters, the American people, shall withhold the requisite means, or, in some authoritative manner, direct the contrary. I trust this will not be regarded as a menace, but only as the declared purpose of the Union that it *will* constitutionally defend, and maintain itself.

In doing this there needs to be no bloodshed or violence; and there shall be none, unless it be forced upon the national authority. The power confided to me, will be used to hold, occupy, and possess the property, and places belonging to the government, and to collect the duties and imposts; but beyond what may be necessary for these objects, there will be no invasion—no using of force against, or among the people anywhere. Where hostility to the United States, in any interior locality, shall be so great and so universal, as to prevent competent resident citizens from holding the Federal offices, there will be no attempt to force obnoxious strangers among the people for that object. While the strict legal right may exist in the government to enforce the exercise of these offices, the attempt to do so would be so irritating, and so nearly impracticable with all, that I deem it better to forego, for the time, the uses of such offices. . . .

Plainly, the central idea of secession, is the essence of anarchy. A majority, held in restraint by constitutional checks, and limitations, and always changing easily, with deliberate changes of popular opinions and sentiments, is the only true sovereign of a free people. Whoever rejects it, does, of necessity, fly to anarchy or to despotism. Unanimity is impossible; the rule of a minority, as a permanent arrangement, is wholly inadmissable; so that, rejecting the majority principle, anarchy, or despotism in some form, is all that is left.

I do not forget the position assumed by some, that constitutional questions are to be decided by the Supreme Court; nor do I deny that such decisions must be binding in any case, upon the parties to a suit, as to the object of that suit, while they are also entitled to very high respect and consideration, in all parallel cases, by all other departments of the government. And while it is obviously possible that such decision may be erroneous in any given case, still the evil effect following it, being limited to that particular case, with the chance that it may be over-ruled, and never become a precedent for other cases, can better be borne than could the evils of a different practice. At the same time the candid citizen must confess that if the policy of the government, upon vital questions, affecting the whole people, is to be irrevocably fixed by decisions of the Supreme Court, the instant they are made, in ordinary litigation between parties, in personal actions, the people will have ceased, to be their own rulers, having, to that extent, practically resigned their government, into the hands of that eminent tribunal. Nor is there, in this view, any assault upon the court, or the judges. It is a duty, from which they may not shrink, to decide cases properly brought before them; and it is no fault of theirs, if others seek to turn their decisions to political purposes.

One section of our country believes slavery is *right*, and ought to be extended, while the other believes it is *wrong*, and ought not to be extended. This is the only substantial dispute. The fugitive slave clause of the Constitution, and the law for the suppression of the foreign slave trade, are each as well enforced, perhaps, as any law can ever be in a community where the moral sense of the people imperfectly supports the law itself. The great body of the people abide by the dry legal obligation in both cases, and a few break over in each. This, I think, cannot be perfectly cured; and it would be worse in both cases *after* the separation of the sections, than before. The foreign slave trade, now imperfectly suppressed, would be ultimately revived without restriction, in one section; while fugitive slaves, now only partially surrendered, would not be surrendered at all, by the other.

Physically speaking, we cannot separate. We cannot remove our respective sections from each other, nor build an impassable wall between them. A husband and wife may be divorced, and go out of the presence, and beyond the reach of each other; but the different parts of our country cannot do this. They cannot but remain face to face; and intercourse, either amicable or hostile, must continue between them. Is it possible then to make that intercourse more advantageous, or more satisfactory, *after* separation than *before*? Can aliens make treaties easier than friends can make laws? Can treaties be more faithfully enforced between aliens, than laws can among friends? Suppose you go to war, you cannot fight always; and when, after much loss on both sides, and no gain on either, you cease fighting, the identical old questions, as to terms of intercourse, are again upon you.

This country, with its institutions, belongs to the people who inhabit it. Whenever they shall grow weary of the existing government, they can exercise their *constitutional* right of amending it, or their *revolutionary* right to dismember, or overthrow it. I can not be ignorant of the fact that many worthy, and patriotic citizens are desirous of having the national constitution amended. While I make no recommendation of amendments, I fully recognize the rightful authority of the people over the whole subject, to be exercised in either of the modes prescribed in the instrument itself; and I should, under existing circumstances, favor, rather than oppose, a fair opportunity being afforded the people to act upon it. . . .

Why should there not be a patient confidence in the ultimate justice of the people? Is there any better, or equal hope, in the world? In our present differences, is either party without faith of being in the right? If the Almighty Ruler of nations, with his eternal truth and justice, be on your side of the North, or on yours of the South, that truth, and that justice, will surely prevail, by the judgment of this great tribunal, the American people.

By the frame of the government under which we live, this same people have wisely given their public servants but little power for mischief; and have, with equal wisdom, provided for the return of that little to their own hands at very short intervals.

While the people retain their virtue, and vigilance, no administration, by any extreme of wickedness or folly, can very seriously injure the government, in the short space of four years.

My countrymen, one and all, think calmly and *well*, upon this whole subject. Nothing valuable can be lost by taking time. If there be an object to *hurry* any of you, in hot haste, to a step which you would never take *deliberately*, that object will be frustrated by taking time; but no good object can be frustrated by it. Such of you as are now dissatisfied, still have the old Constitution unimpaired, and, on the sensitive point, the laws of your own framing under it; while the new administration will have no immediate power, if it would, to change either. If it were admitted that you who are dissatisfied, hold the right side in the dispute, there still is no single good reason for precipitate action. Intelligence, patriotism, Christianity, and a firm reliance on Him, who has never yet forsaken this favored land, are still competent to adjust, in the best way, all our present difficulty.

In *your* hands, my dissatisfied fellow countrymen, and not in *mine*, is the momentous issue of civil war. The government will not assail *you*. You can have no conflict, without being yourselves the aggressors. *You* have no oath registered in Heaven to destroy the government, while *I* shall have the most solemn one to "preserve, protect and defend" it.

I am loth to close. We are not enemies, but friends. We must not be enemies. Though passion may have strained, it must not break our bonds of affection. The mystic chords of memory, stretching from every battle-field, and patriot grave, to every living heart and hearthstone, all over this broad land, will yet swell the chorus of the Union, when again touched, as surely they will be, by the better angels of our nature.

V

The Protest Against
Social Darwinism

Social Darwinism, with its individualistic, competitive, and laissez-faire corollaries, reigned as the dominant philosophy in America in the decades after the close of the Civil War. Its doctrines squared perfectly with the needs of the conservative business-oriented society of that time. The virtue and inevitability of social Darwinism were taught by spokesmen from many parts of the society: William Graham Sumner from Yale, the Reverend Josiah Strong from the Protestant pulpit, and Andrew Carnegie from his desk in Pittsburgh were among its leading disciples.

But the philosophy of social Darwinism and its economic, social, and political consequences soon came under attack from a wide variety of critics. It is impossible to set forth the ideas of all the significant opponents of social Darwinism. Instead, selections from three representative forms of protest—the reform Darwinism of Lester Frank Ward, the Utopian socialism of Edward Bellamy, and the reform movement known as populism—will be presented. This material indicates the nature and extent of the opposition to social Darwinism in this nation at the end of the nineteenth century and demonstrates the indigenous, non-Marxist roots of these liberal collectivist protests.

Lester Frank Ward was unknown to the American public during his lifetime. His writings did, however, exert a profound influence on American sociology, which was then emerging as a separate academic discipline. Ward accepted the basic evolutionary doctrines of Herbert Spencer, but he refused to apply them to man's mental processes. His reform Darwinism distinguished between the wasteful, directionless competition of the animal world and man's mental capacity for controlling his environment.

Ward's importance lies in the fact that he was "the first and most formidable of a number of thinkers who attacked the unitary assumptions of social Darwinism and natural-law laissez-faire individualism."[1] In *The Psychic Factors of Civilization* Ward favored social planning and rule by a trained elite of social scientists—a "sociocracy." American

[1] Richard Hofstadter, *Social Darwinism in American Thought* (rev. ed.; Boston: The Beacon Press, 1955), p. 68.

liberalism in the twentieth century never fully accepted Ward's solutions for social and economic problems, but it was deeply affected by the general collectivist nature of his thought.

The significance of Edward Bellamy's Utopian socialism rests not in its effect on American society—its influence was distinctly ephemeral —but in the fact that the popularity of his ideas during the last years of the nineteenth century indicates the total disenchantment with the competitive system on the part of many citizens. Bellamy's socialist Utopia, portrayed in great detail in his romantic novel *Looking Backward: 2000–1887*, envisioned a collectivized society in which all traces of competition had been removed.

Bellamy's indictment of social Darwinism was complete. In a speech entitled "Plutocracy or Nationalism—Which?" given before the Boston Nationalist Club, he stated: "The final plea for any form of brutality in these days is that it tends to the survival of the fittest; and very properly this plea has been advanced in favor of the system which is the sum of all brutalities."

But while Bellamy rejected the philosophy of social Darwinism, he did not reject its materialistic goals. By nationalizing industry into one great publicly owned trust and collectivizing all aspects of social relations, Bellamy believed, wealth could be greatly increased for all members of the society. In *Looking Backward*, Dr. Leete, the spokesman for the Utopia of the year 2000, explained to Julian West, the representative of 1887, the basic weakness of individualism and the strength of collectivism:

> The broad shoulders of the nation . . . bear now like a feather the burden that broke the backs of the women of your day. Their misery came, with all your other miseries, from that incapacity for cooperation which followed from the individualism on which your social system was founded, from your inability to perceive that you could make ten times more profit out of your fellow man by uniting with them than by contending with them.[2]

The American farmers in the three decades following the close of the Civil War suffered through a period of almost continual economic crisis. Falling agricultural prices, rising interest rates, and drought plagued rural America. To combat the economic distress, the farmers organized and became increasingly politically active. The Grange, the Greenback Party, and the Farmers' Alliance were manifestations of the rural discontent of the 1860's to 1880's. But the most important and

[2] (Boston: Houghton Mifflin Company, 1887), p. 120.

successful of the farm protest movements was populism. Building upon the organizational achievements of the Farmers' Alliance, populism became an important political force during the 1890's.

Populism, with its roots deep in agricultural and small-town America, had almost no urban intellectual support to provide it with a well-thought-out political philosophy. Its more literate spokesmen, such as Ignatius Donnelly, W. H. ("Coin") Harvey, and Mary E. Lease, did produce an abundance of novels, pamphlets, and pseudosocial science tracts which stated their grievances, program for reform, and generally emotional and conspiratorial world view. Populism, however, lacked a Lester Ward or an Edward Bellamy to supply it with an intellectual and theoretical grounding.

But, for all its naïveté, populism had a definite program for political and economic change, and that program has had a deep impact on the subsequent history of this nation. The People's Party platform of 1892 is the best single statement of populist objectives. In that document the Populist Party called for a variety of political reforms: the secret ballot, the direct election of Senators, and the initiative and referendum.

The populists did not believe, however, that a few political changes would end the wrongs they found in American society. They understood surprisingly well the economic basis of their complaints, and they turned to the national government for the solution of many of their difficulties. In addition to their most celebrated panacea—the unlimited coinage of silver and gold at a 16 to 1 ratio—the populist platform called for a number of fundamental economic reforms: a national graduated income tax, the nationalization of railroad, telephone, and telegraphic services, an eight-hour day for government employees, and the prohibition of the use of private police forces against striking workers.

"Populism," Richard Hofstadter has written, "was the first political movement of practical importance in the United States to insist that the federal government has some responsibility for the common weal; indeed, it was the first such movement to attack seriously the problems created by industrialism."[3] Populism's perception of the economic nature of many of society's ills and its belief in action by the national government to remedy these difficulties foreshadowed the views of twentieth-century liberalism. Its program signaled the decline of American liberalism's faith in laissez-faire and ushered in a new era of belief in positive central government involvement in the nation's economy.

[3] *The Age of Reform* (New York: Alfred A. Knopf, 1956), p. 61.

28. WARD

Reform Darwinism

Lester Frank Ward (1841–1913) was born in Joliet, Illinois, and lived for the first two decades of his life in Illinois and Iowa. He came east in 1861 and, when the Civil War broke out, enlisted in the Union Army. Wounded at Chancellorsville, Ward was discharged and obtained employment with the Treasury Department in Washington, D.C. During the next seven years he received AB, AM, and LLB degrees from George Washington University. In 1881 he left the Treasury Department and joined the United States Geological Survey first as a geologist and later as a paleontologist. Ward made important scholarly contributions in these fields, but his fame derives primarily from his significance as a founder of American sociology. His books in this field include: *Dynamic Sociology* (1883), *Outlines of Sociology* (1897), *Pure Sociology* (1903), and *Applied Sociology* (1906). The following selection is from Ward's second published work on sociology, *The Psychic Factors of Civilization.** Ward spent the last years of his life, 1906–13, as a professor of sociology at Brown University.

Thus far attention has been chiefly confined to the science of society contemplated from the psychologic standpoint. But every applied science has its corresponding art. And although the social art is none other than this same government of which it has already been necessary to say so much, still, our social synthesis would be incomplete without some more special inquiry into the essential character of that art as a product of the combined consciousness, will, and intellect of society. Existing governments, it must be confessed, after all that can be said in their favor, realize this only to a very feeble extent. The social consciousness is as yet exceedingly faint. . . . The social will is, therefore, merely a mass of conflicting desires which largely neutralize one another

* (Boston: Ginn and Company, Publishers, 1892), pp. 313–27.

and result in little advance movement in one settled direction. The social intellect proves a poor guide, not because it is not sufficiently vigorous, but because knowledge of those matters which principally concern society is so limited, while that which exists is chiefly lodged in the minds of those individuals who are allowed no voice in the affairs of state.

. . . I have pointed out what I regard as the one certain correction possible to apply to this state of things, and have entered into a logically arranged demonstration of this point. "The universal diffusion of the maximum amount of the most important knowledge" was the formula reached for the expression of the result, and it was shown that its attainment is not only practicable but easy and simple whenever the social intelligence shall reach the stage at which its importance is distinctly recognized. It is only after the mind of society, as embodied in its consciousness, will, and intellect, shall, through the application of this formula for a sufficiently prolonged period to produce the required result, come to stand to the social organism in somewhat the relation that the individual mind stands to the individual organism, that any fully developed art of government can be expected to appear. . . . It will be the product of the inventive faculty perfected through the inventive genius, and systematized by scientific discovery under the influence of the scientific method and spirit.

Contrasted with this the governments of the past and present may be regarded as empirical. Useful, as is all empirical art, necessary, and adapted in a manner to their age and country, they have served and are serving a purpose in social development and civilization. They have taken on a number of different forms, of which the principal ones are called either monarchies or democracies. These terms, however, never very precise, have now become in most cases wholly misleading. The monarchies of Europe, with perhaps two exceptions, are now all democracies, if there are any such, and some of those that still prefer to be called monarchies are more democratic than some that call themselves republics. And in America, where none of the governments have the monarchical form, some of them are decidedly autocratic and elections are either a signal for revolution or else a mere farce. So that the names by which governments are known are wholly inadequate indexes to their true character. A more exact classification would be into *autocracies*, *aristocracies*, and *democracies*. By aristocracy would then be meant a ruling class, not necessarily superior, but held to be so. Most monarchies belong to this class. The aristocracy consists not merely of the royal family or dynasty, but of the nobles, clergy, and other privileged persons, for all such really belong to the ruling class. Most European countries have passed through the first two of these stages into the third. Some may be considered as still in the second, while most half-civilized, barbarous, or savage nations have not emerged from the first.

. . . [T]he intellect was developed as an aid to the will in furthering the personal ends of the individual, and . . . among the many modes of acquisition government played a leading part. This is more especially the case in the stages of autocracy and aristocracy. It becomes less so in that of democracy, where it is confined to the professional politician and the "legal fraternity." Most of the attacks upon government that it is now so fashionable to make are based upon the vivid manner in which history portrays the doings of the ruling class during the stages of autocracy and aristocracy, and those who make them seem to forget that in all fully enlightened nations this stage has been passed and that of democracy has been fairly reached. But the fear and dread of government still lingers, and its ghost still perpetually rises and will not down. Although modern governments, chiefly on account of the known odium in which they are held, scarcely dare carry out the emphatically declared will of those who create them, and hesitate to take a step forward for fear of being forthwith overthrown by a sweeping plebiscite, still they are the objects of the most jealous vigilance and violent denunciation. Their power for usefulness is thus greatly weakened, and social progress and reform are slow.

It must not, however, be inferred that human nature has been changed by the transition from autocracy and aristocracy to democracy. The spirit of self-aggrandizement is undiminished, but the methods of accomplishing it have been changed. Just as society by the establishment of the institution of government put an end to the internecine strifes that threatened its existence, so also by the overthrow of autocracy and aristocracy it wrested from the autocrat and the aristocrat his power to subsist upon the masses. But the keen egoism of the astute individual immediately sought other means to better his condition at the expense of those less gifted with this irrepressible mental power or less favorably circumstanced for its exercise. What could not be secured through statecraft must be gained through some other species of craft. And soon was found in the very weakness of government the means of accomplishing far more than could ever be accomplished by the aid of the strongest form of government. What could no longer be attained

through the universal or complete social organization has become easy
of attainment through some one or other of the many kinds of partial
or incomplete social organizations. . . . With the rigid system which has
grown up for the protection of the individual in his legal vested rights
there is nothing in the way of advancing to almost any length in this
direction.

The reaction in the direction of democracy, obeying the rhythmic
law of social progress, aimed at, and to a large extent attained, a fourth
stage which may be appropriately called *physiocracy*. Indeed, it may
be said to consist of little else than that which was demanded by the
French school of political economists who styled themselves Physio-
crats. Neglecting some of their special tenets arising out of local
conditions in France, this movement was not essentially different from
that which was soon after introduced into England and made such
rapid progress that it took complete possession of the public mind and
has furnished the foundation of the political philosophy of that
country and of the social and economic science taught from the high
chairs of learning wherever the English language is spoken. This
physiocracy, as a habit of thought rather than a form of government,
now goes by the name of individualism, and is carried so far by many
as to amount to a practical anarchism, reducing all government to the
action of so-called natural laws.

The general result is that the world, having passed through the
stages of autocracy and aristocracy into the stage of democracy, has,
by a natural reaction against personal power, so far minimized the
governmental influence that the same spirit which formerly used
government to advance self is now ushering in a fifth stage, viz., that
of *plutocracy*, which thrives well in connection with a weak democracy
or physiocracy, and aims to supersede it entirely. Its strongest hold is
the wide-spread distrust of all government, and it leaves no stone
unturned to fan the flame of misarchy. Instead of demanding more and
stronger government it demands less and feebler. Shrewdly clamoring
for individual liberty, it perpetually holds up the outrages committed
by governments in their autocratic and aristocratic stages, and falsely
insists that there is imminent danger of their reënactment. *Laissez faire*
and the most extreme individualism, bordering on practical anarchy
in all except the enforcement of existing proprietary rights, are loudly
advocated, and the public mind is thus blinded to the real condition of
things. The system of political economy that sprang up in France and
England at the close of the aristocratic stage in those countries is still

taught in the higher institutions of learning. It is highly favorable to the spread of plutocracy, and is pointed to by those who are to profit by that system of government as the invincible scientific foundation upon which it rests. Many honest political economists are still lured by the specious claims of this system and continue to uphold it, and at least one important treatise on social science, that of Herbert Spencer, defends it to the most extreme length. Thus firmly intrenched, it will require a titanic effort on the part of society to dislodge this baseless prejudice, and rescue itself once more from the rapacious jaws of human egoism under the crafty leadership of a developed and instructed rational faculty.

Under the system as it now exists the wealth of the world, however created, and irrespective of the claims of the producer, is made to flow toward certain centers of accumulation, to be enjoyed by those holding the keys to such situations. The world appears to be approaching a stage at which those who labor, no matter how skilled, how industrious, or how frugal, will receive, according to the "iron law" formulated by Ricardo, only so much for their services as will enable them "to subsist and to perpetuate their race." The rest finds its way into the hands of a comparatively few, usually non-producing, individuals, whom the usages and laws of all countries permit to claim that they own the very sources of all wealth and the right to allow or forbid its production.

These are great and serious evils, compared with which all the crimes, recognized as such, that would be committed if no government existed, would be as trifles. The underpaid labor, the prolonged and groveling drudgery, the wasted strength, the misery and squalor, the diseases resulting, and the premature deaths that would be prevented by a just distribution of the products of labor, would in a single year outweigh all the so-called crime of a century, for the prevention of which, it is said, government alone exists. This vast theater of woe is regarded as wholly outside the jurisdiction of government, while the most strenuous efforts are put forth to detect and punish the perpetrators of the least of the ordinary recognized crimes. This ignoring of great evils while so violently striking at small ones is the mark of an effete civilization, and warns us of the approaching dotage of the race.

Against the legitimate action of government in the protection of society from these worst of its evils, the instinctive hostility to government, or misarchy, above described, powerfully militates. In the face of it the government hesitates to take action, however clear the right or the method. But, as already remarked, this groundless over-caution against an impossible occurrence would not, in and of itself, have sufficed to prevent government from redressing such palpable wrongs. It has been nursed and kept alive for a specific purpose. It has formed the chief argument of those whose interests require the maintenance of the existing social order in relation to the distribution of wealth. Indeed, it is doubtful whether, without the incessant reiteration given to it by this class, it could have persisted to the present time. This inequitable economic system has itself been the product of centuries of astute management on the part of the shrewdest heads, with a view to securing by legal devices that undue share of the world's products which was formerly the reward of superior physical strength. It is clear to this class that their interests require a policy of strict non-interference on the part of government in what they call the natural laws of political economy, and they are quick to see that the old odium that still lingers among the people can be made a bulwark of strength for their position. They therefore never lose an opportunity to appeal to it in the most effective manner. Through the constant use of this *argumentum ad populum* the anti-government sentiment, which would naturally have smoldered and died out after its cause ceased to exist, is kept perpetually alive.

The great evils under which society now labors have grown up during the progress of intellectual supremacy. They have crept in stealthily during the gradual encroachment of organized cunning upon the domain of brute force. Over that vanishing domain, government retains its power, but it is still powerless in the expanding and now all-embracing field of psychic influence. No one ever claimed that in the trial of physical strength the booty should fall to the strongest. In all such cases the arm of government is stretched out and justice is enforced. But in those manifold, and far more unequal struggles now going on between mind and mind, or rather between the individual and an organized system, the product of ages of thought, it is customary to say that such matters must be left to regulate themselves, and that the fittest must be allowed to survive. Yet, to anyone who will candidly consider the matter, it must be clear that the first and principal acts of government openly and avowedly prevented, through forcible inter-ference, the natural results of all trials of physical strength. These much-talked-of laws of nature are violated every time the highway robber is arrested and sent to jail.

Primitive government, when only brute force was employed, was strong enough to secure the just and equitable distribution of wealth.

To-day, when mental force is everything, and physical force is nothing, it is powerless to accomplish this. This alone proves that government needs to be strengthened in its primary quality—the protection of society. There is no reasoning that applies to one kind of protection that does not apply equally to the other. It is utterly illogical to say that aggrandizement by physical force should be forbidden while aggrandizement by mental force or legal fiction should be permitted. It is absurd to claim that injustice committed by muscle should be regulated, while that committed by brain should be unrestrained.

While the modern plutocracy is not a form of government in the same sense that the other forms mentioned are, it is, nevertheless, easy to see that its power is as great as any government has ever wielded. The test of governmental power is usually the manner in which it taxes the people, and the strongest indictments ever drawn up against the worst forms of tyranny have been those which recited their oppressive methods of extorting tribute. But tithes are regarded as oppressive, and a fourth part of the yield of any industry would justify a revolt. Yet to-day there are many commodities for which the people pay two and three times as much as would cover the cost of production, transportation, and exchange at fair wages and fair profits. The monopolies in many lines actually tax the consumer from 25 to 75 per cent of the real value of the goods. Imagine an excise tax that should approach these figures! . . . [U]nder the operation of either monopoly or aggressive competition the price of everything is pushed up to the maximum limit that will be paid for the commodity in profitable quantities, and this wholly irrespective of the cost of production. No government in the world has now or ever had the power to enforce such an extortion as this. It is a governing power in the interest of favored individuals, which exceeds that of the most powerful monarch or despot that ever wielded a scepter.

What then is the remedy? How can society escape this last conquest of power by the egoistic intellect? It has overthrown the rule of brute force by the establishment of government. It has supplanted autocracy by aristocracy and this by democracy, and now it finds itself in the coils of plutocracy. Can it escape? Must it go back to autocracy for a power sufficient to cope with plutocracy? No autocrat ever had a tithe of that power. Shall it then let itself be crushed? It need not. There is one power and only one that is greater than that which now chiefly rules society. That power is society itself. There is one form of government that is stronger than autocracy or aristocracy or democracy, or even plutocracy, and that is *sociocracy*.

The individual has reigned long enough. The day has come for society to take its affairs into its own hands and shape its own destinies. The individual has acted as best he could. He has acted in the only way he could. With a consciousness, will, and intellect of his own he could do nothing else than pursue his natural ends. He should not be denounced nor called any names. He should not even be blamed. Nay, he should be praised, and even *imitated*. Society should learn its great lesson from him, should follow the path he has so clearly laid out that leads to success. It should imagine itself an individual, with all the interests of an individual, and becoming fully *conscious* of these interests it should pursue them with the same indomitable *will* with which the individual pursues his interests. Not only this, it must be guided, as he is guided, by the social *intellect*, armed with all the knowledge that all individuals combined, with so great labor, zeal, and talent have placed in its possession, constituting the social intelligence.

Sociocracy will differ from all other forms of government that have been devised, and yet that difference will not be so radical as to require a revolution. Just as absolute monarchy passed imperceptibly into limited monarchy, and this, in many states without even a change of name has passed into more or less pure democracy, so democracy is capable of passing as smoothly into sociocracy, and without taking on this unfamiliar name or changing that by which it is now known. For, though paradoxical, democracy, which is now the weakest of all forms of government, at least in the control of its own internal elements, is capable of becoming the strongest. Indeed, none of the other forms of government would be capable of passing directly into a government by society. Democracy is a phase through which they must first pass on any route that leads to the ultimate social stage which all governments must eventually attain if they persist.

How then, it may be asked, do democracy and sociocracy differ? How does society differ from the people? If the phrase "the people" really meant the people, the difference would be less. But that shibboleth of democratic states, where it means anything at all that can be described or defined, stands simply for the majority of qualified electors, no matter how small that majority may be. There is a sense in which the action of a majority may be looked upon as the action of society. At least, there is no denying the right of the majority to act for society, for to do this would involve either the denial of the right of government to act at all, or the admission of the right of a minority to act for society. But a majority acting for society is a different thing from society acting for itself, even though, as must always be the case, it acts through an agency chosen by its members. All democratic governments are largely party governments. The electors range themselves on one side or the other of some party line, the winning side considers itself the state as much as Louis the Fourteenth did. The losing party usually then regards the government as something alien to it and hostile, like an invader, and thinks of nothing but to gain strength enough to overthrow it at the next opportunity. While various issues are always brought forward and defended or attacked, it is obvious to the looker-on that the contestants care nothing for these, and merely use them to gain an advantage and win an election.

From the standpoint of society this is child's play. A very slight awakening of the social consciousness will banish it and substitute something more business-like. Once get rid of this puerile gaming spirit and have attention drawn to the real interests of society, and it will be seen that upon nearly all important questions all parties and all citizens are agreed, and that there is no need of this partisan strain upon the public energies. This is clearly shown at every change in the party complexion of the government. The victorious party which has been denouncing the government merely because it was in the hands of its political opponents boasts that it is going to revolutionize the country in the interest of good government, but the moment it comes into power and feels the weight of national responsibility it finds that it has little to do but carry out the laws in the same way that its predecessors had been doing.

There is a vast difference between all this outward show of partisanship and advocacy of so-called principles, and attention to the real interests and necessary business of the nation, which latter is what the government must do. It is a social duty. The pressure which is brought to enforce it is the power of the social will. But in the factitious excitement of partisan struggles where professional politicians and demagogues on the one hand, and the agents of plutocracy on the other, are shouting discordantly in the ears of the people, the real interests of society are, temporarily at least, lost sight of, clouded and obscured, and men lose their grasp on the real issues, forget even their own best interests, which, however selfish, would be a far safer guide, and the general result usually is that these are neglected and nations continue in the hands of mere politicians who are easily managed by the shrewd representatives of wealth.

Sociocracy will change all this. Irrelevant issues will be laid aside. The important objects upon which all but an interested few are agreed will receive their proper degree of attention, and measures will be considered in a non-partisan spirit with the sole purpose of securing these objects. Take as an illustration the postal telegraph question. No one not a stockholder in an existing telegraph company would prefer to pay twenty-five cents for a message if he could send it for ten cents. Where is the room for discussing a question of this nature? What society wants is the cheapest possible system. It wants to know with certainty whether a national postal telegraph system would secure this universally desired object. It is to be expected that the agents of the present telegraph companies would try to show that it would not succeed. This is according to the known laws of psychology as set forth in this work. But why be influenced by the interests of such a small number of persons, however worthy, when all the rest of mankind are interested in the opposite solution? The investigation should be a disinterested and strictly scientific one, and should actually settle the question in one way or the other. If it was found to be a real benefit, the system should be adopted. There are to-day a great number of these strictly social questions before the American people, questions which concern every citizen in the country, and whose solution would doubtless profoundly affect the state of civilization attainable on this continent. Not only is it impossible to secure this, but it is impossible to secure an investigation of them on their real merits. The same is true of other countries, and in general the prevailing democracies of the world are incompetent to deal with problems of social welfare.

The more extreme and important case referred to a few pages back may make the distinction still more clear. It was shown, and is known to all political economists, that the prices of most of the staple commodities consumed by mankind have no necessary relation to the cost of producing them and placing them in the hands of the consumer. It is always the highest price that the consumer will pay rather than do without. Let us suppose that price to be on an average double what it would cost to produce, transport, exchange, and deliver the goods, allowing in each of these transactions a fair compensation for all services rendered. Is there any member of society who would prefer to pay two dollars for what is thus fairly worth only one? Is there any sane ground for arguing such a question? Certainly not. The individual cannot correct this state of things. No democracy can correct it. But a government that really represented the interests of society would no more tolerate it than an individual would tolerate a continual extortion of money on the part of another without an equivalent.

And so it would be throughout. Society would inquire in a business way without fear, favor, or bias, into everything that concerned its welfare, and if it found obstacles it would remove them, and if it found opportunities it would improve them. In a word, society would do under the same circumstances just what an intelligent individual would do. It would further, in all possible ways, its own interests. . . .

29. BELLAMY

"Plutocracy or Nationalism—Which?"

Edward Bellamy (1850–1898) was born and spent most of his life in Chicopee Falls, Massachusetts. He received his education in the schools of that community and briefly attended Union College. Bellamy spent his eighteenth year traveling in Europe, and it was at this time that he first became interested in social and economic issues. Upon his return to the United States he studied law and was admitted to the bar; his first love, however, was writing. For a time he worked for the New York *Evening Post* and later founded a newspaper in Springfield, Massachusetts, with his brother. Still dissatisfied, he turned to writing short stories and novels. The most famous and important of his writings is *Looking Backward: 2000–1887* (1888). In the wake of the popularity and financial success of this book, Nationalist Clubs were created in many parts of the country to popularize the doctrines propounded by its author. Bellamy wrote and lectured and for a few years edited a nationalist magazine, the *New Nation*. This selection is taken from a speech given by Bellamy to the Nationalist Club at Tremont Temple, Boston, on May 31, 1889.

When Rome was the world's center, it used to be said that all roads led to Rome; so now, when the burden upon the heart of the world is the necessity of evolving a better society, it may be said that all lines of thought lead to the social question. For the sake of clearness, however, I shall this afternoon take up but a single thread of a single line of argument, namely, the economic. I shall speak of the present tendency to the concentration of the industrial and commercial business of the country in few and constantly fewer hands. The "Trust," or "Syndicate," in which this tendency finds its fullest expression, is recognized as one of the most significant phenomena of the day. In seeking a comparison for the bewildering effect produced by the appearance of the Trust above the business horizon, one can only think of the famous comets of past centuries and the terrors their rays diffused, turning nations into flocks of sheep and perplexing kings with fear of change. The advent of the Trust marks a crisis more important than a hundred presidential elections rolled into one—no less a crisis, in fact, than the beginning of the end of the competitive system in industry. And the end is going to be rather near the beginning. It is in vain that the newspapers sit up nights with the patient and the legislatures feed it with tonics. It is moribund. The few economists who still seriously defend the competitive system are heroically sacrificing their reputations in the effort to mask the evacuation of a position which, as nobody knows better than our hard-headed captains of industry, has become untenable. Surely there have been few, if any, events in history on which the human race can be so unreservedly congratulated as the approaching doom of the competitive system. From the beginning, Christianity has been at odds with its fundamental principle—the principle that the only title to the means of livelihood is the strength and cunning to get and keep. Between Christianity and the competitive system a sort of *modus vivendi* has indeed been patched up, but Christianity has not thriven upon it, and the friends of Christianity are today vigorously repudiating it. As for the humane and philanthropic spirit, it has always found itself set at naught, and practically dammed up, by a system of which sordid self-seeking is so absolutely the sole idea that kindliness, humanity and generous feeling simply will not mix with it, while charity deranges the whole machine.

The final plea for any form of brutality in these days is that it tends to the survival of the fittest; and very properly this plea has been advanced in favor of the system which is the sum of all brutalities. But the retort is prompt and final. If this were indeed so, if the richest were the best, there would never have been any social question. Disparities of condition would have been willingly endured, which were recognized as corresponding to virtue or public service. But so far is this from being the case that the competitive system seems rather to tend to the survival of the unfittest. Not that the rich are worse than the poor, but that the competitive system tends to develop what is worst in the character of all, whether rich or poor. The qualities which it discourages are the noblest and most generous that men have, and the qualities which it rewards are those selfish and sordid instincts which humanity can only hope to rise above by outgrowing. But perhaps the explanation of the panic which the critical condition of the competitive system excites in some quarters lies in a belief that whatever may be said as to the immoral aspects of it, it is nevertheless so potent a machine for the production of wealth as to be indispensable. If such a belief be entertained, it is certainly the most groundless of superstitions. The problem before any system of national industry is to get the greatest result out of the natural resources of a country and the capital and labor of a people. In what way then, let us inquire, has the competitive system undertaken to solve this problem? It would seem a matter of obvious common sense that it should of course proceed upon some carefully digested and elaborated system of work to begin with. We should expect to see a close and constant oversight to secure perfect cooperation and coordination between all departments of work and all the workers. But in fact the competitive system offers nothing of the sort. Instead of a carefully digested plan of operation, there is no general plan at all; there are as many plans as there are workers, some twenty millions. There is no general oversight even of an advisory sort. Every worker not only has his own plan but is his own commander-in-chief. Not only is there no cooperation between the workers, but each is doing all he possibly can to hinder those who are working near him. Finally, not only are they not working in cooperation, but they are not even working for the same end—that is, the general wealth; but each to get the most for himself. And this he does, as frequently as not, by courses not only not contributory to the general wealth, but destructive of it.

If one of you should apply the same method of planlessness, lack of oversight and utter lack of cooperation, to your own factory or farm, your friends would have you in an asylum in twenty-four hours, and be called long suffering at that. Not a man in the country would undertake to cultivate a quarter of an acre, not a woman would undertake Spring cleaning, without more plan, more system for economy of effort, than goes to the correlated management of the industries of the United States.

If you would form a vivid conception of the economical absurdity of the competitive system in industry, consider merely the fact that its only method of improving the quality or reducing the price of goods is by overdoing their production. Cheapness, in other words, can only result under competition from duplication and waste of effort. But things which are produced with waste of effort are really dear, whatever they may be called. Therefore, goods produced under competition are made cheap only by being made dear. Such is the *reductio ad absurdum* of the system. It is in fact often true that the goods we pay the least for are in the end the most expensive to the nation owing to the wasteful competition which keeps down the price. All waste must in the end mean loss and, therefore, about once in seven years the country has to go into insolvency as the result of a system which sets three men to fighting for work which one man could do.

To speak of the moral iniquities of competition would be to enter on too large a theme for this time, and I only advert in passing to one feature of our present industrial system in which it would be hard to say whether inhumanity or economic folly predominated, and refer to the grotesque manner in which the burden of work is distributed. The industrial press-gang robs the cradle and the grave, takes the wife and mother from the fireside, and old age from the chimney-corner, while at the same time hundreds of thousands of strong men fill the land with clamors for an opportunity to work. The women and children are delivered to the task-masters, while the men can find nothing to do. There is no work for the fathers but there is plenty for the babies.

What then is the secret of this alarm over the approaching doom of a system under which nothing can be done properly without doing it twice, which can do no business without overdoing it, which can produce nothing without over-production, which in a land full of want cannot find employment for strong and eager hands, and finally which gets along at all only at the cost of a total collapse every few years, followed by a lingering convalescence?

When a bad king is mourned by his people, the conclusion must be that the heir to the throne is a worse case still. That appears to be, in fact, the explanation of the present distress over the decay of the competitive system. It is because there is fear of going from bad to worse, and that the little finger of combination will be thicker than the loins of competition; that while the latter system has chastised the people with whips, the Trust will scourge them with scorpions. Like the children of Israel in the desert, this new and strange peril causes the timid to sigh even for the iron rule of Pharaoh. Let us see if there be not also in this case a promised land, by the prospect of which faint hearts may be encouraged.

Let us first enquire whether a return to the old order of things, the free competitive system, is possible. A brief consideration of the causes which have led to the present world-wide movement for the substitution of combination in business for competition will surely convince any one that, of all revolutions, this is the least likely to go backward. It is a result of the increase in the efficiency of capital in great masses, consequent upon the inventions of the last and present generations. In former epochs the size and scope of business enterprises were subject to natural restrictions. There were limits to the amount of capital that could be used to advantage by one management. Today there are no limits, save the earth's confines, to the scope of any business undertaking; and not only no limit to the amount of capital that can be used by one concern, but an increase in the efficiency and security of the business proportionate to the amount of capital in it. The economies in management resulting from consolidation, as well as the control over the market resulting from the monopoly of a staple, are also solid business reasons for the advent of the Trust. It must not be supposed, however, that the principle of combination has been extended to those businesses only which call themselves Trusts. That would be greatly to under-estimate the movement. There are many forms of combination less close than the Trust, and comparatively few businesses are now conducted without some understanding approaching to a combination with its former competitors—a combination tending constantly to become closer.

From the time that these new conditions began to prevail, the small businesses have been disappearing before the larger; the process has not been so rapid as people fancy whose attention has but lately been called to it. For twenty years past the great corporations have been carrying on a war of extermination against the swarm of small industrial enterprises which are the red blood corpuscles of a free competitive system and with the decay of which it dies. While the economists have been wisely debating whether we could dispense with the principle of individual initiative in business, that principle has passed away, and now belongs to history. Except in a few obscure corners of the business world, there is at present no opportunity for individual initiative in business unless backed by a large capital; and the size of the capital needed is rapidly increasing. Meanwhile, the same increase in the efficiency of capital in masses, which has destroyed the small businesses, has reduced the giants which have destroyed them to the necessity of making terms with one another. As in Bulwer Lytton's fancy of the coming race, the people of the Vril-ya had to give up war because their arms became so destructive as to threaten mutual annihilation, so the modern business world finds that the increase in the size and powers of the organizations of capital demands the suppression of competition between them, for the sake of self-preservation.

The first great group of business enterprises which adopted the principle of combining, instead of competing, made it necessary for every other group sooner or later to do the same or perish. For as the corporation is more powerful than the individual, so the syndicate overtops the corporation. The action of governments to check this logical necessity of economical evolution can produce nothing more than eddies in a current which nothing can check. Every week sees some new tract of what was once the great open sea of competition, wherein merchant adventurers used to fare forth with little capital besides their courage and come home loaded—every week now sees some new tract of this once open sea inclosed, dammed up, and turned into the private fish-pond of a syndicate.

I would also incidentally call your attention to the fact that these syndicates are largely foreign. Our new industrial lords are largely to be absentees. The British are invading the United States in these days with a success brilliantly in contrast with their former failures in that line. It is no wonder in these days, when the political basis of aristocracy is going to pieces, that foreign capitalists should rush into a market where industrial dukedoms, marquisates and baronies, richer than ever a king distributed to his favorites, are for sale. To say that from the present look of things the substantial consolidation of the various groups of industries in the country, under a few score great syndicates, is likely to be complete within fifteen years, is certainly not to venture a wholly rash statement.

So great an economic change as is involved in taking the conduct of the country's industries out of the hands of the people, and concentrating them in the management of a few great Trusts, could not, of course, be without important social reaction; and this is a reaction which is going to affect peculiarly what is called, in the hateful jargon of classes which we hope some day to do away with, the middle class. It is no longer a question merely for the poor and uneducated what they are to do with their work; but for the educated and well-to-do, also, where they are to find business to do and business investments to make. This difficulty cannot fail constantly to increase, as one tract after another of the formerly free field of competition is inclosed by a new syndicate. The middle class, the business class, is being turned into a proletarian class.

It is not difficult to forecast the ultimate issue of the concentration of industry if carried out on the lines at present indicated. Eventually, and at no very remote period, society must be divided into a few hundred families of prodigious wealth on the one hand, a professional class dependent upon their favor but excluded from equality with them and reduced to the state of lackeys; and underneath a vast population of working men and women, absolutely without hope of bettering a condition which would year by year sink them more and more hopelessly into serfdom.

This is not a pleasant picture, but I am sure it is not an exaggerated statement of the social consequences of the syndicate system carried out according to the plans of its managers. Are we going to permit the American people to be rounded up, corralled and branded as the dependents of some hundreds of great American and English families? It is well never to despair of the Republic, but it is well to remember that republics are saved not by a vague confidence in their good luck, but by the clear vision and courageous action of their citizens.

What, then, is the outcome? What way lies the Promised Land which we may reach? For back to Egypt we cannot go. The return to the old system of free competition and the day of small things is not a possibility. It would involve a turning backward of the entire stream of modern material progress.

If the nation does not wish to turn over its industries—and that means its liberties as well—to an industrial oligarchy, there is but one alternative; it must assume them itself. Plutocracy or Nationalism is the choice which, within ten years, the people of the United States will have virtually made.

Pray observe, ladies and gentlemen, that your argument is not with me, or with those of us who call ourselves Nationalists. We are not forcing upon you this alternative. The facts of the present state and tendencies of national affairs are doing it. Your controversy is with them, not with us. Convince yourself and your friends that this talk about the invasion and appropriation of the field of general business by Trusts and Syndicates is all nonsense; satisfy yourself from a careful study of the news of the day that there is really no tendency toward the concentration in the hands of a comparatively few powerful organizations of the means of the nation's livelihood, and you can afford to disregard us entirely. Nothing is more certain than that we cannot make a revolution with mere words, or unless the facts are with us. Once admit, however, that the Trusts and Syndicates are facts, and that business is rapidly being concentrated in their hands, and if you do not propose to submit to the state of things which these admitted facts portend, you have no choice but to be Nationalists. The burning issue of the period now upon us is to be, is already, Nationalism against Plutocracy. In its fierce heat the ties of old party allegiances are destined ere long to dissolve like wax.

There have been many movements for a nobler order of society which should embody and illustrate brotherly love, but they have failed because the time was not right; that is to say, because the material tendencies of the age did not work with the moral. Today they work together. Today it matters little how weak the voice of the preacher may be, for the current of affairs, the logic of events, is doing his work and preaching his sermon for him. This is why there is ground today for a higher-hearted hope that a great deliverance for humanity is at hand than was ever before justified. When sun and moon together pull the sea, a mighty tide is sure to come. So today, when the spiritual and economic tendencies of the time are for once working together; when the spirit of this age, and the divine spirit of all ages, for once are on the same side, hope becomes reason, and confidence is but common sense. Many, perhaps, have a vague idea of what Nationalism is, and may wish to know in just what ways our national assumption of the industries of the country is going to affect the people beneficially. Briefly it may be said that the result of this action will be to make the nation an equal industrial partnership of its members as it already is an equal political partnership. The people will have formed themselves into a great joint stock company for the general business of maintaining and enjoying life. In this company every man and woman will be an equal stockholder, and the annual dividends will constitute their means of subsistence. While all share alike in the profits of the business, all will share according to their strength in its service, the nation undertaking to provide employment for all adapted to their gifts and guaranteeing the industrious against the idle by making industrial service obligatory. In effect the nation will then have become a universal insurance company for the purpose of assuring all its members against want, oppression, accident, or disability of whatever sort. It will be a mighty trust holding all the assets of society, moral, intellectual, and material, not only for the use of the present and passing generation, but for the benefit of the future race, looking to the ends of the world and the judgment of God. This is Nationalism.

Economically, it will be observed that the Nationalization of industry presents the logical, conclusive, and complete form of the evolution from competition toward combination which is now in progress. Every economical argument for the partial consolidation of industry already being effected, together with many new ones, tends to prove that a complete National consolidation would create a system better adapted to wealth production than any the world has seen.

It is important to state that while the economic movement toward consolidation is greatly hastening the nationalization of industries, that result will belong strictly to another line of evolution—the political. That is to say, the National idea—which is that of the union of a people to use the collective strength for the common protection and welfare,—distinctly and logically involved from the beginning the eventual nationalization of industry and the placing of the livelihood of the people under the national guarantee. If this be the true conception of a nation, then how preposterous is the notion that the mere exclusive possession, as against foreign nations, of a tract of land, in any true sense constitutes nationality. The house-lot is not a house. Such a community has merely secured a place on which to build a nation, that is all. The nation may be built or not. If it is built, it will consist in a social structure so roofed over and meetly joined together and so arranged within in all its details, as to provide in the highest possible degree for the happiness and welfare of all its people. Where are any such nations? you may well ask. And I reply that there are none, and never have been any. We consider that the time is now arrived for building such nations, and that the first such nation will be built in America. We call ourselves Nationalists because we have faith in this true nation that is to be, and have given our hearts and our allegiance to it while yet it is unborn. . . .

30. POPULIST PARTY

Expanding the People's Power

The agrarian protest of the post-Civil War period reached its peak of influence between 1890 and 1896. By 1890 the many Farmers' Alliances had combined into three major organizations—the Northwestern Alliance, the Southern Alliance, and the Colored Alliance. In South Carolina, Tennessee, and Georgia the Alliances secured control of the Democratic Party, and in Nebraska, Minnesota, Kansas, and South Dakota they cooperated with the Democrats to gain control of the state governments. Alliance leaders, made bold by their successes and convinced that the two major political parties could not function as instruments of reform, decided to form a third party. The People's Party, or Populist Party, met in convention at Omaha, Nebraska, on July 4, 1892. Its platform,* largely written by Ignatius Donnelly of Minnesota, set forth a ringing demand for political, social, and economic reform.

Assembled upon the 116th anniversary of the Declaration of Independence, the People's Party of America, in their first national convention, invoking upon their action the blessing of Almighty God, put forth in the name and on behalf of the people of this country, the following preamble and declaration of principles:

PREAMBLE

The conditions which surround us best justify our cooperation; we meet in the midst of a nation brought to the verge of moral, political, and material ruin. Corruption dominates the ballot-box, the Legislature, the Congress, and touches even the ermine of the bench. The people are demoralized; most of the states have been compelled to isolate the voters at the polling places to prevent universal intimidation and bribery. The newspapers are largely subsidized or muzzled, public opinion silenced, business prostrated, homes covered with mortgages,

* *The World Almanac, 1893*, pp. 83–85.

labor impoverished, and the land concentrating in the hands of capitalists. The urban workmen are denied the right to organize for self-protection, imported pauperized labor beats down their wages, a hireling standing army, unrecognized by our laws, is established to shoot them down, and they are rapidly degenerating into European conditions. The fruits of the toil of millions are boldly stolen to build up colossal fortunes for a few, unprecedented in the history of mankind; and the possessors of those, in turn, despite the Republic and endanger liberty. From the same prolific womb of governmental injustice we breed the two great classes—tramps and millionaires.

The national power to create money is appropriated to enrich bondholders; a vast public debt payable in legal tender currency has been funded into gold-bearing bonds, thereby adding millions to the burdens of the people.

Silver, which has been accepted as coin since the dawn of history, has been demonetized to add to the purchasing power of gold by decreasing the value of all forms of property as well as human labor, and the supply of currency is purposely abridged to fatten usurers, bankrupt enterprise, and enslave industry. A vast conspiracy against mankind has been organized on two continents, and it is rapidly taking possession of the world. If not met and overthrown at once it forebodes terrible social convulsions, the destruction of civilization, or the establishment of an absolute despotism.

We have witnessed for more than a quarter of a century the struggles of the two great political parties for power and plunder, while grievous wrongs have been inflicted upon the suffering people. We charge that the controlling influences dominating both these parties have permitted the existing dreadful conditions to develop without serious effort to prevent or restrain them. Neither do they now promise us any substantial reform. They have agreed together to ignore, in the coming campaign, every issue but one. They propose to drown the outcries of a plundered people with the uproar of a sham battle over the tariff, so that capitalists, corporations, national banks, rings, trusts, watered stock, the demonetization of silver and the oppressions of the usurers may all be lost sight of. They propose to sacrifice our homes, lives, and children on the altar of mammon; to destroy the multitude in order to secure corruption funds from the millionaires.

Assembled on the anniversary of the birthday of the nation, and filled with the spirit of the grand general and chief who established our independence, we seek to restore the government of the Republic to the hands of "the plain people," with which class it originated. We assert our purposes to be identical with the purposes of the National Constitution; to form a more perfect union and establish justice, insure domestic tranquillity, provide for the common defence, promote the general welfare, and secure the blessings of liberty for ourselves and our posterity.

We declare that this Republic can only endure as a free government while built upon the love of the whole people for each other and for the nation; that it cannot be pinned together by bayonets; that the civil war is over, and that every passion and resentment which grew out of it must die with it, and that we must be in fact, as we are in name, one united brotherhood of free men.

Our country finds itself confronted by conditions for which there is no precedent in the history of the world; our annual agricultural productions amount to billions of dollars in value, which must, within a few weeks or months, be exchanged for billions of dollars' worth of commodities consumed in their production; the existing currency supply is wholly inadequate to make this exchange; the results are falling prices, the formation of combines and rings, the impoverishment of the producing class. We pledge ourselves that if given power we will labor to correct these evils by wise and reasonable legislation, in accordance with the terms of our platform.

We believe that the power of government—in other words, of the people—should be expanded (as in the case of the postal service) as rapidly and as far as the good sense of an intelligent people and the teachings of experience shall justify, to the end that oppression, injustice, and poverty shall eventually cease in the land.

While our sympathies as a party of reform are naturally upon the side of every proposition which will tend to make men intelligent, virtuous, and temperate, we nevertheless regard these questions, important as they are, as secondary to the great issues now pressing for solution, and upon which not only our individual prosperity but the very existence of free institutions depend; and we ask all men to first help us to determine whether we are to have a republic to administer before we differ as to the conditions upon which it is to be administered, believing that the forces of reform this day organized will never cease to move forward until every wrong is remedied and equal rights and equal privileges securely established for all the men and women of this country.

PLATFORM

We declare, therefore—

First.—That the union of the labor forces of the United States this day consummated shall be permanent and perpetual; may its spirit enter into all hearts for the salvation of the Republic and the uplifting of mankind.

Second.—Wealth belongs to him who creates it, and every dollar taken from industry without an equivalent is robbery. "If any will not work, neither shall he eat." The interests of rural and civic labor are the same; their enemies are identical.

Third.—We believe that the time has come when the railroad corporations will either own the people or the people must own the railroads, and should the government enter upon the work of owning and managing all railroads, we should favor an amendment to the Constitution by which all persons engaged in the government service shall be placed under a civil-service regulation of the most rigid character, so as to prevent the increase of the power of the national administration by the use of such additional government employés.

FINANCE.—We demand a national currency, safe, sound, and flexible, issued by the general government only, a full legal tender for all debts, public and private, and that without the use of banking corporations, a just, equitable, and efficient means of distribution direct to the people, at a tax not to exceed 2 per cent. per annum, to be provided as set forth in the sub-treasury plan of the Farmers' Alliance, or a better system; also by payments in discharge of its obligations for public improvements.

1. We demand free and unlimited coinage of silver and gold at the present legal ratio of 16 to 1.

2. We demand that the amount of circulating medium be speedily increased to not less than $50 per capita.

3. We demand a graduated income tax.

4. We believe that the money of the country should be kept as much as possible in the hands of the people, and hence we demand that all State and national revenues shall be limited to the necessary expenses of the government, economically and honestly administered.

5. We demand that postal savings banks be established by the government for the safe deposit of the earnings of the people and to facilitate exchange.

TRANSPORTATION.—Transportation being a means of exchange and a public necessity, the government should own and operate the railroads in the interest of the people. The telegraph, telephone, like the post-office system, being a necessity for the transmission of news, should be owned and operated by the government in the interest of the people.

LAND.—The land, including all the natural sources of wealth, is the heritage of the people, and should not be monopolized for specu-lative purposes, and alien ownership of land should be prohibited. All land now held by railroads and other corporations in excess of their actual needs, and all lands now owned by aliens should be reclaimed by the government and held for actual settlers only.

EXPRESSION OF SENTIMENTS

Your Committee on Platform and Resolutions beg leave unanimously to report the following:

Whereas, Other questions have been presented for our consideration, we hereby submit the following, not as a part of the Platform of the People's Party, but as resolutions expressive of the sentiment of this Convention:

1. *Resolved*, That we demand a free ballot and a fair count in all elections, and pledge ourselves to secure it to every legal voter without Federal intervention, through the adoption by the States of the unperverted Australian or secret ballot system.

2. *Resolved*, That the revenue derived from a graduated income tax should be applied to the reduction of the burden of taxation now levied upon the domestic industries of this country.

3. *Resolved*, That we pledge our support to fair and liberal pensions to ex-Union soldiers and sailors.

4. *Resolved*, That we condemn the fallacy of protecting American labor under the present system, which opens our ports to the pauper and criminal classes of the world and crowds out our wage-earners; and we denounce the present ineffective laws against contract labor, and demand the further restriction of undesirable emigration.

5. *Resolved*, That we cordially sympathize with the efforts of organized workingmen to shorten the hours of labor, and demand a rigid enforcement of the existing eight-hour law on Government work, and ask that a penalty clause be added to the said law.

6. *Resolved*, That we regard the maintenance of a large standing army of mercenaries, known as the Pinkerton system, as a menace to our liberties, and we demand its abolition; and we condemn the recent invasion of the Territory of Wyoming by the hired assassins of pluto-cracy, assisted by Federal officers.

7. *Resolved*, That we commend to the favorable consideration of the people and the reform press the legislative system known as the initiative and referendum.

8. *Resolved*, That we favor a constitutional provision limiting the office of President and Vice-President to one term, and providing for the election of Senators of the United States by a direct vote of the people.

9. *Resolved*, That we oppose any subsidy or national aid to any private corporation for any purpose.

10. *Resolved*, That this convention sympathizes with the Knights of Labor* and their righteous contest with the tyrannical combine of clothing manufacturers of Rochester, and declares it to be the duty of all who hate tyranny and oppression to refuse to purchase the goods made by the said manufacturers, or to patronize any merchants who sell such goods.

---

* [An American labor organization formed in 1869. It reached its peak of influence and size in the 1880's but soon collapsed as a result of factional and financial weaknesses.—Ed.]

VI

The Law as an Instrument of Social Change

American law at the end of the nineteenth century increasingly reflected the social, economic, and political views of the nation's conservative interests. The tradition of natural law supplemented by nineteenth-century historical jurisprudence combined to provide the legal defense for conservatism. These legal philosophies emphasized the fixed, certain nature of law and the absence of judicial discretion in deciding cases.

Individualism, competition, laissez-faire, and the rights of property were the main tenets of post-Civil War conservatism. Legal rules and the biases of judges who operated behind the pretense of neutrality secured and enforced these basic conservative doctrines. The Supreme Court of the United States was the most important instrument for implementing these beliefs. From the last decade of the nineteenth century until 1937 the Court persistently applied conservative principles to its interpretation of American constitutional law.

America's legal conservatism was never without its opponents, even during the period of its greatest influence. The work of these critics in attacking the conservative legal order and in developing a different conception of law constitutes an important body of American liberal thought during the late nineteenth and early twentieth centuries.

Oliver Wendell Holmes, Jr., holds a central place in the history of this development. His importance rests in large measure on his essentially destructive criticism of this nation's nineteenth-century legal order. In two essays, "The Path of the Law" and "Natural Law," Holmes attacked the main doctrines of the established legal system: its belief in the basic importance of logic and history and its acceptance of natural law.

While not rejecting the importance of logic, Holmes denied that it was the dominant characteristic of the law. On the opening page of his celebrated work *The Common Law*, Holmes singled out for criticism this overemphasis on logic and stated his own views on the sources of the law:

The life of the law has not been logic: it has been experience. The felt necessities of the time, the prevalent moral and political theories, intuitions

243

of public policy avowed or unconscious, even the prejudices which judges share with their fellow men, have had a good deal more to do than the syllogism in determining the rules by which men should be governed.[1]

Holmes was also sharply critical of the role judges played in the legal system of his time. Behind the façade of certainty and judicial impartiality supplied by rules and logic, judges allowed their private conceptions of right and wrong to influence public policy. Their behavior violated the central principle governing Holmes' legal thought: "The first requirement of a sound body of law is that it should correspond with the actual feelings and demands of the community, whether right or wrong."[2]

It was from this conception of the law that Holmes developed his belief in judicial self-restraint. The determination of public policy is to be left to the legislative branch of government; judges are not to substitute their private views for those of the majority of the people as expressed through national and state legislatures. In his dissenting opinion in Lochner v. New York, 198 U.S. 45, 75 (1905), a case involving the constitutionality of a New York State maximum hours law for bakers, Holmes expressed his philosophy of judicial self-restraint:

> This case is decided upon an economic theory which a large part of the community does not entertain. If it were a question whether I agreed with that theory, I should desire to study it further and long before making up my mind. But I do not conceive that to be my duty, because I strongly believe that my agreement or disagreement has nothing to do with the right of a majority to embody their opinion in law.

It is ironic that Holmes should have influenced and been idolized by several generations of American liberals, for he had no program of reform and, indeed, was skeptical and even sarcastic about reformers and their plans. "I have no belief in panaceas and almost none in sudden ruin,"[3] he once stated. In a more critical vein he wrote of socialism: "The notion that with socialized property we should have women free and a piano for everybody seems to me an empty humbug."[4]

---

[1] *The Common Law* (Boston: Little, Brown, 1881), p. 1.
[2] *Ibid.*, p. 41.
[3] Oliver Wendell Holmes, Jr., "Law and the Court," in *Collected Legal Papers* (New York: Harcourt, Brace and Company, 1921), p. 295.
[4] Holmes, "Ideals and Doubts," *ibid.*, p. 306.

But Holmes' influence on twentieth-century liberalism came not in his positive proposals for social reform but in his undermining of the established legal tradition and in his espousal of judicial self-restraint. His criticism enabled positive legal reformers such as Roscoe Pound and Louis Brandeis to build new, socially oriented judicial philosophies upon the debris of the old way of thought; his belief in judicial self-restraint permitted liberal reformers to circumscribe the powers of the courts and allow legislatures the freedom to experiment with new social and economic policies. The triumph of Holmes' doctrine of restraint came in the wake of the battle over President Roosevelt's Court Reform Plan of 1937. Since that year the Supreme Court has not declared unconstitutional a single national law based on Congress' power over interstate commerce.

Roscoe Pound, like Holmes, was also a critic of nineteenth-century American law. His early writings are replete with attacks on the supposed certainty of the law and the nonsubjective mechanical functioning of judges. In addition, there is in much of Pound's work criticism of the excessive individualism of this nation's laws. But Pound was not content with being merely a critic. Far more than Holmes he busied himself with the task of constructing a new jurisprudence that would suit the needs of a twentieth-century industrial society.

Pound's criticism of the needless individualism of American law and his call for a more collective conception of law founded on social and economic knowledge is clearly brought out in his *Introduction to the Philosophy of Law*. Pound's moderation—his gradualist approach to legal reform—obscures the profound impact he has exerted on America's legal system. More than any other man, Pound led American jurisprudence into the twentieth century; he provided the theoretical justification for the vast amount of social and economic legislation adopted in this century and for the recognition by courts of the interrelationship of the law and the social sciences.

31. HOLMES

"The Path of the Law"

Oliver Wendell Holmes, Jr. (1841–1935), the son of the famous New England literary personality of the mid-nineteenth century, was born in Boston and received his early education from private tutors. He was graduated from Harvard College in 1861, several months after the outbreak of the Civil War, and immediately enlisted as a lieutenant with the 20th Massachusetts Volunteers. He was wounded three times during the war, twice seriously at Ball's Bluff in 1861 and at Antietam in 1862. Following his discharge from service Holmes entered Harvard Law School and received his LLB in 1866. He engaged in private law practice in Boston from 1873 until 1882 and then briefly taught law at Harvard. Much of his prestige as a legal scholar at this time stemmed from the Lowell Lectures he delivered in 1880, which were published in book form the following year as *The Common Law*. In 1882, at the age of forty-one, Holmes was appointed associate justice of the supreme judicial court of Massachusetts, and he continued to hold this position until 1899, when he was elevated to chief justice of the court. Finally, in 1902, President Theodore Roosevelt nominated the jurist to the United States Supreme Court, where Holmes served for twenty-nine years until his retirement in January, 1932.

This selection* from Justice Holmes' writings is taken from his important and influential 1897 essay "The Path of the Law."

When we study law we are not studying a mystery but a well known profession. We are studying what we shall want in order to appear before judges, or to advise people in such a way as to keep them out of court. The reason why it is a profession, why people will pay lawyers to argue for them or to advise them, is that in societies like ours the command of the public force is intrusted to the judges in

* *Harvard Law Review*, X (1896–97), pp. 457–61, 464–69, 473–74.

certain cases, and the whole power of the state will be put forth, if necessary, to carry out their judgments and decrees. People want to know under what circumstances and how far they will run the risk of coming against what is so much stronger than themselves, and hence it becomes a business to find out when this danger is to be feared. The object of our study, then, is prediction, the prediction of the incidence of the public force through the instrumentality of the courts.

The means of the study are a body of reports, of treatises, and of statutes, in this country and in England, extending back for six hundred years, and now increasing annually by hundreds. In these sibylline leaves are gathered the scattered prophecies of the past upon the cases in which the axe will fall. These are what properly have been called the oracles of the law. Far the most important and pretty nearly the whole meaning of every new effort of legal thought is to make these prophecies more precise, and to generalize them into a thoroughly connected system. The process is one, from a lawyer's statement of a case, eliminating as it does all the dramatic elements with which his client's story has clothed it, and retaining only the facts of legal import, up to the final analyses and abstract universals of theoretic jurisprudence. The reason why a lawyer does not mention that his client wore a white hat when he made a contract, while Mrs. Quickly would be sure to dwell upon it along with the parcel gilt goblet and the sea-coal fire, is that he forsees that the public force will act in the same way whatever his client had upon his head. It is to make the prophecies easier to be remembered and to be understood that the teachings of the decisions of the past are put into general propositions and gathered into text-books, or that statutes are passed in a general form. The primary rights and duties with which jurisprudence busies itself again are nothing but prophecies. One of the many evil effects of the confusion between legal and moral ideas, about which I shall have something to say in a moment, is that theory is apt to get the cart before the horse, and to consider the right or the duty as something existing apart from and independent of the consequences of its breach, to which certain sanctions are added afterward. But, as I shall try to show, a legal duty so called is nothing but a prediction that if a man does or omits certain things he will be made to suffer in this or that way by judgment of the court;— and so of a legal right.

The number of our predictions when generalized and reduced to a system is not unmanageably large. They present themselves as a finite body of dogma which may be mastered within a reasonable time. It is a great mistake to be frightened by the ever increasing number of reports. The reports of a given jurisdiction in the course of a generation take up pretty much the whole body of the law, and restate it from the present point of view. We could reconstruct the corpus from them if all that went before were burned. The use of the earlier reports is mainly historical, a use about which I shall have something to say before I have finished.

I wish, if I can, to lay down some first principles for the study of this body of dogma or systematized prediction which we call the law, for men who want to use it as the instrument of their business to enable them to prophesy in their turn, and, as bearing upon the study, I wish to point out an ideal which as yet our law has not attained.

The first thing for a business-like understanding of the matter is to understand its limits, and therefore I think it desirable at once to point out and dispel a confusion between morality and law, which sometimes rises to the height of conscious theory, and more often and indeed constantly is making trouble in detail without reaching the point of consciousness. You can see very plainly that a bad man has as much reason as a good one for wishing to avoid an encounter with the public force, and therefore you can see the practical importance of the distinction between morality and law. A man who cares nothing for an ethical rule which is believed and practised by his neighbors is likely nevertheless to care a good deal to avoid being made to pay money, and will want to keep out of jail if he can.

I take it for granted that no hearer of mine will misinterpret what I have to say as the language of cynicism. The law is the witness and external deposit of our moral life. Its history is the history of the moral development of the race. The practice of it, in spite of popular jests, tends to make good citizens and good men. When I emphasize the difference between law and morals I do so with reference to a single end, that of learning and understanding the law. For that purpose you must definitely master its specific marks, and it is for that that I ask you for the moment to imagine yourselves indifferent to other and greater things.

I do not say that there is not a wider point of view from which the distinction between law and morals becomes of secondary or no importance, as all mathematical distinctions vanish in presence of the infinite. But I do say that that distinction is of the first importance for the object which we are here to consider,—a right study and mastery of the law as a business with well understood limits, a body of dogma enclosed within definite lines. I have just shown the practical reason for saying so. If you want to know the law and nothing else, you must look at it as a bad man, who cares only for the material consequences which such knowledge enables him to predict, not as a good one, who finds his reasons for conduct, whether inside the law or outside of it, in the vaguer sanctions of conscience. The theoretical importance of the distinction is no less, if you would reason on your subject aright. The law is full of phraseology drawn from morals, and by the mere force of language continually invites us to pass from one domain to the other without perceiving it, as we are sure to do unless we have the boundary constantly before our minds. The law talks about rights, and duties, and malice, and intent, and negligence, and so forth, and nothing is easier, or, I may say, more common in legal reasoning, than to take these words in their moral sense, at some stage of the argument, and so to drop into fallacy. For instance, when we speak of the rights of man in a moral sense, we mean to mark the limits of interference with individual freedom which we think are prescribed by conscience, or by our ideal, however reached. Yet it is certain that many laws have been enforced in the past, and it is likely that some are enforced now, which are condemned by the most enlightened opinion of the time, or which at all events pass the limit of interference as many consciences would draw it. Manifestly, therefore, nothing but confusion of thought can result from assuming that the rights of man in a moral sense are equally rights in the sense of the Constitution and the law. No doubt simple and extreme cases can be put of imaginable laws which the statute-making power would not dare to enact, even in the absence of written constitutional prohibitions, because the community would rise in rebellion and fight; and this gives some plausibility to the proposition that the law, if not a part of morality, is limited by it. But this limit of power is not coextensive with any system of morals. For the most part it falls far within the lines of any such system, and in some cases may extend beyond them, for reasons drawn from the habits of a particular people at a particular time. I once heard the late Professor Agassiz say that a German population would rise if you added two cents to the price of a glass of beer. A statute in such a case would be empty words, not because it was wrong, but because it could not be enforced. No one will deny that wrong statutes can be and are enforced, and we should not all agree as to which were the wrong ones.

The confusion with which I am dealing besets confessedly legal conceptions. Take the fundamental question, What constitutes the law? You will find some text writers telling you that it is something different from what is decided by the courts of Massachusetts or England, that it is a system of reason, that it is a deduction from principles of ethics or admitted axioms or what not, which may or may not coincide with the decisions. But if we take the view of our friend the bad man we shall find that he does not care two straws for the axioms or deductions, but that he does want to know what the Massachusetts or English courts are likely to do in fact. I am much of his mind. The prophecies of what the courts will do in fact, and nothing more pretentious, are what I mean by the law. . . .

So much for the limits of the law. The next thing which I wish to consider is what are the forces which determine its content and its growth. You may assume, with Hobbes and Bentham and Austin, that all law emanates from the sovereign, even when the first human beings to enunciate it are the judges, or you may think that law is the voice of the Zeitgeist, or what you like. It is all one to my present purpose. Even if every decision required the sanction of an emperor with despotic power and a whimsical turn of mind, we should be interested none the less, still with a view to prediction, in discovering some order, some rational explanation, and some principle of growth for the rules which he laid down. In every system there are such explanations and principles to be found. It is with regard to them that a second fallacy comes in, which I think it important to expose.

The fallacy to which I refer is the notion that the only force at work in the development of the law is logic. In the broadest sense, indeed, that notion would be true. The postulate on which we think about the universe is that there is a fixed quantitative relation between every phenomenon and its antecedents and consequents. If there is such a thing as a phenomenon without these fixed quantitative relations, it is a miracle. It is outside the law of cause and effect, and as such transcends our power of thought, or at least is something to or from which we cannot reason. The condition of our thinking about the universe is that it is capable of being thought about rationally, or, in other words, that every part of it is effect and cause in the same sense in which those parts are with which we are most familiar. So in the broadest sense it is true that the law is a logical development, like everything else. The danger of which I speak is not the admission that the principles governing other phenomena also govern the law, but the notion that a given system, ours, for instance, can be worked out like mathematics from some general axioms of conduct. This is the natural error of the schools, but it is not confined to them. I once heard a very eminent judge say that he never let a decision go until he was absolutely sure that it was right. So judicial dissent often is blamed, as if it meant simply that one side or the other were not doing their sums right, and, if they would take more trouble, agreement inevitably would come.

This mode of thinking is entirely natural. The training of lawyers is a training in logic. The processes of analogy, discrimination, and deduction are those in which they are most at home. The language of judicial decision is mainly the language of logic. And the logical method and form flatter that longing for certainty and for repose which is in every human mind. But certainty generally is illusion, and repose is not the destiny of man. Behind the logical form lies a judgment as to the relative worth and importance of competing legislative grounds, often an inarticulate and unconscious judgment, it is true, and yet the very root and nerve of the whole proceeding. You can give any conclusion a logical form. You always can imply a condition in a contract. But why do you imply it? It is because of some belief as to the practice of the community or of a class, or because of some opinion as to policy, or, in short, because of some attitude of yours upon a matter not capable of exact quantitative measurement, and therefore not capable of founding exact logical conclusions. Such matters really are battle grounds where the means do not exist for determinations that shall be good for all time, and where the decision can do no more than embody the preference of a given body in a given time and place. We do not realize how large a part of our law is open to reconsideration upon a slight change in the habit of the public mind. No concrete proposition is self-evident, no matter how ready we may be to accept it, not even Mr. Herbert Spencer's. "Every man has a right to do what he wills, provided he interferes not with a like right on the part of his neighbors." . . .

I think that the judges themselves have failed adequately to recognize their duty of weighing considerations of social advantage. The duty is inevitable, and the result of the often proclaimed judicial aversion to deal with such considerations is simply to leave the very ground and foundation of judgments inarticulate, and often unconscious, as I have said. When socialism first began to be talked about, the comfortable classes of the community were a good deal frightened. I suspect that this fear has influenced judicial action both here and in England, yet it is certain that it is not a conscious factor in the decisions to which I refer. I think that something similar has led people who no longer hope to control the legislatures to look to the courts as expounders of the Constitutions, and that in some courts new principles have been discovered outside the bodies of those instruments, which may be generalized into acceptance of the economic doctrines which prevailed about fifty years ago, and a wholesale prohibition of what a tribunal of lawyers does not think about right. I cannot but believe that if the training of lawyers led them habitually to consider more definitely and explicitly the social advantage on which the rule they lay down must be justified, they sometimes would hesitate where now they are confident, and see that really they were taking sides upon debatable and often burning questions.

So much for the fallacy of logical form. Now let us consider the present condition of the law as a subject for study, and the ideal toward which it tends. We still are far from the point of view which I desire to see reached. No one has reached it or can reach it as yet. We are only at the beginning of a philosophical reaction, and of a reconsideration of the worth of doctrines which for the most part still are taken for granted without any deliberate, conscious, and systematic questioning of their grounds. The development of our law has gone on for nearly a thousand years, like the development of a plant, each generation taking the inevitable next step, mind, like matter, simply obeying a law of spontaneous growth. It is perfectly natural and right that it should have been so. Imitation is a necessity of human nature, as has been illustrated by a remarkable French writer, M. Tarde, in an admirable book, "Les Lois de l'Imitation." Most of the things we do, we do for no better reason than that our fathers have done them or that our neighbors do them, and the same is true of a larger part than we suspect of what we think. The reason is a good one, because our short life gives us no time for a better, but it is not the best. It does not follow, because we all are compelled to take on faith at second hand most of the rules on which we base our action and our thought, that each of us may not try to set some corner of his world in the order of reason, or that all of us collectively should not aspire to carry reason as far as it will go throughout the whole domain. In regard to the law, it is true, no doubt, that an evolutionist will hesitate to affirm universal validity for his social ideals, or for the principles which he thinks should be embodied in legislation. He is content if he can prove them best for here and now. He may be ready to admit that he knows nothing about an absolute best in the cosmos, and even that he knows next to nothing about a permanent best for men. Still it is true that a body of law is more rational and more civilized when every rule it contains is referred articulately and definitely to an end which it subserves, and when the grounds for desiring that end are stated or are ready to be stated in words.

At present, in very many cases, if we want to know why a rule of law has taken its particular shape, and more or less if we want to know why it exists at all, we go to tradition. We follow it into the Year Books, and perhaps beyond them to the customs of the Salian Franks, and somewhere in the past, in the German forests, in the needs of Norman kings, in the assumptions of a dominant class, in the absence of generalized ideas, we find out the practical motive for what now best is justified by the mere fact of its acceptance and that men are accustomed to it. The rational study of law is still to a large extent the study of history. History must be a part of the study, because without it we cannot know the precise scope of rules which it is our business to know. It is a part of the rational study, because it is the first step toward an enlightened scepticism, that is, toward a deliberate reconsideration of the worth of those rules. When you get the dragon out of his cave on to the plain and in the daylight, you can count his teeth and claws, and see just what is his strength. But to get him out is only the first step. The next is either to kill him, or to tame him and make him a useful animal. For the rational study of the law the black-letter man may be the man of the present, but the man of the future is the man of statistics and the master of economics. It is revolting to have no better reason for a rule of law than that so it was laid down in the time of Henry IV. It is still more revolting if the grounds upon which it was laid down have vanished long since, and the rule simply persists from blind imitation of the past. . . .

I trust that no one will understand me to be speaking with disrespect of the law, because I criticise it so freely. I venerate the law, and especially our system of law, as one of the vastest products of the human mind. No one knows better than I do the countless number of great intellects that have spent themselves in making some addition or improvement, the greatest of which is trifling when compared with the mighty whole. It has the final title to respect that it exists, that it is not a Hegelian dream, but a part of the lives of men. But one may criticise even what one reveres. Law is the business to which my life is devoted, and I should show less than devotion if I did not do what in me lies to improve it, and, when I perceive what seems to me the ideal of its future, if I hesitated to point out and to press toward it with all my heart.

Perhaps I have said enough to show the part which the study of history necessarily plays in the intelligent study of the law as it is to-day. . . . We must beware of the pitfall of antiquarianism, and must remember that for our purposes our only interest in the past is for the light it throws upon the present. I look forward to a time when the part played by history in the explanation of dogma shall be very small, and instead of ingenious research we shall spend our energy on a study of the ends sought to be attained and the reasons for desiring them. As a step toward that ideal it seems to me that every lawyer ought to seek an understanding of economics. The present divorce between the schools of political economy and law seems to me an evidence of how much progress in philosophical study still remains to be made. In the present state of political economy, indeed, we come again upon history on a larger scale, but there we are called on to consider and weigh the ends of legislation, the means of attaining them, and the cost. We learn that for everything we have to give up something else, and we are taught to set the advantage we gain against the other advantage we lose, and to know what we are doing when we elect. . . .

32. HOLMES
"Natural Law"

The doctrine of natural law has existed as part of Western philosophical thought since the time of ancient Rome, but Holmes remained unimpressed by these credentials. In a 1918 essay,* Holmes turned his devastating skepticism to the subject of natural law.

It is not enough for the knight of romance that you agree that his lady is a very nice girl—if you do not admit that she is the best that God ever made or will make, you must fight. There is in all men a

* "Natural Law," 32 *Harvard Law Review*, pp. 40–44; copyright 1918 by The Harvard Law Review Association. By permission.

demand for the superlative, so much so that the poor devil who has no other way of reaching it attains it by getting drunk. It seems to me that this demand is at the bottom of the philosopher's effort to prove that truth is absolute and of the jurist's search for criteria of universal validity which he collects under the head of natural law.

I used to say, when I was young, that truth was the majority vote of that nation that could lick all others. Certainly we may expect that the received opinion about the present war will depend a good deal upon which side wins, (I hope with all my soul it will be mine), and I think that the statement was correct in so far as it implied that our test of truth is a reference to either a present or an imagined future majority in favor of our view. If, as I have suggested elsewhere, the truth may be defined as the system of my (intellectual) limitations, what gives its objectivity is the fact that I find my fellow man to a greater or less extent (never wholly) subject to the same *Can't Helps*. If I think that I am sitting at a table I find that the other persons present agree with me; so if I say that the sum of the angles of a triangle is equal to two right angles. If I am in a minority of one they send for a doctor or lock me up; and I am so far able to transcend the to me convincing testimony of my senses or my reason as to recognize that if I am alone probably something is wrong with my works.

Certitude is not the test of certainty. We have been cock-sure of many things that were not so. If I may quote myself again, property, friendship, and truth have a common root in time. One can not be wrenched from the rocky crevices into which one has grown for many years without feeling that one is attacked in one's life. What we most love and revere generally is determined by early associations. I love granite rocks and barberry bushes, no doubt because with them were my earliest joys that reach back through the past eternity of my life. But while one's experience thus makes certain preferences dogmatic for oneself, recognition of how they came to be so leaves one able to see that others, poor souls, may be equally dogmatic about something else. And this again means scepticism. Not that one's belief or love does not remain. Not that we would not fight and die for it if important —we all, whether we know it or not, are fighting to make the kind of a world that we should like—but that we have learned to recognize that others will fight and die to make a different world, with equal sincerity or belief. Deep-seated preferences can not be argued about— you can not argue a man into liking a glass of beer—and therefore, when differences are sufficiently far reaching, we try to kill the other man rather than let him have his way. But that is perfectly consistent with admitting that, so far as appears, his grounds are just as good as ours.

The jurists who believe in natural law seem to me to be in that naïve state of mind that accepts what has been familiar and accepted by them and their neighbors as something that must be accepted by all men everywhere. No doubt it is true that, so far as we can see ahead, some arrangements and the rudiments of familiar institutions seem to be necessary elements in any society that may spring from our own and that would seem to us to be civilized—some form of permanent association between the sexes—some residue of property individually owned—some mode of binding oneself to specified future conduct—at the bottom of all, some protection for the person. But without speculating whether a group is imaginable in which all but the last of these might disappear and the last be subject to qualifications that most of us would abhor, the question remains as to the *Ought* of natural law.

It is true that beliefs and wishes have a transcendental basis in the sense that their foundation is arbitrary. You can not help entertaining and feeling them, and there is an end of it. As an arbitrary fact people wish to live, and we say with various degrees of certainty that they can do so only on certain conditions. To do it they must eat and drink. That necessity is absolute. It is a necessity of less degree but practically general that they should live in society. If they live in society, so far as we can see, there are further conditions. Reason working on experience does tell us, no doubt, that if our wish to live continues, we can do it only on those terms. But that seems to me the whole of the matter. I see no *a priori* duty to live with others and in that way, but simply a statement of what I must do if I wish to remain alive. If I do live with others they tell me that I must do and abstain from doing various things or they will put the screws on to me. I believe that they will, and being of the same mind as to their conduct I not only accept the rules but come in time to accept them with sympathy and emotional affirmation and begin to talk about duties and rights. But for legal purposes a right is only the hypostasis of a prophecy— the imagination of a substance supporting the fact that the public force will be brought to bear upon those who do things said to contravene it—just as we talk of the force of gravitation accounting for the conduct of bodies in space. One phrase adds no more than the other to what we know without it. No doubt behind these legal rights is the fighting will of the subject to maintain them, and the spread of his emotions to the general rules by which they are maintained; but that does not seem to me the same thing as the supposed *a priori* discernment of a duty or the assertion of a preëxisting right. A dog will fight for his bone.

The most fundamental of the supposed preëxisting rights—the right to life—is sacrificed without a scruple not only in war, but whenever the interest of society, that is, of the predominant power in the community, is thought to demand it. Whether that interest is the interest of mankind in the long run no one can tell, and as, in any event, to those who do not think with Kant and Hegel it is only an interest, the sanctity disappears. I remember a very tender-hearted judge being of opinion that closing a hatch to stop a fire and the destruction of a cargo was justified even if it was known that doing so would stifle a man below. It is idle to illustrate further, because to those who agree with me I am uttering commonplaces and to those who disagree I am ignoring the necessary foundations of thought. The *a priori* men generally call the dissentients superficial. But I do agree with them in believing that one's attitude on these matters is closely connected with one's general attitude toward the universe. Proximately, as has been suggested, it is determined largely by early associations and temperament, coupled with the desire to have an absolute guide. Men to a great extent believe what they want to—although I see in that no basis for a philosophy that tells us what we should want to want.

Now when we come to our attitude toward the universe I do not see any rational ground for demanding the superlative—for being dissatisfied unless we are assured that our truth is cosmic truth, if there is such a thing—that the ultimates of a little creature on this little earth are the last word of the unimaginable whole. If a man sees no reason for believing that significance, consciousness and ideals are more than marks of the finite, that does not justify what has been familiar in French sceptics; getting upon a pedestal and professing to look with haughty scorn upon a world in ruins. The real conclusion is that the part can not swallow the whole—that our categories are not, or may not be, adequate to formulate what we can not know. If we believe that we come out of the universe, not it out of us, we must admit that we do not know what we are talking about when we speak of brute matter. We do know that a certain complex of energies can wag its tail and another can make syllogisms. These are among the powers of the unknown, and if, as maybe, it has still greater powers that we can not understand, as Fabre in his studies of instinct would have us believe, studies that gave Bergson one of the strongest strands for his philosophy and enabled Maeterlinck to make us fancy for a moment that we heard a clang from behind phenomena—if this be true, why should we not be content? Why should we employ the energy that is furnished to us by the cosmos to defy it and shake our fist at the sky? It seems to me silly.

That the universe has in it more than we understand, that the private soldiers have not been told the plan of campaign, or even that there is one, rather than some vaster unthinkable to which every predicate is an impertinence, has no bearing upon our conduct. We still shall fight—all of us because we want to live, some, at least, because we want to realize our spontaneity and prove our powers, for the joy of it, and we may leave to the unknown the supposed final valuation of that which in any event has value to us. It is enough for us that the universe has produced us and has within it, as less than it, all that we believe and love. If we think of our existence not as that of a little god outside, but as that of a ganglion within, we have the infinite behind us. It gives us our only but our adequate significance. A grain of sand has the same, but what competent person supposes that he understands a grain of sand? That is as much beyond our grasp as man. If our imagination is strong enough to accept the vision of ourselves as parts inseverable from the rest, and to extend our final interest beyond the boundary of our skins, it justifies the sacrifice even of our lives for ends outside of ourselves. The motive, to be sure, is the common wants and ideals that we find in man. Philosophy does not furnish motives, but it shows men that they are not fools for doing what they already want to do. It opens to the forlorn hopes on which we throw ourselves away, the vista of the farthest stretch of human thought, the chords of a harmony that breathes from the unknown.

33. POUND

Sociology and Law

Roscoe Pound (1870–1964) was born in Lincoln, Nebraska, and studied botany at the University of Nebraska. He received three degrees in this field from the school and then spent a single year at the Harvard Law School. Despite this background, Pound went on to become the most important and influential figure in twentieth-century American jurisprudence. He taught at the University of Nebraska Law School from 1890 to 1907 and served as dean during his last four years at the school. Pound then taught briefly at both Northwestern and Chicago law schools before accepting a professorship at Harvard Law School in 1910. From 1916 until 1936 Pound served as dean of the law school—the first non-Harvard graduate to hold that position. He resigned in 1936 to accept a professorship at Harvard that permitted him to teach courses anywhere in the university. From 1946 to 1949 he was an adviser to the Nationalist Chinese government on the reform of that nation's legal system. Upon his return to the United States he taught at the law school of the University of California at Los Angeles before returning to Harvard in 1953, where he spent the final decade of his life working daily in his office at the law school.

The scope of Pound's learning was incredible. In addition to his encyclopedic knowledge of law and botany, he was accomplished in the social sciences and had mastered French, Spanish, Italian, German, Greek, Latin, Hebrew, and Sanskrit. He knew some Russian and at the age of seventy-six undertook the study of Chinese. Pound was a prolific writer of articles and books. Some of his most important works on law include: *The Spirit of the Common Law* (1921), *Interpretation of Legal History* (1923), *Justice According to Law* (1951), and *An Introduction to the Philosophy of Law*,* from which the following selection has been taken.

. . . If we turn to the ideas which have obtained in conscious thinking about the end of law, we may recognize three which have held the ground successively in legal history and a fourth which is beginning

* (New Haven: Yale University Press, 1922), pp. 72–92.

to assert itself. The first and simplest idea is that law exists in order to keep the peace in a given society; to keep the peace at all events and at any price. This is the conception of what may be called the stage of primitive law. It puts satisfaction of the social want of general security, stated in its lowest terms, as the purpose of the legal order. So far as the law goes, other individual or social wants are ignored or are sacrified to this one. Accordingly the law is made up of tariffs of exact compositions for every detailed injury instead of principles of exact reparation, of devices to induce or coerce submission of controversies to adjudication instead of sanctions, of regulation of self-help and self-redress instead of a general prohibition thereof, and of mechanical modes of trial which at any rate do not admit of argument instead of rational modes of trial involving debate and hence dispute and so tending to defeat the purpose of the legal order. In a society organized on the basis of kinship, in which the greater number of social wants were taken care of by the kin-organizations, there are two sources of friction; the clash of kin-interests, leading to controversies of one kindred with another, and the kinless man, for whom no kin-organization is responsible, who also has no kin-organization to stand behind him in asserting his claims. Peace between kindreds and peace between clansmen and the growing mass of non-gentile population is the unsatisfied social want to which politically organized society must address itself. The system of organized kindreds gradually breaks down. Groups of kinsmen cease to be the fundamental social units. Kin-organization is replaced by political organization as the primary agency of social control. The legal unit comes to be the free citizen or the free man. In this transition regulation of self-redress and prevention of private war among those who have no strong clan-organizations to control them or respond for them are demanded by the general security. The means of satisfying these social wants are found in a legal order conceived solely in terms of keeping the peace.

Greek philosophers came to conceive of the general security in broader terms and to think of the end of the legal order as preservation of the social *status quo*. They came to think of maintaining the general security mediately through the security of social institutions. They thought of law as a device to keep each man in his appointed groove in society and thus prevent friction with his fellows. The virtue on which they insisted was *sophrosyne*, knowing the limits which nature fixes for human conduct and keeping within them. The vice which they denounced was *hybris*, wilful bondbreaking—wilful transgression of the socially appointed bounds. This mode of thinking follows the substitution of the city-state political organization of society for the kin-organization. The organized kindreds were still powerful. An aristocracy of the kin-organized and kin-conscious, on the one hand, and a mass of those who had lost or severed their ties of kinship, or had come from without, on the other hand, were in continual struggle for social and political mastery. Also the politically ambitious individual and the masterful aristocrat were continually threatening the none too stable political organization through which the general security got a precarious protection. The chief social want, which no other social institution could satisfy, was the security of social institutions generally. In the form of maintenance of the social *status quo* this became the Greek and thence the Roman and medieval conception of the end of law.

Transition from the idea of law as a device to keep the peace to the idea of law as a device to maintain the social *status quo* may be seen in the proposition of Heraclitus, that men should fight for their laws as for the walls of their city. In Plato the idea of maintaining the social order through the law is fully developed. The actual social order was by no means what it should be. Men were to be reclassified and everyone assigned to the class for which he was best fitted. But when the classification and the assignment had been made the law was to keep him there. It was not a device to set him free that he might find his own level by free competition with his fellows and free experiment with his natural powers. It was a device to prevent such disturbances of the social order by holding each individual to his appointed place. As Plato puts it, the shoemaker is to be only a shoemaker and not a pilot also; the farmer is to be only a farmer and not a judge as well; the soldier is to be only a soldier and not a man of business besides; and if a universal genius who through wisdom can be everything and do everything comes to the ideal city-state, he is to be required to move on. Aristotle puts the same idea in another way, asserting that justice is a condition in which each keeps within his appointed sphere; that we first take account of relations of inequality, treating individuals according to their worth, and then secondarily of relations of equality in the classes into which their worth requires them to be assigned. When St. Paul exhorted wives to obey their husbands, and servants to obey their masters, and thus everyone to exert himself to do his duty in the class where the social order had put him, he expressed this Greek conception of the end of law.

Roman lawyers made the Greek philosophical conception into a juristic theory. For the famous three precepts to which the law is reduced in Justinian's Institutes come to this: Everyone is to live honorably; he is to "preserve moral worth in his own person" by conforming to the conventions of the social order. Everyone is to respect the personality of others; he is not to interfere with those interests and powers of action, conceded to others by the social order, which make up their legal personality. Everyone is to render to everyone else his own; he is to respect the acquired rights of others. The social system has defined certain things as belonging to each individual. Justice is defined in the Institutes as the set and constant purpose of giving him these things. It consists in rendering them to him and in not interfering with his having and using them within the defined limits. This is a legal development of the Greek idea of harmoniously maintaining the social *status quo*. The later eastern empire carried it to the extreme. Stability was to be secured by rigidly keeping everyone to his trade or calling and his descendants were to follow him therein. Thus the harmony of society and the social order would not be disturbed by individual ambition.

In the Middle Ages the primitive idea of law as designed only to keep the peace came back with Germanic law. But the study of Roman law presently taught the Roman version of the Greek conception and the legal order was thought of once more as an orderly maintenance of the social *status quo*. This conception answered to the needs of medieval society, in which men had found relief from anarchy and violence in relations of service and protection and a social organization which classified men in terms of such relations and required them to be held to their functions as so determined. Where the Greeks thought of a stationary society corrected from time to time with reference to its nature or ideal, the Middle Ages thought of a stationary society resting upon authority and determined by custom or tradition. To each, law was a system of precepts existing to maintain this stationary society as it was.

In the feudal social order reciprocal duties involved in relations established by tradition and taken to rest on authority were the significant legal institutions. With the gradual disintegration of this order and the growing importance of the individual in a society engaged in discovery, colonization and trade, to secure the claims of individuals to assert themselves freely in the new fields of human activity which were opening on every side became a more pressing social want than to maintain the social institutions by which the system of reciprocal duties was enforced and the relations involving those duties were preserved. Men did not so much desire that others perform for them the duties owing in some relation, as that others keep hands off while they achieved what they might for themselves in a world that continually afforded new opportunities to the active and the daring. The demand was no longer that men be kept in their appointed grooves. Friction and waste were apprehended, not from men getting out of these grooves, but from attempts to hold them there by means devised to meet the needs of a different social order whereby they were made to chafe under arbitrary restraint and their powers were not utilized in the discovery and exploitation of the resources of nature, to which human powers were to be devoted in the succeeding centuries. Accordingly the end of law comes to be conceived as a making possible of the maximum of individual free self-assertion.

Transition to the newer way of thinking may be seen in the Spanish jurist-theologians of the sixteenth century. Their juristic theory was one of natural limits of activity in the relations of individuals with each other, that is, of limits to human action which expressed the rational ideal of man as a moral creature and were imposed upon men by reason. This theory differs significantly from the idea of antiquity, although it goes by the old name. The Greeks thought of a system of limiting men's activities in order that each might be kept in the place for which he was best fitted by nature—the place in which he might realize an ideal form of his capacities—and thus to preserve the social order as it stands or as it shall stand after a rearrangement. The sixteenth-century jurists of the Counter-Reformation held that men's activities were naturally limited, and hence that positive law might and should limit them in the interest of other men's activities, because all men have freedom of will and ability to direct themselves to conscious ends. Where Aristotle thought of inequalities arising from the different worth of individual men and their different capacities for the things which the social order called for, these jurists thought of a natural (i.e., ideal) equality, involved in the like freedom of will and the like power of conscious employment of one's faculties inherent in all men. Hence law did not exist to maintain the social *status quo* with all its arbitrary restraints on the will and on employment of individual powers; it existed rather to maintain the natural equality which often was threatened or impaired by the traditional restrictions on individual activity. Since this natural equality was conceived positively as an ideal equality in opportunity to do things, it could easily pass into a conception of free individual self-assertion as the thing sought, and of the legal order as existing to make possible the maximum thereof in a world abounding in undiscovered resources, undeveloped lands and unharnessed natural forces. The latter idea took form in the seventeenth century and prevailed for two centuries thereafter, culminating in the juristic thought of the last generation.

Law as a securing of natural equality became law as a securing of natural rights. The nature of man was expressed by certain qualities possessed by him as a moral, rational creature. The limitations on human activity, of which the Spanish jurist-theologians had written, got their warrant from the inherent moral qualities of men which made it right for them to have certain things and do certain things. These were their natural rights and the law existed simply to protect and give effect to these rights. There was to be no restraint for any other purpose. Except as they were to be compelled to respect the rights of others, which the natural man or ideal man would do without compulsion as a matter of reason, men were to be left free. In the nineteenth century this mode of thought takes a metaphysical turn. The ultimate thing for juristic purposes is the individual consciousness. The social problem is to reconcile conflicting free wills of conscious individuals independently asserting their wills in the varying activities of life. The natural equality becomes an equality in freedom of will. . . . [T]he end of law is to secure the greatest possible general individual self-assertion; to let men do freely everything they may consistently with a like free doing of everything they may by their fellow men. This is indeed a philosophy of law for discoverers and colonizers and pioneers and traders and entrepreneurs and captains of industry. Until the world became crowded, it served well to eliminate friction and to promote the widest discovery and utilization of the natural resources of human existence.

Looking back at the history of this conception, which has governed theories of the end of law for more than two hundred years, we may note that it has been put to three uses. It has been used as a means of clearing away the restraints upon free economic activity which accumulated during the Middle Ages as incidents of the system of relational duties and as expressions of the idea of holding men to their place in a static social order. This negative side played an important part in the English legislative reform movement in the last century. The English utilitarians insisted upon removal of all restrictions upon individual free action beyond those necessary for securing like freedom on the part of others. This, they said, was the end of legislation. Again it has been used as a constructive idea, as in the seventeenth and eighteenth centuries, when a commercial law which gave effect to what men did as they willed it, which looked at intention and not at form, which interpreted the general security in terms of the security of transactions and sought to effectuate the will of individuals to bring about legal results, was developed out of Roman law and the custom of merchants through juristic theories of natural law. Finally it was used as a stabilizing idea, as in the latter part of the nineteenth century, when men proved that law was an evil, even if a necessary evil, that there should be as little law made as possible, since all law involved restraint upon free exertion of the will, and hence that jurist and legislator should be content to leave things legal as they are and allow the individual "to work out in freedom his own happiness or misery" on that basis.

When this last stage in the development of the idea of law as existing to promote or permit the maximum of free individual self-assertion had been reached, the juristic possibilities of the conception had been exhausted. There were no more continents to discover. Natural resources had been discovered and exploited and the need was for conservation of what remained available. The forces of nature had been harnessed to human use. Industrial development had reached large proportions, and organization and division of labor in our economic order had gone so far that anyone who would could no longer go forth freely and do anything which a restless imagination and daring ambition suggested to him as a means of gain. Although lawyers went on repeating the old formula, the law began to move in another direction. The freedom of the owner of property to do upon it whatever he liked, so he did not overstep his limits or endanger the public health or safety, began to be restricted. Nay, the law began to make men act affirmatively upon their property in fashions which it dictated, where the general health was endangered by non-action. The power to make contracts began to be limited where industrial conditions made abstract freedom of contract defeat rather than advance full individual human life. The power of the owner to dispose freely of his property began to be limited in order to safeguard the security of the social institutions of marriage and the family. Freedom of appropriating *res nullius* and of using *res communes* came to be abridged in order to conserve the natural resources of society. Freedom of engaging in lawful callings came to be restricted, and an elaborate process of education and examination to be imposed upon those who would engage in them, lest there be injury to the public health, safety or morals. A regime in which anyone might freely set up a corporation to engage in a public service, or freely compete in such service, was superseded by one of legal exemption of existing public utilities from destructive competition. In a crowded world, whose resources had been exploited, a system of promoting the maximum of individual self-assertion had come to produce more friction than it relieved and to further rather than to eliminate waste.

At the end of the last and the beginning of the present century, a new way of thinking grew up. Jurists began to think in terms of human wants or desires rather than of human wills. They began to think that what they had to do was not simply to equalize or harmonize wills, but, if not to equalize, at least to harmonize the satisfaction of wants. They began to weigh or balance and reconcile claims or wants or desires, as formerly they had balanced or reconciled wills. They began to think of the end of law not as a maximum of self-assertion, but as a maximum satisfaction of wants. Hence for a time they thought of the problem of ethics, of jurisprudence, and of politics as chiefly one of valuing; as a problem of finding criteria of the relative value of interests. In jurisprudence and politics they saw that we must add practical problems of the possibility of making interests effective through governmental action, judicial or administrative. But the first question was one of the wants to be recognized—of the interests to be recognized and secured. Having inventoried the wants or claims or interests which are asserting and for which legal security is sought, we were to value them, select those to be recognized, determine the limits within which they were to be given effect in view of other recognized interests, and ascertain how far we might give them effect by law in view of the inherent limitations upon effective legal action. This mode of thinking may be seen, concealed under different terminologies, in more than one type of jurist in the last three decades.

Three elements contributed to shift the basis of theories as to the end of law from wills to wants, from a reconciling or harmonizing of wills to a reconciling or harmonizing of wants. The most important part was played by psychology which undermined the foundation of the metaphysical will-philosophy of law. Through the movement for unification of the social sciences, economics also played an important part, especially indirectly through the attempts at economic interpretation of legal history, reinforcing psychology by showing the extent to which law had been shaped by the pressure of economic wants. Also the differentiation of society, involved in industrial organization, was no mean factor, when classes came to exist in which claims to a minimum human existence, under the standards of the given civilization, became more pressing than claims to self-assertion. Attention was turned from the nature of law to its purpose, and a functional attitude, a tendency to measure legal rules and doctrines and institutions by the extent to which they further or achieve the ends for which law exists, began to replace the older method of judging law by criteria drawn from itself. In this respect the thought of the present is more like that of the seventeenth and eighteenth centuries than that of the nineteenth century. French writers have described this phenomenon as a "revival of juridical idealism." But in truth the social utilitarianism of today and the natural-law philosophy of the seventeenth and eighteenth centuries have only this in common: Each has its attention fixed upon phenomena of growth; each seeks to direct and further conscious improvement of the law. . . .

VII

The Positive State:
Progressivism and the New Deal

The protest movements of the last three decades of the nineteenth century—greenbackers, nationalists, populists—developed in the midst of continuing economic crisis, especially in the nation's agricultural economy. But from 1896 until the close of World War I, America experienced a period of economic growth and prosperity. This prosperity did not, however, put an end to the demand for economic, social, and political reform. On the contrary, the nation entered into a time of sustained and widespread reform known as the Progressive Era.

Progressivism affected every part of the United States, except perhaps the South, but it was by no means a unified or organized phenomenon. It was, for one thing, geographically divided into fairly distinct Western and Eastern branches. The progressivism of Wisconsin's Senator Robert M. La Follette, for example, differed in style, interest, and program from the urban Eastern progressivism of Theodore Roosevelt.

In addition, progressives gave different emphases to the importance of political, social, and economic problems, though concern with one area did not preclude interest in the others. Some progressives sought political reforms such as the direct primary, the direct election of Senators, initiative, referendum and recall, and the short ballot. Much of the energy of political reform was directed at the municipal level; campaigns against corruption, the movement for home rule, and the commission and city manager plans of government were the major manifestations of this form of progressivism.

Other progressives stressed the social problems of the nation. They demanded a broad program of legislation by state and national governments designed to secure greater social justice in the United States. Child labor laws, maximum hours and minimum wage laws for women, and workmen's compensation legislation were the most important features of the progressive proposals.

But economic issues were, perhaps, the preeminent interest of American progressives. They demanded and obtained the creation of state commissions to regulate the rates and services of railroads and other public utilities. At the national level the progressives were successful

271

in obtaining more rigorous enforcement of the Sherman Anti-Trust Act under Presidents Roosevelt, Taft, and Wilson; legislation to strengthen the powers of the Interstate Commerce Commission in respect to the nation's railroads; and the passage of the Federal Reserve Act in 1913 and the Clayton Anti-Trust and Federal Trade Commission acts in 1914.

The rapid pace of industrialization in the decades after the Civil War had drastically altered the character of the American economy. Concentration of economic power in the hands of giant corporations and, to a lesser extent, in the trade unions frightened the American middle class. The doctors, lawyers, clerical personnel, salesmen, and farmers who provided the bulk of progressivism's support remained unorganized and hence did not reap the financial rewards which followed from organization. "The central theme in Progressivism," Richard Hofstadter has written, "was the revolt against the industrial discipline: the Progressive movement was the complaint of the un-organized against the consequences of organization."[1]

Theodore Roosevelt and Woodrow Wilson were the most significant political leaders of the progressive movement, and in the 1912 Presidential election Roosevelt's philosophy, "New Nationalism," clashed directly with Wilson's "New Freedom." Roosevelt stressed the need for social reform legislation and for national control and regulation of the economy. Wilson, on the contrary, warned of the dangers of concentrated power in the national government and called instead for a concerted effort to destroy monopoly and to restore competition. In brief, Roosevelt stood for the use of government power to obtain social and economic justice while Wilson favored a continuation of the laissez-faire policies of the nineteenth century with government authority being used only to destroy unfair privilege.

The direct influence of Herbert Croly's *The Promise of American Life* on the thinking of Theodore Roosevelt has been greatly overstated. He did read the book soon after its publication in 1909, but the general ideas developed by Croly had been forming in Roosevelt's mind before this date. *The Promise of American Life*, nonetheless, is the most important expression of progressive political thought and a book which states the prevalent philosophy of much of twentieth-century liberalism. Throughout the nineteenth century, Croly contended, the American people believed that the promise of America would be automatically

[1] *The Age of Reform* (New York: Alfred A. Knopf, 1956), pp. 214–15.

brought about by following the Jeffersonian doctrines of small, limited government and free competition. In an industrial age, however, such a philosophy could only work against the fulfillment of America's promise: it would injure the welfare of the many and favor the special economic interests. Croly called upon progressives to reject their historic attachment to Jefferson's ideas and to accept a new nationalism —a belief in the Hamiltonian philosophy of government intervention in the nation's economic life.

Woodrow Wilson gradually abandoned his dedication to laissez-faire during his tenure as President and, in effect, adopted a position closer to that of Roosevelt and Croly. In 1916 Wilson first gave his support to national child labor laws and workmen's compensation legislation and obtained the enactment of these proposals from the Congress. Certainly the political pressures of the impending Presidential election influenced Wilson's thinking, but so also had the ideas of his most influential adviser, Louis D. Brandeis. Brandeis, like Wilson, believed in the virtue of a competitive economic order, but his sense of social justice also led him to favor the use of governmental power to promote the welfare of the less privileged members of society. His testimony before the United States Commission on Industrial Relations in 1915 reveals his acute desire for economic and social justice and enumerates some of the reforms Brandeis believed necessary to bring about this more just America.

The progressive movement came to a close as America gradually became involved in the Great War that was raging in Europe. Progressivism was briefly but unsuccessfully revived as a political party in the 1924 Presidential election, but it was not until after the country had slipped into its worst economic depression that it once again embarked on an extended program of domestic reform.

It can hardly be maintained that Franklin Roosevelt's New Deal was a well-thought-out philosophy of reform. In his first Inaugural Address Roosevelt said that the nation demanded action in this period of economic ruin, and he committed his administration to undertake whatever steps were necessary to solve the crisis. Roosevelt's actions as President were frankly pragmatic. He advocated a large number of programs, some of which were contradictory, in search of policies that would alleviate the economic distress. By 1936 the President had transformed the Democratic Party from the party of Jefferson and Jackson to that of Hamilton by continuing and extending the Hamiltonian nationalism which had emerged as the liberal philosophy during the progressive period.

If the New Deal had a philosopher, it was John Dewey; and if it had a philosophy, it was Dewey's experimentalism—a system of thought stated in his 1935 book *Liberalism and Social Action*. Dewey's experimentalism and Roosevelt's New Deal opposed the old order of laissez-faire individualism and favored peaceful democratic change through the positive use of governmental authority. Roosevelt, however, never accepted Dewey's contention that centralized planning in a socialized economy was necessary to achieve the highest possible development of each individual. Both expressed the belief that man's intelligence could successfully be applied to the solution of social and economic problems, though Dewey believed that the New Deal had not gone far enough in its use of "socially organized intelligence."

34. CROLY
The New Nationalism

Born in New York City into a middle-class intellectual family, Herbert Croly (1869–1930) was an unlikely person to become an intellectual leader of Eastern American progressivism. Croly's early interests were distinctly nonpolitical. He entered Harvard College in 1886 and studied philosophy and religion but did not complete his degree even though he was intermittently a student at the school for eleven years. His early writings dealt with literary and aesthetic topics, and for six years he served as editor of the *Architectural Record*. Croly increasingly turned to political subjects, and in 1909 he published his influential study *The Promise of American Life*, from which the following selection* is taken. In the next decade Croly was a leading spokesman for the progressive movement and a strong supporter of Theodore Roosevelt. In addition to *The Promise of American Life*, Croly also wrote *Progressive Democracy* (1914) and along with Walter Weyl and Walter Lippmann founded and coedited the *New Republic* magazine.

WHAT IS THE PROMISE OF AMERICAN LIFE?

The average American is nothing if not patriotic. . . . The faith of Americans in their own country is religious, if not in its intensity, at any rate in its almost absolute and universal authority. It pervades the air we breathe. As children we hear it asserted or implied in the conversation of our elders. Every new stage of our educational training provides some additional testimony on its behalf. Newspapers and novelists, orators and playwrights, even if they are little else, are at least loyal preachers of the Truth. The skeptic is not controverted; he is overlooked. It constitutes the kind of faith which is the implication, rather than the object, of thought, and consciously or unconsciously it enters largely into our personal lives as a formative influence. We

* (New York: The Macmillan Company, 1909), pp. 1–5, 8–13, 16–18, 20–24.

may distrust and dislike much that is done in the name of our country by our fellow-countrymen; but our country itself, its democratic system, and its prosperous future are above suspicion. . . .

The higher American patriotism . . . combines loyalty to historical tradition and precedent with the imaginative projection of an ideal national Promise. The Land of Democracy has always appealed to its more enthusiastic children chiefly as a land of wonderful and more than national possibilities. . . . This vision of a better future is not, perhaps, as unclouded for the present generation of Americans as it was for certain former generations; but in spite of a more friendly acquaintance with all sorts of obstacles and pitfalls, our country is still figured in the imagination of its citizens as the Land of Promise. They still believe that somehow and sometime something better will happen to good Americans than has happened to men in any other country; and this belief, vague, innocent, and uninformed though it be, is the expression of an essential constituent in our national ideal. The past should mean less to a European than it does to an American, and the future should mean more. To be sure, American life cannot with impunity be wrenched violently from its moorings any more than the life of a European country can; but our American past, compared to that of any European country, has a character all its own. Its peculiarity consists, not merely in its brevity, but in the fact that from the beginning it has been informed by an idea. From the beginning Americans have been anticipating and projecting a better future. From the beginning the Land of Democracy has been figured as the Land of Promise. Thus the American's loyalty to the national tradition rather affirms than denies the imaginative projection of a better future. An America which was not the Land of Promise, which was not informed by a prophetic outlook and a more or less constructive ideal, would not be the America bequeathed to us by our forefathers. In cherishing the Promise of a better national future the American is fulfilling rather than imperiling the substance of the national tradition.

When, however, Americans talk of their country as the Land of Promise, a question may well be raised as to precisely what they mean. They mean, of course, in general, that the future will have something better in store for them individually and collectively than has the past or the present; but a very superficial analysis of this meaning discloses certain ambiguities. What are the particular benefits which this better future will give to Americans either individually or as a nation? And how is this Promise to be fulfilled? Will it fulfill itself, or does it imply certain responsibilities? If so, what responsibilities? When we speak of a young man's career as promising, we mean that his abilities and opportunities are such that he is likely to become rich or famous or powerful; and this judgment does not of course imply, so far as we are concerned, any responsibility. It is merely a prophecy based upon past performances and proved qualities. But the career, which from the standpoint of an outsider is merely an anticipation, becomes for the young man himself a serious task. For him, at all events, the better future will not merely happen. He will have to do something to deserve it. It may be wrecked by unforeseen obstacles, by unsuspected infirmities, or by some critical error of judgment. So it is with the Promise of American life. From the point of view of an immigrant this Promise may consist of the anticipation of a better future, which he can share merely by taking up his residence on American soil; but once he has become an American, the Promise can no longer remain merely an anticipation. It becomes in that case a responsibility, which requires for its fulfillment a certain kind of behavior on the part of himself and his fellow-Americans. And when we attempt to define the Promise of American life, we are obliged, also, to describe the kind of behavior which the fulfillment of the Promise demands.

The distinction between the two aspects of America as a Land of Promise made in the preceding paragraph is sufficiently obvious, but it is usually slurred by the average good American patriot. The better future, which is promised for himself, his children, and for other Americans, is chiefly a matter of confident anticipation. He looks upon it very much as a friendly outsider might look on some promising individual career. The better future is understood by him as something which fulfills itself. He calls his country, not only the Land of Promise, but the Land of Destiny. It is fairly launched on a brilliant and successful career, the continued prosperity of which is prophesied by the very momentum of its advance. As Mr. H. G. Wells says in "The Future in America," "When one talks to an American of his national purpose, he seems a little at a loss; if one speaks of his national destiny, he responds with alacrity." The great majority of Americans would expect a book written about "The Promise of American Life" to contain chiefly a fanciful description of the glorious American future—a sort of Utopia up-to-date, situated in the land of Good-Enough, and flying the Stars and Stripes. They might admit in words that the achievement of this glorious future implied certain responsibilities, but they would not regard the admission either as startling or novel. Such responsibilities were met by our predecessors; they will be met by our followers. Inasmuch as it is the honorable American past which prophesies on behalf of the better American future, our national responsibility consists fundamentally in remaining true to traditional ways of behavior, standards, and ideals. What we Americans have to do in order to fulfill our national Promise is to keep up the good work—to continue resolutely and cheerfully along the appointed path.

The reader who expects this book to contain a collection of patriotic prophecies will be disappointed. I am not a prophet in any sense of the word, and I entertain an active and intense dislike of the foregoing mixture of optimism, fatalism, and conservatism. To conceive the better American future as a consummation which will take care of itself,—as the necessary result of our customary conditions, institutions, and ideas,—persistence in such a conception is admirably designed to deprive American life of any promise at all. The better future which Americans propose to build is nothing if not an idea which must in certain essential respects emancipate them from the past. American history contains much matter for pride and congratulation, and much matter for regret and humiliation. On the whole, it is a past of which the loyal American has no reason to feel ashamed, chiefly because it has throughout been made better than it was by the vision of a better future; and the American of to-day and to-morrow must remain true to that traditional vision. He must be prepared to sacrifice to that traditional vision even the traditional American ways of realizing it. Such a sacrifice is, I believe, coming to be demanded; and unless it is made, American life will gradually cease to have any specific Promise. . . .

. . . No more explicit expression has ever been given to the way in which the Land of Promise was first conceived by its children than in the "Letters of an American Farmer." This book was written by a French immigrant, Hector St. John de Crèvecœur before the Revolution, and is informed by an intense consciousness of the difference between conditions in the Old and in the New World. "What, then, is an American, this new man?" asks the Pennsylvanian farmer. "He is either a European or the descendant of a European; hence the strange mixture of blood, which you will find in no other country. . . .

"He becomes an American by being received in the broad lap of our great *Alma Mater*. Here individuals of all nations are melted into a new race of men, whose labors and prosperity will one day cause great changes in the world. Here the rewards of his industry follow with equal steps the progress of his labor; this labor is founded on the basis of *self-interest;* can it want a stronger allurement? Wives and children, who before in vain demanded a morsel of bread, now fat and frolicsome, gladly help their father to clear those fields, whence exuberant crops are to arise to feed them all; without any part being claimed either by a despotic prince, a rich abbot, or a mighty lord. . . . The American is a new man, who acts upon new principles; he must therefore entertain new ideas and form new opinions. From involuntary idleness, servile dependence, penury, and useless labor, he has passed to toils of a very different nature rewarded by ample subsistence. This is an American."

Although the foregoing is one of the first, it is also one of the most explicit descriptions of the fundamental American; and it deserves to be analyzed with some care. According to this French convert the American is a man, or the descendant of a man, who has emigrated from Europe chiefly because he expects to be better able in the New World to enjoy the fruits of his own labor. The conception implies, consequently, an Old World, in which the ordinary man cannot become independent and prosperous, and, on the other hand, a New World in which economic opportunities are much more abundant and accessible. America has been peopled by Europeans primarily because they expected in that country to make more money more easily. To the European immigrant—that is, to the aliens who have been converted into Americans by the advantages of American life—the Promise of America has consisted largely in the opportunity which it offered of economic independence and prosperity. Whatever else the better future, of which Europeans anticipate the enjoyment in America, may contain, these converts will consider themselves cheated unless they are in a measure relieved of the curse of poverty.

This conception of American life and its Promise is as much alive to-day as it was in 1780. Its expression has no doubt been modified during four generations of democratic political independence, but the modification has consisted of an expansion and a development rather than of a transposition. The native American, like the alien immigrant, conceives the better future which awaits himself and other men in America as fundamentally a future in which economic prosperity will be still more abundant and still more accessible than it has yet been either here or abroad. No alteration or attenuation of this demand has been permitted. With all their professions of Christianity their national idea remains thoroughly worldly. They do not want either for themselves or for their descendants an indefinite future of poverty and deprivation in this world, redeemed by beatitude in the next. The Promise, which bulks so large in their patriotic outlook, is a promise of comfort and prosperity for an ever increasing majority of good Americans. At a later stage of their social development they may come to believe that they have ordered a larger supply of prosperity than the economic factory is capable of producing. Those who are already rich and comfortable, and who are keenly alive to the difficulty of distributing these benefits over a larger social area, may come to tolerate the idea that poverty and want are an essential part of the social order. But as yet this traditional European opinion has found few echoes in America, even among the comfortable and the rich. The general belief still is that Americans are not destined to renounce, but to enjoy.

Let it be immediately added, however, that this economic independence and prosperity has always been absolutely associated in the American mind with free political institutions. The "American Farmer" traced the good fortune of the European immigrant in America, not merely to the abundance of economic opportunity, but to the fact that a ruling class of abbots and lords had no prior claim to a large share of the products of the soil. He did not attach the name of democracy to the improved political and social institutions of America, and when the political differences between Great Britain and her American colonies culminated in the Revolutionary War, the converted "American Farmer" was filled with anguish at this violent assertion of the "New Americanism." Nevertheless he was fully alive to the benefits which the immigrant enjoyed from a larger dose of political and social freedom; and so, of course, have been all the more intelligent of the European converts to Americanism. A certain number of them, particularly during the early years, came over less for the purpose of making money than for that of escaping from European political and religious persecution. America has always been conventionally conceived, not merely as a land of abundant and accessible economic opportunities, but also as a refuge for the oppressed; and the immigrant ships are crowded both during times of European famine and during times of political revolution and persecution.

Inevitably, however, this aspect of the American Promise has undergone certain important changes since the establishment of our national independence. When the colonists succeeded in emancipating themselves from political allegiance to Great Britain, they were confronted by the task of organizing a stable and efficient government without encroaching on the freedom, which was even at that time traditionally associated with American life. The task was by no means an easy one, and required for its performance the application of other political principles than that of freedom. The men who were responsible for this great work were not, perhaps, entirely candid in recognizing the profound modifications in their traditional ideas which their constructive political work had implied; but they were at all events fully aware of the great importance of their addition to the American idea. That idea, while not ceasing to be at bottom economic, became more than ever political and social in its meaning and contents. The Land of Freedom became in the course of time also the Land of Equality. The special American political system, the construction of which was predicted in the "Farmer's" assertion of the necessary novelty of American modes of thought and action, was made explicitly, if not uncompromisingly, democratic; and the success of this democratic political system was indissolubly associated in the American mind with the persistence of abundant and widely distributed economic prosperity. Our democratic institutions became in a sense the guarantee that prosperity would continue to be abundant and accessible. In case the majority of good Americans were not prosperous, there would be grave reasons for suspecting that our institutions were not doing their duty.

The more consciously democratic Americans became, however, the less they were satisfied with a conception of the Promised Land, which went no farther than a pervasive economic prosperity guaranteed by free institutions. The amelioration promised to aliens and to future Americans was to possess its moral and social aspects. The implication was, and still is, that by virtue of the more comfortable and less trammeled lives which Americans were enabled to lead, they would constitute a better society and would become in general a worthier set of men. The confidence which American institutions placed in the American citizen was considered equivalent to a greater faith in the excellence of human nature. In our favored land political liberty and economic opportunity were by a process of natural education inevitably making for individual and social amelioration. In Europe the people did not have a fair chance. Population increased more quickly than economic opportunities, and the opportunities which did exist were largely monopolized by privileged classes. Power was lodged in the hands of a few men, whose interest depended upon keeping the people in a condition of economic and political servitude; and in this way a divorce was created between individual interest and social stability and welfare. The interests of the privileged rulers demanded the perpetuation of unjust institutions. The interest of the people demanded a revolutionary upheaval. In the absence of such a revolution they had no sufficient inducement to seek their own material and moral improvement. The theory was proclaimed and accepted as a justification for this system of popular oppression that men were not to be trusted to take care of themselves—that they could be kept socially useful only by the severest measures of moral, religious, and political discipline. The theory of the American democracy and its practice was proclaimed to be the antithesis of this European theory and practice. The people were to be trusted rather than suspected and disciplined. They must be tied to their country by the strong bond of self-interest. Give them a fair chance, and the natural goodness of human nature would do the rest. Individual and public interest will, on the whole, coincide, provided no individuals are allowed to have special privileges. Thus the American system will be predestined to success by its own adequacy, and its success will constitute an enormous stride towards human amelioration. Just because our system is at bottom a thorough test of the ability of human nature to respond admirably to a fair chance, the issue of the experiment is bound to be of more than national importance. The American system stands for the highest hope of an excellent worldly life that mankind has yet ventured,—the hope that men can be improved without being fettered, that they can be saved without even vicariously being nailed to the cross. . . .

HOW THE PROMISE IS TO BE REALIZED

In the preceding section I have been seeking to render justice to the actual achievements of the American nation. A work of manifest individual and social value has been wrought; and this work, not only explains the expectant popular outlook towards the future, but it partially determines the character as distinguished from the continued fulfillment of the American national Promise. The better future, whatever else it may bring, must bring at any rate a continuation of the good things of the past. The drama of its fulfillment must find an appropriate setting in the familiar American social and economic scenery. No matter how remote the end may be, no matter what unfamiliar sacrifices may eventually be required on its behalf, the substance of the existing achievement must constitute a veritable beginning, because on no other condition can the attribution of a peculiar Promise to American life find a specific warrant. On no other condition would our national Promise constitute more than an admirable but irrelevant moral and social aspiration.

The moral and social aspiration proper to American life is, of course, the aspiration vaguely described by the word democratic; and the actual achievement of the American nation points towards an adequate and fruitful definition of the democratic ideal. Americans are usually satisfied by a most inadequate verbal description of democracy, but their national achievement implies one which is much more comprehensive and formative. In order to be true to their past, the increasing comfort and economic independence of an ever increasing proportion of the population must be secured, and it must be secured by a combination of individual effort and proper political organization. Above all, however, this economic and political system must be made to secure results of moral and social value. It is the seeking of such results which converts democracy from a political system into a constructive social ideal; and the more the ideal significance of the American national Promise is asserted and emphasized, the greater will become the importance of securing these moral and social benefits.

The fault in the vision of our national future possessed by the ordinary American does not consist in the expectation of some continuity of achievement. It consists rather in the expectation that the familiar benefits will continue to accumulate automatically. In his mind the ideal Promise is identified with the processes and conditions which hitherto have very much simplified its fulfillment, and he fails sufficiently to realize that the conditions and processes are one thing and the ideal Promise quite another. Moreover, these underlying social and economic conditions are themselves changing, in such wise that hereafter the ideal Promise, instead of being automatically fulfilled, may well be automatically stifled. For two generations and more the American people were, from the economic point of view, most happily situated. They were able, in a sense, to slide down hill into the valley of fulfillment. Economic conditions were such that, given a fair start, they could scarcely avoid reaching a desirable goal. But such is no longer the case. Economic conditions have been profoundly modified, and American political and social problems have been modified with them. The Promise of American life must depend less than it did upon the virgin wilderness and the Atlantic Ocean, for the virgin wilderness has disappeared, and the Atlantic Ocean has become merely a big channel. The same results can no longer be achieved by the same easy methods. Ugly obstacles have jumped into view, and ugly obstacles are peculiarly dangerous to a person who is sliding down hill. The man who is clambering up hill is in a much better position to evade or overcome them. Americans will possess a safer as well as a worthier vision of their national Promise as soon as they give it a house on a hill-top rather than in a valley. . . .

. . . A numerous and powerful group of reformers has been collecting whose whole political policy and action is based on the conviction that the "common people" have not been getting the Square Deal to which they are entitled under the American system; and these reformers are carrying with them a constantly increasing body of public opinion. A considerable proportion of the American people is beginning to exhibit economic and political, as well as personal, discontent. A generation ago the implication was that if a man remained poor and needy, his poverty was his own fault, because the American system was giving all its citizens a fair chance. Now, however, the discontented poor are beginning to charge their poverty to an unjust political and economic organization, and reforming agitators do not hesitate to support them in this contention. Manifestly a threatened obstacle has been raised against the anticipated realization of our national Promise. Unless the great majority of Americans not only have, but believe they have, a fair chance, the better American future will be dangerously compromised.

The conscious recognition of grave national abuses casts a deep shadow across the traditional American patriotic vision. The sincere and candid reformer can no longer consider the national Promise as destined to automatic fulfillment. The reformers themselves are, no doubt, far from believing that whatever peril there is cannot be success-fully averted. They make a point of being as patriotically prophetic as the most "old-fashioned Democrat." They proclaim even more loudly their conviction of an indubitable and a beneficent national future. But they do not and cannot believe that this future will take care of itself. As reformers they are bound to assert that the national body requires for the time being a good deal of medical attendance, and many of them anticipate that even after the doctors have discontinued their daily visits the patient will still need the supervision of a sanitary specialist. He must be persuaded to behave so that he will not easily fall ill again, and so that his health will be permanently improved. Consequently, just in so far as reformers are reformers they are obliged to abandon the traditional American patriotic fatalism. The national

Promise has been transformed into a closer equivalent of a national purpose, the fulfillment of which is a matter of conscious work.

The transformation of the old sense of a glorious national destiny into the sense of a serious national purpose will inevitably tend to make the popular realization of the Promise of American life both more explicit and more serious. As long as Americans believed they were able to fulfill a noble national Promise merely by virtue of maintaining intact a set of political institutions and by the vigorous individual pursuit of private ends, their allegiance to their national fulfillment remained more a matter of words than of deeds; but now that they are being aroused from their patriotic slumber, the effect is inevitably to disentangle the national idea and to give it more dignity. The redemption of the national Promise has become a cause for which the good American must fight, and the cause for which a man fights is a cause which he more than ever values. The American idea is no longer to be propagated merely by multiplying the children of the West and by granting ignorant aliens permission to vote. Like all sacred causes, it must be propagated by the Word and by that right arm of the Word, which is the Sword.

The more enlightened reformers are conscious of the additional dignity and value which the popularity of reform has bestowed upon the American idea, but they still fail to realize the deeper implications of their own programme. In abandoning the older conception of an automatic fulfillment of our national destiny, they have abandoned more of the traditional American point of view than they are aware. The traditional American optimistic fatalism was not of accidental origin, and it cannot be abandoned without involving in its fall some other important ingredients in the accepted American tradition. Not only was it dependent on economic conditions which prevailed until comparatively recent times, but it has been associated with certain erroneous but highly cherished political theories. It has been wrought into the fabric of our popular economic and political ideas to such an extent that its overthrow necessitates a partial revision of some of the most important articles in the traditional American creed.

The extent and the character of this revision may be inferred from a brief consideration of the effect upon the substance of our national Promise of an alteration in its proposed method of fulfillment. The substance of our national Promise has consisted, as we have seen, of an improving popular economic condition, guaranteed by democratic political institutions, and resulting in moral and social amelioration.

These manifold benefits were to be obtained merely by liberating the enlightened self-interest of the American people. The beneficent result followed inevitably from the action of wholly selfish motives—provided, of course, the democratic political system of equal rights was maintained in its integrity. The fulfillment of the American Promise was considered inevitable because it was based upon a combination of self-interest and the natural goodness of human nature. On the other hand, if the fulfillment of our national Promise can no longer be considered inevitable, if it must be considered as equivalent to a conscious national purpose instead of an inexorable national destiny, the implication necessarily is that the trust reposed in individual self-interest has been in some measure betrayed. No preëstablished harmony can then exist between the free and abundant satisfaction of private needs and the accomplishment of a morally and socially desirable result. The Promise of American life is to be fulfilled—not merely by a maximum amount of economic freedom, but by a certain measure of discipline; not merely by the abundant satisfaction of individual desires, but by a large measure of individual subordination and self-denial. And this necessity of subordinating the satisfaction of individual desires to the fulfillment of a national purpose is attached particularly to the absorbing occupation of the American people,—the occupation, viz.: of accumulating wealth. The automatic fulfillment of the American national Promise is to be abandoned, if at all, precisely because the traditional American confidence in individual freedom has resulted in a morally and socially undesirable distribution of wealth.

In making the concluding statement of the last paragraph I am venturing, of course, upon very debatable ground. Neither can I attempt in this immediate connection to offer any justification for the statement which might or should be sufficient to satisfy a stubborn skeptic. I must be content for the present with the bare assertion that the prevailing abuses and sins, which have made reform necessary, are all of them associated with the prodigious concentration of wealth, and of the power exercised by wealth, in the hands of a few men. I am far from believing that this concentration of economic power is wholly an undesirable thing, and I am also far from believing that the men in whose hands this power is concentrated deserve, on the whole, any exceptional moral reprobation for the manner in which it has been used. In certain respects they have served their country well, and in almost every respect their moral or immoral standards are those of the great majority of their fellow-countrymen. But it is none the less true that the political corruption, the unwise economic organization, and the legal support afforded to certain economic privileges are all under existing conditions due to the malevolent social influence of individual and incorporated American wealth; and it is equally true that these abuses, and the excessive "money power" with which they are associated, have originated in the peculiar freedom which the American tradition and organization have granted to the individual. Up to a certain point that freedom has been and still is beneficial. Beyond that point it is not merely harmful; it is by way of being fatal. Efficient regulation there must be; and it must be regulation which will strike, not at the symptoms of the evil, but at its roots. The existing concentration of wealth and financial power in the hands of a few irresponsible men is the inevitable outcome of the chaotic individualism of our political and economic organization, while at the same time it is inimical to democracy, because it tends to erect political abuses and social inequalities into a system. The inference which follows may be disagreeable, but it is not to be escaped. In becoming responsible for the subordination of the individual to the demand of a dominant and constructive national purpose, the American state will in effect be making itself responsible for a morally and socially desirable distribution of wealth.

The consequences, then, of converting our American national destiny into a national purpose are beginning to be revolutionary. When the Promise of American life is conceived as a national ideal, whose fulfillment is a matter of artful and laborious work, the effect thereof is substantially to identify the national purpose with the social problem. What the American people of the present and the future have really been promised by our patriotic prophecies is an attempt to solve that problem. They have been promised on American soil comfort, prosperity, and the opportunity for self-improvement; and the lesson of the existing crisis is that such a Promise can never be redeemed by an indiscriminate individual scramble for wealth. The individual competition, even when it starts under fair conditions and rules, results, not only, as it should, in the triumph of the strongest, but in the attempt to perpetuate the victory; and it is this attempt which must be recognized and forestalled in the interest of the American national purpose. The way to realize a purpose is, not to leave it to chance, but to keep it loyally in mind, and adopt means proper to the importance and the difficulty of the task. No voluntary association of individuals, resourceful and disinterested though they be, is competent to assume the responsibility. The problem belongs to the American national democracy, and its solution must be attempted chiefly by means of official national action. . . .

35. BRANDEIS

Industrial Democracy

Louis D. Brandeis (1856–1941) was born in Louisville, Kentucky. He was the son of Jewish immigrant parents from Bohemia. Without prior college training he entered Harvard Law School at the age of nineteen and was graduated two years later with an academic average of .97, one of the highest ever attained in the history of that institution. Brandeis amassed a personal fortune as a corporation lawyer, but toward the end of the nineteenth century he turned his energies to the progressive movement and served as the "people's attorney" for a variety of causes. He continued this work during the early years of the twentieth century and eventually served as Woodrow Wilson's adviser. President Wilson appointed Brandeis to the United States Supreme Court in 1916, and he remained on the Court until his retirement in 1939. Collections of his writings are to be found in *The Social and Economic Views of Mr. Justice Brandeis* (1930) and *The Curse of Bigness* (1934). This selection* is taken from the testimony given by Brandeis on January 23, 1915, before the United States Commission on Industrial Relations under the chairmanship of Senator Thomas J. Walsh of Montana, also a close adviser to President Wilson.

CHAIRMAN WALSH. Have the large corporations increased the wages as rapidly as the prices of commodities have increased, or shortened working-hours as rapidly as the development of the industry would warrant?

MR. BRANDEIS. It is difficult to answer that comprehensively. I should feel quite certain that in some respects they had not—certain corporations, and very prominent ones, have not increased wages as

* *United States Commission on Industrial Relations, Industrial Relations: Final Report and Testimony, United States Senate, 64th Congress, 1st Session*, VIII (1916), pp. 7658–63.

rapidly as the profits of the organization warranted, nor have they reduced hours. But I think that is true also of many corporations that are small.

CHAIRMAN WALSH. Does the corporate type of organization tend to produce a higher grade of workmen and citizens?

MR. BRANDEIS. I should think not.

CHAIRMAN WALSH. Have the large corporations acted as a bulwark to prevent the growth of trade unions, from your observation, Mr. Brandeis?

MR. BRANDEIS. Yes.

CHAIRMAN WALSH. I wish you would state what information you have, generally, of course, upon which you base that answer.

MR. BRANDEIS. I think that the large industrial corporations have found this possible. That is true of the trusts and true also of large corporations which are not among those technically known as trusts, but which have powerful financial organizations; for instance, the Steel Trust, the Tobacco Trust, the Sugar Trust. It seems to me that they have possessed the power against which, in the main, the unions —union organizations have struggled in vain. There have been a very large number, undoubtedly, of other employers who were not large, who had exactly the same desires and the same economic views as those who control these great corporations, but they had not the power of resistance, the power of endurance, and the influence and connections, which enabled them to make their will law. It was a difference, not of motive in the main, but of conditions.

CHAIRMAN WALSH. Have you observed the extent to which potential control over labor conditions is concentrated in the hands of financial directors of large corporations?

MR. BRANDEIS. To a certain extent. I think that goes necessarily with the control of the corporations themselves. There has been undoubtedly great financial concentration—direct to a certain extent and indirect to a greater extent—and that influence which came from the concentration in comparatively few hands of a deciding voice in important financial and industrial questions almost necessarily affects the labor problems, as it does other problems, although it may not have been the design primarily to deal with the labor problem.

CHAIRMAN WALSH. Have you observed the extent to which this potential control is exercised in connection with labor matters? Do you know of individual instances in which the control is directly used?

MR. BRANDEIS. Well, the report of the Stanley investigating committee indicated that it had been used quite effectively in the steel trade.

CHAIRMAN WALSH. Do such financial directors, in your opinion, Mr. Brandeis, have sufficient knowledge of industrial conditions and social conditions to qualify them to direct labor policies involving hundreds of thousands of men?

MR. BRANDEIS. I should think most of them did not; but what is perhaps more important or fully as important is the fact that neither these same men nor anybody else can properly deal with these problems without a far more intimate knowledge of the facts than it is possible for men to get who undertake to have a voice in so many different businesses. They are prevented from obtaining an understanding not so much because of their point of view or motive, but because of human limitations. These men have endeavored to cover far more ground than it is possible for men to cover properly, and without an intimate knowledge of the facts they cannot possibly deal with the problems involved.

CHAIRMAN WALSH. Does the fact that many large corporations with thousands of stockholders, among whom are large numbers of employees, in any way whatever affect the policy of large corporations?

MR. BRANDEIS. I do not believe that the holding of stock by employees —what is practically almost an insignificant participation, considering their percentage to the whole body of stockholders in large corporations —improves the condition of labor in those corporations. I think its effect is rather the opposite.

CHAIRMAN WALSH. I wish you would elucidate that a little, if you will, please, Mr. Brandeis; state the reasons for it.

MR. BRANDEIS. Perhaps I would have to go a little further into my general feeling in this respect—

CHAIRMAN WALSH. I wish you would do so, Mr. Brandeis.

MR. BRANDEIS.—As to the causes of the difficulty and of the unrest.

CHAIRMAN WALSH. I wish you would please do so.

MR. BRANDEIS. My observation leads me to believe that while there are many contributing causes to unrest, that there is one case which is fundamental. That is the necessary conflict—the contrast between our political liberty and our industrial absolutism. We are as free politically, perhaps, as free as it is possible for us to be. Every male has his voice and vote; and the law has endeavored to enable, and has succeeded practically, in enabling him to exercise his political franchise without fear. He therefore has his part; and certainly can secure an adequate part in the government of the country in all of its political relations; that is, in all relations which are determined directly by legislation or governmental administration.

On the other hand, in dealing with industrial problems the position of the ordinary worker is exactly the reverse. The individual employee has no effective voice or vote. And the main objection, as I see it, to the very large corporation is, that it makes possible—and in many cases makes inevitable—the exercise of industrial absolutism. It is not merely the case of the individual worker against the employer which, even if he is a reasonably sized employer, presents a serious situation calling for the interposition of a union to protect the individual. But we have the situation of an employer so potent, so well organized, with such concentrated forces and with such extraordinary powers of reserve and the ability to endure against strikes and other efforts of a union, that the relatively loosely organized masses of even strong unions are unable to cope with the situation. We are dealing here with a question, not of motive, but of condition. Now, the large corporation and the managers of the powerful corporation are probably in large part actuated by motives just the same as an employer of a tenth of their size. Neither of them, as a rule, wishes to have his liberty abridged; but the smaller concern usually comes to the conclusion that it is necessary that it should be, where an important union must be dealt with. But when a great financial power has developed—when there exists these powerful organizations, which can successfully summon forces from all parts of the country, which can afford to use tremendous amounts of money in any conflict to carry out what they deem to be their business principle, and can also afford to suffer large losses—you have necessarily a condition of inequality between the two contending forces. Such contests, though undertaken with the best motives and with strong conviction on the part of the corporate managers that they are seeking what is for the best interests not only of the company but of the community, lead to absolutism. The result, in the cases of these large corporations, may be to develop a benevolent absolutism, but it is an absolutism all the same; and it is that which makes the great corporation so dangerous. There develops within the State a state so powerful that the ordinary social and industrial forces existing are insufficient to cope with it.

I noted, Mr. Chairman, that the question you put to me concerning the employees of these large corporations related to their physical condition. Their mental condition is certainly equally important.

Unrest, to my mind, never can be removed—and fortunately never can be removed—by mere improvement of the physical and material condition of the workingman. If it were possible we should run great risk of improving their material condition and reducing their manhood. We must bear in mind all the time, that however much we may desire material improvement and must desire it for the comfort of the individual, that the United States is a democracy, and that we must have, above all things, men. It is the development of manhood to which any industrial and social system should be directed. We Americans are committed not only to social justice in the sense of avoiding things which bring suffering and harm, like unjust distribution of wealth; but we are committed primarily to democracy. The social justice for which we are striving is an incident of our democracy, not the main end. It is rather the result of democracy—perhaps its finest expression— but it rests upon democracy, which implies the rule by the people. And therefore the end for which we must strive is the attainment of rule by the people, and that involves industrial democracy as well as political democracy. That means that the problem of a trade should be no longer the problems of the employer alone. The problems of his business, and it is not the employer's business alone, are the problems of all in it. The union cannot shift upon the employer the responsibility for conditions, nor can the employer insist upon determining, according to his will, the conditions which shall exist. The problems which exist are the problems of the trade; they are the problems of employer and employee. Profit sharing, however liberal, cannot meet the situation. That would mean merely dividing the profits of business. Such a division may do harm or it might do good, dependent on how it is applied.

There must be a division not only of profits, but a division also of responsibilities. The employees must have the opportunity of participating in the decisions as to what shall be their condition and how the business shall be run. They must learn also in sharing that responsibility that they, too, must bear the suffering arising from grave mistakes, just as the employer must. But the right to assist in making the decisions, the right of making their own mistakes, if mistakes there must be, is a privilege which should not be denied to labor. We must insist upon labor sharing the responsibilities for the result of the business.

Now, to a certain extent we are gradually getting it—in smaller businesses. The grave objection to the large business is that, almost inevitably, the form of organization, the absentee stockholdings, and its remote directorship prevent participation, ordinarily, of the employees in such management. The executive officials become stewards in charge of the details of the operation of the business, they alone coming into direct relation with labor. Thus we lose that necessary co-operation which naturally flows from contact between employers and employees—and which the American aspirations for democracy demand. It is in the resultant absolutism that you will find the fundamental cause of prevailing unrest; no matter what is done with the superstructure, no matter how it may be improved in one way or the other, unless we eradicate that fundamental difficulty, unrest will not only continue, but, in my opinion, will grow worse. . . .

CHAIRMAN WALSH. For the purpose of illustration, take a corporation such as the Steel Corporation and explain what you mean by the democratization of industry, and to apply it to a concrete corporation, take that one.

MR. BRANDEIS. I think the difficulty of applying it to that corporation, I mean a corporation as large as that and as powerful as that, is this: The unit is so large that it is almost inconceivable that the men in control can be made to realize the necessity of yielding a part of their power to the employee.

Now, when they resist a particular labor policy—for instance, the unionization of shops—and they do resist it violently, most of the officials do so in absolute good faith, convinced that they are doing what they ought to do. They have in mind the excesses of labor unions and their obligations to stockholders to protect the property; and having those things in mind and exaggerating, no doubt, the dangers of the situation, they conclude that they cannot properly submit to so-called union demands. They are apt to believe that it is "un-American" to do so—and declare it to be contrary to our conceptions of liberty, and the rest. And they believe they are generally sincere in their statements.

The possession of almost absolute power makes them believe this. It is exactly the same condition that presents itself often in the political world.

No doubt the Emperor of Russia means just as well toward each of his subjects as most rulers of a constitutional government or the executives of a republic. But he is subject to a state of mind that he cannot overcome. The fact that he possesses the power and that he is the final judge of what is right or wrong prevents his seeing clearly and doing that which is necessary to give real liberty and freedom.

It is almost inconceivable to my mind that a corporation with powers so concentrated as the Steel Corporation could get to a point where it would be willing to treat with the employees on equal terms. And unless they treat on equal terms then there is no such thing as democratization. The treatment on equal terms with them involves not merely the making of a contract; it must develop into a continuing relation. The making of a contract with a union is a long step. It is collective bargaining—a great advance. But it is only the first step. In order that collective bargaining should result in industrial democracy it must go further and create practically an industrial government—a relation between employer and employee where the problems as they arise from day to day, or from month to month, or from year to year, may come up for consideration and solution as they come up in our political government.

In that way conditions are created best adapted to securing proper consideration of any question arising. The representative of each party is heard—and strives to advance the interest he represents. It is the conflict of these opposing forces which produces the contract ultimately. But adequately to solve the trade problems there must be some machinery which will deal with these problems as they arise from day to day. You must create something akin to a government of the trade before you reach a real approach to democratization. You must create a relation of employer to employee similar to that which exists in the trade under the protocol with the preferential union shop.

CHAIRMAN WALSH. Past experience indicates that large corporations can be trusted to bring about these reforms themselves?

MR. BRANDEIS. I think all of our human experience shows that no one with absolute power can be trusted to give it up even in part. That has been the experience with political absolutism; it must prove the same with industrial absolutism. Industrial democracy will not come by gift. It has got to be won by those who desire it. And if the situation is such that a voluntary organization like a labor union is powerless to bring about the democratization of a business, I think we have in this fact some proof that the employing organization is larger than is consistent with the public interest. I mean by larger, is more powerful, has a financial influence too great to be useful to the State; and the State must in some way come to the aid of the workingmen if democratization is to be secured.

CHAIRMAN WALSH. Are the workmen employed by large corporations in a position to work out their own salvation by trade-union organization today?

MR. BRANDEIS. I think our experience, taking the steel trade as an example, has certainly shown that they are not. And this is true also of many other lines of business. Even in case of corporations very much smaller than the Steel Corporation, where the unions have found it impossible to maintain their position against the highly centralized, well-managed, highly financed company. Such corporations as a means of overcoming union influence and democratization frequently grant their employees more in wages and comforts than the union standard demands. But "man cannot live by bread alone." Men must have industrial liberty as well as good wages.

CHAIRMAN WALSH. Do you believe that the existing State and Federal legislation is adequately and properly drawn to provide against abuses in industry, so far as the employees are concerned?

MR. BRANDEIS. I have grave doubt as to how much can be accomplished by legislation, unless it be to set a limit upon the size of corporate units. I believe in dealing with this labor problem as in dealing with the problem of credit. We must meet this question.

CHAIRMAN WALSH. Of what? Excuse me.

MR. BRANDEIS. Size. And in dealing with the problem of industrial democracy there underlies all of the difficulties the question of the concentration of power. This factor so important in connection with the subject of credit and in connection with the subject of trusts and monopolies is no less important in treating the labor problem. As long as there is such concentration of power no effort of the workingmen to secure democratization will be effective. The statement that size is not a crime is entirely correct when you speak of it from the point of motive. But size may become such a danger in its results to the community that the community may have to set limits. A large part of our protective legislation consists of prohibiting things which we find are dangerous, according to common experience. Concentration of power has been shown to be dangerous in a democracy, even though that power may be used beneficently. For instance, on our public highways we put a limit on the size of an autotruck, no matter how well it is run. It may have the most skillful and considerate driver, but its mere size may make it something which the community cannot tolerate, in view of the other uses of the highway and the danger inherent in its occupation to so large an extent by a single vehicle.

CHAIRMAN WALSH. Commissioner Lennon has a few questions he would like to ask.

COMMISSIONER LENNON. Mr. Brandeis, in speaking with regard to the physical betterment that has come about in some instances in these great industries, did you mean to indicate that these physical betterments were not something of an element toward progress, toward democratic manhood?

MR. BRANDEIS. I think they contribute a very material amount, provided they do not result in a bribe to forgo that which is more important.

COMMISSIONER LENNON. Now, to apply it to the work that the unions have done for physical betterment, increase of wages and limitation of the hours, and the elimination of children like in the coal industry.

MR. BRANDEIS. Oh, I think those are all positive gains, unqualified gains.

COMMISSIONER LENNON. Gains for manhood?

MR. BRANDEIS. They are all gains for manhood; and we recognize that manhood is what we are striving for in America. We are striving for democracy; we are striving for the development of men. It is absolutely essential in order that men may develop that they be properly fed and properly housed, and that they have proper opportunities of education and recreation. We cannot reach our goal without those things. But we may have all those things and have a nation of slaves. . . .

36. ROOSEVELT

The New Deal

Franklin D. Roosevelt (1882–1945), thirty-second President of the United States, was born in Hyde Park, New York, on January 30, 1882. He received his AB degree from Harvard College in 1905 and studied law at Columbia University from 1904 to 1907. Roosevelt practiced law in New York City from 1907 to 1910, when he was elected to the New York state senate as a Democrat from a normally Republican district in upstate Dutchess County. Reelected in 1912, Roosevelt resigned his seat the following year to accept an appointment from President Wilson as Assistant Secretary of the Navy. He held that position until 1920, when he received the nomination of the Democratic Party for Vice President on the ticket with Presidential candidate James M. Cox. Although the Republicans swept the national election, Franklin Roosevelt emerged as a bright new star in Democratic Party politics. But a year later, in August, 1921, Roosevelt was stricken with infantile paralysis, and he was forced to spend the next seven years recuperating from the illness, never recovering the use of his paralyzed legs. He nonetheless reentered political life in 1929 and was elected to the first of two terms as governor of New York. Following these triumphs, Roosevelt was nominated and elected President of the United States in 1932 and was subsequently reelected three times—America's only four-term President.

This selection* presents the full text of President Roosevelt's first Inaugural Address. Delivered on March 4, 1933, the address came at a time when the nation had slumped to the lowest point in the economic crisis which had gripped it since 1929.

I am certain that my fellow Americans expect that on my induction into the Presidency I will address them with a candor and a decision which the present situation of our nation impels. This is pre-eminently the time to speak the truth, the whole truth, frankly and boldly. Nor need we shrink from honestly facing conditions in our country today. This great nation will endure as it has endured, will revive and will prosper. So, first of all, let me assert my firm belief that the only thing we have to fear is fear itself—nameless, unreasoning, unjustified terror which paralyzes needed efforts to convert retreat into advance. In every dark hour of our national life a leadership of frankness and vigor has met with that understanding and support of the people themselves which is essential to victory. I am convinced that you will again give that support to leadership in these critical days.

In such a spirit on my part and on yours we face our common difficulties. They concern, thank God, only material things. Values have shrunken to fantastic levels; taxes have risen; our ability to pay has fallen; government of all kinds is faced by serious curtailment of income; the means of exchange are frozen in the currents of trade; the withered leaves of industrial enterprise lie on every side; farmers find no markets for their produce; the savings of many years in thousands of families are gone.

More important, a host of unemployed citizens face the grim problem

* *The Public Papers and Addresses of Franklin D. Roosevelt*, Samuel I. Rosenman, ed., II (New York: Random House, 1938), pp. 11–16.

of existence, and an equally great number toil with little return. Only a foolish optimist can deny the dark realities of the moment.

Yet our distress comes from no failure of substance. We are stricken by no plague of locusts. Compared with the perils which our fore-fathers conquered because they believed and were not afraid, we still have much to be thankful for. Nature still offers her bounty and human efforts have multiplied it. Plenty is at our doorstep, but a generous use of it languishes in the very sight of the supply. Primarily, this is because the rulers of the exchange of mankind's goods have failed through their own stubbornness and their own incompetence, have admitted their failure, and abdicated. Practices of the unscrupulous money changers stand indicted in the court of public opinion, rejected by the hearts and minds of men.

True, they have tried, but their efforts have been cast in the pattern of an outworn tradition. Faced by failure of credit they have proposed only the lending of more money. Stripped of the lure of profit by which to induce our people to follow their false leadership, they have resorted to exhortations, pleading tearfully for restored confidence. They know only the rules of a generation of self-seekers. They have no vision, and when there is no vision the people perish.

The money changers have fled from their high seats in the temple of our civilization. We may now restore that temple to the ancient truths. The measure of the restoration lies in the extent to which we apply social values more noble than mere monetary profit.

Happiness lies not in the mere possession of money; it lies in the joy of achievement, in the thrill of creative effort. The joy and moral stimulation of work no longer must be forgotten in the mad chase of evanescent profits. These dark days will be worth all they cost us if they teach us that our true destiny is not to be ministered unto but to minister to ourselves and to our fellow-men.

Recognition of the falsity of material wealth as the standard of success goes hand in hand with the abandonment of the false belief that public office and high political position are to be valued only by the standards of pride of place and personal profit; and there must be an end to a conduct in banking and in business which too often has given to a sacred trust the likeness of callous and selfish wrongdoing.

Small wonder that confidence languishes, for it thrives only on honesty, on honor, on the sacredness of obligations, on faithful protection, on unselfish performance; without them it cannot live.

Restoration calls, however, not for changes in ethics alone. This Nation asks for action, and action now.

Our greatest primary task is to put people to work. This is no unsolvable problem if we face it wisely and courageously. It can be accomplished in part by direct recruiting by the Government itself, treating the task as we would treat the emergency of a war, but at the same time, through this employment, accomplishing greatly needed projects to stimulate and reorganize the use of our natural resources.

Hand in hand with this, we must frankly recognize the overbalance of population in our industrial centers and, by engaging on a national scale in a redistribution, endeavor to provide a better use of the land for those best fitted for the land. The task can be helped by definite efforts to raise the values of agricultural products and with this the power to purchase the output of our cities. It can be helped by preventing realistically the tragedy of the growing loss through foreclosure of our small homes and our farms. It can be helped by insistence that the Federal, State and local governments act forthwith on the demand that their cost be drastically reduced. It can be helped by the unifying of relief activities which today are often scattered, uneconomical and unequal. It can be helped by national planning for and supervision of all forms of transportation and of communications and other utilities which have a definitely public character. There are many ways in which it can be helped, but it can never be helped merely by talking about it. We must act, and act quickly.

Finally, in our progress toward a resumption of work we require two safeguards against a return of the evils of the old order: there must be a strict supervision of all banking and credits and investments, there must be an end to speculation with other people's money; and there must be provision for an adequate but sound currency.

These are the lines of attack. I shall presently urge upon a new Congress in special session, detailed measures for their fulfillment, and I shall seek the immediate assistance of the several States.

Through this program of action we address ourselves to putting our own national house in order and making income balance outgo. Our international trade relations, though vastly important, are, in a point of time and necessity secondary to the establishment of a sound national economy. I favor as a practical policy the putting of first things first. I shall spare no effort to restore world trade by international economic readjustment, but the emergency at home cannot wait on that accomplishment.

The basic thought that guides these specific means of national recovery is not narrowly nationalistic. It is the insistence, as a first consideration, upon the interdependence of the various elements in and parts of the United States—a recognition of the old and permanently important manifestation of the American spirit of the pioneer. It is the way to recovery. It is the immediate way. It is the strongest assurance that the recovery will endure.

In the field of world policy I would dedicate this Nation to the policy of the good neighbor—the neighbor who resolutely respects himself and, because he does so, respects the rights of others—the neighbor who respects his obligations and respects the sanctity of his agreements in and with a world of neighbors.

If I read the temper of our people correctly, we now realize as we have never realized before, our interdependence on each other; that we cannot merely take, but we must give as well; that if we are to go forward, we must move as a trained and loyal army willing to sacrifice for the good of a common discipline, because without such discipline, no progress is made, no leadership becomes effective. We are, I know, ready and willing to submit our lives and property to such discipline, because it makes possible a leadership which aims at a larger good. This I propose to offer, pledging that the larger purposes will bind upon us all as a sacred obligation with a unity of duty hitherto evoked only in time of armed strife.

With this pledge taken, I assume unhesitatingly the leadership of this great army of our people, dedicated to a disciplined attack upon our common problems.

Action in this image and to this end is feasible under the form of government which we have inherited from our ancestors. Our Constitution is so simple and practical that it is possible always to meet extraordinary needs by changes in emphasis and arrangement without loss of essential form. That is why our constitutional system has proved itself the most superbly enduring political mechanism the modern world has produced. It has met every stress of vast expansion of territory, of foreign wars, of bitter internal strife, of world relations.

It is to be hoped that the normal balance of Executive and legislative authority may be wholly adequate to meet the unprecedented task before us. But it may be that an unprecedented demand and need for undelayed action may call for temporary departure from that normal balance of public procedure.

I am prepared under my constitutional duty to recommend the

measures that a stricken Nation in the midst of a stricken world may require.

These measures, or such other measures as the Congress may build out of its experience and wisdom, I shall seek, within my constitutional authority, to bring to speedy adoption.

But in the event that the Congress shall fail to take one of these two courses, and in the event that the national emergency is still critical, I shall not evade the clear course of duty that will then confront me. I shall ask the Congress for the one remaining instrument to meet the crisis—broad Executive powei to wage a war against the emergency as great as the power that would be given to me if we were in fact invaded by a foreign foe.

For the trust reposed in me I will return the courage and the devotion that befit the time. I can do no less.

We face the arduous days that lie before us in the warm courage of national unity; with the clear consciousness of seeking old and precious moral values; and with the clean satisfaction that comes from the stern performance of duty by old and young alike. We aim at the assurance of a rounded and permanent national life.

We do not distrust the future of essential democracy. The people of the United States have not failed. In their need they have registered a mandate that they want direct, vigorous action. They have asked for discipline and direction under leadership. They have made me the present instrument of their wishes. In the spirit of the gift I take it.

In this dedication of a Nation we humbly ask the blessing of God. May He protect each and every one of us. May He guide me in the days to come.

37. DEWEY
Intelligence in Politics

John Dewey (1859–1952), the foremost American educator and philosopher of his time, was born in Burlington, Vermont. He attended the local public schools and received his AB degree from the University of

Vermont in 1879 and his PhD from Johns Hopkins University in 1884. Dewey taught philosophy at the University of Michigan from 1884 to 1888 and again from 1889 to 1894, and at the University of Minnesota during the 1888–89 academic year. He served as the chairman of the philosophy department at the University of Chicago from 1894 to 1904 and as director of the school of education at Chicago from 1902 to 1904. In 1904 he accepted a professorship in the department of philosophy at Columbia University and remained in this position until his retirement in 1930. Throughout his life Dewey was active in a variety of academic, political, and civic organizations. He served terms as president of both the American Psychological Association and the American Philosophical Association and was an honorary life president of the National Education Association. He was an honorary vice-chairman of the New York State Liberal Party and was active in such organizations as the League for Industrial Democracy, the Committee for Cultural Freedom, and the International League for Academic Freedom. Dewey was the author of about 300 books and articles. His most important books include: *Democracy and Education* (1916), *Reconstruction in Philosophy* (1920), *Human Nature and Conduct* (1922), *Experience and Nature* (1925), *The Public and Its Problems* (1927), *The Quest for Certainty* (1929), *Logic: The Theory of Inquiry* (1938), and *Freedom and Culture* (1939).

The following selection* is taken from the final chapter of *Liberalism and Social Action.*

Nothing is blinder than the supposition that we live in a society and world so static that either nothing new will happen or else it will happen because of the use of violence. Social change is here as a fact, a fact having multifarious forms and marked in intensity. Changes that are revolutionary in effect are in process in every phase of life. Transformations in the family, the church, the school, in science and art, in economic and political relations, are occurring so swiftly that imagination is baffled in attempt to lay hold of them. Flux does not have to be created. But it does have to be directed. It has to be so controlled that it will move to some end in accordance with the principles of life, since life itself is development. Liberalism is committed to an end that is at once enduring and flexible: the liberation of individuals so that realization of their capacities may be the law of their life. It is committed to the use of freed intelligence as the method of directing change. In any case, civilization is faced with the problem of uniting the changes that are going on into a coherent pattern of social organization. The liberal spirit is marked by its own picture

* (New York: G. P. Putnam's Sons, 1935), pp. 56–58, 61–65, 70–71, 79–81, 86–93.

of the pattern that is required: a social organization that will make possible effective liberty and opportunity for personal growth in mind and spirit in all individuals. Its present need is recognition that established material security is a prerequisite of the ends which it cherishes, so that, the basis of life being secure, individuals may actively share in the wealth of cultural resources that now exist and may contribute, each in his own way, to their further enrichment.

The fact of change has been so continual and so intense that it overwhelms our minds. We are bewildered by the spectacle of its rapidity, scope and intensity. It is not surprising that men have protected themselves from the impact of such vast change by resorting to what psycho-analysis has taught us to call rationalizations, in other words, protective fantasies. The Victorian idea that change is a part of an evolution that necessarily leads through successive stages to some preordained divine far-off event is one rationalization. The conception of a sudden, complete, almost catastrophic, transformation, to be brought about by the victory of the proletariat over the class now dominant, is a similar rationalization. But men have met the impact of change in the realm of actuality, mostly by drift and by temporary, usually incoherent, improvisations. Liberalism, like every other theory of life, has suffered from the state of confused uncertainty that is the lot of a world suffering from rapid and varied change for which there is no intellectual and moral preparation.

Because of the lack of mental and moral preparation the impact of swiftly moving changes produced, as I have just said, confusion, uncertainty and drift. Change in patterns of belief, desire and purpose has lagged behind the modification of the external conditions under which men associate. Industrial habits have changed most rapidly; there has followed at considerable distance, change in political relations; alterations in legal relations and methods have lagged even more, while changes in the institutions that deal most directly with patterns of thought and belief have taken place to the least extent. This fact defines the primary, though not by any means the ultimate, responsibility of a liberalism that intends to be a vital force. Its work is first of all education, in the broadest sense of that term. Schooling is a part of the work of education, but education in its full meaning includes all the influences that go to form the attitudes and dispositions (of desire as well as of belief), which constitute dominant habits of mind and character. . . .

When, then, I say that the first object of a renascent liberalism is education, I mean that its task is to aid in producing the habits of mind and character, the intellectual and moral patterns, that are somewhere near even with the actual movements of events. It is, I repeat, the split between the latter as they have externally occurred and the ways of desiring, thinking, and of putting emotion and purpose into execution that is the basic cause of present confusion in mind and paralysis in action. The educational task cannot be accomplished merely by working upon men's minds, without action that effects actual change in institutions. The idea that dispositions and attitudes can be altered by merely "moral" means conceived of as something that goes on wholly inside of persons is itself one of the old patterns that has to be changed. Thought, desire and purpose exist in a constant give and take of interaction with environing conditions. But resolute thought is the first step in that change of action that will itself carry further the needed change in patterns of mind and character.

In short, liberalism must now become radical, meaning by "radical" perception of the necessity of thoroughgoing changes in the set-up of institutions and corresponding activity to bring the changes to pass. For the gulf between what the actual situation makes possible and the actual state itself is so great that it cannot be bridged by piecemeal policies undertaken *ad hoc*. The process of producing the changes will be, in any case, a gradual one. But "reforms" that deal now with this abuse and now with that without having a social goal based upon an inclusive plan, differ entirely from effort at re-forming, in its literal sense, the institutional scheme of things. The liberals of more than a century ago were denounced in their time as subversive radicals, and only when the new economic order was established did they become apologists for the *status quo* or else content with social patchwork. If radicalism be defined as perception of need for radical change, then today any liberalism which is not also radicalism is irrelevant and doomed.

But radicalism also means, in the minds of many, both supporters and opponents, dependence upon use of violence as the main method of effecting drastic changes. Here the liberal parts company. For he is committed to the organization of intelligent action as the chief method. Any frank discussion of the issue must recognize the extent to which those who decry the use of any violence are themselves willing to resort to violence and are ready to put their will into operation. Their fundamental objection is to change in the economic institution that now exists, and for its maintenance they resort to the use of the force that is placed in their hands by this very institution. They do not need to advocate the use of force; their only need is to employ it. Force, rather than intelligence, is built into the procedures of the existing social system, regularly as coercion, in times of crisis as overt violence. The legal system, conspicuously in its penal aspect, more subtly in civil practice, rests upon coercion. Wars are the methods recurrently used in settlement of disputes between nations. One school of radicals dwells upon the fact that in the past the transfer of power in one society has either been accomplished by or attended with violence. But what we need to realize is that physical force is used, at least in the form of coercion, in the very set-up of our society. That the competitive system, which was thought of by early liberals as the means by which the latent abilities of individuals were to be evoked and directed into socially useful channels, is now in fact a state of scarcely disguised battle hardly needs to be dwelt upon. That the control of the means of production by the few in legal possession operates as a standing agency of coercion of the many, may need emphasis in statement, but is surely evident to one who is willing to observe and honestly report the existing scene. It is foolish to regard the political state as the only agency now endowed with coercive power. Its exercise of this power is pale in contrast with that exercised by concentrated and organized property interests.

It is not surprising in view of our standing dependence upon the use of coercive force that at every time of crisis coercion breaks out into open violence. In this country, with its tradition of violence fostered by frontier conditions and by the conditions under which immigration went on during the greater part of our history, resort to violence is especially recurrent on the part of those who are in power. In times of imminent change, our verbal and sentimental worship of the Constitution, with its guarantees of civil liberties of expression, publication and assemblage, readily goes overboard. Often the officials of the law are the worst offenders, acting as agents of some power that rules the economic life of a community. What is said about the value of free speech as a safety valve is then forgotten with the utmost of ease: a comment, perhaps, upon the weakness of the defense of freedom of expression that values it simply as a means of blowing-off steam.

It is not pleasant to face the extent to which, as matter of fact, coercive and violent force is relied upon in the present social system as a means of social control. It is much more agreeable to evade the fact. But unless the fact is acknowledged as a fact in its full depth and breadth, the meaning of dependence upon intelligence as the alternative method of social direction will not be grasped. Failure in acknowledgment signifies, among other things, failure to realize that those who propagate the dogma of dependence upon force have the sanction of much that is already entrenched in the existing system. They would but turn the use of it to opposite ends. The assumption that the method of intelligence already rules and that those who urge the use of violence are introducing a new element into the social picture may not be hypocritical but it is unintelligently unaware of what is actually involved in intelligence as an alternative method of social action. . . .

. . . I wish to say something about the operation of intelligence in our present political institutions, as exemplified by current practices of democratic government. I would not minimize the advance scored in substitution of methods of discussion and conference for the method of arbitrary rule. But the better is too often the enemy of the still better. Discussion, as the manifestation of intelligence in political life, stimulates publicity; by its means sore spots are brought to light that would otherwise remain hidden. It affords opportunity for promulgation of new ideas. Compared with despotic rule, it is an invitation to individuals to concern themselves with public affairs. But discussion and dialectic, however indispensable they are to the elaboration of ideas and policies after ideas are once put forth, are weak reeds to depend upon for systematic origination of comprehensive plans, the plans that are required if the problem of social organization is to be met. There was a time when discussion, the comparison of ideas already current so as to purify and clarify them, was thought to be sufficient in discovery of the structure and laws of physical nature. In the latter field, the method was displaced by that of experimental observation guided by comprehensive working hypotheses, and using all the resources made available by mathematics.

But we still depend upon the method of discussion, with only incidental scientific control, in politics. Our system of popular suffrage, immensely valuable as it is in comparison with what preceded it, exhibits the idea that intelligence is an individualistic possession, at best enlarged by public discussion. Existing political practice, with its complete ignoring of occupational groups and the organized knowledge and purposes that are involved in the existence of such groups, manifests a dependence upon a summation of individuals quantitatively, similar to Bentham's purely quantitative formula of the greatest sum of pleasures of the greatest possible number. The formation of parties or, as the eighteenth-century writers called them, factions, and the system of party government is the practically necessary counterweight to a numerical and atomistic individualism. The idea that the conflict of parties will, by means of public discussion, bring out necessary public truths is a kind of political watered-down version of the Hegelian dialectic, with its synthesis arrived at by a union of antithetical conceptions. The method has nothing in common with the procedure of organized coöperative inquiry which has won the triumphs of science in the field of physical nature. . . .

It is frequently asserted that the method of experimental intelligence can be applied to physical facts because physical nature does not present conflicts of class interests, while it is inapplicable to society because the latter is so deeply marked by incompatible interests. It is then assumed that the "experimentalist" is one who has chosen to ignore the uncomfortable fact of conflicting interests. Of course, there *are* conflicting interests; otherwise there would be no social problems. The problem under discussion is precisely *how* conflicting claims are to be settled in the interest of the widest possible contribution to the interests of all—or at least of the great majority. The method of democracy—inasfar as it is that of organized intelligence—is to bring these conflicts out into the open where their special claims can be seen and appraised, where they can be discussed and judged in the light of more inclusive interests than are represented by either of them separately. There is, for example, a clash of interests between munition manufacturers and most of the rest of the population. The more the respective claims of the two are publicly and scientifically weighed, the more likely it is that the public interest will be disclosed and be made effective. There is an undoubted objective clash of interests between finance-capitalism that controls the means of production and whose profit is served by maintaining relative scarcity, and idle workers and hungry consumers. But what generates violent strife is failure to bring the conflict into the light of intelligence where the conflicting interests can be adjudicated in behalf of the interest of the great majority. Those most committed to the dogma of inevitable force recognize the need for intelligently discovering and expressing the dominant social interest up to a certain point and then draw back. The "experimentalist" is one who would see to it that the method depended upon by all in some degree in every democratic community be followed through to completion.

In spite of the existence of class conflicts, amounting at times to veiled civil war, any one habituated to the use of the method of science will view with considerable suspicion the erection of actual human beings into fixed entities called classes, having no overlapping interests and so internally unified and externally separated that they are made the protagonists of history—itself hypothetical. Such an idea of classes is a survival of a rigid logic that once prevailed in the sciences of nature, but that no longer has any place there. This conversion of abstractions into entities smells more of a dialectic of concepts than of a realistic examination of facts, even though it makes more of an emotional appeal to many than do the results of the latter. To say that all past historic social progress has been the result of coöperation and not of conflict would be also an exaggeration. But exaggeration against exaggeration, it is the more reasonable of the two. And it is no exaggeration to say that the measure of civilization is the degree in which the method of coöperative intelligence replaces the method of brute conflict. . . .

The final argument in behalf of the use of intelligence is that as are the means used so are the actual ends achieved—that is, the consequences. I know of no greater fallacy than the claim of those who hold to the dogma of the necessity of brute force that this use will be the method of calling genuine democracy into existence—of which they profess themselves the simon-pure adherents. It requires an unusually credulous faith in the Hegelian dialectic of opposites to think that all of a sudden the use of force by a class will be transmuted into a democratic classless society. Force breeds counterforce; the Newtonian law of action and reaction still holds in physics, and violence is physical. To profess democracy as an ultimate ideal and the suppression of democracy as a means to the ideal may be possible in a country that has never known even rudimentary democracy, but when professed in a country that has anything of a genuine democratic spirit in its traditions, it signifies desire for possession and retention of power by a class, whether that class be called Fascist or Proletarian. In the light of what happens in non-democratic countries, it is pertinent to ask whether the rule of a class signifies the dictatorship of the majority, or dictatorship over the chosen class by a minority party; whether dissenters are allowed even within the class the party claims to represent; and whether the development of literature and the other arts proceeds according to a formula prescribed by a party in conformity with a doctrinaire dogma of history and of infallible leadership, or whether artists are free from regimentation? Until these questions are satisfactorily answered, it is permissible to look with considerable suspicion upon those who assert that suppression of democracy is the road to the adequate establishment of genuine democracy. The one exception—and that apparent rather than real—to dependence upon organized intelligence as the method for directing social change is found when society through an authorized majority has entered upon the path of social experimentation leading to great social change, and a minority refuses by force to permit the method of intelligent action to go into effect. Then force may be intelligently employed to subdue and disarm the recalcitrant minority.

There may be some who think I am unduly dignifying a position held by a comparatively small group by taking their arguments as seriously as I have done. But their position serves to bring into strong relief the alternatives before us. It makes clear the meaning of renascent liberalism. The alternatives are continuation of drift with attendant improvisations to meet special emergencies; dependence upon violence; dependence upon socially organized intelligence. The first two alternatives, however, are not mutually exclusive, for if things are allowed to drift the result may be some sort of social change effected by the use of force, whether so planned or not. Upon the whole, the recent policy of liberalism has been to further "social legislation"; that is, measures which add performance of social services to the older functions of government. The value of this addition is not to be despised. It marks a decided move away from *laissez faire* liberalism, and has considerable importance in educating the public mind to a realization of the possibilities of organized social control. It has helped to develop some of the techniques that in any case will be needed in a socialized economy. But the cause of liberalism will be lost for a considerable period if it is not prepared to go further and socialize the forces of production, now at hand, so that the liberty of individuals will be supported by the very structure of economic organization. . . .

Since liberation of the capacities of individuals for free, self-initiated expression is an essential part of the creed of liberalism, liberalism that is sincere must will the means that condition the achieving of its ends. Regimentation of material and mechanical forces is the only way by which the mass of individuals can be released from regimentation and consequent suppression of their cultural possibilities. The eclipse of liberalism is due to the fact that it has not faced the alternatives and adopted the means upon which realization of its professed aims depends. Liberalism can be true to its ideals only as it takes the course that leads to their attainment. The notion that organized social control of economic forces lies outside the historic path of liberalism shows that liberalism is still impeded by remnants of its earlier *laissez faire* phase, with its opposition of society and the individual. The thing which now dampens liberal ardor and paralyzes its efforts is the conception that liberty and development of individuality as ends exclude the use of organized social effort as means. Earlier liberalism regarded the separate and competing economic action of individuals as the means to social well-being as the end. We must reverse the perspective and see that socialized economy is the means of free individual development as the end.

That liberals are divided in outlook and endeavor while reactionaries are held together by community of interests and the ties of custom is well-nigh a commonplace. Organization of standpoint and belief among liberals can be achieved only in and by unity of endeavor. Organized unity of action attended by consensus of beliefs will come about in the degree in which social control of economic forces is made the goal of liberal action. The greatest educational power, the greatest force in shaping the dispositions and attitudes of individuals, is the social medium in which they live. The medium that now lies closest to us is that of unified action for the inclusive end of a socialized economy. The attainment of a state of society in which a basis of material security will release the powers of individuals for cultural expression is not the work of a day. But by concentrating upon the task of securing a socialized economy as the ground and medium for release of the impulses and capacities men agree to call ideal, the now scattered and often conflicting activities of liberals can be brought to effective unity.

It is no part of my task to outline in detail a program for renascent liberalism. But the question of "what is to be done" cannot be ignored. Ideas must be organized, and this organization implies an organization of individuals who hold these ideas and whose faith is ready to translate itself into action. Translation into action signifies that the general creed of liberalism be formulated as a concrete program of action. It is in organization for action that liberals are weak, and without this organization there is danger that democratic ideals may go by default. Democracy has been a fighting faith. When its ideals are reënforced by those of scientific method and experimental intelligence, it cannot be that it is incapable of evoking discipline, ardor and organization. To narrow the issue for the future to a struggle between Fascism and Communism is to invite a catastrophe that may carry civilization down in the struggle. Vital and courageous democratic liberalism is the one force that can surely avoid such a disastrous narrowing of the issue. I for one do not believe that Americans living in the tradition of Jefferson and Lincoln will weaken and give up without a whole-hearted effort to make democracy a living reality. This, I repeat, involves organization. . . .

It would be fantastic folly to ignore or to belittle the obstacles that stand in the way. But what has taken place, also against great odds, in the scientific and industrial revolutions, is an accomplished fact; the way is marked out. It may be that the way will remain untrodden. If so, the future holds the menace of confusion moving into chaos, a chaos that will be externally masked for a time by an organization of force, coercive and violent, in which the liberties of men will all but disappear. Even so, the cause of the liberty of the human spirit, the cause of opportunity of human beings for full development of their powers, the cause for which liberalism enduringly stands, is too precious and too ingrained in the human constitution to be forever obscured. Intelligence after millions of years of errancy has found itself as a method, and it will not be lost forever in the blackness of night. The business of liberalism is to bend every energy and exhibit every courage so that these precious goods may not even be temporarily lost but be intensified and expanded here and now.

VIII

Liberalism
Since World War II

In the years since the close of World War II, American liberals have primarily been concerned with two basic issues. They have sought, first, to expand the social welfare state initiated by the New Deal; and, second, they have actively supported the extension of constitutional rights for individuals and minority groups by the United States Supreme Court and the Congress.

The struggle for the expansion of the welfare state proved to be a particularly long and not entirely successful one. In the immediate postwar period President Truman obtained continued Congressional support for programs that had been established during the New Deal— minimum wages, social security benefits, and low income housing— but met with crushing defeat in those areas of domestic reform that were new and most controversial—federal aid to education, a national program of health insurance, and the Brannan farm subsidy plan. The entrenched power in the Congress of conservative opponents of domestic reform, the indifference to social and economic problems on the part of an increasingly affluent American public, and the onset of the Korean War in June, 1950, combined to put an end to President Truman's Fair Deal.

The election of Dwight D. Eisenhower to the Presidency in 1952, the first Republican administration in two decades, symbolized the triumph of postwar conservatism and brought an end to the national political leadership for domestic reform that both Presidents Roosevelt and Truman had supplied. In fairness, it must be said that President Eisenhower supported legislation for federal aid to education, though his proposals were defeated in the Congress. Further, a major breakthrough in federal support for urban renewal took place during the Eisenhower years with the enactment of the Housing Act of 1954.

The prevailing mood of the 1950's was, however, one of private indulgence and opposition to an expanded role for government in the nation's social and economic life. Only under the pressure of domestic events—the growth of the civil rights movement, for example—and of liberal criticism did the public mood gradually change. Perhaps the most important and influential liberal commentator in contemporary

America is John Kenneth Galbraith. Beginning in the late 1950's and continuing throughout the 1960's, Galbraith has attacked America's commitment to private spending and its antagonism toward government spending for domestic purposes. Most important, he was one of the first public figures to direct the nation's attention to the existence of poverty in an otherwise affluent America. In his many writings and speeches Galbraith has repeatedly called for a revision of the country's thinking about public expenditures so that a large-scale program of governmental spending might be undertaken to eliminate poverty. In advocating a governmental solution to poverty, Galbraith has placed himself squarely within the tradition of twentieth-century American liberalism, which has consistently favored the use of governmental authority to meet domestic problems.

The issue of poverty and domestic reform was stressed by John F. Kennedy during his brief tenure as President. While public recognition and support for his reform proposals increased during the early 1960's, a recalcitrant Congress successfully blocked passage of most of Kennedy's legislative program. It was not until after President Kennedy's death and the overwhelming victory of Lyndon B. Johnson in the 1964 national election that the logjam of domestic reform legislation was finally broken. Aid to education, Medicare, and anti-poverty legislation were among the major laws enacted during 1964 and 1965 as part of President Johnson's domestic program.

President Johnson succeeded in making major changes in the national government's commitment to help eliminate the social and economic problems of the nation, but many of his programs, especially in the area of poverty and aid to the cities, were underfinanced and hence unable to achieve their stated purposes. The 1968 Report of the National Advisory Commission on Civil Disorders documented the seriousness of the racial problem in America's large cities and called for a massive new attack on the causes of this condition: white racism, blighted housing, inadequate health and welfare programs, and widespread unemployment in the ghettos. Thus, the demand for a continuation of domestic reform remained strong in the closing years of the 1960's, but it was uncertain whether the nation and the Congress would respond to the call.

While liberalism's success with domestic reform has been limited, it has, on the contrary, met with good fortune in the field of legal rights for individuals and minority groups. The United States Supreme Court has spearheaded the extension of these constitutional rights and has been the leading force in advancing American liberalism since the mid-1950's.

Having the Supreme Court play this role in behalf of liberalism has not been without its intellectual difficulties, however. At least since the time of Jefferson, liberals have attacked the Court for its undemocratic and conservative nature. Eugene V. Rostow, in his essay "The Democratic Character of Judicial Review," attempted to reevaluate the Supreme Court's power of judicial review and to associate this doctrine with American liberal democratic theory. Rostow first denied the contention made by critics of judicial review that only a system of legislative supremacy accords with the tenets of democracy. He further refused to acknowledge the claim that the people's belief in democracy fades if the power of judicial review is used to control their decisions, and he saw no historic justification for the fear that the people would destroy the independence of the Supreme Court as a reaction to judicial review.

Rostow's argument in behalf of judicial review is partly historical (that it was intended by the framers of the Constitution) and partly pragmatic (that it is necessary to have the courts protect the interests of those individuals and groups who do not have influence in the legislative chambers). Most important, Rostow is concerned with the individual and group rights guaranteed by the Bill of Rights and the Fourteenth Amendment, and he views the Supreme Court as the only institution of government capable of representing these nonmajority interests.

To support his contention that the Supreme Court should actively protect individual rights, Rostow maintains that the Court is an educational body engaged in a continuing debate with the American public over important matters of public policy. It uses its power of review to formulate important principles of law for the society. Rostow sees nothing undemocratic in this procedure; to the contrary, it can be a method by which democracy is advanced in this nation:

> The reciprocal relation between the Court and the community in the formation of policy may be a paradox to those who believe that there is something undemocratic in the power of judicial review. But the work of the Court can have, and when wisely exercised does have, the effect not of inhibiting but of releasing and encouraging the dominantly democratic forces of American life.

Under the intellectual and personal leadership of Chief Justice

Warren the Supreme Court has accepted the task of implementing the philosophy advocated by Rostow. During the tenure of Chief Justice Earl Warren the Supreme Court has decided cases involving a wide variety of civil liberty and civil rights problems: obscenity; freedom of speech, association, press, travel, and religion; church-state relations; the procedural rights of the criminally accused; and alleged discrimination against the Negro and the urban dweller. In the great majority of these cases the Court has upheld the individual or group claim to the existence of a constitutional liberty or right.

The cases of *Brown* v. *Board of Education*, *Reynolds* v. *Sims*, and *Miranda* v. *Arizona* are three of the most important of these decisions: each has brought about dramatic changes in the legal, political, and social system of the United States. In the Brown case, involving a series of challenges to state education segregation laws, the Supreme Court overturned the "separate but equal" interpretation of the Fourteenth Amendment established in the 1896 case of *Plessy* v. *Ferguson*. Writing for a unanimous Court, Chief Justice Warren cited sociological and psychological studies to support his argument and concluded that "in the field of public education the doctrine of 'separate but equal' has no place. Separate educational facilities are inherently unequal."

In *Reynolds* v. *Sims* the Supreme Court upheld the claim that the system of representation used for electing the legislatures of a number of states violated the equal protection clause of the Fourteenth Amendment. Writing for an eight-man majority, Chief Justice Warren concluded that the Fourteenth Amendment required that the principle of "equal representation for equal numbers of people" be applied to the election of all state legislators: "the Equal Protection Clause requires that the seats in both houses of a bicameral state legislature must be apportioned on a population basis."

Throughout most of American history the major criminal procedure requirements of the Bill of Rights had been held to apply only to the national government. But in the early 1960's the Supreme Court decided a number of cases that compelled the states to follow these constitutional standards. The right to counsel and the protection against self-incrimination, for example, were interpreted to be part of the liberty guaranteed to the individual against state government by the due process clause of the Fourteenth Amendment.

In 1965 the Supreme Court began a new examination into the issue of police confessions. *Escobedo* v. *Illinois* extended the right to counsel to include the period of interrogation and abandoned the test of voluntariness for the use of confessions in state courts. But the decision in the Escobedo case raised more questions than it answered. Did the Court intend to outlaw all police interrogations and confessions? Or would the Court accept these practices only where a suspect had been expressly told of his constitutional protection against self-incrimination and his right to counsel? Would the state have to provide counsel to an indigent accused?

Two years after *Escobedo* v. *Illinois*, the Supreme Court provided answers to these and other questions. In *Miranda* v. *Arizona*, Chief Justice Warren clearly outlined the procedures necessary if confessions were to meet constitutional standards. The most important of these rules were stated by the Chief Justice at the beginning of his opinion:

> Prior to any questioning, the person must be warned that he has a right to remain silent, that any statement he does make may be used as evidence against him, and that he has a right to the presence of an attorney, either retained or appointed. The defendant may waive effectuation of these rights, provided the waiver is made voluntarily, knowingly and intelligently. If, however, he indicates in any manner and at any stage of the process that he wishes to consult with an attorney before speaking there can be no questioning.

While the Supreme Court has been the most active of the three branches of the federal government in advancing liberalism in post-World War II America, it would be wrong to ignore the significant role played by the President and the Congress in the area of civil rights. Viewed in the perspective of twentieth-century American liberalism, the recent actions by the elected branches of government seem doubly remarkable. Neither Theodore Roosevelt nor Woodrow Wilson suggested any legislation designed to assist America's Negro minority, and Franklin Roosevelt proposed only the enactment of an antilynch law in the late 1930's. A filibuster in the United States Senate prevented the passage of this modest proposal; but no civil rights bill passed the Congress from the time of Reconstruction until 1957.

President Truman deserves credit for first defining the nature of the civil rights problem in this nation and for proposing legislation to remedy the situation. His program was based on the 1947 report of his Committee on Civil Rights, *To Secure These Rights*. The report called for the strengthening of the role of the Justice Department and the FBI in civil rights matters, the enactment of antilynch and antipoll tax laws, and the creation of a Fair Employment Practices Commission.

When Congress refused to act on these proposals, President Truman used his executive powers to reorganize the civil rights section of the Justice Department and to have the FBI assist private parties in civil rights cases. In addition, he issued executive orders in 1948 which led to the end of segregation in the armed services and in employment in all government agencies.

Finally, in 1957 Congress, too, joined in the struggle against racial discrimination, enacting in little more than a decade five civil rights laws. Most important were the Civil Rights Act of 1964, which outlawed discrimination in interstate businesses providing public accommodations; the Civil Rights Act of 1965, which eliminated the remaining state barriers to Negro voting in the South; and the Civil Rights Act of 1968, which strengthened federal laws dealing with civil rights crimes and outlawed racial discrimination in the sale or rental of most categories of homes and apartments.

38. GALBRAITH
Poverty Amid Affluence

John Kenneth Galbraith (1908–), who has also used the pseudonyms Hershel McLandrass and Mark Epernay, is Paul M. Warburg professor of economics at Harvard University. He has been called America's most influential economist, though Professor Galbraith humbly denies this singular importance. The United States has its good neighbor to the north to thank for Galbraith's beginnings. He was born in Iona Station, Ontario, Canada, in 1908 and received his BS degree from the University of Toronto in 1931 before coming south to take advanced degrees at the University of California. Galbraith served two tours of duty with the federal government. From 1942 to 1943 he was a deputy administrator in the Office of Price Administration and from 1961 to 1963 American ambassador to India. Galbraith taught at Princeton University and was a member of the board of editors of *Fortune* magazine before coming to Harvard in 1948. He has written widely on economic and political issues and has been active in Democratic Party affairs. Galbraith's books include: *American Capitalism* (1952), *A Theory of Price Control* (1952), *The Great Crash* (1955), *The Affluent Society* (1958), *The Liberal Hour* (1960), *Economic Development* (1963), and *The New Industrial State* (1967). The following selection* is taken from a 1964 article by Galbraith, "Let Us Begin: An Invitation to Action on Poverty."

The misfortune of the liberal is that he must suffer the censure of both his friends and his enemies. His friends are particularly severe, for, naturally enough, they hold him to much higher standards of intellectual deportment than those with whom they disagree. I speak here from experience. Because, a few years ago, I wrote a book which described our society as affluent I have ever since been accused of believing that there are no poor people left in the United States. This charge comes, to be sure, from those who have not read the book but as every author is aware this accounts for a distressingly large majority of the voting population and a not insignificant fraction of the more eloquent critics. I continue to hope that those who have been more profligate of their energy will recall that one of my principal purposes was to urge that growing wealth would not, of itself, solve the problem of poverty. Instead, with increased well-being, the position of those left behind would become ever more shameful—an anachronism from which we would be able to divert our eyes only with ever-increasing determination. But my purpose here is not to defend myself but—in the deeper tradition of American liberalism—to dwell on the shortcomings of other people.

The problem of poverty in the United States is the problem of people who for reasons of location, education, health, environment in youth or mental deficiency, or race are not able to participate effectively— or at all—in the economic life of the nation. Being barred from participation they are denied the income that accrues to participants. So they live in deprivation.

Those who argue that a steady expansion in economic output is a necessary condition for the elimination of poverty have a valid case. People who are able to participate in the economy must have a chance for jobs. And there also continues to be good reason for seeking a broad and equitable distribution of the revenues from production. . . .

But on one elementary point there must be no doubt. If the head of a family is stranded deep on the Cumberland Plateau, or if he never went to school, or if he has no useful skill, or if his health is broken, or if he succumbed as a youngster to a slum environment, or if opportunity is denied to him because he is a Negro, then he will be poor and his family will be poor and that will be true no matter how opulent everyone else becomes. A very large part of the very worst poverty is the affliction of people who are unable to make a useful contribution to the economy. Being unable to contribute they receive nothing. They will continue to receive nothing no matter how rapidly the economy expands.

Equally there must be no doubt that the means for rescuing these people or their children—investment to conserve and develop resources, assistance in relocation of workers, assistance to new industries, vastly improved education, training and retraining, medical and mental care, youth employment, counseling, urban recreational facilities, housing, slum abatement, and the assurance of full civic equality—will require public effort and public funds. This must be honest effort and not pilot projects which are a modern device for simulating action without spending money. Poverty can be made to disappear. It won't be accomplished simply by stepping up the growth rate any more than it will be accomplished by incantation or ritualistic washing of the feet. Growth is only for those who can take advantage of it.

We have, of course, no hope of erasing this blot on our social life if we are affected by the thinking of that new and interesting cult which call themselves the modern conservatives. As to this, I suppose, there will be general agreement the modern conservative is not even especially modern. He is engaged, on the contrary, in one of man's oldest, best financed, most applauded, and, on the whole, least successful exercises in moral philosophy. That is the search for a superior moral justification for selfishness. It is an exercise which always involves a certain number of internal contradictions and even a few absurdities. The conspicuously wealthy turn up urging the character-building value of privation for the poor. The man who has struck it rich in minerals, oil, or other bounties of nature is found explaining the debilitating effect of unearned income from the state. The corporation executive who is a superlative success as an organization man weighs in on the evils of bureaucracy. Federal aid to education is feared by those who live in suburbs that could easily forgo this danger, and by people whose children are in private schools. Socialized medicine is condemned by men emerging from Walter Reed Hospital. Social Security is viewed with alarm by those who have the comfortable cushion of an inherited income. Those who are immediately threatened by public efforts to meet their needs— whether widows, small farmers, hospitalized veterans, or the unemployed—are almost always oblivious to their danger.

The first three or four times that I read *The Conscience of a Conservative* I confess that I was slightly attracted by the vision of a young, two-fisted man of my own age, up from the ranks, self-reliant, self-made, accepting the risk of illness without income, disdaining any organized provision for his old age, asking only that he might keep safe from the tax collector what he earned by the sweat of his own brow. I continue to think of this as the work of a detached scholar. But, in the purely literary way that one writer explores the psyche of another, I wonder if some personal anxieties are not eased by identification with a really good department store.

I have no thought of reproach here. My own interest in the Harvard retirement plan slumped appallingly when my books began to appear on the best-seller lists and my wife, quite unexpectedly, became the beneficiary of the small remnants of a New England fortune founded, we believe, on the development of a better horse blanket. Why, we wondered, should the Internal Revenue Service share so handsomely in the royalties when it had had no part in the lonely agonies of composition? Should not the spirit of enterprise that produced those blankets be better rewarded in the present generation? For one fleeting moment Young Americans for Freedom had their chance.

It is not conservatives, however, but liberals who are the object of my present interest. It is to them, conservatives will be relieved to realize, that I address my word of reproach.

The elimination of poverty at home and its mitigation abroad are jobs for liberals. They will not be accomplished unless liberalism is a determined faith. . . .

It is especially important that liberals not be defensive about the public tasks that lie ahead. These are becoming more and not less urgent. . . .

. . . There is no case for redundant bases, unneeded manpower, or unused services. The quarrel is with those who see in sound public service some danger to society. In fact the public services are one of the two great forces in the fiscal system working for economic equity and social stability.

We have long recognized that the progressive income tax is one such force. In the last quarter of the last century and the first quarter of this century, the concentration of wealth proceeded at a rapid, even appalling, rate in the United States. There seemed to be good ground for the Marxist prediction that this concentration would, in the end, destroy the vitality of capitalism and bring its destruction. The income tax was a major step in arresting this trend and thus annulling Marx's prediction. Conservatives have many reasons to be grateful for the Taft family but there can be little doubt that its greatest single monument is William Howard Taft's successful bid for a constitutional amendment permitting the progressive income tax. . . .

But we need to bear in mind that the incidence of public services is similar to that of the progressive income tax. It also strongly favors the least fortunate.

Thus the well-to-do family can escape to the country. It is the poor who need parks and whose children need swimming pools. Only the poor live in the slums and require the myriad of services that, we may hope, will one day mitigate urban congestion and public squalor. The well-to-do live in communities that have good schools; it is the schools of slum dwellers and wage and salary workers which would be principally improved by federal aid to education. Colleges and universities are more accessible to the rich than to the poor. It is the masses and not the classes who use mass transportation. The elderly couple of less than average income would be the major beneficiary of medicare. Social security, minimum-wages enforcement, youth employment are all most important for the least well-to-do. It is poor children who play in dirty streets. It is their father who gets laid off when public works are suddenly cut back.

Even the protective functions of the state are most important for those in the lower income brackets. Lethal serum and poison drugs do, one gathers, work rather democratically on rich and poor alike. But many of us could probably survive a certain amount of exploitation in our prescriptions, fraud in our food packaging, mendacity in our dental advertising, or thimblerigging in our securities. We live in parts of cities where epidemics are less likely. The family that struggles to make ends meet, the widow with life-insurance money around loose, the dwellers in urban tenements need the protection of an alert FTC, FDA, SEC, and Public Health Service.

Public services have, to use the economist's word, a strong redistributional effect. And this effect is strongly in favor of those with lower incomes. Those who clamor the loudest for public economy are those for whom public services do the least. Tax reduction that curtails or limits public services has a double effect in comforting the comfortable and afflicting the poor.

This is something which liberals should not forget. I venture to think there is an even stronger lesson for the man of goodwill and good income who, regardless of political disposition, counts himself a good and compassionate citizen. When he is tempted by a crusade against public expenditure, he should remember that the sacrifice is not his. This is all the more true, for the crusaders almost invariably exclude defense expenditures, the one large outlay that even the most affluent corporation finds a convenient source of revenue.

In recent times there has been a noticeable reluctance to base social policy on differences in personal income—or even to admit that they exist. Politicians now avoid the subject. As pornography has become ever more popular, inequality has become obscene. Ours is a classless society; we must not set the poor against the rich, or possibly vice versa.

This is great nonsense. There are wide differences in ability to pay in our society. There are also wide differences in the benefit from public services. These are facts of life to be treated without rancor but with full candor. The progressive income tax is a powerful force for equality and the stability of our economic institutions. So are public services. To suppose that public services are of equal benefit to people of all income, and hence that there is equality of sacrifice in curtailment, is to work a fraud on the poorest of our citizens.

My impression is that poverty will be eliminated primarily by energetic action along lines on which we are already working—on civil rights, education, slum abatement, the rest. . . .

To the best of knowledge there is no place in the world where a well-educated population is really poor. If so, let us here in the United States select, beginning next year, the hundred lowest-income counties (or, in the case of urban slums, more limited areas of substantial population and special need) and designate them as special educational districts. These would be equipped (or re-equipped) with a truly excellent and comprehensive school plant, including both primary and secondary schools, transportation, and the best in recreational facilities. The employment on construction in this part of the task would be well-adjusted to the areas of unemployment.

Next, in the manner of the Peace Corps, but with ample pay, an elite body of teachers would be assembled—ready to serve in the most remote areas, tough enough and well-trained enough to take on the worst slums, proud to go to Harlan County or to Harlem. By this one step we would overcome the present difficulty in getting good teachers to go where they are most needed. I would think that the minimum salary for men and women qualifying for this Corps should be around $12,000.

Finally, the scheme should include modest educational grants to families to feed and clothe children for school and to compensate for their earnings. Breakfast should be available for children who need it in addition to lunch. Perhaps there should be an issue of efficient and attractive clothing. Specifically qualified members of the Corps would be available for counseling on home conditions, following up on truancy and delinquency, and otherwise insuring that these youngsters overcome the environment to which the accident of birth committed them. Those who need it would be provided with medical and psychiatric care. The year following, the program would be enlarged and extended to the next 150 or two hundred most abysmal areas. It would come to cover as quickly as possible the areas of need. But it would not go beyond areas of low income or, as in the case of the slums, of special educational problems.

This is not federal aid to education. It is an attack on poverty by what I would judge to be the most effective single step that could be taken. Can anyone argue that youngsters with these facilities and this training would share the dismal fate of their parents? As incomes rise above a specified level, the schools would be returned to the localities in accordance with a cost-sharing formula that would take account of increasing ability to pay. Those who fear federal control of education are amply protected. The effort would not affect them.

There are adequate precedents for such action. Some ten years ago it was sadly evident that our highways were heading for trouble. In the richer states they were fairly good. Elsewhere they were too few, too narrow, and too slow. One day soon the vehicles would be backing up into Detroit itself. Then we would have only an interlocked mass of metal full of sound but devoid of movement. The consequences for business would be far from agreeable. Foreseeing this crisis, the federal government stepped in. Disdaining to be bound by the time-honored formulae for sharing costs with the states, it proceeded, subject to some fairly transparent disguises, to contribute up to 90 per cent of the cost of the new highways. General Motors did not object. Ford did not object. Chrysler did not object. The National Association of Manufacturers was acquiescent. Mr. Lucius Clay, the father of the scheme, was at no time stigmatized as a radical promoter of big government. Confident of the same approval, I would urge that we finance in the same way this frontal attack on the areas where education is worst, is needed most, and has the most to offer.

39. ROSTOW

Judicial Review and Democracy

Eugene V. Rostow (1913–) received an AB degree from Yale College in 1933 and an LLB from Yale Law School in 1937. He has been a member of the Yale Law School faculty since 1938 and served as dean of that school from 1955 to 1965. Rostow served as an adviser to the Department of State from 1942 to 1944 and as assistant executive director of the United Nation's Economic Commission for Europe from 1949 to 1950. In September, 1966, President Johnson appointed him to be Undersecretary of State for Political Affairs. He has taught at Cambridge University and at several leading law schools and universities in the United States. Rostow is the author of many articles and reviews, and his books include: *Planning for Freedom* (1959), *The Sovereign Prerogative: The Supreme Court and the Quest for Law* (1962), and *Law, Power and the Pursuit of Peace* (1968). This selection* is from his 1952 article "The Democratic Character of Judicial Review."

It would require an uncommon portion of fortitude in the judges to do their duty as faithful guardians of the Constitution, where legislative invasions of it had been instigated by the major voice of the community.
— *Alexander Hamilton*

A theme of uneasiness, and even of guilt colors the literature about judicial review. Many of those who have talked, lectured, and written about the Constitution have been troubled by a sense that judicial review is undemocratic. Why should a majority of nine Justices appointed for life be permitted to outlaw as unconstitutional the acts of elected officials or of officers controlled by elected officials? Judicial review, they have urged, is an undemocratic shoot on an otherwise respectable tree. It should be cut off, or at least kept pruned and in-

* 66 *Harvard Law Review*, 193–200, 209–10 (all footnotes omitted). Copyright 1952 by The Harvard Law Review Association. By permission of the publisher and the author.

conspicuous. The attack has gone further. Reliance on bad political doctrine, they say, has produced bad political results. The strength of the courts has weakened other parts of the government. The judicial censors are accused of causing laxness and irresponsibility in the state and national legislatures, and political apathy in the electorate. At the same time, we are warned, the participation of the courts in this essentially political function will inevitably lead to the destruction of their independence and thus compromise all other aspects of their work.

The idea that judicial review is undemocratic is not an academic issue of political philosophy. Like most abstractions, it has far-reaching practical consequences. I suspect that for some judges it is the main-spring of decision, inducing them in many cases to uphold legislative and executive action which would otherwise have been condemned. Particularly in the multiple opinions of recent years, the Supreme Court's self-searching often boils down to a debate within the bosoms of the Justices over the appropriateness of judicial review itself.

The attack on judicial review as undemocratic rests on the premise that the Constitution should be allowed to grow without a judicial check. The proponents of this view would have the Constitution mean what the President, the Congress, and the state legislatures say it means. In this way, they contend, the electoral process would determine the course of constitutional development, as it does in countries with plenipotentiary parliaments.

But the Constitution of the United States does not establish a parliamentary government, and attempts to interpret American government in a parliamentary perspective break down in confusion or absurdity. One may recall, in another setting, the anxious voice of the *Washington Post* urging President Truman to resign because the Republican Party had won control of the Congress in the 1946 elections.

It is a grave oversimplification to contend that no society can be democratic unless its legislature has sovereign powers. The social quality of democracy cannot be defined by so rigid a formula. Government and politics are after all the arms, not the end, of social life. The purpose of the Constitution is to assure the people a free and democratic society. The final aim of that society is as much freedom as possible for the individual human being. The Constitution provides society with a mechanism of government fully competent to its task, but by no means universal in its powers. The power to govern is parcelled out between the states and the nation and is further divided among the three main branches of all governmental units. By custom as well as constitutional practice, many vital aspects of community life are beyond the direct reach of government—for example, religion, the press, and, until recently at any rate, many phases of educational and cultural activity. The separation of powers under the Constitution serves the end of democracy in society by limiting the roles of the several branches of government and protecting the citizen, and the various parts of the state itself, against encroachments from any source. The root idea of the Constitution is that man can be free because the state is not.

The power of constitutional review, to be exercised by some part of the government, is implicit in the conception of a written constitution delegating limited powers. A written constitution would promote discord rather than order in society if there were no accepted authority to construe it, at the least in cases of conflicting action by different branches of government or of constitutionally unauthorized governmental action against individuals. The limitation and separation of powers, if they are to survive, require a procedure for independent mediation and construction to reconcile the inevitable disputes over the boundaries of constitutional power which arise in the process of government. British Dominions operating under written constitutions have had to face the task pretty much as we have, and they have solved it in similar ways. Like institutions have developed in other federal systems.

So far as the American Constitution is concerned, there can be little real doubt that the courts were intended from the beginning to have the power they have exercised. The Federalist Papers are unequivocal; the Debates as clear as debates normally are. The power of judicial review was commonly exercised by the courts of the states, and the people were accustomed to judicial construction of the authority derived from colonial charters. Constitutional interpretation by the courts, Hamilton said, does not

> by any means suppose a superiority of the judicial to the legislative power. It only supposes that the power of the people is superior to both; and that where the will of the legislature, declared in its statutes, stands in opposition to that of the people, declared in the Constitution, the judges ought to be governed by the latter rather than the former. They ought to regulate their decisions by the fundamental laws, rather than by those which are not fundamental.

Hamilton's statement is sometimes criticized as a verbal legalism. But it has an advantage too. For much of the discussion has complicated the problem without clarifying it. Both judges and their critics have wrapped themselves so successfully in the difficulties of particular cases that they have been able to evade the ultimate issue posed in the Federalist Papers.

Whether another method of enforcing the Constitution could have been devised, the short answer is that no such method has developed. The argument over the constitutionality of judicial review has long since been settled by history. The power and duty of the Supreme Court to declare statutes or executive action unconstitutional in appropriate cases is part of the living Constitution. "The course of constitutional history," Mr. Justice Frankfurter recently remarked, has cast responsibilities upon the Supreme Court which it would be "stultification" for it to evade. The Court's power has been exercised differently at different times: sometimes with reckless and doctrinaire enthusiasm; sometimes with great deference to the status and responsibilities of other branches of the government; sometimes with a degree of weakness and timidity that comes close to the betrayal of trust. But the power exists, as an integral part of the process of American government. The Court has the duty of interpreting the Constitution in many of its most important aspects, and especially in those which concern the relations of the individual and the state. The political proposition underlying the survival of the power is that there are some phases of American life which should be beyond the reach of any majority, save by constitutional amendment. In Mr. Justice Jackson's phrase, "One's right to life, liberty, and property, to free speech, a free press, freedom of worship and assembly, and other fundamental rights may not be submitted to vote; they depend on the outcome of no elections." Whether or not this was the intention of the Founding Fathers, the unwritten Constitution is unmistakable.

If one may use a personal definition of the crucial word, this way of policing the Constitution is not undemocratic. True, it employs appointed officials, to whom large powers are irrevocably delegated. But democracies need not elect all the officers who exercise crucial authority in the name of the voters. Admirals and generals can win or lose wars in the exercise of their discretion. The independence of judges in the administration of justice has been the pride of communities which aspire to be free. Members of the Federal Reserve Board have the lawful power to plunge the country into depression or inflation. The list could readily be extended. Government by referendum or town meeting is not the only possible form of democracy. The task of democracy is not to have the people vote directly on every issue, but to assure their ultimate responsibility for the acts of their representatives, elected or appointed. For judges deciding ordinary litigation the ultimate responsibility of the electorate has a special meaning. It is a responsibility for the quality of the judges and for the substance of their instructions, never a responsibility for their decisions in particular cases. It is hardly characteristic of law in democratic society to encourage bills of attainder, or to allow appeals from the courts in particular cases to legislatures or to mobs. Where the judges are carrying out the function of constitutional review, the final responsibility of the people is appropriately guaranteed by the provisions for amending the Constitution itself, and by the benign influence of time, which changes the personnel of courts. Given the possibility of constitutional amendment, there is nothing undemocratic in having responsible and independent judges act as important constitutional mediators. Within the narrow limits of their capacity to act, their great task is to help maintain a pluralist equilibrium in society. They can do much to keep it from being dominated by the states or the Federal Government, by Congress or the President, by the purse or the sword.

In the execution of this crucial but delicate function, constitutional review by the judiciary has an advantage thoroughly recognized in both theory and practice. The power of the courts, however final, can only be asserted in the course of litigation. Advisory opinions are forbidden, and reefs of self-limitation have grown up around the doctrine that the courts will determine constitutional questions only in cases of actual controversy, when no lesser ground of decision is available, and when the complaining party would be directly and personally injured by the assertion of the power deemed unconstitutional. Thus the check of judicial review upon the elected branches of government must be a mild one, limited not only by the detachment, integrity, and good sense of the Justices, but by the structural boundaries implicit in the fact that the power is entrusted to the courts. Judicial review is inherently adapted to preserving broad and flexible lines of constitutional growth, not to operating as a continuously active factor in legislation or executive decisions.

The division and separation of governmental powers within the American federal system provides the community with ample power to act, without compromising its pluralist structure. The Constitution formalizes the principle that a wide dispersal of authority among the institutions of society is the safest foundation for social freedom. It was accepted from the beginning that the judiciary would be one of the chief agencies for enforcing the restraints of the Constitution. In a letter to Madison, Jefferson remarked of the Bill of Rights:

> In the arguments in favor of a declaration of rights, you omit one which has great weight with me; the legal check which it puts into the hands of the judiciary. This is a body, which, if rendered independent and kept strictly to their own department, merits great confidence for their learning and integrity. In fact, what degree of confidence would be too much, for a body composed of such men as Wythe, Blair and Pendleton? On characters like these, the *'civium ardor prava pubentium'* would make no impression.

Jefferson, indeed, went further. He regretted the absence in the Constitution of a direct veto power over legislation entrusted to the judiciary, and wished that no legislation could take effect for a year after its final enactment. Within such constitutional limits, Jefferson believed, American society could best achieve its goal of responsible self-government. "I have no fear," he wrote, "but that the result of our experiment will be, that men may be trusted to govern themselves without a master."

Democracy is a slippery term. I shall make no effort at a formal definition here. Certainly as a matter of historical fact some societies with parliamentary governments have been and are "democratic" by standards which Americans would accept, although it is worth noting that almost all of them employ second chambers, with powers at least of delay, and indirect devices for assuring continuity in the event of a parliamentary collapse, either through the crown or some equivalent institution, like the presidency in France. But it would be scholastic pedantry to define democracy in such a way as to deny the title of "democrat" to Jefferson, Madison, Lincoln, Brandeis, and others who have found the American constitutional system, including its tradition of judicial review, well adapted to the needs of a free society. As Mr. Justice Brandeis said,

> the doctrine of the separation of powers was adopted by the Convention of 1787, not to promote efficiency but to preclude the exercise of arbitrary power. The purpose was, not to avoid friction, but, by means of the

inevitable friction incident to the distribution of governmental powers among three departments, to save the people from autocracy.

It is error to insist that no society is democratic unless it has a government of unlimited powers, and that no government is democratic unless its legislature has unlimited powers. Constitutional review by an independent judiciary is a tool of proven use in the American quest for an open society of widely dispersed powers. In a vast country, of mixed population, with widely different regional problems, such an organization of society is the surest base for the hopes of democracy....

The reciprocal relation between the Court and the community in the formation of policy may be a paradox to those who believe that there is something undemocratic in the power of judicial review. But the work of the Court can have, and when wisely exercised does have, the effect not of inhibiting but of releasing and encouraging the dominantly democratic forces of American life. The historic reason for this paradox is that American life in all its aspects is an attempt to express and to fulfill a far-reaching moral code. Some observers find this a handicap to coldly realistic policy making. Others see in it the essential greatness and appealing power of America as an idea and a world force. The prestige and authority of the Supreme Court derive from the fact that it is accepted as the ultimate interpreter of the American code in many of its most important applications.

40. WARREN

Equality in Education

Earl Warren (1891–   ), fourteenth Chief Justice of the United States, was appointed to that position by President Dwight D. Eisenhower in the fall of 1953 following the death of Chief Justice Frederick M. Vinson. Warren reached this honored position after more than three decades of political and legal service in California. Born in Los Angeles, Warren received his legal training at the University of California Law School and entered private practice in the San Francisco-Oakland area in 1914. He served as an infantry lieutenant in World War I and after his return to California held the positions of deputy city attorney of Oakland and first deputy and chief deputy district attorney of Alameda County. From 1925 to 1939 he was Alameda County district attorney and in 1938 was elected attorney general of California. He held the governorship of the state for three terms from 1942 until 1953, when he resigned to become Chief Justice. The 1948 national Republican convention nominated Warren for Vice President of the United States on its unsuccessful ticket headed by New York's Governor Thomas E. Dewey.

One of the first and most difficult cases the Warren Court had to decide was *Brown* v. *Board of Education*.* In 1952 the Supreme Court first heard arguments in five cases dealing with the constitutionality of education segregation laws in South Carolina, Virginia, Delaware, Kansas, and the District of Columbia. In June, 1953, the Court announced that reargument of the cases would take place that fall. The task which immediately fell to the new Chief Justice was to guide the Court in its handling of this most complex and emotional subject. At issue was the constitutional validity of the "separate but equal" doctrine first stated by the Supreme Court in the 1896 case of *Plessy* v. *Ferguson*. The Court's decision affected the school systems of seventeen states and the District of Columbia and involved approximately 40 percent of the nation's school population—some 8 million white and 2.5 million black children. The selection contains most of Chief Justice Warren's opinion for a unanimous Court.

These cases come to us from the States of Kansas, South Carolina, Virginia, and Delaware. They are premised in different facts and different local conditions, but a common legal question justifies their consideration together in this consolidated opinion.

In each of these cases, minors of the Negro race, through their legal representatives, seek the aid of the courts in obtaining admission to the public schools of their community on a nonsegregated basis. In each instance, they had been denied admission to schools attended by white children under laws requiring or permitting segregation according to race. This segregation was alleged to deprive the plaintiffs of the equal protection of the laws under the Fourteenth Amendment. In each of the cases other than the Delaware case, a three-judge federal district court denied relief to the plaintiffs on the so-called "separate but equal" doctrine announced by this Court in Plessy v. Ferguson, 163 U.S. 537. Under that doctrine, equality of treatment is accorded when the races are provided substantially equal facilities, even though these facilities be separate. In the Delaware case, the Supreme Court of Delaware

* 347 U.S. 483, 486–95 (1954).

adhered to that doctrine, but ordered that the plaintiffs be admitted to the white schools because of their superiority to the Negro schools.

The plaintiffs contend that segregated public schools are not "equal" and cannot be made "equal," and that hence they are deprived of the equal protection of the laws. Because of the obvious importance of the question presented, the Court took jurisdiction. Argument was heard in the 1952 Term, and reargument was heard this Term on certain questions propounded by the Court.

Reargument was largely devoted to the circumstances surrounding the adoption of the Fourteenth Amendment in 1868. It covered exhaustively consideration of the Amendment in Congress, ratification by the states, then existing practices in racial segregation, and the views of proponents and opponents of the Amendment. This discussion and our own investigation convince us that, although these sources cast some light, it is not enough to resolve the problem with which we are faced. At best, they are inconclusive. The most avid proponents of the post-war Amendments undoubtedly intended them to remove all legal distinctions among "all persons born or naturalized in the United States." Their opponents, just as certainly, were antagonistic to both the letter and the spirit of the Amendments and wished them to have the most limited effect. What others in Congress and the state legislatures had in mind cannot be determined with any degree of certainty.

An additional reason for the inconclusive nature of the Amendment's history, with respect to segregated schools, is the status of public education at that time. In the South, the movement toward free common schools, supported by general taxation, had not yet taken hold. Education of white children was largely in the hands of private groups. Education of Negroes was almost nonexistent, and practically all of the race were illiterate. In fact, any education of Negroes was forbidden by law in some states. Today, in contrast, many Negroes have achieved outstanding success in the arts and sciences as well as in the business and professional world. It is true that public education had already advanced further in the North, but the effect of the Amendment on Northern States was generally ignored in the congressional debates. Even in the North, the conditions of public education did not approximate those existing today. The curriculum was usually rudimentary; ungraded schools were common in rural areas; the school term was but three months a year in many states; and compulsory school attendance was virtually unknown. As a consequence, it is not surprising that there should be so little in the history of the Fourteenth Amendment relating to its intended effect on public education.

In the first cases in this Court construing the Fourteenth Amendment, decided shortly after its adoption, the Court interpreted it as proscribing all state-imposed discriminations against the Negro race. The doctrine of "separate but equal" did not make its appearance in this Court until 1896 in the case of Plessy v. Ferguson, involving not education but transportation. American courts have since labored with the doctrine for over half a century. In this Court, there have been six cases involving the "separate but equal" doctrine in the field of public education. In Cumming v. County Board of Education, 175 U.S. 528, and Gong Lum v. Rice, 275 U.S. 78, the validity of the doctrine itself was not challenged. In more recent cases all on the graduate school level, inequality was found in that specific benefits enjoyed by the white students were denied to Negro students of the same educational qualifications. Missouri ex rel Gaines v. Canada, 305 U.S. 337; Sipuel v. Oklahoma, 332 U.S. 631; Sweatt v. Painter, 339 U.S. 629; McLaurin v. Oklahoma State Regents, 339 U.S. 637. In none of these cases was it necessary to reexamine the doctrine to grant relief to the Negro plaintiff. And in Sweatt v. Painter . . . the Court expressly reserved decision on the question whether Plessy v. Ferguson should be held inapplicable to public education.

In the instant cases, that question is directly presented. Here, unlike Sweatt v. Painter, there are findings below that the Negro and white schools involved have been equalized, or are being equalized, with respect to buildings, curricula, qualifications and salaries of teachers, and other "tangible" factors. Our decision, therefore, cannot turn on merely a comparison of these tangible factors in the Negro and white schools involved in each of the cases. We must look instead to the effect of segregation itself on public education.

In approaching this problem, we cannot turn the clock back to 1868 when the Amendment was adopted, or even to 1896 when Plessy v. Ferguson was written. We must consider public education in the light of its full development throughout the Nation. Only in this way can it be determined if segregation in public schools deprives these plaintiffs of the equal protection of the laws.

Today, education is perhaps the most important function of state and local governments. Compulsory school attendance laws and the great expenditures for education both demonstrate our recognition of the importance of education to our democratic society. It is required in the performance of our most basic public responsibilities, even service in the armed forces. It is the very foundation of good citizenship. Today it is a principal instrument in awakening the child to cultural values, in preparing him for later professional training, and in helping him to adjust normally to his environment. In these days, it is doubtful that any child may reasonably be expected to succeed in life if he is denied the opportunity of an education. Such an opportunity, where the state has undertaken to provide it, is a right which must be made available to all on equal terms.

We come then to the question presented: Does segregation of children in public schools solely on the basis of race, even though the physical facilities and other "tangible" factors may be equal, deprive the children of the minority group of equal educational opportunities? We believe that it does.

In Sweatt v. Painter . . . in finding that a segregated law school for Negroes could not provide them equal educational opportunities, this Court relied in large part on "those qualities which are incapable of objective measurement but which make for greatness in a law school." In McLaurin v. Oklahoma State Regents . . . the Court, in requiring that a Negro admitted to a white graduate school be treated like all other students, again resorted to intangible considerations: ". . . his ability to study, to engage in discussions and exchange views with other students, and, in general, to learn his profession." Such considerations apply with added force to children in grade and high schools. To separate them from others of similar age and qualifications solely because of their race generates a feeling of inferiority as to their status in the community that may affect their hearts and minds in a way unlikely ever to be undone. The effect of this separation on their educational opportunities was well stated by a finding in the Kansas case by a court which nevertheless felt compelled to rule against the Negro plaintiffs:

"Segregation of white and colored children in public schools has a detrimental effect upon the colored children. The impact is greater when it has the sanction of the law; for the policy of separating the races is usually interpreted as denoting the inferiority of the Negro group. A sense of inferiority affects the motivation of a child to learn. Segregation with the sanction of law, therefore, has a tendency to retard the educational and mental development of Negro children and to deprive them of some of the benefits they would receive in a racially integrated school system." Whatever may have been the extent of psychological knowledge at the time of Plessy v. Ferguson, this finding is amply supported by modern authority.* Any language in Plessy v. Ferguson contrary to this finding is rejected.

We conclude that in the field of public education the doctrine of "separate but equal" has no place. Separate educational facilities are inherently unequal. Therefore, we hold that the plaintiffs and others similarly situated for whom the actions have been brought are, by reason of the segregation complained of, deprived of the equal protection of the laws guaranteed by the Fourteenth Amendment. . . .

41. WARREN
One Man, One Vote

Reynolds v. *Sims*† was one of a number of cases concerned with malapportionment of state legislatures that the United States Supreme Court decided in 1964. A federal district court in Alabama had voided a sixty-year-old apportionment law under which each of Alabama's 35 counties received one seat in the state senate. The population of these counties ranged from 635,000 to 15,000 a population variance ratio of approximately 41 to 1. The ratio in the lower house of the state legislature was about 16 to 1. A special session of the Alabama legislature passed two alternative apportionment plans which slightly altered the older scheme and were to be employed in case the federal judiciary objected to the original system. The district court allowed the 1962 election to be conducted under the provisions of these two laws. The new legislature refused to act on the apportionment issue, and an appeal from the district court's decision reached the Supreme Court. The selection presents excerpts from Chief Justice Warren's opinion for the Court.

* K. B. Clark, Effect of Prejudice and Discrimination on Personality Development (Midcentury White House Conference on Children and Youth) (1950); Witmer and Kotinsky, Personality in the Making (1952), c. VI; Deutscher and Chein, The Psychological Effects of Enforced Segregation: A Survey of Social Science Opinion, 26 J. Psychol. 259 (1948); Chein, What are the Psychological Effects of Segregation Under Conditions of Equal Facilities?, 3 Int. J. Opinion and Attitude Res. 229 (1949); Brameld, Educational Costs, in Discrimination and National Welfare (McIver, ed., 1949), 44–48; Frazier, The Negro in the United States (1949), 674–681. And see generally Myrdal, An American Dilemma (1944).

† 377 U.S. 533, 561–68 (1964).

III

A predominant consideration in determining whether a State's legislative apportionment scheme constitutes an invidious discrimination violative of rights asserted under the Equal Protection Clause is that the rights allegedly impaired are individual and personal in nature. As stated by the Court in United States v. Bathgate, 246 U.S. 220, 227, "[t]he right to vote is personal. . . ." While the result of a court decision in a state legislative apportionment controversy may be to require the restructuring of the geographical distribution of seats in a state legislature, the judicial focus must be concentrated upon ascertaining whether there has been any discrimination against certain of the State's citizens which constitutes an impermissible impairment of their constitutionally protected right to vote. Like Skinner v. Oklahoma, 316 U.S. 535, such a case "touches a sensitive and important area of human rights," and "involves one of the basic civil rights of man," presenting questions of alleged "invidious discriminations . . . against groups or types of individuals in violation of the constitutional guaranty of just and equal laws." 316 U.S., at 536, 541. Undoubtedly, the right of suffrage is a fundamental matter in a free and democratic society. Especially since the right to exercise the franchise in a free and unimpaired manner is preservative of other basic civil and political rights, any alleged infringement of the right of citizens to vote must be carefully and meticulously scrutinized. Almost a century ago, in Yick Wo v. Hopkins, 118 U.S. 356, the Court referred to "the political franchise of voting" as "a fundamental political right, because preservative of all rights." 118 U.S., at 370.

Legislators represent people, not trees or acres. Legislators are elected by voters, not farms or cities or economic interests. As long as ours is a representative form of government, and our legislatures are those instruments of government elected directly by and directly representative of the people, the right to elect legislators in a free and unimpaired fashion is a bedrock of our political system. It could hardly be gainsaid that a constitutional claim had been asserted by an allegation that certain otherwise qualified voters had been entirely prohibited from voting for members of their state legislature. And, if a State should provide that the votes of citizens in one part of the State should be given two times, or five times, or 10 times the weight of votes of citizens in another part of the State, it could hardly be contended that the right to vote of those residing in the disfavored areas had not been effectively diluted. It would appear extraordinary to suggest that a State could be constitutionally permitted to enact a law providing that certain of the State's voters could vote two, five, or 10 times for their legislative representatives, while voters living elsewhere could vote only once. And it is inconceivable that a state law to the effect that, in counting votes for legislators, the votes of citizens in one part of the State would be multiplied by two, five, or 10, while the votes of persons in another area would be counted only at face value, could be constitutionally sustainable. Of course, the effect of state legislative districting schemes which give the same number of representatives to unequal numbers of constituents is identical. Overweighting and overvaluation of the votes of those living here has the certain effect of dilution and undervaluation of the votes of those living there. The resulting discrimination against those individual voters living in disfavored areas is easily demonstrable mathematically. Their right to vote is simply not the same right to vote as that of those living in a favored part of the State. Two, five, or 10 of them must vote before the effect of their voting is equivalent to that of their favored neighbor. Weighting the votes of citizens differently, by any method or means, merely because of where they happen to reside, hardly seems justifiable. One must be ever aware that the Constitution forbids "sophisticated as well as simple-minded modes of discrimination." Lane v. Wilson, 307 U.S. 268, 275; Gomillion v. Lightfoot, 364 U.S. 339, 342. As we stated in Wesberry v. Sanders:

> "We do not believe that the Framers of the Constitution intended to permit the same vote-diluting discrimination to be accomplished through the device of districts containing widely varied numbers of inhabitants. To say that a vote is worth more in one district than in another would . . . run counter to our fundamental ideas of democratic government. . . ."

State legislatures are, historically, the fountainhead of representative government in this country. A number of them have their roots in colonial times, and substantially antedate the creation of our Nation and our Federal Government. In fact, the first formal stirrings of American political independence are to be found, in large part, in the views and actions of several of the colonial legislative bodies. With the birth of our National Government, and the adoption and ratification of the Federal Constitution, state legislatures retained a most important place in our Nation's governmental structure. But representative government is in essence self-government through the medium of elected representatives of the people, and each and every citizen has an inalienable right to full and effective participation in the political processes of his State's legislative bodies. Most citizens can achieve this participation only as qualified voters through the election of legislators to represent them. Full and effective participation by all citizens in state government requires, therefore, that each citizen have an equally effective voice in the election of members of his state legislature. Modern and viable state government needs, and the Constitution demands, no less.

Logically, in a society ostensibly grounded on representative government, it would seem reasonable that a majority of the people of a State could elect a majority of that State's legislators. To conclude differently, and to sanction minority control of state legislative bodies, would appear to deny majority rights in a way that far surpasses any possible denial of minority rights that might otherwise be thought to result. Since legislatures are responsible for enacting laws by which all citizens are to be governed, they should be bodies which are collectively responsive to the popular will. And the concept of equal protection has been traditionally viewed as requiring the uniform treatment of persons standing in the same relation to the governmental action questioned or challenged. With respect to the allocation of legislative representation, all voters, as citizens of a State, stand in the same relation regardless of where they live. Any suggested criteria for the differentiation of citizens are insufficient to justify any discrimination, as to the weight of their votes, unless relevant to the permissible purposes of legislative apportionment. Since the achieving of fair and effective representation for all citizens is concededly the basic aim of legislative apportionment, we conclude that the Equal Protection Clause guarantees the opportunity for equal participation by all voters in the election of state legislators. Diluting the weight of votes because of place of residence impairs basic constitutional rights under the Fourteenth Amendment just as much as invidious discriminations based upon factors such as race, Brown v. Board of Education, 347 U.S. 483, or economic status, Griffin v. People of State of Illinois, 351 U.S. 12, Douglas v. People of State of California, 372 U.S. 353. Our constitutional system amply provides for the protection of minorities by means other than giving them majority control of state legislatures. And the democratic ideals of equality and majority rule, which have served this Nation so well in the past, are hardly of any less significance for the present and the future.

We are told that the matter of apportioning representation in a state legislature is a complex and many-faceted one. We are advised that

States can rationally consider factors other than population in apportioning legislative representation. We are admonished not to restrict the power of the States to impose differing views as to political philosophy on their citizens. We are cautioned about the dangers of entering into political thickets and mathematical quagmires. Our answer is this: a denial of constitutionally protected rights demands judicial protection; our oath and our office require no less of us. As stated in Gomillion v. Lightfoot:

> "When a State exercises power wholly within the domain of state interest, it is insulated from federal judicial review. But such insulation is not carried over when state power is used as an instrument for circumventing a federally protected right."

To the extent that a citizen's right to vote is debased, he is that much less a citizen. The fact that an individual lives here or there is not a legitimate reason for overweighting or diluting the efficacy of his vote. The complexions of societies and civilizations change, often with amazing rapidity. A nation once primarily rural in character becomes predominantly urban. Representation schemes once fair and equitable become archaic and outdated. But the basic principle of representative government remains, and must remain, unchanged—the weight of a citizen's vote cannot be made to depend on where he lives. Population is, of necessity, the starting point for consideration and the controlling criterion for judgment in legislative apportionment controversies.

A citizen, a qualified voter, is no more nor less so because he lives in the city or on the farm. This is the clear and strong command of our Constitution's Equal Protection Clause. This is an essential part of the concept of a government of laws and not of men. This is the heart of Lincoln's vision of "government of the people, by the people, [and] for the people." The Equal Protection Clause demands no less than substantially equal state legislative representation for all citizens, of all places as well as of all races.

IV

We hold that, as a basic constitutional standard, the Equal Protection Clause requires that the seats in both houses of a bicameral state legislature must be apportioned on a population basis. Simply stated, an individual's right to vote for state legislators is unconstitutionally impaired when its weight is in a substantial fashion diluted when compared with votes of citizens living in other parts of the State. . . .

42. WARREN

Rights of the Accused

Miranda v. *Arizona** was one of four cases decided collectively by the Supreme Court in 1966. All were concerned with the admissibility of confessions. Miranda had been convicted of kidnapping and rape on the basis of a confession secured by Arizona police officials after two hours of questioning during which time he had not been told of his constitutional rights to counsel and to remain silent. The excerpts presented in the selection are taken from Chief Justice Warren's majority opinion for a closely divided (5 to 4) Supreme Court.

The cases before us raise questions which go to the roots of our concepts of American criminal jurisprudence: the restraints society must observe consistent with the Federal Constitution in prosecuting individuals for crime. More specifically, we deal with the admissibility of statements obtained from an individual who is subjected to custodial police interrogation and the necessity for procedures which assure that the individual is accorded his privilege under the Fifth Amendment to the Constitution not to be compelled to incriminate himself. . . .

I

The constitutional issue we decide in each of these cases is the admissibility of statements obtained from a defendant questioned while in custody or otherwise deprived of his freedom of action in any significant way. In each, the defendant was questioned by police officers, detectives, or a prosecuting attorney in a room in which he was cut off from the outside world. In none of these cases was the defendant given a full and effective warning of his rights at the outset of the interrogation process. In all the cases, the questioning elicited oral admissions, and in three of them, signed statements as well which were admitted at their trials. They all thus share salient features—incom-

* 384 U.S. 436, 439, 467–75, 478–79 (1966).

municado interrogation of individuals in a police-dominated atmosphere, resulting in self-incriminating statements without full warnings of constitutional rights. . . .

III

Today, then, there can be no doubt that the Fifth Amendment privilege is available outside of criminal court proceedings and serves to protect persons in all settings in which their freedom of action is curtailed in any significant way from being compelled to incriminate themselves. We have concluded that without proper safeguards the process of in-custody interrogation of persons suspected or accused of crime contains inherently compelling pressures which work to undermine the individual's will to resist and to compel him to speak where he would not otherwise do so freely. In order to combat these pressures and to permit a full opportunity to exercise the privilege against self-incrimination, the accused must be adequately and effectively apprised of his rights and the exercise of those rights must be fully honored.

It is impossible for us to foresee the potential alternatives for protecting the privilege which might be devised by Congress or the States in the exercise of their creative rule-making capacities. Therefore we cannot say that the Constitution necessarily requires adherence to any particular solution for the inherent compulsions of the interrogation process as it is presently conducted. Our decision in no way creates a constitutional straitjacket which will handicap sound efforts at reform, nor is it intended to have this effect. We encourage Congress and the States to continue their laudable search for increasingly effective ways of protecting the rights of the individual while promoting efficient enforcement of our criminal laws. However, unless we are shown other procedures which are at least as effective in apprising accused persons of their right of silence and in assuring a continuous opportunity to exercise it, the following safeguards must be observed.

At the outset, if a person in custody is to be subjected to interrogation, he must first be informed in clear and unequivocal terms that he has the right to remain silent. For those unaware of the privilege, the warning is needed simply to make them aware of it—the threshold requirement for an intelligent decision as to its exercise. More important, such a warning is an absolute prerequisite in overcoming the inherent pressures of the interrogation atmosphere. It is not just the subnormal or woefully ignorant who succumb to an interrogator's imprecations, whether implied or expressly stated, that the interrogation will continue until a confession is obtained or that silence in the face of accusation is itself damning and will bode ill when presented to a jury. Further, the warning will show the individual that his interrogators are prepared to recognize his privilege should he choose to exercise it.

The Fifth Amendment privilege is so fundamental to our system of constitutional rule and the expedient of giving an adequate warning as to the availability of the privilege so simple, we will not pause to inquire in individual cases whether the defendant was aware of his rights without a warning being given. Assessments of the knowledge the defendant possessed, based on information as to his age, education, intelligence, or prior contact with authorities, can never be more than speculation; a warning is a clearcut fact. More important, whatever the background of the person interrogated, a warning at the time of the interrogation is indispensable to overcome its pressures and to insure that the individual knows he is free to exercise the privilege at that point in time.

The warning of the right to remain silent must be accompanied by the explanation that anything said can and will be used against the individual in court. This warning is needed in order to make him aware not only of the privilege, but also of the consequences of forgoing it. It is only through an awareness of these consequences that there can be any assurance of real understanding and intelligent exercise of the privilege. Moreover, this warning may serve to make the individual more acutely aware that he is faced with a phase of the adversary system— that he is not in the presence of persons acting solely in his interest.

The circumstances surrounding in-custody interrogation can operate very quickly to overbear the will of one merely made aware of his privilege by his interrogators. Therefore, the right to have counsel present at the interrogation is indispensable to the protection of the Fifth Amendment privilege under the system we delineate today. Our aim is to assure that the individual's right to choose between silence and speech remains unfettered throughout the interrogation process. A once-stated warning, delivered by those who will conduct the interrogation, cannot itself suffice to that end among those who most require knowledge of their rights. A mere warning given by the interrogators is not alone sufficient to accomplish that end. Prosecutors themselves claim that the admonishment of the right to remain silent without more "will benefit only the recidivist and the professional." Brief for the National District Attorneys Association as *amicus curiae*, p. 14. Even preliminary advice given to the accused by his own attorney can be swiftly overcome by the secret interrogation process. Cf. Escobedo v. State of Illinois, 378 U.S. 478, 485, n. 5. Thus, the need for counsel to protect the Fifth Amendment privilege comprehends not merely a right to consult with counsel prior to questioning, but also to have counsel present during any questioning if the defendant so desires.

The presence of counsel at the interrogation may serve several significant subsidiary functions as well. If the accused decides to talk to his interrogators, the assistance of counsel can mitigate the dangers of untrustworthiness. With a lawyer present the likelihood that the police will practice coercion is reduced, and if coercion is nevertheless exercised the lawyer can testify to it in court. The presence of a lawyer can also help to guarantee that the accused gives a fully accurate statement to the police and that the statement is rightly reported by the prosecution at trial. See Crooker v. State of California, 357 U.S. 433, 443–448 (Douglas, J., dissenting).

An individual need not make a pre-interrogation request for a lawyer. While such request affirmatively secures his right to have one, his failure to ask for a lawyer does not constitute a waiver. No effective waiver of the right to counsel during interrogation can be recognized unless specifically made after the warnings we here delineate have been given. The accused who does not know his rights and therefore does not make a request may be the person who most needs counsel. As the California Supreme Court has aptly put it:

"Finally, we must recognize that the imposition of the requirement for the request would discriminate against the defendant who does not know his rights. The defendant who does not ask for counsel is the very defendant who most needs counsel. We cannot penalize a defendant who, not understanding his constitutional rights, does not make the formal request and by such failure demonstrates his helplessness. To require the request would be to favor the defendant whose sophistication or status had fortuitously prompted him to make it." People v. Dorado, 62 Cal.2d 338, 351.

In Carnley v. Cochran, 369 U.S. 506, 513, we stated: "[I]t is settled that where the assistance of counsel is a constitutional requisite, the right to be furnished counsel does not depend on a request." This proposition applies with equal force in the context of providing counsel to protect an accused's Fifth Amendment privilege in the face of interrogation. Although the role of counsel at trial differs from the role during interrogation, the differences are not relevant to the question whether a request is a prerequisite.

Accordingly we hold that an individual held for interrogation must be clearly informed that he has the right to consult with a lawyer and to have the lawyer with him during interrogation under the system for protecting the privilege we delineate today. As with the warnings of the right to remain silent and that anything stated can be used in evidence against him, this warning is an absolute prerequisite to interrogation. No amount of circumstantial evidence that the person may have been aware of this right will suffice to stand in its stead. Only through such a warning is there ascertainable assurance that the accused was aware of this right.

If an individual indicates that he wishes the assistance of counsel before any interrogation occurs, the authorities cannot rationally ignore or deny his request on the basis that the individual does not have or cannot afford a retained attorney. The financial ability of the individual has no relationship to the scope of the rights involved here. The privilege against self-incrimination secured by the Constitution applies to all individuals. The need for counsel in order to protect the privilege exists for the indigent as well as the affluent. In fact, were we to limit these constitutional rights to those who can retain an attorney, our decisions today would be of little significance. The cases before us as well as the vast majority of confession cases with which we have dealt in the past involve those unable to retain counsel. While authorities are not required to relieve the accused of his poverty, they have the obligation not to take advantage of indigence in the administration of justice. Denial of counsel to the indigent at the time of interrogation while allowing an attorney to those who can afford one would be no more supportable by reason or logic than the similar situation at trial and on appeal struck down in Gideon v. Wainwright, 372 U.S. 335, and Douglas v. People of State of California, 372 U.S. 353.

In order fully to apprise a person interrogated of the extent of his rights under this system then, it is necessary to warn him not only that he has the right to consult with an attorney, but also that if he is indigent a lawyer will be appointed to represent him. Without this additional warning, the admonition of the right to consult with counsel would often be understood as meaning only that he can consult with a lawyer if he has one or has the funds to obtain one. The warning of a right to counsel would be hollow if not couched in terms that would convey to the indigent—the person most often subjected to interrogation

—the knowledge that he too has a right to have counsel present. As with the warnings of the right to remain silent and of the general right to counsel, only by effective and express explanation to the indigent of this right can there be assurance that he was truly in a position to exercise it.

Once warnings have been given, the subsequent procedure is clear. If the individual indicates in any manner, at any time prior to or during questioning, that he wishes to remain silent, the interrogation must cease. At this point he has shown that he intends to exercise his Fifth Amendment privilege; any statement taken after the person invokes his privilege cannot be other than the product of compulsion, subtle or otherwise. Without the right to cut off questioning, the setting of in-custody interrogation operates on the individual to overcome free choice in producing a statement after the privilege has been once invoked. If the individual states that he wants an attorney, the interrogation must cease until an attorney is present. At that time, the individual must have an opportunity to confer with the attorney and to have him present during any subsequent questioning. If the individual cannot obtain an attorney and he indicates that he wants one before speaking to police, they must respect his decision to remain silent.

This does not mean, as some have suggested, that each police station must have a "station house lawyer" present at all times to advise prisoners. It does mean, however, that if police propose to interrogate a person they must make known to him that he is entitled to a lawyer and that if he cannot afford one, a lawyer will be provided for him prior to any interrogation. If authorities conclude that they will not provide counsel during a reasonable period of time in which investigation in the field is carried out, they may refrain from doing so without violating the person's Fifth Amendment privilege so long as they do not question him during that time.

If the interrogation continues without the presence of an attorney and a statement is taken, a heavy burden rests on the government to demonstrate that the defendant knowingly and intelligently waived his privilege against self-incrimination and his right to retained or appointed counsel. Escobedo v. State of Illinois, 378 U.S. 478, 490, n. 14. This Court has always set high standards of proof for the waiver of constitutional rights, Johnson v. Zerbst, 304 U.S. 458, and we reassert these standards as applied to in-custody interrogation. Since the State is responsible for establishing the isolated circumstances under which the interrogation takes place and has the only means of making available corroborated evidence of warnings given during incommunicado interrogation, the burden is rightly on its shoulders.

An express statement that the individual is willing to make a statement and does not want an attorney followed closely by a statement could constitute a waiver. But a valid waiver will not be presumed simply from the silence of the accused after warnings are given or simply from the fact that a confession was in fact eventually obtained. . . .

In dealing with statements obtained through interrogation, we do not purport to find all confessions inadmissible. Confessions remain a proper element in law enforcement. Any statement given freely and voluntarily without any compelling influences is, of course, admissible in evidence. The fundamental import of the privilege while an individual is in custody is not whether he is allowed to talk to the police without the benefit of warnings and counsel, but whether he can be interrogated. There is no requirement that police stop a person who enters a police station and states that he wishes to confess to a crime, or a person who calls the police to offer a confession or any other statement he desires to make. Volunteered statements of any kind are not barred by the Fifth Amendment and their admissibility is not affected by our holding today.

To summarize, we hold that when an individual is taken into custody or otherwise deprived of his freedom by the authorities in any significant way and is subjected to questioning, the privilege against self-incrimination is jeopardized. Procedural safeguards must be employed to protect the privilege and unless other fully effective means are adopted to notify the person of his right of silence and to assure that the exercise of the right will be scrupulously honored, the following measures are required. He must be warned prior to any questioning that he has the right to remain silent, that anything he says can be used against him in a court of law, that he has the right to the presence of an attorney, and that if he cannot afford an attorney one will be appointed for him prior to any questioning if he so desires. Opportunity to exercise these rights must be afforded to him throughout the interrogation. After such warnings have been given, and such opportunity afforded him, the individual may knowingly and intelligently waive these rights and agree to answer questions or make a statement. But unless and until such warnings and waiver are demonstrated by the prosecution at trial, no evidence obtained as a result of interrogation can be used against him. . . .

Suggestions for Further Reading

BAILYN, BERNARD, *Ideological Origins of the American Revolution*. Cambridge: Harvard University Press, 1967. The outstanding work on the intellectual background of the revolution.

——— *The Origins of American Politics*. New York: Knopf, 1968. American politics and political ideas in the first half of the eighteenth century.

BEARD, CHARLES, *An Economic Interpretation of the Constitution*. New York: Macmillan, 1913. The famous and influential study of the American Constitution.

BECKER, CARL, *The Declaration of Independence*. New York: Knopf, 1942. An excellent study of the history and philosophy of the Declaration.

BENSON, LEE, *The Concept of Jacksonian Democracy*. Princeton: Princeton University Press, 1961. New perspectives on Jacksonian Democracy with New York State as the case study.

COMMAGER, HENRY S., *The American Mind*. New Haven: Yale University Press, 1950. A study of American thought from the 1880's to the mid-twentieth century.

CORWIN, EDWIN S., "The 'Higher Law' Background of American Constitutional Law," *Harvard Law Review*, XLII (1928–29), 149–85, 365–409; reprinted by Cornell University Press (1955). Scholarship and historical writing at its best. The evolution of "higher law" thought from Greece and Rome to the nineteenth century and its influence on the American Constitution.

ERNST, JAMES E., *The Political Thought of Roger Williams*. Seattle: University of Washington Press, 1929. Still the best study of Williams' political thought.

FORCEY, CHARLES, *The Crossroads of Liberalism*. New York: Oxford University Press, 1961. American progressivism between 1900 and 1925 through the ideas of Herbert Croly, Walter Weyl, and Walter Lippmann.

HARTZ, LOUIS, *The Liberal Tradition in America*. New York: Harcourt, Brace, 1955. A provocative and influential interpretation of America's political tradition.

HOFSTADTER, RICHARD, *The Age of Reform.* New York: Knopf, 1955. An exciting analysis of the political ideas of populism, progressivism, and the New Deal.

—— *The American Political Tradition.* New York: Knopf, 1948. Interpretive essays of famous American political leaders with an emphasis on their ideas.

—— *Social Darwinism in American Thought, 1860–1915.* Philadelphia: University of Pennsylvania Press, 1944. Herbert Spencer's American supporters and opponents—William Graham Sumner, Henry George, Lester Ward, and others.

KENYON, CECELIA, "Men of Little Faith: The Anti-Federalists on the Nature of Representative Government," *William and Mary Quarterly,* 12 (1955), 3d series, 3–43. An important and controversial interpretation of anti-Federalist political thought.

MASON, ALPHEUS T., *The States Rights Debate: Anti-Federalism and the Constitution.* Englewood Cliffs, N.J.: Prentice-Hall, 1964. Original source material and interpretive essays on anti-Federalism and its leading supporters.

MCDONALD, FOREST, *We the People: The Economic Origins of the Constitution.* Chicago: University of Chicago Press, 1958. A reexamination of Charles Beard's economic interpretation of the Constitution.

NOBLE, DAVID W., *The Paradox of Progressive Thought.* Minneapolis: University of Minnesota Press, 1958. An analysis of the ideas of major progressive thinkers including Herbert Croly, Thorstein Veblen, and Walter Rauschenbush.

PETERSON, MERRILL D., *The Jefferson Image in the American Mind.* New York: Oxford University Press, 1960. An examination of Jefferson's influence on subsequent periods of American history.

ROSSITER, CLINTON, *Seedtime of the Republic.* New York: Harcourt, Brace, 1953. Seventeenth- and eighteenth-century political ideas and personalities.

SCHLESINGER, ARTHUR M., Jr., *The Age of Jackson.* Boston: Little, Brown, 1945. The politics, personalities, and ideas of the Jacksonians.

SMITH, J. ALLEN, *The Spirit of American Government.* New York: Macmillan, 1912. Next to Beard's *Economic Interpretation* the most important statement of the political ideas of America's progressive historians.

SWISHER, CARL B., *Roger B. Taney.* New York: Macmillan, 1935. Still the best study of a generally neglected figure in American political history.

WHITE, MORTON, *Social Thought in America: The Revolt 'Against Formalism.* New York: Viking, 1949. An analysis of the social thought of such influential progressives as Charles Beard, Thorstein Veblen, and Oliver W. Holmes, Jr.